*Uncle John's*

# CURIOUSLY COMPELLING BATHROOM READER®

# Uncle John's
# CURIOUSLY COMPELLING BATHROOM READER

## By the Bathroom Readers' Institute

Bathroom Readers' Press
Ashland, Oregon

# OUR "REGULAR" READERS RAVE!

"*Uncle John's Bathroom Reader* has added a new dimension to my bathroom visits. Thank you."
—**Mitchell A.**

"I have never in my 71 years had a book that I carry with me at all times. Since I've had a copy of the *Bathroom Reader*, I don't even watch a lot of TV!"
—**Robert T.**

"I would just like to thank you for making me laugh. Since discovering your great series, I find myself visiting my bathroom more often. There is need of a new invention: Armrests in the toilet!"
—**Caroline Q.**

"I think these books are the best in the world. I take them to school and show all my friends. Thank you for making my visits to the bathroom fun."
—**Bobby R.**

"You guys are the funniest I've ever read!"
—**Suzanne P.**

"Just thought I'd let you know what a great job you're doing. My whole family enjoys your books and our tradition has been to buy one, then two books at Christmastime for reading the next year. You've become so popular that we now have at least three new books in the bathroom, and it's only June!"
—**Martha O.**

"I absolutely love your books. But oddly, I've never read them in the bathroom. As soon as I get one, I have to read it cover to cover. Keep up the good work!"
—**Leanne P.**

# UNCLE JOHN'S CURIOUSLY COMPELLING BATHROOM READER®

For information, write:
The Bathroom Readers' Institute,
P.O. Box 1117, Ashland, OR 97520
*www.bathroomreader.com*
888-488-4642

Cover design by Michael Brunsfeld,
San Rafael, CA (*Brunsfeldo@comcast.net*)

Special thank you to Gary Martin, M.O. (Master of Origami)

BRI "technician" on the back cover: Larry Kelp

*Uncle John's Curiously Compelling Bathroom Reader®*
by the Bathroom Readers' Institute

ISBN-13: 978-1-59223-679-4
ISBN-10: 1-59223-679-0

Library of Congress Catalog Card Number:
2006932282

Printed in the United States of America
Third Printing
3 4 5 6 7 8 9 10 09 08 07

# THANK YOU!

*The Bathroom Readers' Institute sincerely thanks the people
whose advice and assistance made this book possible.*

Gordon Javna
John Dollison
Thom Little
Brian Boone
Amy Miller
Jay Newman
Julia Papps
Malcolm Hillgartner
Jahnna Beecham
Michael Brunsfeld
Angela Kern
Sharilyn Hovind
Jeff Altemus
Gideon Javna
Sydney Stanley
JoAnn Padgett
Jolly Jeff Cheek
Scarab Media
Jef Fretwell
Connie Vazquez
Kristine Hemp
Nancy Toeppler
Dan Schmitz
Kyle Coroneos
Sheila & Rad

Gary Martin
Claudia Bauer
Jennifer Thornton
Jennifer B. & Melinda A.
Laurel Graziano
Mana, Dylan & Chandra
Maggie Javna
(Mr.) Mustard Press
Rick Overton
Steven Style Group
Kristen Vanberg
John Burns
Allen Orso
Shobha Grace
Matthew Furber
Jo Scheer
Eddie Deezen
Alan Nathanson
Keziah Veres
Michelle Sedgwick
Maggie McLaughlin
Raincoast Books
Chris Olsen
Porter the Wonder Dog
Thomas Crapper

\*    \*    \*

"If one cannot enjoy reading a book over and over again, there is
no use in reading it at all."

—**Oscar Wilde**

# CONTENTS

Because the BRI understands your reading needs, we've
divided the contents by length as well as subject.

Short—a quick read

Medium—2 to 3 pages

Long—for those extended visits, when something
a little more involved is required

* Extended—for those leg-numbing experiences

\*      \*      \*

## DO NOT CALL IN EVENT OF EMERGENCY

The Office of Homeland Security operates a secret emergency hotline that connects to the governors of all 50 states. In 2006 the number was placed on the national "Do Not Call" registry. Reason: the line was being barraged by telemarketers. Wisconsin governor Jim Doyle says the phone rang once during the early days of the Iraq War. In a panic, he grabbed the phone, thinking he was about to hear instructions or grave news. Instead, he was asked if he was unhappy with his long distance service.

# GREETINGS FROM "CURIOSITY CENTRAL"

Annnnnnnd...we're back!

Wow! It's hard to believe it's time to write another introduction, but here it is—*Uncle John's Curiously Compelling Bathroom Reader*, our 19th edition (we've already rented our tuxes for next year's 20th anniversary celebration).

But there's plenty of reason to celebrate this year. Our insatiable curiosity has taken us to new heights in our continuing quest to bring you obscure knowledge and eye-popping trivia.

If you're an old friend, welcome back. If you're new, welcome to the family. And speaking of family, our little team at the BRI is tighter and happier than ever. We truly had a great time putting this *Bathroom Reader* together. Sure, it was a lot of work, what with all of the researching and compiling and writing and revising we've done over the last 12 months. But every single day one of our crackpot staffers would crack the rest of us up. That's especially important during the final push to get the book to press, or "crunch time," as we affectionately call it. Our little red schoolhouse becomes a bunker: the kitchen table is covered with (somewhat) healthy junk food; we drink gallons of coffee; John D. brings his cot to zonk out on in the back room; and Uncle John groans a lot.

So what compelling topics do we have in store for you? Too many great ones to list, but here are some of our favorites:

• **Long-lost history:** Lincoln's duel, the first trans-Pacific flight, and roving gangs of robots.

• **Music, music, music:** the two weeks in 1927 that put country music on the map, and the shrieking birth of punk rock.

• **Follies, flubs, and fabulous hoaxes:** stupid campaign promises, the college kids who beat the Vegas casinos at their own game, and "Bunga Bunga!"

- **Humanity's fascination with food:** how nutmeg brought the world together and how the potato nearly ripped it apart.

- **Canadian lore:** The United States government's top secret plans to invade its friendliest neighbor. (Really!)

- **Helpful hints:** how to store your collectibles, why you should wash your hands, and how to get home safe if you're stranded in the wilderness.

And now, before I sign off, let me send a big *Bathroom Reader* thank you—

- To our inhouse writers, John D, Thom, Brian (our robot pirate zombie), and Jumpin' Jay.

- To our outhouse team featuring the writing talents of Malcolm and Jahnna, Jolly Jeff, Gideon, Kyle, Jef, Matthew, and to Angie, who keeps finding those amazing running feet (the little facts at the bottom of every page).

- To our production staff featuring the amazing Amy, whose calm demeanor and editing prowess helped make this book the best ever. To our mystical Julia, who somehow manages to manage it all. To our number-one reliever, Jeff A., copyeditors Sharilyn, Claudia, and Kristen, shipping diva Shobha Grace. And to Michael B., whose covers keep getting better!

- To Sydney, JoAnn, and the friendly folks at Banta.

- And last but most, **TO YOU!** You're the reason we make these books, and we'll bring you them with a smile year after year.

Keep on reading. And as always,

*Go with the Flow!*

**Uncle John and the BRI Staff**

P.S. Porter the Wonder Dog says…nothing. (He's a *dog!*)

# YOU'RE MY INSPIRATION

*It's always interesting to find out where the architects of
pop culture get their ideas. These may surprise you.*

**E**LVIS PRESLEY. Most of the King's biographers attribute
his singing style to black gospel and country music. But Elvis
wanted to reach a wider audience, so he based his early
vocal stylings on pop crooner Dean Martin. (For evidence, listen
to Elvis's first recording of "Love Me Tender.")

**THE MICHELIN MAN.** In 1898 André Michelin's brother
reported seeing a stack of tires that strangely resembled a human
figure. That inspired Michelin to commission French artist
O'Galop to paint a man made of tires. (The first Michelin Man
was named Bibendum. He was much fatter than today's version
and smoked a cigar.)

**SHELLEY WINTERS.** Born Shirley Schrift, the actress—who
starred in more than 70 films, including *Lolita* (1962) and *The Posei-
don Adventure* (1972)—changed her name when she got to Hollywood in 1943. Her mother's maiden name was Winter, and she
took the first name from her favorite poet, Percy Bysshe Shelley.

**COLUMBIA PICTURES LOGO.** In 1993 Columbia hired New
Orleans artist Michael Deas to update their logo—a woman in a
toga, holding a torch (the original 1924 model was rumored to be
actress Evelyn Venable). So who's the new model? Actress Annette
Bening has claimed it's her…but it's not. The real model: a 31-
year-old Louisiana woman named Jenny Joseph. "When I go to
the movies," she says, "I get my 15 minutes of fame. The kids get a
kick out of it."

**THE OLD MAN AND THE SEA.** The title character in Ernest
Hemingway's 1952 novella was inspired by a Cuban fisherman
named Gregorio Fuentes. In the 1930s, Hemingway hired Fuentes
to watch over his boat, and the two formed a friendship that lasted
30 years. Ironically, Fuentes outlived the author by many years,
dying in 2002 at the age of 104. In all those years, he never read
*The Old Man and the Sea.*

# GAME SHOW GOOFS

*Being on a game show may look easy from the comfort
of your living room, but under those hot television lights,
contestants' mouths sometimes disconnect from their brains.*

**Anne Robinson:** What insect is commonly found hovering above lakes?
**Contestant:** Crocodiles.
                    *—The Weakest Link*

**Alex Trebek:** If a Japanese *isha* (doctor) asks you to stick out your *shita*, he means this.
**Contestant:** What is…your behind?
                    *—Jeopardy!*

**Anne Robinson:** Who is the only Marx brother that remained silent throughout all their films?
**Contestant:** Karl.
                    *—The Weakest Link*

**Todd Newton:** Bourbon whiskey is named after Bourbon County, located in what state?
**Contestant:** England.
                    *—Press Your Luck*

**The Puzzle:** TOM HANKS AS _ORREST GUMP
**Contestant:** Tom Hanks as Morris Gump.
                    *—Wheel of Fortune*

**Richard Dawson:** Name something a blind man might use.
**Contestant:** A sword.
                    *—Family Feud*

**Eamonn Holmes:** Name the playwright commonly known by the initials G.B.S.
**Contestant:** William Shakespeare?
                    *—National Lottery Jet Set*

**Steve Wright:** What is the capital of Australia? And it's not Sydney.
**Contestant:** Sydney.
                    *—Steve Wright Radio Show*

**Bob Eubanks:** What is your husband's favorite cuisine?
**Contestant:** *All in the Family.*
                    *—The Newlywed Game*

**Kevin O'Connell:** What moos?
**Contestant:** A car.
                    *—Go*

**Richard Dawson:** Name an occupation whose members must get tired of smiling.
**Contestant:** Game show host.
                    *—Family Feud*

---

**Sean Connery has a tattoo that says "Mum and Dad."**

# RANDOM ORIGINS

*You know what these are…but do you know where they came from?*

## HAMSTERS

The natural habitat of Golden or Syrian hamsters, as the pet variety is known, is limited to one area: the desert outside the city of Aleppo, Syria. (Their name in the local Arabic dialect translates to "saddlebags," thanks to the pouches in their mouths that they use to store food.) In 1930 a zoologist named Israel Aharoni found a nest containing a female and a litter of 11 babies in the desert and brought them back to his lab at the Hebrew University of Jerusalem. The mother died on the trip home; so did seven of her babies. Virtually all of the millions of domesticated Golden hamsters in the world are descended from the four that survived.

## MAIL-ORDER CATALOGS

In September 1871, a British major named F. B. McCrea founded the Army & Navy Cooperative in London to supply goods to military personnel at the lowest possible price. Its first catalog was issued in February 1872…six months before an American named Aaron Montgomery Ward put his first catalog in the mail.

## ALUMINUM

The Earth's crust contains more aluminum than any other metallic element, yet it was not discovered or extracted until the mid-1820s—when it was so expensive to extract that it was actually considered a precious metal. Then, in 1886, two different inventors—Charles Hall, an American, and Paul Héroult, a Frenchman—discovered a process by which aluminum could be extracted much more cheaply using electricity. The Hall-Héroult process reduced the price of aluminum to less than 1% of its previous cost. But it wasn't until World War I, when German designer Hugo Junkers started building airplanes out of metal instead of the traditional wood and fabric, that aluminum came into its own. Today the world uses more aluminum than any other metal except iron and steel.

# WHAT WORLD CITY...?

*Some facts to consider before your next vacation.*

**H**as the most billionaires? Moscow, with 33.

**Has the most people?** Tokyo. Population: 34 million.

**Is the most densely populated?** Manila, the Philippines, with 108,000 people per square mile.

**Has the most skyscrapers?** New York City—it has 47 buildings that are more than 600 feet tall.

**Is the deadliest?** Caracas, Venezuela, reportedly has the highest murder rate in the world: 100 per 100,000 people a year.

**Is the highest?** Potosí, Bolivia, at an elevation of 13,000 feet. The lowest is Jericho, Israel, at 1,000 feet below sea level.

**Eats out the most?** Paris has about 8,000 restaurants—more than any other city.

**Has suffered the most hurricanes?** Grand Cayman, Cayman Islands, which has been hit 61 times since 1871.

**Is the oldest?** Byblos, Lebanon. It was founded around 5000 B.C. Brasilia, Brazil, founded in 1960, is the world's youngest major city.

**Has the worst air?** According to *Guinness World Records*, Mexico City has the most air pollution.

**Costs the most?** Oslo, Norway, has the highest cost of living.

**Is the most cultured?** Amsterdam, the Netherlands, has the most museums per square mile.

**Drinks the most?** Per capita, Maun, Botswana, consumes the most alcohol.

**Drives the most?** Suva, Fiji, has 668 cars for every 1,000 people.

**Has the most bridges?** Hamburg, Germany—more than 2,300.

**Is the most wired?** Seoul, South Korea, has the most Internet traffic.

**Is the most "wired"?** Wellington, New Zealand. It has the most coffee shops per capita.

---

**What about pepper?** Salt is mentioned more than 30 times in the Bible.

# OOPS!

*Everyone's amused by tales of outrageous blunders—probably because
it's comforting to know that someone's screwing up even worse than
we are. So go ahead and feel superior for a few minutes.*

## STICKIN' IT TO 'EM

"One of Britain's most prestigious art galleries put a block of slate on display, topped by a small piece of wood, in the mistaken belief it was a work of art. The Royal Academy included the chunk of stone and the small bone-shaped wooden stick in its summer exhibition in London. But the slate was actually a *plinth*— a slab on which a pedestal is placed—and the stick was designed to prop up a sculpture. The sculpture itself—of a human head— was nowhere to be seen. The Academy explained the error by saying the parts were sent to the exhibitors separately. 'Given their separate submission,' it said in a statement, 'the two parts were judged independently. The head was rejected. The base was thought to have merit and was accepted.'"

—*Telegraph* (U.K.)

## HOLY WATER

"People in Pope John Paul II's hometown of Wadowice, Poland, believed a miracle had happened when water began spouting from the base of a statue of the Pontiff. Word soon spread across the country with pilgrims travelling from all over to the tiny town to fill up bottles with the liquid. But their belief in what they thought was a 'godly experience' was shattered by town mayor Eva Filipiak, who admitted the local water council had installed an ordinary water pipe beneath the statue. 'We didn't mean anything by it,' said Filipiak, 'it was just supposed to make the statue look prettier.'"

—**Ananova**

## HITTING THE DUMB-FECTA

"Roger Loughran, a horse-racing jockey, stood tall and proud in the saddle of Central House at the end of the Paddy Power Dial-A-Bet Chase in December 2005, and waved his whip at the packed grandstand. He was celebrating his first win as a professional jockey. Just

Hair is the second-fastest growing tissue in the body. The fastest is bone marrow.

for good measure, he swung a looping underarm punch into the air. There was just one problem: they still had 80 meters to run. The 26-year-old had mistaken the end of a running rail for the winning post, and as he eased up on Central House, Hi Cloy and Fota Island galloped past, relegating him to third place. It was an extraordinary, humiliating error, which reduced the crowd to near-silence. Some catcalls followed, but as Loughran returned to the paddock to unsaddle, there was more sympathy than anger."

—Buzzle.com

## PUT THE METAL TO THE PEDAL

"A Michigan man destroyed his car after putting his toolbox on the gas pedal. The accident occurred when the man, whose identity was not released, attempted to free his car from a muddy field by placing the toolbox on the accelerator, then getting behind the car to push it free. The man later said he was lost, and when he backed into a field to turn around, the car got stuck in the mud, said Lt. James McDonagh. 'After several attempts to free the car, the man then placed his toolbox on the accelerator, exited the vehicle, and attempted to push it free,' McDonagh said. The full-size Mercury sedan then accelerated across a cut soybean field with the man running behind. The car reached an estimated speed of 100 mph and traveled a half-mile, sometimes becoming airborne. The car then struck a tree, crushing it back to the windshield."

—*Battle Creek Enquirer*

## HOP-ALONG

"An artist who chained his legs together to draw a picture of the image was forced to hop 12 hours through the desert after realizing he lost the key and couldn't unlock the restraints. Trevor Corneliusien, 26, tightly wrapped and locked a long, thick chain around his bare ankles while camping north of Baker, California. 'It took him over 12 hours because he had to hop through boulders and sand,' Deputy Ryan Ford said. Corneliusien finally made it to a gas station and called the sheriff's department, which sent paramedics and deputies with bolt cutters. His legs were bruised but he was otherwise in good health. And the drawing? 'He brought it with him,' Ford said. 'It was a pretty good depiction of how a chain would look wrapped around your legs.'"

—Breitbart.com

New York City has 722 miles of subway track.

# WARNING LABELS

*Some things in life should go without saying, but there's always the occasional genius who needs to be told not to use a vacuum cleaner to pick up something that's on fire.*

**On a bottle of dog shampoo:** "Contents should not be fed to fish."

**On a baking pan:** "Ovenware will get hot when used in oven."

**On a blanket:** "Not to be used as protection from a tornado."

**On a fishing lure with a three-pronged hook:** "Harmful if swallowed."

**On a 12-inch CD rack:** "Do not use as a ladder."

**On a carpenter's drill:** "Not intended for use as a dental drill."

**On a knife set:** "Never try to catch a falling knife."

**On a package of earplugs:** "These earplugs are non-toxic, but may interfere with breathing if caught in windpipe."

**On a Japanese food processor:** "Not to be used for the other use."

**On a cocktail napkin with a mini map of Hilton Head, South Carolina:** "Not to be used for navigation."

**On an insect spray:** "This product not tested on animals."

**On a box of birthday candles:** "DO NOT use soft wax as ear plugs or for any other function that involves insertion into a body cavity."

**On a child's scooter:** "This product moves when used."

**Inside a six-inch plastic bag:** "Do not climb inside this bag and zip it up. Doing so will cause injury or death."

**On a paint remover that heats up to 1,000°:** "Do not use heat gun as a hair dryer."

**On a shower cap:** "Fits one head."

**On a can of pepper spray:** "May irritate eyes."

**On a toilet:** "Recycled flush water unsafe for drinking."

The shortest complete sentence in the English language: "Go."

# ANIMAL HOUSES

*College: home of higher education, world-class research…and fraternities.*

S tudents at Northwestern University in Illinois started a new fraternity named Zeta Zeta Zeta, better known by its Greek letters, ZZZ. Members say they are dedicated to "encouraging excellence through sleep," and are open to both men and women "regardless of race, gender, or sleeping orientation."

• Chi Omega, a sorority at Kent State University in Ohio, was placed on probation after the group held a formal dinner-dance where they gave a student an award for being the "blackest member" of the sorority. She was white. The sorority issued an apology, saying it was just a joke.

• California State University, Chico, began an investigation when someone reported (anonymously) that while watching a pornographic movie they recognized the room in which the "actors" were being filmed: it was the living room of the Phi Kappa Tau fraternity house on campus. Not only that, some of the "actors" were members of the fraternity. Officials at the school announced that all activities at the fraternity—whose motto is "Where Character Counts"—would be suspended.

• Student body president Mark Morice at Southeastern Louisiana University was arrested after he convinced his fraternity brothers to steal all the copies of the university newspaper before anyone could read it. The paper had an article critical of Morice's handling of school funds and questioning his ethics.

• Three Kappa Alpha members at the University of Missouri–Columbia were arrested in 2006 after a fireworks prank resulted in a near-fatal explosion. The trio had loaded up a Civil War-era cannon with fireworks, expecting the blast to shoot out the end of the barrel, but instead, the entire cannon blew up. An eight-inch chunk flew across the street and crashed through the roof of an apartment building, finally coming to rest on a Ping-Pong table that was being used by visiting students from China.

# FOOD ORIGINS

*When Uncle John was a kid, the basic food groups were meat, bread, vegetables, and dairy products. Uncle John always wondered why they left out the other basic food groups: coffee, candy, cold soup, fish sticks, corn dogs, and salad dressing.*

## CAPPUCCINO

In Vienna, a *Kapuziner* is a cup of espresso with a few drops of cream stirred in. The drink gets its name from the Catholic order of *Kapuzin* friars, who wore a brown habit or robe that was about the same color as the drink. (In English, the friars are known as Capuchins.) In the late 1800s, Austrian soldiers stationed in northern Italy introduced Kapuziners there; the Italians renamed them *cappuccinos*. When high-pressure espresso machines were introduced in 1906, the Italians put their own stamp on the drink by making it with steamed, foamy milk, and plenty of it, instead of just a little bit of cream.

## VICHYSSOISE

Don't let the French name fool you—this leek-and-potato soup (pronounced *vi-she-swaz*) is as American as apple pie. Louis Diat, the head chef of New York's Ritz-Carlton Hotel, came up with this cold soup in 1917 while looking for something to serve to customers in the sweltering heat of New York summers.

## FISH STICKS

Clarence Birdseye single-handedly invented the frozen-food industry in the late 1920s when he figured out how to freeze food without ruining its flavor, texture, or nutritional value (you have to freeze it *quickly*). His early machines worked best with food that was cut into slender pieces, and one of the first foods he came up with was a knockoff of a French delicacy called *goujonettes de sole*: sole fillets baked or fried in bread crumbs and a light batter. Birdseye switched to cheaper fish (cod), fried it in a heavier batter, and scored a hit: If you had a freezer in the 1930s, more likely than not it contained a box or two of fish sticks.

There are roughly 1,300 kernels in a pound of corn.

## LICORICE ALLSORTS

You might not recognize these candies by name, but you'd know them by sight—they're the variety of licorice candies that are sold as a mixture of colors, shapes, and sizes. The candies were created by the Bassetts company of England in the late 1800s. The original plan was to sell each shape separately, but that plan was foiled in 1899 when a salesman named Charlie Thompson spilled a carefully arranged tray of the pieces during a sales call. The buyer actually *preferred* the candies all mixed up…and as it turned out, so did everyone else: The candies sold better as a mixture than they ever did individually.

## WISH-BONE SALAD DRESSING

When Phillip Sollomi returned from fighting in World War II in 1945, he opened a restaurant in Kansas City, Missouri. The house specialty was fried chicken, so he named the restaurant "The Wish-bone." In 1948 he started serving his mother's Sicilian salad dressing; it was so popular that customers asked for bottles to take home. So he started bottling it…and soon demand was so strong that he had to make it in batches of 50 gallons at a time. In 1957 he sold the salad dressing business to the Lipton Tea Company, and today Wish-Bone is the bestselling Italian dressing in the United States.

## CORN DOGS

Even if he wasn't the very first person to dip a hot dog in corn meal batter and deep fry it, Neil Fletcher was the guy who popularized the dish when he began selling it at the Texas State Fair in 1942. Those early dogs were served on plates; it wasn't until four years later that Ed Waldmire, a soldier stationed at the Amarillo Airfield, became the first person to put the corn dog on a "stick" (the first ones were actually metal cocktail forks, later replaced by wooden sticks)

\*     \*     \*

**Alternative energy:** A 2006 study found that the average American walks about 900 miles a year. Another study found that Americans drink an average of 22 gallons of beer a year. That means that, on average, Americans get about 41 miles per gallon.

Mark Twain received a patent for "improved suspenders" in 1871.

# LOST ATTRACTIONS

*As a kid growing up in New Jersey, Uncle John often went to Palisades Amusement Park. Then one day they announced they were tearing it down to build an apartment complex. Many areas have an attraction like that—it's an important part of the cultural landscape for decades...and then it's gone.*

**A**TTRACTION: The Hippodrome
**LOCATION:** New York City
**STORY:** When it opened in 1905, it was called "the largest theater in the world." With a seating capacity of 5,300, only the biggest acts—in both size and popularity—performed there: Harry Houdini, diving horses, the circus, 500-person choirs. But the daily upkeep for such a mammoth theater, coupled with the cost of staging huge shows, forced a change. In 1923 it became a vaudeville theater and then, in 1928, it was sold to RKO and turned into a movie theater. It then became an opera house. Then a sports arena. The Hippodrome was finally torn down in 1939.
**WHAT'S THERE NOW:** An office building and parking garage.

**ATTRACTION:** Aquatarium
**LOCATION:** St. Petersburg, Florida
**STORY:** Housed in a 160-foot-tall transparent geodesic dome, the 17-acre Aquatarium opened in 1964. Tourists came from far and wide to visit this aquarium, which overlooked the Gulf of Mexico and was home to porpoises, sea lions, and pilot whales. But it rapidly started losing customers—and money—when the bigger and better Walt Disney World opened in nearby Orlando in 1971. In 1976 sharks were brought in and the site was renamed Shark World to capitalize on the popularity of *Jaws*, but it didn't help.
**WHAT'S THERE NOW:** Condominiums.

**ATTRACTION:** Pink and White Terraces
**LOCATION:** Lake Rotomahana, New Zealand
**STORY:** Called the eighth wonder of the world, the Terraces were once New Zealand's most popular and famous tourist attraction. They were two naturally occurring "staircases" of silica shelves that looked like pink and white marble. Each terrace (they were

two miles apart) was formed over thousands of years. Geysers spouted silica-laden hot water which flowed downhill and then crystallized into terraces as it cooled. But on June 10, 1886, a nearby volcano —Mount Tarawera—erupted, spewing lava, hot mud, and boulders. The eruption destroyed the village of Te Wairoa, killing 153 people, and the hot magma completely destroyed the terraces.

**WHAT'S THERE NOW:** Shapeless rock.

**ATTRACTION:** Jantzen Beach
**LOCATION:** Portland, Oregon
**STORY:** When it opened in 1928, this 123-acre amusement park on an island in the middle of the Columbia River was the largest in the United States. It housed a merry-go-round from the 1904 World's Fair, four swimming pools, a fun house, a train, and the Big Dipper—a huge wooden roller coaster. More than 30 million people visited "the Coney Island of the West" over its lifetime. But after World War II, attendance started to decline and continued steadily downward until the park finally closed in 1970.

**WHAT'S THERE NOW:** A shopping mall.

**ATTRACTION:** Palisades Amusement Park
**LOCATION:** Cliffside Park and Fort Lee, New Jersey
**STORY:** Built on steep cliffs on the west side of the Hudson River, it began in 1898 as a grassy park for picnics and recreation. In 1908 it was renamed Palisades Amusement Park and rides and attractions were added. It boasted a 400-by-600-foot saltwater pool ("world's largest"); the Cyclone, one of the biggest roller coasters in the country; and then in the 1950s, rock 'n' roll shows. Attendance grew during that period because of heavy advertising on TV and in comic books. (There was a hole in the fence behind the music stage kept open to let kids sneak in to avoid paying the 25-cent admission fee.) By 1967, the park had gotten *too* popular. The city of Cliffside Park was tired of park-related traffic, litter, and parking problems, so it rezoned the site for housing (it has great views of Manhattan). The park was shut down for good in 1971. Plans to retain the saltwater pool were scrapped when vandals destroyed it.

**WHAT'S THERE NOW:** High-rise apartment buildings.

---

It cost $3 million to build the *Titanic*...and $100 million to make the movie.

**ATTRACTION:** Crystal Palace

**LOCATION:** London, England

**STORY:** This massive 750,000 square foot structure originally housed the Great Exhibition of 1851, then was moved from Hyde Park to south London in 1854. Designed to evoke ancient Greek structures, the Crystal Palace featured dozens of columns, girders, and arches made of iron, and 900,000 square feet of glass. The building and surrounding grounds housed artwork and treasures from all over the world, including 250-foot-high fountains (requiring two water towers), gardens, and life-size replicas of dinosaurs. The coronation of King George V was held there, as was the annual English soccer championship. But after 1900, attendance started to dwindle. The Palace was closed on Sundays, the only day most Londoners had off from work. Then, in 1936, the Palace caught fire. The blaze was visible for miles. The building wasn't properly insured, so there wasn't enough to pay for rebuilding. All that was left were the water towers, later demolished during World War II out of fear Germany could use them to more easily locate London.

**WHAT'S THERE NOW:** A sports-arena complex.

**ATTRACTION:** Old Man of the Mountain

**LOCATION:** Cannon Mountain, New Hampshire

**STORY:** In 1805 surveyors Francis Whitcomb and Luke Brooks discovered this rock formation in the White Mountains of New Hampshire. Viewed from the correct angle, it had the appearance of a man's face. It jutted out 1,200 feet above Profile Lake and was estimated to be 40 feet tall and 25 feet wide. Nineteenth-century politician Daniel Webster and novelist Nathaniel Hawthorne wrote about the Old Man and helped make it a state icon. The Old Man graces New Hampshire's state quarter and a postage stamp. Signs of deterioration were first noted in 1906, and ever since, various methods—including cables and spikes—have been used to keep the face in place. But they didn't work. In 2003, the Old Man finally collapsed and crumbled.

**WHAT'S THERE NOW:** A rocky cliff. Viewfinders looking at the former landmark superimpose an image of the Old Man when it was intact to show visitors what it looked like.

---

The main cluster of riders in a bicycle race is called a *peloton*.

# DUMB JOCKS

*Heinrich Heine once said, "There are more fools in the world than there are people." We don't exactly know what he meant by that. And chances are, neither do these sports stars.*

"I have nothing to say, and I'll only say it once."
—**Floyd Smith,**
**Buffalo Sabres coach**

"I've had to overcome a lot of diversity."
—**Drew Gooden,**
**Cleveland Cavaliers player**

"If the NBA was on channel five and a bunch of frogs making love were on channel four, I'd watch the frogs, even if they were coming in fuzzy."
—**Bobby Knight,**
**college basketball coach**

"Play some Picasso."
—**Chris Morris,**
**New Jersey Nets player,**
**to a pianist while trying**
**to impress a date**

"Most of my clichés aren't original."
—**Chuck Knox,**
**NFL coach**

"If I go down, I'm going down standing up."
—**Chuck Person,**
**San Antonio Spurs player**

"The only thing that keeps this organization from being recognized as one of the finest in baseball is wins and losses at the Major League level."
—**Chuck LaMar,**
**Tampa Bay Devil Rays GM**

"I was in a no-win situation, so I'm glad that I won rather than lost."
—**Frank Bruno,**
**heavyweight boxer**

"We can't have stupidity in our locker room and we can't have stupidity on the ice. The stupidity has all been used up, plus some, in the NHL this year. The stupidity meter is broken."
—**Jeremy Roenick,**
**Philadelphia Flyers player**

"Therapy can be a good thing. It can be therapeutic."
—**Alex Rodriguez,**
**New York Yankees player**

"Surprise me."
—**Yogi Berra, when asked**
**by his wife where he**
**wanted to be buried**

---

In Canada, milk is sold in plastic bags as well as in jugs.

# AAAAH! ROBOTS!

*If you think robots are a thing of the future, think again. Scientists have been coming up with new uses for robots for years and…they're here.*

## WHAT IS A ROBOT?

The word "robot" conjures up images of the human-looking machines in sci-fi movies and TV shows, but it simply refers to "a machine that can perform physical tasks." Although robots are programmed to do specific things or to react to their surroundings, which may give the impression of intelligence, they are always controlled by humans, either by programming or by direct control. And they seldom look human—they can look like almost anything, from a mechanical arm to a box on wheels. But robot technology is changing rapidly, and the "droids" and "replicants" of science-fiction may someday become reality. Until then, scientists are still on the lookout for new and inventive ways to use robots…like these:

**TREASURE-BOT.** In 1993 Chilean inventor Manuel Salinas built Arturito, a robot made up of a metal body on all-terrain wheels, with a probe and a tiny radar dish. Salinas planned to use the robot to get government work locating and destroying landmines—leftovers from border disputes with Bolivia and Peru. But since then, he's used Arturito (a Spanish take on R2-D2 from *Star Wars*) in many other ways. In July 2005, Arturito led Chilean police to the missing body of a man under 12 feet of cement. Later that year, the robot found a stash of weapons and bombs hidden by a criminal gang, and then found buried treasure on an island off the Chilean coast. Arturito can also detect deposits of copper, water, and petroleum as deep as 600 feet underground.

**CANCER-BOT.** Enterix, an Australian medical technology company, has built a robot named Grace that can detect bowel cancer faster than conventional methods and at a 98% accuracy rate. It analyzes tissue samples in five seconds, reducing the need for invasive colonoscopies. Enterix estimates that if Grace were run 24 hours a day, Australia's entire population could be screened for bowel cancer in just one year.

**A lion's roar is louder than a jackhammer.**

**SAVIOR-BOT.** While filming *The Passion of the Christ*, actor Jim Caviezel (playing Jesus) risked hypothermia enduring 15-hour days hanging on a cross wearing only a loincloth. So filmmakers constructed a body double: a $220,000 robot that looked like Caviezel and was able to move its head and limbs convincingly.

**BEER-BOT.** Students at the Technical University of Darmstadt in Holland built a robot that can pour the perfect glass of beer. It takes the small, table-top robotic arm—"Hermann"—one minute, 11 seconds to pour, at the perfect angle, a proper mix of beer and froth. Amazingly, it cost less than $100 to build.

**DIET-BOT.** Researchers at MIT created a nuclear-powered robot dog to help dieters. It monitors a pedometer worn by the dieter, counting calories (based on a programmed meal plan) and recording how much the person has walked. At the end of the day, the user asks the robot, "How am I doing?" If the dieter ate well and exercised, the dog wags its tail and jumps up and down. If not, the dog whines and lays down.

## BOTS GONE WILD

• In 1942 science-fiction writer Isaac Asimov proposed three "laws of robotics" to ensure the safety of humankind. The first law: "A robot may not injure a human being, or, through inaction, allow a human being to come to harm." In 2006 Japan made Asimov's law an *actual* law. The country that gave us *Godzilla* is developing robot nurses (for elder care), but they fear robot rebellion. So all robots must now have sensors to prevent them from running into people, be made of soft materials, and include emergency shut-off buttons.

• Robot researchers at the Magna Science Center in Rotherham, England, were alarmed when one of their experiments, a robot that can "think" and act on its own, tried to escape the laboratory. Professor Noel Sharkey left the robot, "Gaak," alone for 15 minutes in a small closet. Gaak apparently forced its way out, went down an access ramp and out the front door of the center, and made it into the parking garage before being struck by a car. "There's no need to worry," Sharkey said. "Although they can escape they are perfectly harmless and won't be taking over just yet."

# "BUNGA BUNGA!"

*Sophomoric clown or a brilliant satirist of British imperialism? Either way, Horace de Vere Cole was responsible for one of the best pranks in history.*

## HIS MAJESTY REQUESTS...

In the years before World War I, Britain had the most powerful navy in the world. And the HMS *Dreadnought*, armed with 10 large guns and powered by a steam engine, was the pride of the fleet. Considered the superweapon of its day, the huge battleship lay anchored under the tightest security in Weymouth. Few outside the Navy's top officers had ever stepped on board, much less toured its "top-secret" state-of-the-art weaponry.

On February 10, 1910, Sir William May, the ship's captain, received a telegram from the Foreign Office, signed by Under-Secretary Sir Charles Hardinge, announcing the impending arrival of the emperor of Abyssinia and his court in England. The emperor was to receive the royal treatment, including a tour of the HMS *Dreadnought*. The captain immediately ordered his officers and crew to prepare to greet the emperor with all due pomp and circumstance. Guns were polished, decks swabbed, and uniforms washed and pressed in anticipation of the royal tour.

## V.I.P. TREATMENT

But the telegram was a fake—it was sent by a practical joker named Horace de Vere Cole. A few days later, he and five co-conspirators (including author Virginia Woolf and her brother) blackened their faces and hands with burnt cork, glued false beards to their chins, donned long red robes topped with makeshift turbans (all rented), and took a cab to London's Paddington Station. Brazenly declaring that he was a state official named "Herbert Cholmondley," Cole talked the stationmaster into giving them a VIP train to Weymouth, where the delegation was met with a full honor guard and a brass band.

An Abyssinian flag couldn't be found (no one knew what one looked like), so one from Zanzibar was used instead. And the band played the Zanzibar national anthem, since that was the only African anthem they knew. (The pranksters didn't know the difference.) The Navy had no translator either: fortunately, the delegation supplied their own, and his translations were so eloquent that none of the navy officers noticed that the language spoken by the "Abyssinians" bore a striking resemblance to fractured Latin. And as they were shown all of the ship's accoutrements, they shouted "Bunga Bunga!" in approval at everything they saw.

There were a few anxious moments. One was when the pranksters realized one of the Navy officers knew Woolf. But the officer never caught on. Another came when their "interpreter" sneezed and almost blew off his whiskers. Again, no one noticed. Weather almost sank the prank, too: Rain began to fall as the delegation arrived at the *Dreadnought*; Cole managed to talk their way onto a lower deck just as their makeup started to run.

Finally, Cole decided it was time to get out. They refused lunch (they weren't sure what dietary restrictions might go along with their made-up religion) and left quickly on the excuse that there were no prayer mats for their daily devotionals.

The delegation was given a military escort back to their train. Still in disguise and under Naval supervision, the "Abyssinians" requested that waiters serving them dinner wear white gloves. (The train stopped and was held up in Reading to purchase the gloves.)

## SHIP OF FOOLS

Five days later a photograph appeared in the *Daily Mirror*, showing the "Abyssinian" delegation with their Naval hosts. In the accompanying article, Cole exposed the hoax and ridiculed the Navy for being so gullible. All over London, sailors were harassed with cries of "Bunga Bunga!" The Admiralty was furious, but its attempt to charge Cole and his party with treason (the delegation had seen top-secret areas of the ship) was hooted down in Parliament and the press. After all, as people pointed out, the only "treasonous" thing they'd done was make the Admiralty and its officers look like fools. Besides, the only actual crime committed was sending a telegram under a fake name.

The Navy decided to not press charges, but still felt that somebody had to be punished. As the pranksters were all upper class, they could get away with a symbolic act to settle the dispute as gentlemen. Naval officers visited Cole and gave him six symbolic taps on the buttocks with a cane. Cole insisted he be allowed to do the same to the officers. Amazingly, the officers agreed.

# TOO RISKY
# FOR GUINNESS

*Some world records are amazing, some are funny, some are ridiculous.
Here's a look at some folks who risked life and limb to make it into
Guinness World Records...only to get tossed back out again.*

**B**ACKGROUND
When Ross and Norris McWhirter started keeping track of
world records for the Guinness Brewing Company in 1955,
they had to come up with guidelines for what kinds of records
they'd allow in their book. Sex was out. So was anything having to
do with crime or hard liquor (the book was sponsored by a brew-
ery, so some beer-related records were permitted). They did allow
many categories that were inherently dangerous, such as sword
swallowing and fire eating, but as people attempted to break those
records, the McWhirters became concerned that people might
actually kill themselves in the attempt...and Guinness would be
to blame. So in the late 1970s they started to "retire" (and later
revive) some of the more dangerous categories. Here are a few
examples:

## HOT-WATER-BOTTLE BURSTING

**Record Holder:** Italian actor and bodybuilder Franco Columbu

**Details:** Using only his lung power, in August 1979, Columbu
inflated a rubber hot-water bottle to the bursting point (28.5
pounds per square inch of air pressure) in 23 seconds.

**What Happened:** Columbu's name and record made it into the
1980 edition, but by the 1981 edition they were gone, replaced
with the following notice: "Contests involving the bursting of hot-
water bottles with sheer lung power are regarded as medically most
inadvisable, and the category has been discontinued."

**Update:** For a while *Guinness* replaced hot-water-bottle bursting
with weather-balloon blowing, but today the hot-water bottles
are back in. The current record holder is George Christen, who,
in 2000, inflated a hot-water bottle to the bursting point in

52.68 seconds—almost 30 seconds *slower* than Columbu's record.

## BURIAL ALIVE (VOLUNTARY)

**Record Holder:** Hendrick Luypaerts of Hechtel, Belgium

**Details:** In April 1974, Luypaerts climbed into a coffin 6'6" long, 33½" wide, and 25" deep, and was buried alive beneath almost 10 feet of dirt. He stayed there for 101 days and 37 minutes, with only a small tube for air, water, food, and…uh…bathroom needs connecting him to the surface. (*Guinness* says the record for *involuntary* burial alive is six years and five months, set by two Polish men who were trapped in a demolished World War II bunker from January 1945 until June 1951.)

**What Happened:** In 1979 the *Guinness* referees announced that future claims would be inadmissible "unless the depth of the coffin is a minimum two meters below ground with a maximum length of two meters, width of 70 centimeters, height of 100 centimeters, and a maximum aperture of 10 centimeters for feeding and communication." Then the following year they dumped the category altogether.

**Update:** In 1998 a British man named Geoff Smith broke the record by staying underground for 147 days in honor of his deceased mother, who had set the European record of being buried alive for 101 days. But *Guinness* refused to recognize Smith's attempt, saying the category was too dangerous. Smith had to settle for recognition from *Ripley's Believe It or Not*, but says he doesn't mind. "Although the feat is not recognized by *Guinness*, everyone in the world knows who I am now after what I've done," he says.

**Related Note:** The category "Most Cockroaches in a Coffin" is still open. Any takers? (You have to get in the coffin with the cockroaches.) Current record: 20,050 cockroaches.

## SWORD SWALLOWING

**Record Holder:** "Count Desmond" of Binghamton, New York

**Details:** Desmond set the record in 1981 by swallowing thirteen 23" swords, but injured himself in the process.

**What Happened:** *Guinness* officials acknowledged the attempt …then retired the category. "We don't want Count Desmond trying any more, saying he cut his guts out for *Guinness*," the book's American editor, David Boehm, explained.

**Update:** As of 1999, sword swallowing is back in, with a twist—literally. The new category is called "Most Swords Swallowed and Twisted." Current record holder: Brad Byers of Moscow, Idaho. On August 13, 1999, he swallowed ten 27" swords and rotated them a full 180° in his esophagus. But, according to *Guinness*, "Brad says he once cut his epiglottis so badly that he couldn't eat or drink for 48 hours."

## BICYCLE EATING

**Record Holder:** French entertainer Michel Lotito, also known as *Monsieur Mangetout* ("Mr. Eat All")

**Details:** Between March 17, 1977, and April 2, 1977, Mangetout devoured one entire bicycle, including the tires, which he consumed by cutting them into strips and making a "stew."

**What Happened:** Monsieur Mangetout's category was closed, but unlike some other discontinued dangerous categories, *Guinness* continued to print the record in subsequent editions. Why? "The ultimate in stupidity—the eating of a bicycle—has been recorded since it is unlikely to attract competition," the *Guinness* people wrote.

**Update:** Mangetout, who claims to devour two pounds of metal in a typical day, has blown past his old record: Since 1977 he has consumed a Cessna 150 aircraft, several televisions, shopping carts, and 17 more items. Today he's listed under the category "strangest diet." Is there anything Lotito won't eat? "I don't eat hard-boiled eggs or bananas," he says. "They make me sick."

## NEW CATEGORIES

• **Fastest Car Driven While Blindfolded:** 144.75 mph, by Mike Newman at North Yorkshire, U.K., in August 2003.

• **Scorpion Eating:** 35,000 by Rene Alvarenga of El Salvador. He averages 25 poisonous scorpions a day.

• **Fastest Motorcycle Driven While Blindfolded:** 164.87 mph, by Billy Baxter at Wiltshire, U.K., in August 2003.

• **Most Rattlesnakes Held in the Mouth at One Time:** Eight, by Jackie Bibby in Orlando, Florida, in May 2001.

---

The town of Levan—in the center of Utah—is "navel" spelled backwards.

# FLUBBED HEADLINES

*These are 100% honest-to-goodness headlines. Can you figure out what the writers were trying to say?*

Man Eating Piranha Mistakenly Sold as Pet Fish

**Nuns Forgive Break-In, Assault Suspect**

*MAN WITH ONE ARM CHEATS ON OTHER HALF*

Home Depot Purchases Wallpaper, Blinds Retailers

NATION SPLIT ON BUSH AS UNITER OR DIVIDER

**Man Is Fatally Slain**

*UTAH GIRL DOES WELL IN DOG SHOWS*

Smithsonian May Cancel Bombing of Japan Exhibits

*POLL SAYS 53% BELIEVE THAT MEDIA OFFEN MAKES MISTAKES*

*Some Pieces of Rock Hudson Sold at Auction*

Blind Woman Gets New Kidney From Dad She Hasn't Seen in Years

A REASON FOR ODOR FOUND AT SEWER PLANT

Judges Appear More Lenient on Crack Cocaine

*William Kelly Was Fed Secretary*

*TV Networks Agree to Police Violence*

Autos Killing 110 a Day, Let's Resolve to Do Better

DEALERS WILL HEAR CAR TALK AT NOON

**Bush Planning Mars Trip**

ARAFAT SWEARS IN CABINET

*Something Went Wrong in Jet Crash, Expert Says*

LANSING RESIDENTS CAN DROP OFF TREES

**Sewer District Plans Emergency Backup**

*Man Accused of Shooting Neighbor, Dog Held for Trial*

First actor to appear on the cover of *Time* magazine: Charlie Chaplin, in 1925.

# BOX OFFICE BLOOPERS

*Everyone loves bleepers…er, bloppers…er, we mean bloopers.*
*Here are a few great ones from the silver screen.*

**Movie:** *Goldfinger* (1964)
**Scene:** Dressed as Army soldiers, Goldfinger's crew breaks into Fort Knox and disables personnel with nerve gas.
**Blooper:** They're wearing Air Force insignias on their Army uniforms.

**Movie:** *The Sound of Music* (1965)
**Scene:** Maria (Julie Andrews) is riding on a bus singing "I Have Confidence in Me."
**Blooper:** The bus is supposed to be moving…but the mountains in the background never change.

**Movie:** *Free Willy* (1993)
**Scene:** Randolph and Jesse are sitting inside by a window reading a book together.
**Blooper:** At the beginning of the scene, the sun is shining brightly. Two minutes later, it's pitch black outside.

**Movie:** *Crash* (2004)
**Scene:** Officer Ryan (Matt Dillon) is talking on the phone about his father's health insurance.
**Blooper:** Ryan is a patrolman, but he's wearing sergeant stripes.

**Movie:** *Annie Hall* (1977)
**Scene:** The end credits.
**Blooper:** Christopher Walken's name is listed as "Christopher Wlaken."

**Movie:** *9 to 5* (1980)
**Scene:** Violet (Lily Tomlin) gets stopped by the police for a broken taillight.
**Blooper:** When the car pulls away, both taillights are working fine.

Nearly three-fourths of all the fresh water in the world is in Canada.

**Movie:** *Napoleon Dynamite* (2004)
**Scene:** Napoleon dances to a funk song after Pedro's class president speech.
**Blooper:** During the dance, Napoleon's shirt is tucked in, then it's untucked, then tucked back in, then untucked, then tucked in again.

**Movie:** *The Da Vinci Code* (2006)
**Scene:** In a flashback scene, Mary Magdalene (Charlotte Graham) leaves Jerusalem. As she walks, the Dome of the Rock is clearly visible in the background.
**Blooper:** This landmark was built in the 7th century...about 700 years after Mary Magdalene died.

**Movie:** *Charlie's Angels* (2000)
**Scene:** The Angels are fighting the Thin Man (Crispin Glover).
**Blooper:** Just before Dylan (Drew Barrymore) lifts up Alex (Lucy Liu) to kick the Thin Man, she calls her "Lucy," not "Alex."

**Movie:** *Mr. and Mrs. Smith* (2005)
**Scene:** Three BMWs chase Mr. and Mrs. Smith (Brad Pitt and Angelina Jolie).
**Blooper:** The movie is supposed to take place in New York City. So why do we see a street sign reading "Los Angeles City Limits"?

**Movie:** *2001: A Space Odyssey* (1968)
**Scene:** The shuttle crew discovers the monolith on the moon. As they gaze at it, moon dust begins to blow around.
**Blooper:** There is no wind on the moon—it has no atmosphere.

**Movie:** *Romeo + Juliet* (1996)
**Scene:** Romeo (Leonardo DiCaprio) and Juliet (Clare Danes) lie dead.
**Blooper:** Romeo blinks.

**Movie:** *A Night at the Opera* (1935)
**Scene:** Mr. Driftwood (Groucho Marx) complains that his meal at a restaurant in Milan, Italy, costs $9.
**Blooper:** They didn't use dollars in Italy...they used *lire*.

---

Johnny Depp played guitar on the 1998 Oasis album *Be Here Now*.

# INVENTIVE ADVERTISING

*The other day, we were eating delicious Cowboy Burgers at Applebee's when Uncle John remarked that it seems like advertising is becoming more and more intrusive. Then he took a refreshing sip of his ice-cold Pepsi.*

## BEER-FOOT

When the town of Creston, British Columbia, couldn't come up with the $20,000 needed to build a statue of Sasquatch, the Kokanee Brewing Company came to the rescue. But Kokanee's contribution to the statue fund was contingent on one small change in the design. Now Bigfoot can be sighted in downtown Creston...carrying a 12-pack of Kokanee beer.

## HOT CUP OF WHAT?

The advertising company Saatchi & Saatchi came up with a clever idea to help sell Folgers coffee: paint New York City manhole covers so they look like full cups of coffee viewed from above. As the manhole covers emit steam, they look like steaming cups of Folgers coffee. (You know it's Folgers because the logo appears prominently on the street next to the cover.) One problem: The steam that rises out of the manholes doesn't *smell* like coffee, but rather like something much worse and much less appetizing.

## FAUX-LANTHROPY

In 2004 Ben & Jerry's Ice Cream responded to a plea from a group of nuns in Amsterdam, Netherlands, to help the homeless. Displaying incredible generosity, the company gave winter jackets to the city's street people. But every jacket they donated bore the Ben & Jerry's logo.

## PIMP MY DRINK

In 2004 Seagram's Gin "found" its way into popular songs from such hip-hop artists as Twista, Dem Franchize Boyz, and Kanye West. Another performer, Petey Pablo, scored the year's second-most-played rap song, "Freek-a-Leek," which features the lines: "Now I got to give a shout out to Seagram's Gin / 'Cause I'm drinkin' it and they payin' me for it!"

---

Hedgehog urine was once believed to cure baldness.

## AMERICAN GRAFFITI, INC.

Targeting their products to inner-city youth, Sony Music hired graffiti artists to spray-paint ads on walls in many American cities. The ads depicted caricatures of urban kids enjoying Sony music products. City officials, especially in San Francisco, were furious that a major corporation would advocate vandalism and ordered Sony to clean up the walls or face legal action. Sony denied involvement at first, but finally gave in and removed the ads.

## SPAM SPAM SPAM SPAM SPAM SPAM SPAM SPAM!

British comedy troupe Monty Python, who routinely made fun of Spam on their 1970s TV show, was paid by Hormel Foods to display cans of the processed meat in *Spamalot*, their Broadway musical adaptation of the film *Monty Python and the Holy Grail*. (*Spamalot* also featured a paid mention of Yahoo!)

## A NOVEL APPROACH

In her chick-lit book *The Sweetest Taboo*, British novelist Carole Matthews changed the car her heroine drives from a Volkswagen Beetle to a Ford Fiesta. Why? Ford paid her—plus they gave Matthews her own Fiesta (which she named Flossie).

## JO$E, CAN YOU $EE?

In 2005 famed playwright Neil Simon approved a script change in his 1969 play *Sweet Charity*: The original version had the characters simply drinking "tequila." Now they drink "Jose Cuervo's Gran Centenario Premium Tequila." And not only that, the Jose Cuervo logo was displayed prominently on some of the sets.

## BODY LANGUAGE

In 2005 Karolyne Smith of Salt Lake City offered something unusual on eBay: advertising space...on her forehead. She did it, she says, to send her son to private school. GoldenPalace.com, an online casino, chose the "Buy It Now" option for $10,000, and Smith now has a tattoo of the casino's logo on her forehead. "To me, $10,000 is like $1 million," she said. "And it's a small sacrifice to build a better future for my son."

A tiger can cover about 30 feet in a single stride.

# FAMOUS LAST WORDS

*If you could choose your last words, what would they be?*

"Curtain! Fast music! Lights! Ready for the last finale! Great! The show looks good!"
—**Florenz Ziegfeld, Broadway producer, hallucinating on his deathbed**

"It hurts."
—**Charles de Gaulle**

"Dost thou think that I am afraid of it? This will cure all sorrows. What dost thou fear? Strike, man, strike!"
—**Sir Walter Raleigh, to his executioner**

"I'm losing."
—**Frank Sinatra**

"I am not going. Do with me what you like. I am not going. Come on! Come on! Take action! Let's go!"
—**Sitting Bull, to the police who were there to arrest him, just before being shot**

"Vancouver! Vancouver! This is it! This is…"
—**David Johnston, geologist who was killed in the 1980 eruption of Mt. St. Helens**

"I'm tired. I'm going back to bed."
—**George Reeves, who starred as Superman in the 1950s, to his friends before shooting himself**

"Wait until I have finished my problem!"
—**Archimedes, Greek mathematician, to the Roman soldier who captured and killed him**

"No."
—**Alexander Graham Bell, in sign language, to his deaf wife, who pleaded, "Don't leave me."**

"Codeine. Bourbon."
—**Tallulah Bankhead**

"Dammit… Don't you dare ask God to help me!"
—**Joan Crawford, to her housekeeper, who was praying for her**

"Yeah."
—**John Lennon, to the cop in the ambulance, who asked, "Are you John Lennon?"**

Think you know everything about Harry Potter? Okay—when's his birthday? (July 31)

# THE MUSTACHE REPORT

*We found these stories right under our noses.*

## WHY THE LONG FACE?

In 2003 Bhupati Das, from the Indian state of West Bengal, announced his plan to break the world record in "mustache weightlifting." The 48-year-old said he'd been inspired to try it six years earlier when he read about a man who had lifted a typewriter with *his* mustache. "I made up my mind," Das said, "and started nursing my mustache." He "nursed" it to a length of four feet, oiling it twice a day (he had to keep it tucked behind his ears and covered with a cloth while at work). Alas, it was all for naught: He failed to break the *Guinness* world record of 24kg (52.9 lbs.).

## THE STRONG, SILENT TYPE

In 2005 Suzy Walker of Kirkland, Georgia, started going every-where—even to restaurants and movies—with a life-size man-nequin. And the mannequin sported a fake black mustache. She told reporters that she did it because the mannequin, so altered, looked exactly like her husband, a Navy sailor deployed on a submarine. "When I put the mustache on him, I couldn't believe the resemblance," she said. Her husband said he'd become the butt of jokes around the sub, but that he didn't mind—he thought it was funny.

## MUSTACHE PAY

In 2004 police in northern India were offered an extra 65 cents a month if they grew mustaches after a researcher found that officers with mustaches are taken more seriously. But superintendent Mayank Jain said that mustaches would be monitored...to make sure that they didn't give any officers a "mean look."

## SPEED-O

In the 1972 Olympics, mustache-wearing Mark Spitz put on one of the greatest swimming performances in history, winning a record seven gold medals and breaking world records in all seven events. Years later he told *Time* magazine that a Russian coach at the Games had asked him about the mustache. Spitz jokingly replied that it "deflects water away from my mouth, allows my rear end to rise and makes me bullet shaped in the water, and that's what had allowed me to swim so great." The next year, Spitz said, "every Russian male swimmer had a mustache."

## A STASH OF 'STACHE FACTS

• In the 19th century it was illegal for British Army officers to shave their mustaches. The rule was repealed on October 6, 1916.

• According to the MGAA (Mustache Growers Association of America), October 6 is International Mustache Day.

• Medical researchers say mustaches first appear on adolescent males at the corners of the upper lip and then spread to cover the entire area above the lip.

• There are 27 words for "mustache" in Albanian. *Madh* describes a bushy one, *posht* is one that hangs down at the ends, and *fshes* is a long mustache with bristly hairs. (They also have 27 different words for "eyebrows.")

• In 2006 author Dax Herrera (we've never heard of him, either) sold his mustache, called "the Captain," on eBay for $105.

• A *snood* is a type of hair net used to protect and shape mustaches.

• Mustache quiz: How many of the Beatles have mustaches on the cover of *Sgt. Pepper's Lonely Hearts Club Band?* (Answer below.)

• During the Victorian era, wax was often used to keep large mustaches in shape. That created a problem for men drinking hot beverages—the heat would melt the wax into the drinks. In 1830 Englishman Harvey Adams invented the "mustache cup." The cups had a "mustache guard" across the rim, with a small hole that allowed mustached men to safely sip their tea. Mustache cups became popular all over Europe and the United States, and are still made today.

• Quiz answer: All four Beatles have mustaches.

• In 1991 Barbara Mossner of Mount Clemens, Michigan, was ordered to pay her ex-husband $2,800 for damaging his record collection…and for drawing a mustache on his Frank Sinatra poster.

If this page were a nose, these words would be a mustache.

# KNOW YOUR PRODUCE

*Tired of apples and peas? Need a break from prunes and brussels sprouts? Here's a list of unusual fruits and vegetables to look for next time you're at the supermarket.*

**Burro Banana:** A 3- to 5-inch long banana with square sides that tastes kind of lemony when ripe. (There's also an Ice Cream Banana—a creamy banana with a blue skin.)

**Medlar:** A small fruit related to both apples and roses, the medlar is pale, freckled, and radish shaped. It takes so long to ripen that it also ferments, giving it a taste similar to wine.

**Crosnes:** A caterpillar-shaped tuber with a crunch and flavor similar to a Jerusalem artichoke.

**Cherimoya:** A green, bumpy tropical fruit that tastes like a cross between a banana, a pineapple, and a papaya.

**Yuzu:** A yellow Japanese fruit, similar in size and shape to a tangerine, but with a flavor that's stronger than a lemon.

**Lychee:** The lychee looks so much like a nut that it's also known as the lychee nut. Beneath the brown, bumpy shell is a clear or white fruit, said to taste like grapes and cherries drizzled with honey.

**Durian:** A green prickly fruit from Southeast Asia that looks like a hand grenade and smells like stinky feet. It tastes so good that it's known as the "king of fruits."

**Celeriac:** A root that looks like a turnip or a rutabaga, but tastes like celery.

**Pomelo:** A green thick-skinned cousin of the grapefruit. It's not as juicy as a grapefruit, but it can grow as large as a basketball.

**Scorzonera:** A dark, almost black vegetable that has a taste and texture similar to an artichoke.

**Chayote:** A pear-shaped light-green vegetable that tastes like a cross between an apple and a cucumber.

**Kiwano:** Also known as the African horned cucumber and the jelly melon, the kiwano is a yellow-orange, oblong, spiky fruit with lime-green flesh that looks like kiwi fruit but tastes like a mix of lemon, banana, and cucumber.

---

Myth-information: The actual communication from *Apollo 13* was...

# RESEARCH SHOWS...

*Unusual findings from the world of science.*

**FIDGETING MAKES YOU THINNER.** In 2005 researchers at the Mayo Clinic put special movement sensors in 20 subjects' underwear. Ten described themselves as "fidgety"; the other 10 were "couch potatoes." Finding: Fidgety people are less likely to be obese; their extraneous movements burn an average of 350 calories a day, which could work off 10 to 30 pounds a year.

**THINKING MAKES YOU STRONGER.** Researchers at the Cleveland Clinic found that imagining doing exercises (but not doing them) actually boosted muscle strength. The study: They had one group of people imagining moving their pinky muscles for 15 minutes a day for 12 weeks, and another group doing nothing. At the end of the study the second group showed no change, but the first group had a 35% increase in pinky strength.

**HELL ISN'T SO HOT AFTER ALL.** A 2005 "study" determined the temperatures of Heaven and Hell. First, citing Isaiah 30:26, which says that in Heaven "the light of the Moon shall be as the light of the Sun and the light of the Sun shall be sevenfold, as the light of seven days," they did the math and found that heaven would be 525°C, or 977°F. For Hell they used Revelations 21:8, which describes a "lake which burneth with fire and brimstone." Their calculations determined that a lake of molten brimstone (sulphur) must be at or below its boiling point, around 445°C, or 833°F. The study's conclusion: "Heaven is hotter than Hell."

**SPOONS HAVE LEGS.** Scientists at the Burnet Institute in Melbourne, Australia, secretly numbered 70 teaspoons at the facility and tracked their movements over a five-month period. Result: 80% vanished. They said the teaspoons may have disappeared through *counterphenomenological resistentialism*, a belief that inanimate objects have a natural aversion to humans. Or, they said, the spoons may have slipped away to a planet populated by "spoonoid" life forms (they really said that). They also said that people could have simply taken them.

# THE PILGRIMS, PT. I: A CHURCH DIVIDED

*This article started as a short list of facts about the* Mayflower, *the ship that brought the Pilgrims to America in 1620. But after doing a little research, we found ourselves immersed in a much more fascinating story than we anticipated—the tale of the Pilgrims' journey to the New World and religious freedom. Here's Part I, which begins more than a century before the Pilgrims ever set sail.*

## UNHOLY ROMANS

Most modern democracies regard freedom of religion as a basic human right, but if you lived in Europe in the late Middle Ages, it was a very different story. The Roman Catholic Church was the state church in most of Western Europe. Although there were periods of tolerance for other religions scattered throughout the era, intolerance was largely the norm. But by the 16th century, things were beginning to change.

It all began with the Protestant Reformation, which traces its roots to the German monk Martin Luther, who in 1517 nailed his *95 Theses* to the door of the Castle Church in Wittenburg. Sharply critical of the corruption in the Church, Luther's writings (which spread throughout Europe thanks to another new invention, the printing press) ignited the growing contempt for the Church in other countries. By 1534 the discontent had spread to England, where King Henry VIII cut ties with Rome and founded the Church of England, also known as the "Anglican" Church.

## REFORM

But Henry had a personal reason for the break. Luther and the other Reformers broke from Rome on religious principals—they wanted a Church without a pope or bishops, not to mention corruption. The *bible* was supreme, they said, and they wanted it translated into common German (instead of Latin) so that common people could read and interpret it themselves.

Henry's reason: The Pope wouldn't grant him a divorce. His aging wife, Catherine, hadn't given birth to any male heirs, so the king wanted to divorce her and marry his "consort," Anne Boleyn. Henry defied the pope: he divorced Catherine and married Anne anyway…and was promptly excommunicated. So in 1534, he created a new state religion, the Church of England, proclaiming himself as its leader.

## PURITANS AND SEPARATISTS

Henry VIII also had the Bible officially translated into English for the first time. (Seventy years later, in 1611, King James I commissioned a new English version—now known as the King James Bible.) But having the Bible in English just added more fuel to an already growing fire of dissent. Now that people could read the Bible for themselves, they questioned why they needed religious leaders to explain the Scriptures to them at all. By then, some English Protestants had already banded together to "purify" the church from its Roman Catholic traditions. Called Puritans by their enemies, they were shunned—often brutally. Yet they remained loyal to the Church of England, hoping to change it from the inside.

A few of the Puritans, however, saw the attempt as hopeless. For them, the Puritan movement was becoming just as strict and oppressive as the Church of England. These people only wanted to worship as they pleased and be left alone. Seeing no other outlet, they decided to "separate" from both the Puritans and the Church of England, forming congregations in the countryside where they secretly practiced their faith in basements and farmhouses. The punishment for being captured: imprisonment, torture, and in some cases, public execution. This group of religious refugees has been known by—and called themselves—many names: Separatists, Saints, Outcomers…today we refer to them as Pilgrims.

Their first spiritual leader was Richard Clyfton, a parson from Nottinghamshire, England, who spoke openly against the Puritan movement. More importantly, he publicly defied the Church of England. Two young men who attended Clyfton's sermons would one day play very important parts in the settling of America. One was William Brewster, who would lead the Separatists to the Netherlands; the other was William Bradford, who would lead them to America. But before any of that could happen, these "enemies of the state" first had to escape from England.

*To discover more about the Pilgrims, sail over to page 215.*

# WEIRD GHOSTS

*You might not want to read this page with the lights out.*

**WANDERING SOLES.** Employees at a store in Cornwall, England, claim a ghost has taken up residence in the shop. And the ghost, they say, is obsessed with shoes. "I was standing at the counter," says a salesclerk named Helen Honey, "when the top shelf of the display began wobbling. Then a pair of deck shoes jumped off the shelf and landed next to each other. I ran out of the shop, screaming." Locals say the ghost is a former owner of the shop, a butcher, who died in the 1800s.

**MOO!** Residents of Culver, Oregon, have reported driving a winding section of Highway 97 at night and seeing phantom cows appear suddenly in front of them. The ghost cows have glowing green eyes, and the cars pass right through them. (*Moo*-ha-ha!)

**SCARE-A-VISION.** Tracey Taylor of Lower Ince, England, is convinced that her television is haunted. She took a picture of her two-year-old daughter Faith dusting the TV set, and when she got the photos developed, she noticed a mysterious "face" on the screen...even though the set was off. It wasn't a reflection because there was nobody else in the room. Who was it? When Tracey showed the photo to Faith, the child said, "That's Ben."

**POLTER-BARF.** Indiana State University students report seeing a female ghost in their dormitory. What does it do? It throws up. According to folklore professor Nan McEntire, "Barfing Barb," as she's known, has been in the building for decades. Local legend says she's the spirit of a student who died after a night of drinking.

**MEDIUM RARE.** Ercy Cardoso of Viamao, Brazil, was shot and killed in 2003. His girlfriend, Iara Barcelos, was charged with the crime but ultimately acquitted thanks to an unusual witness: a medium hired by Barcelos said Cardoso's ghost appeared to him and dictated two letters swearing to Barcelos's innocence. A spokesman for the court said the ghost's testimony was accepted as evidence because the prosecution never registered an objection.

---

**A spider sheds its skin as many as 15 times during its life.**

# THE AVRO ARROW

*If you're not from Canada, you've probably never heard of the Avro Arrow. If you are from Canada, you may never forget it. Here's the story of the fastest plane that never was.*

## HERE WE GO AGAIN

When the Soviet Union tested its first nuclear weapon in 1949, just four years after the end of World War II, it began to seem like the next world war, this time a *nuclear* war, might be just around the corner. The Soviets were also developing long-range bombers—could they be planning to attack Europe and North America?

Canada's response to the new threat was to develop jet fighters that could intercept and destroy any Soviet bombers before they could attack their targets. The first such aircraft, a jet fighter named the Avro CF-100 Canuck, entered service in 1953. By then, however, the Soviets were already working on a new generation of jet-powered bombers, which would be able to fly higher and faster than any they'd built before. The Royal Canadian Air Force felt they needed a *supersonic* jet fighter to counter the Soviet threat.

## DO IT YOURSELF

Specifically, the RCAF wanted a plane that could fly at Mach 1.5 (one and a half times the speed of sound), climb to 50,000 feet in less than five minutes, and fly for 300 nautical miles without refueling. It also had to be able to fly day or night in any kind of weather. There were no planes in existence or even on the drawing board that could meet those specifications, so in December 1953 the Canadian government awarded Avro Canada Ltd., the builder of the Canuck, a $27 million contract to begin work on developing just such a plane. When completed, it would be the fastest fighter plane ever built.

Building the Arrow, as the plane was called, was problematic from the start. Avro's plan was to design the airframe and then buy the engines, the weapons systems, and the other major components from outside suppliers. But when its first and second choices for jet engines were both discontinued, Avro decided to design the

---

In 1912 the Giants and Yankees played a charity game to raise money for *Titanic* survivors.

engines in-house. The company encountered similar problems with its choices of missile and firing systems. All these setbacks caused the cost of the Arrow to soar, but the RCAF remained committed to the project. While this was happening, the Soviet Union detonated its first hydrogen bomb and rolled out two different kinds of jet-powered bombers. There was no time to waste—in 1955 the Canadian government awarded Avro a $260 million contract to build five test planes, followed by 35 production aircraft.

## TURNING POINT

Avro had never built a supersonic aircraft before, yet it managed to design and build one of the world's most sophisticated aircraft in just under four years. It had accomplished a great deal in a very short period of time, but the timing couldn't have been worse: On the very day that the first flyable prototype was rolled out in front of 12,000 spectators in October 1957, the Soviet Union sent Sputnik, the world's first artificial Earth satellite, into space. If the Soviets were launching satellites, could nuclear-tipped missiles be very far behind? For a time, defense planners wondered if combat aircraft would become obsolete in the missile age. Meanwhile, the Arrow's cost kept climbing.

Earlier that year, Canada and the United States had formed the North American Air Defense Command (NORAD) and they'd already began to coordinate their air defense. Cost: $270 million. NORAD's air defense system called for using Bomarc nuclear-tipped antiaircraft missiles, not fighter planes, to intercept enemy bombers. Could Canada afford both missiles *and* fighters?

In September 1958, the Canadian Department of Defense calculated that even after having spent $300 million on the Arrow, another $871 million was needed to finish the program. That was an astronomical amount of money in 1958, and Canada had far fewer taxpayers than the U.S. did to shoulder the cost. The government decided that rather than build 40 planes as planned, it would commit only to finishing the handful of airplanes currently under construction. The rest of the program was placed under review.

## BLACK FRIDAY

Then, without warning, on the morning of February 20, 1959, the Canadian government announced it was scrapping the Arrow immediately. Avro employees learned of the decision 20 minutes later, and at 4:00 that afternoon it was announced over the P.A. system that all 14,525 of them were out of a job. Another 26,000 Canadians working for Avro subcontractors lost their jobs, too.

## WHAT'S THE PROBLEM?

The irony of the cancellation was that in spite of all the problems, Avro had managed to produce a very sophisticated aircraft that had performed exceptionally well in flight testing. At the time the program was cancelled, the company was only two weeks away from fitting the aircraft with improved jet engines that would likely have made it the fastest fighter plane in the world.

Would the Arrow have broken the world speed record? We'll never know for sure, because shortly after the program was cancelled, the Canadian government ordered everything associated with the program—aircraft, models, tooling, spare parts, even blueprints and photographs—to be destroyed to prevent the technology from falling into the hands of Soviet spies.

Canadian taxpayers had pumped more than $300 million into the project by then, but had literally nothing to show for it. Avro closed its doors; Canada lost its edge in defense aviation and never built another fighter plane. Many of Avro's top designers and engineers went abroad to find work: Some went to Europe and worked on the Concorde, and more than 30 went to NASA and played leading roles in the effort to land *American* men on the moon.

## JET SET

All that survives today are a couple of engines, a cockpit and nose cone, a few diagrams, odd parts, and some historical photos. This near-total destruction of the Arrow, combined with the fact that it was the most advanced fighter of its day, has elevated the plane to mythical status. "Arrow Heads," as fans are known, build replicas, trade conspiracy theories, and dream of what might have been. Wishful thinkers look at the 1959 photo showing the jets lined up outside the factory to be destroyed and note that one plane, RL-202, is not in the picture. Does that mean it's still out there somewhere, waiting to be found? University of Toronto historian Michael Bliss likes to tell his students it's in a barn in Saskatchewan. "It's taken out and flown once a year. By Elvis."

# DIED ON THE JOHN

*From the darker wing of Uncle John's Stall of Fame, here
are some people who took their last breaths in the bathroom.
(Someday we'll probably put Uncle John on the list.)*

In 1016, 27-year-old King Edmund II of England was murdered
in the bathroom. An assassin hid behind the primitive toilet
and, as Edmund sat, the murderer stepped out and quickly
shoved his sword twice "into the king's bowels."

• Another English monarch, King George II, died on the toilet
in 1760 at the age of 77. He woke up at six that morning, drank
some chocolate, and an hour later went to the bathroom, where
he died of a ruptured aorta.

• Evelyn Waugh, one of the greatest English novelists of the
20th century (*Brideshead Revisited, The Loved One*) had just
returned home from Easter Mass. In recent years, the 62-year-old
had put on a lot of weight. He also drank a lot, smoked cigars,
and rarely exercised. He died "straining at stool" in the bathroom, April 10, 1966.

• Perhaps the most famous death-by-toilet is Elvis Presley's. A
combination of weight gain and too many prescription drugs gave
the 42-year-old singer a heart attack while he was "takin' care of
business." (At the time of his death he was reading a book entitled
*The Scientific Search for the Face of Jesus*.)

• Movie producer Don Simpson (*Top Gun, Flashdance*) died in
1996. While rumors persisted that he died of a cocaine overdose,
the truth was more humble and embarrassing: He died of a heart
attack while going to the bathroom.

• It's commonly believed that Catherine the Great of Russia died
after being "crushed" by a horse. True? Na-a-a-a-y. On that fate-
ful day in 1796, she suffered a stroke while sitting on the toilet,
but died in her bed several hours later.

# Q & A: ASK THE EXPERTS

*Everyone's got a question or two they'd like answered—basic stuff, like "Why is the sky blue?" Here are a few of those questions, with answers from some of the nation's top trivia experts.*

## TURNING OVER A NEW LEAF

**Q:** *Why do leaves change color in the fall?*

**A:** "The *carotenoids* (pigments in photosynthesizing cells), which are responsible for the fall colors, are always present in a tree's leaves. During the growing season, however, those colors are eclipsed by the green of chlorophyll. Toward the end of summer, when the chlorophyll production ceases, the other colors of the carotenoids (yellow, orange, red, or purple) become visible." (From *The Handy Science Answer Book*, by the Carnegie Library)

## HOT, BUT NOT

**Q:** *Why do people sweat when they eat really spicy food?*

**A:** "Spicy foods, such as chili peppers, contain a chemical that stimulates the same nerve endings in the mouth as a rise in temperature does. The nerves don't know what caused the stimulation; they just send a message to the brain telling it that the temperature near the face has risen. The brain reacts by activating cooling mechanisms around the face, and one of these mechanisms is perspiration." (From *Ever Wonder Why?*, by Douglas B. Smith)

## REALITY BITES

**Q:** *How come you can't feel a mosquito bite until it starts to itch?*

**A:** "The female mosquito's biting technique is so skillful that most humans cannot feel it. After a minute or two of resting on the skin, she presses her lancets into a nice, juicy capillary—the insertion takes about a minute. It's barely noticeable because the mosquito lubricates her mouthparts with her own saliva before biting. Most of us become aware of the itching only after the mosquito is long gone—not because of the bite or the loss of blood, but because of the saliva left behind. It acts not only as a lubricant, but also as an anesthetic. For most people, the saliva is a blessing, since it allows us to be oblivious to the fact that our blood is being sucked. Unfortunately, it contains anticoagulant components that can cause allergic reactions—the itchy bumps that make us wonder why mosquitoes exist in this otherwise wonderful world." (From *Do Penguins Have Knees?*, by David Feldman)

## YECCH!

Q: *Why do so many kids hate liver and Brussels sprouts?*
A: Short answer: they're disgusting. Long answer: "Liver and Brussels sprouts have unusual textures and odors as well as bland, gray-green coloring. But probably the biggest reason is the strong taste. Children's taste buds are just developing, and haven't matured enough to enjoy these two delicacies. Liver actually tastes more bitter to a kid's taste buds than to an adult's." (From *Funny You Should Ask*, by Marg Meikle)

## METER READERS

Q: *How are TV ratings determined?*
A: "The ACNielsen Corporation does them, sampling a cross section of households from all over the United States. Samples include homes from all 50 states and people of all ages, income groups, geographic areas, ethnicities, and educational levels—all in proportion to their presence in the population at large. Special meters, known as 'set-top meters,' are installed to capture information about what channel is being viewed in about 25,000 households. The data is automatically retrieved by Nielsen computers each night, then relayed via phone lines to the operations center in Florida, and processed that same night for release to the television industry the next day." (Nielsen Media Research)

## UNCLE JOHN'S WEIGHT-LOSS SYSTEM

Q: *Every time you fart, do you lose a little weight?*
A: "Actually, there is some reason to believe that after a good toot you weigh more—slightly. Two of the principal components of flatus are hydrogen and methane, which are both lighter than air. Thus it is conceivable that when you deflate, as it were, you lose buoyancy and add poundage. On the other hand, it is not clear what the ambient pressure of gas in the intestines is—a critical factor, since even a light gas under sufficient compression weighs the same as or more than air." (From *The Straight Dope*, by Cecil Adams)

A group of hares is called a *down*. (A group of hairs is called a *wig*.)

# BIERCE-ISMS

*Author and newspaper columnist Ambrose Bierce (1842–1914)
often peppered his articles with his own humorous—and cynical
—definitions for common words. Here are a few of our favorites.*

**Dentist:** A magician who, putting metal into your mouth, pulls coins out of your pocket.

**Positive:** Mistaken, at the top of one's voice.

**Acquaintance:** A person whom we know well enough to borrow from, but not well enough to lend to.

**Dog:** An additional Deity designed to catch the overflow and surplus of the world's worship.

**Clairvoyant:** A person who has the power of seeing that which is invisible to her patron—namely, that he is a blockhead.

**Revolution:** An abrupt change in the form of misgovernment.

**Corporation:** An ingenious device for obtaining individual profit without individual responsibility.

**Admiration:** Our polite recognition of another's resemblance to ourselves.

**Saint:** A dead sinner, revised and edited.

**Alliance:** The union of two thieves who have their hands so deeply inserted in each other's pockets that they cannot separately plunder a third.

**Responsibility:** A detachable burden easily shifted to the shoulders of God, Fate, Fortune, Luck, or one's neighbor.

**Appeal:** In law, to put the dice into the box for another throw.

**Coward:** One who in a perilous emergency thinks with his legs.

**Famous:** Conspicuously miserable.

**Friendship:** A ship big enough to carry two in fair weather, but only one in foul.

**Husband:** One who, having dined, is charged with the care of the plate.

**Meekness:** Uncommon patience in planning a revenge that is worthwhile.

**Outcome:** A particular type of disappointment.

**Love:** A temporary insanity curable by marriage.

---

Geography fact: Brazil is larger than all 48 contiguous United States combined.

# IT SEEMED LIKE A GOOD IDEA AT THE TIME

*Life is constantly presenting us with interesting challenges. These challenges have many possible solutions…some good, some not so good, and some just plain bad. These belong in the third category.*

## THE KEYS TO SUCCESS

**Challenge:** A tourist at Montana's Glacier National Park wanted to take a picture of a squirrel that had scurried away into its rocky den.

**Bad Idea:** Trying to coax the animal out of its lair, the man dangled his only set of car keys in front of the opening.

**Outcome:** The squirrel darted out, snatched the keys right out of the man's hand, and disappeared back into the ground. Rangers tried to assist the frantic tourist, but the squirrel (and the keys) were nowhere to be found. The man had to call a locksmith out to the park and pay a hefty sum to get his car back on the road.

## BACKFIRING BOOBY TRAP

**Challenge:** A 66-year-old Dutchman had some very important "stuff" in his garden shed and was afraid someone would steal it.

**Bad Idea:** Using some ropes, he devised a booby trap that hung a shotgun inside the door and set it to go off when the door was opened. Then he proudly opened the door to give his friends a demonstration.

**Outcome:** The man was shot in the stomach by his own gun and needed emergency surgery. After he recovered, he went to jail. (Police discovered the "stuff" he was guarding: 15 full-grown marijuana plants.)

## LIGHT ONE CANDLE

**Challenge:** A 29-year-old St. Paul, Minnesota, man, identified only as Robert, wanted to clean the grit out of his bathtub.

**Bad Idea:** He used gasoline to clean the tub, which left the bathroom smelling really bad. To mask the odor, Robert lit aromatic candles.

The cables on the Golden Gate Bridge contain 80,000 miles of steel wire.

**Outcome:** Robert blew up his apartment. He sustained severe burns, but survived. (The apartment did not.)

## DROVE MY CHEVY TO THE LEVEE

**Challenge:** In 1993, 24-year-old James Scott lived on the Illinois side of the Mississippi River. His wife worked on the Missouri side. All Scott wanted to do was "party," but his wife wouldn't let him.

**Bad Idea:** Scott removed some sandbags from a nearby levee, hoping the river would wash out the road that his wife used to take home.

**Outcome:** Not only did Scott wash out the road…he also flooded 14,000 acres, destroying crops as well as dozens of homes and businesses, and causing a local bridge to be closed for more than three months. After bragging about his "success" to his friends, Scott was arrested and sentenced to life in prison (the maximum penalty for "causing a catastrophe").

## IN NEED OF A LIFT

**Challenge:** Somjet Korkeaw, a 42-year-old office worker from Bangkok, Thailand, was leaving work on a Saturday afternoon when he suddenly realized he'd forgotten something and had to return to his office on the 99th floor to get it. Unfortunately, the passenger elevators had already been turned off for the weekend and the stair doors were locked.

**Bad Idea:** He decided to take a small cargo elevator (designed to carry food and documents). It was small, so he had to crouch into a ball to fit, but it was the only way back to the office.

**Outcome:** Korkeaw weighed 150 pounds, far too heavy for the lift to carry. Result: It got stuck between floors. He had to wait, bent over and crammed inside the little box, for more than 40 hours until the building reopened on Monday morning.

## SHELL SHOCK

**Challenge:** A 19-year-old man from Spokane, Washington, wanted to make a necklace out of bullets. The only way to string the necklace together was to punch holes in the live ammunition.

**Bad Idea:** He punched a hole in the live ammunition.

**Outcome:** He survived the explosion, but will never play piano again.

First horror movie: *Dr. Jekyll and Mr. Hyde* (1908).

# FALSE FRIENDS

*What do you call English words that look or sound exactly like words in other languages, but have entirely different meanings? Linguists call them "false friends" because they can get you into trouble. A few examples:*

**Kill** (Mideast): Good friend

**Fatal** (Germany): Annoying

**Lawman** (Surinam): Lunatic

**Sky** (Norway): Cloud

**City** (Czech): Feelings

**Slut** (Sweden): End

**Alone** (Italy): Halo

**Bless!** (Iceland): Goodbye!

**Fart** (Turkey): Exaggerating

**Bog** (Russia): God

**Arse** (Turkey): Violin bow

**Turd** (Iran): Fragile

**Chew** (Ethiopia): Salt

**Brat** (Russia): Brother

**Dad** (Albania): Wet nurse

**Blubber** (Netherlands): Sun

**Babe** (Swaziland): Priest

**Beast** (Iran): Twenty

**Santa** (Mideast): Wart

**After** (Germany): Anus

**Made** (Netherlands): Maggot

**Pasta** (Portugal): Briefcase

**Bizarro** (Spain): Brave

**Bank** (Netherlands): Bench

**Pies** (Poland): Dog

**Mama** (Georgia): Father

**Kiss** (Sweden): Urine

**Mist** (Germany): Manure

**King** (Estonia): Shoe

**Bean** (Ireland): Woman

**Sex** (Sweden): Six

**Billion** (France): Trillion

**Travesty** (Greece): Transvestite

**Big** (Netherlands): Piglet

**Flint** (Sweden): Bald head

**Ale** (Finland): Discount

**Four** (France): Oven

**Bimbo** (Japan): Poor person

**Groin** (France): Snout

**Helmet** (Finland): Pearls

**Bra** (Sweden): Good

**Air** (Indonesia): Water

**Coin** (Scotland): Dogs

**Cat** (Indonesia): Paint

Shh! The word "listen" contains the same letters as the word "silent".

# SNAKES ON A...

*Get these @\*%$\*%& snakes off this @\*%$\*%& page!*

## BED

B A woman in Leith, Scotland, was cleaning her bedroom when she went to remove her son's toy snake from the bed. Only problem: It wasn't a toy. The snake lunged at her, then slid under the sheets. The terrified woman jumped up on a chair and called her fiancé, who rushed home and was able to catch the two-foot-long reptile. It turned out to be be a harmless corn snake. They don't know how it got into the bed.

## ...CAN

In 2005 a woman in Florida required three days in the hospital after she was bitten on the leg by a poisonous snake...in her toilet. Alicia Bailey said the snake—which disappeared and was not recovered—was a water moccasin, and a large one. She also said the incident had a lasting impact. "We're currently very uncomfortable in our home," she said, "and toilet shy."

## ...STATUE

A 16-foot-long albino king cobra was found wrapped around a statue of the the Hindu goddess Amman in a Malaysian temple in 2006. King cobras are incredibly fearsome: They can make a third of their body length vertical (meaning one this large could look eye-to-eye with a human) and can deliver enough venom to kill an elephant. But seeing one is a good omen in Hindu mythology, and over the next two days more than 30,000 people passed through the temple to see the snake, leaving offerings of milk and eggs. After two days in the temple, the snake slithered away, having injured no one.

## ...ALLIGATOR

In 2005 rangers in Florida's Everglades National Park were stunned to find a 6-foot-long alligator protruding from the stomach of a 13-foot-long snake. Both were dead. The Burmese python had swallowed the alligator whole, and the alligator had then apparently tried to claw its way out—its tail and back legs protruded from the snake's ruptured belly. Burmese pythons thrive in the Everglades, but they aren't native; they started out as escaped pets. Scientists call the find "an ominous sign" that the non-native snakes could dangerously disrupt the area's ecosystem by replacing the alligator as the top predator. But maybe not: The python's head was missing, causing one biologist to surmise that another alligator may have come along and bitten it off.

## ...CAT

Another Burmese python made the news in 2006, when Interlachen, Florida, resident Nicole Salvatore walked into a friend's house. The friend wasn't home, but a 12-foot-long python was... and it was eating her friend's cat. The cat was dead by the time the owner, Dianne Turner, arrived home. Amazingly, Florida Fish and Wildlife officials advised Turner that she was not allowed to kill the snake. "All we could do was stand there and watch that snake eat the cat," Salvatore said. The python had escaped from its outdoor pen in a neighbor's yard. (The kitty's name: Burrito.)

## ...YES, A PLANE

Pilot Monty Coles of West Virginia was about to land his Piper Cherokee in Ohio in 2006 when a snake stuck its head out of the instrument panel. Coles was 3,000 feet in the air at the time. He swatted at the four-foot-long snake, causing it to drop to the floor near his feet. As it started to slither away, Coles grabbed it behind its head. "It coiled all around my arm," he said after landing, "and its tail grabbed hold of a lever on the floor and started pulling." Coles radioed for permission to make an emergency landing: "They came back and asked what my problem was. I told them I had one hand full of snake and the other hand full of plane." He added, "Nothing in any of the manuals ever described anything like this."

\*　　\*　　\*

### TOUGH GUY

"Valentin Grimaldo, 40, was bitten by a poisonous coral snake near Encino, Texas. He survived by biting the snake's head off, slitting its body lengthwise, and using the skin for a tourniquet until help arrived."　　　　　—News of the Weird

# STRANGE LAWSUITS

*Think you can't sue your neighbor just for being a jerk?
These days it seems like people will sue each other over
anything. Here are a few real-life examples.*

**PLAINTIFF:** Rena Young

**DEFENDANT:** Taylor Ostergaard and Lindsey Zilletti, two 18-year-old girls

**LAWSUIT:** One night in July 2005, Ostergaard and Zilletti baked plates of chocolate chip cookies and handed them out to their neighbors in Durango, Colorado. When they left the plate of cookies on Young's doorstep and knocked on her door around 10:30 p.m., the woman became so terrified by "the shadowy figures who banged on her door" that she called the police. According to the cops, no crime had been committed, but Young was still agitated. She went to the hospital the next morning with what she thought was a heart attack (doctors said it was an anxiety attack). Ostergaard and Zilletti both wrote letters of apology, but Young sued them, claiming the apologies rang false.

**VERDICT:** The judge ordered the girls to pay $930 to cover Young's medical bills. He acknowledged that no crime had been committed, but thought that 10:30 p.m. was too late for the girls to be out.

**PLAINTIFF:** Austin Aitken

**DEFENDANT:** NBC

**LAWSUIT:** Aitken was a regular viewer of NBC's gross-out game show *Fear Factor*, which often makes contestants eat disgusting things, such as worms, insects, or animals' internal organs. Aitken had no problem watching people eat worms and animal parts, but claimed a 2005 episode where contestants ate rats chopped up in a blender made his blood pressure rise, made him dizzy and light-headed, and ultimately, made him vomit. So he sued NBC for $2.5 million. "It's barbaric, some of the things they ask these individuals to do," Aitken said.

**VERDICT:** Thrown out of court.

**PLAINTIFF:** Louise Kelsey of Melbourne, Australia

**DEFENDANT:** Park Hyatt Hotel

**LAWSUIT:** In 2005 Kelsey, 58, filed suit against the hotel, where she had earlier worked as a maid. The suit said that in 2001 Kelsey was working in the hotel when a guest, a Uruguayan soccer player in town for a World Cup match, suddenly grabbed her and kissed her. She claimed the kiss led to her suffering post-traumatic stress disorder, which made her legally blind a year later.

**VERDICT:** At first the Park Hyatt fought the case, bringing in a doctor to testify that it must have been "the most powerful kiss in history," but later agreed to an out-of-court settlement.

**PLAINTIFF:** Jirra Collings Ware of Sydney, Australia

**DEFENDANT:** OAMPS Insurance Brokers

**LAWSUIT:** Ware was fired in 2005 after repeatedly showing up for work drunk. He sued, claiming that he suffers from Attention Deficit Disorder, and his employer should have done more to accommodate the illness.

**VERDICT:** Ware won the case and was awarded $7,300.

**PLAINTIFF:** LPGA caddie Gary Robinson

**DEFENDANT:** LPGA golfer Jackie Gallagher-Smith

**LAWSUIT:** Robinson sued his boss in 2005, saying that she had tricked him into a sexual relationship just so she could have a child. Shortly after he was hired by Gallagher-Smith, who was married, she began making advances toward him. At first he wrote it off as "innocent playful activity," but it turned into a physical relationship, he said, and in July she became pregnant…but refuses to acknowledge him as the father. "I hope to get retribution for the emotional pain and suffering," he says, "and eventually get some rights to the child." Gallagher-Smith's lawyer said the case was nothing more than an attempt at extortion.

**VERDICT:** Case dropped. The suit was filed in the state of Florida, where the law says a child born into a marriage is a product of that marriage. That meant Robinson had no rights and couldn't demand a DNA test. In 2006 he dropped the case.

# G.E. COLLEGE BOWL

*The G.E. College Bowl was a quiz show that appeared on TV from 1959 to 1970. Teams from colleges all over the country competed for the national title. Are you as smart as the college kids of yesteryear? Test yourself on these sample questions from the show. (Answers are on page 514.)*

## HOW TO PLAY

*The G.E. College Bowl* was played by two teams of four college students each, representing two different schools—the University of Minnesota vs. UCLA, for example.

• Each player on each team had a buzzer. When the moderator (originally Allen Ludden, who also hosted *Password*) read the first question, called the "Tossup" question, the first player to press the buzzer got to try to answer it. Subject categories included General Knowledge, Literature, Science and Mathematics, Geography, and four areas of History: American, European, Ancient, and General.

• If the student gave the correct answer to the Tossup question, their team got five points and a chance to answer a Bonus question on the same subject for additional points.

• If the first team answered the Tossup incorrectly, the other team got a chance to answer it. If their answer was correct, they got to answer the Bonus question.

• Only individuals could answer Tossup questions, but the entire team could confer on Bonus questions.

So, you think you're ready to give it a try? Below are some questions taken from the original TV show.

## LITERATURE

**Tossup Question:** When the fictional character, Napoleon, and his cohorts win the battle at Manor Farm, they rename the farm. What name do they give it?

**Bonus Questions:**

**1.** What English poet wrote, "'Tis better to have loved and lost, Than never to have loved at all."

**2.** The author of "Prometheus Unbound" and the author of *Frankenstein* were related somehow. How?

---

**Ancient ruler: The tape measure was patented in 1868.**

**3.** The old man in Ernest Hemingway's *The Old Man and the Sea* has a name. What is it?

**4.** Which Beat movement author wrote the following: "We gotta go and never stop going till we get there. Where we going, man? I don't know, but we gotta go."

**5.** William Sydney Porter polished his writing skills while serving a prison sentence for embezzling bank funds. When he got out of the slammer he became better known by what pen name?

## SCIENCE & MATHEMATICS

**Tossup Question:** What does a chronometer measure?

**Bonus Questions:**

**1.** Which of the following is moving faster: a ship traveling at 40 knots, or a car traveling 46 miles per hour?

**2.** What's the common name for the part of your body where the ulnar nerve rests against the medial condyle of the humerus?

**3.** If you buy a dog for $40, sell it for $50, buy it back for $60, and sell it again for $70, how much money have you made or lost?

**4.** *Selenography* is the name for the scientific study of what?

**5.** It's 50° Fahrenheit outside. Within two degrees, what will the reading be on a metric (Celsius) thermometer?

## GENERAL KNOWLEDGE

**Tossup Question:** A pair of aces and a pair of eights are known as the "dead man's hand" in poker. Who was holding this hand when he died?

**Bonus Questions:**

**1.** Where are the Islands of Langerhans located?

**2.** The wife of a duke is called a duchess. The wife of a count is called a countess. What is the wife of an earl called?

**3.** An *algophobe* is afraid of what?

**4.** Coracles, galleons, caravels, and triremes are all types of what?

**5.** If you had a *Musca domestica* in your house, would you 1) eat it, 2) kill it, or 3) tell it to clean your house?

*Ready for more? Turn to page 303 for another round of G.E. College Bowl.*

A turtle's shell is sensitive enough to feel a twig brush across it.

# LIFE'S A GAMBLE

*We'll give you 5 to 1 odds that even if you're a regular gambler, you don't know the origins of these games.*

B LACKJACK
**Description:** Players add up the numbers on the cards they are dealt and try to get as close to 21 points without going over. Face cards count as 10; aces count as 11 or 1.

**History:** Originally called *vingt-et-un,* or "twenty-one," blackjack is believed to have been invented in France in the early 1700s. Today it's one of the most popular casino card games in the world, but it took a while to catch on. A casino in Evansville, Indiana, introduced it to the United States in 1910. The only way gambling houses could get poker players to give the game a try was by awarding bonus payouts for valuable hands. The biggest payout of all, $10 for every $1 bet, went to the player who held the ace of spades and either of the black jacks. The name that resulted—*blackjack*—lasted a lot longer than the bonus payouts did.

## KENO

**Description:** A game similar to Bingo, except that players get to pick their own numbers instead of being stuck with the ones printed on their bingo card. After a player picks several numbers, the house randomly picks 20 numbers between 1 and 80; if the house picks most or all of the player's numbers, the player wins a payout. Many state lotteries operate along similar lines.

**History:** This game was invented in China during the Han Dynasty (202 B.C. to 220 A.D.), reportedly when a city came under siege and had to raise money for the army to defend it. Why burden people with an extra tax when you can get them to contribute voluntarily? So officials devised a lottery system instead, one in which 20 out of a possible 120 Chinese characters were chosen at random. Players selected 10 characters of their own, and prizes went to anyone who had at least 5 matching characters. The game saved the city and became popular over so large an area that homing pigeons were used to send messages to people telling them whether they'd won or lost. That's how the Chinese version of the game became known as *Pok Kop Piu*, or "White Pigeon Ticket."

The American version of the game dates back to 1928, when some Chinese men asked a Butte, Montana, bar owner named Joseph Lyden to organize a game of White Pigeon Ticket for them. Lyden dropped the Chinese characters in favor of numbers and renamed the game Keno (from a French game called *quine*, which means "five winning numbers"). He's also the guy who brought the game to Las Vegas after casino gambling was legalized in 1931.

## SLOT MACHINES

**Description:** You don't know what a slot machine is?

**History:** Mechanical poker machines were popular in taverns as far back as the 1880s: the player put in a nickel and pulled a lever, which caused five rotating reels with playing cards painted on them to spin and deal a poker hand. These machines didn't give direct cash payouts—there are too many different winning combinations in poker for the machine to be able to pay them all. Instead, when you got a winning hand you showed it to the bartender. He poured you a free drink, made you a sandwich, or gave you whatever other prize was listed next to the machine.

Then in 1887, a man named Charles Fey built a much simpler machine called the Liberty Bell. It had only three reels and only five possible symbols: horseshoes, diamonds, spades, hearts, and bells. The simpler design made automated payouts possible: when a player got three bells, they won the highest jackpot of all—ten whole nickels! Mobster Bugsy Siegel was the first in Las Vegas to put slot machines in his casino, the Flamingo Hotel, in 1947. At the time they were little more than novelty items designed to keep wives and girlfriends busy while the men played poker or blackjack or shot craps. Today they're computerized, and they bring in between 60% and 80% of a typical casino's total profits.

## VIDEO POKER

**Description:** Just like it sounds—a video-game version of poker. You put in your money, the machine deals your "cards" onto a video screen, and you play poker as if you were sitting at a poker table.

**History:** Another descendant of the early mechanical poker machine, video poker was invented after slot machine manufacturer Si Redd saw the Pong video game in the early 1970s. "We just copied it," he told an interviewer in 2001. Redd started out making both blackjack and poker machines, but dropped blackjack after gamblers realized that their money lasted a lot longer in the poker machines.

As with slot machines when they were first introduced, Redd thought video poker was little more than a novelty; he figured people entering the casino would play a few games before getting down to more serious gambling. Wrong again—gamblers too intimidated to play at the poker tables made video poker machines a mainstay.

## THE BIG SIX WHEEL/WHEEL OF FORTUNE

**Description:** If you're familiar with TV's *Wheel of Fortune*, you already know how this game works. The only differences are that in casinos the wheel is mounted vertically, not horizontally the way it is on TV, and the dealer spins it instead of the players. Pegs divide the wheel into 54 different sections that offer different payouts according to how many times they appear on the wheel. Sections that pay $1 for every dollar wagered are scattered all over the wheel, but there may be only one or two sections that pay $20. When the wheel is spun, the pegs rub against an arrow pointer that slows the wheel down; the winning section is the one the arrow is pointing at when the wheel stops spinning.

**History:** The wheel of fortune is so old that nobody knows for sure how it originated. One story, most likely apocryphal, is that Roman soldiers invented the game as a means of divvying up the battlefield spoils of defeated enemies. Rather than fight over who got what, each soldier inscribed a mark in a section of the wheel of an overturned chariot. A spear was stuck into the ground next to the wheel to serve as a marker, and then the wheel was spun. The booty in question went to the person whose mark was closest to the spear when the wheel stopped spinning. From there the game is said to have spread to harvest festivals and other public gatherings, where the large wheel made it possible for crowds of people to follow the action. Roulette, which means "small wheel" in French, may have started out as a more portable version of the same game.

# UNCLE JOHN'S STALL OF FAME

*Uncle John is amazed—and pleased—by the creative ways
people get involved with bathrooms, toilets, toilet paper,
etc. That's why he created the "Stall of Fame."*

**H**onoree: Patricia Bernard, a game show contestant
**Notable Achievement:** Making game show history…in
the ladies' room
**True Story:** In 1976 Bernard was an audience member on the
game show *The Price Is Right*. And she knew her chances of getting on the show were slim—out of 350 hopefuls, only 9 are
chosen to play. So she thought she could safely sneak away for a
bathroom break. You can probably guess what happened next:
"Patricia Bernard! Come on down!" The camera panned the audience looking for her…to no avail. Her stunned husband, who'd
been sitting next to her, jumped up and yelled, "Hold on, I'll go
get her!" and ran out of the studio. Amused, host Bob Barker said
into his microphone, "It had to happen some time, folks. She's in
the little girls' room. Well, if she can't come to us, let's all go to
her." Then Barker started walking down the aisle, followed by several contestants. Thankfully, before they reached the bathroom,
the Bernards ran back into the studio to the cheers of the audience. (No word on how she did on the show.)

**Honorees:** Li Zhaoxing, a Chinese diplomat, and Taro Aso, a
Japanese diplomat
**Notable Achievement:** Successfully practicing "toilet diplomacy"
**True Story:** In Malaysia in 2006, during summit talks to improve
the tense relationship between China and Japan, Aso was using
the men's room when Li happened to walk in. With the press
corps waiting outside, the two talked about state matters…for 20
minutes. Then they exited (one at a time) and went to their
respective seats for the "formal" set of meetings. Once there, Aso
announced to his colleagues, "I just met Li in the toilet and we
had a good discussion." Asked later whether Aso knew that Li

The term "Dixieland" is rumored to come from…

was already in the restroom, he dismissed it as pure coincidence, adding, "But it was awfully cold in the conference room."

**Honoree:** Yellowcard, a rock group from Jacksonville, Florida
**Notable Achievement:** Turning the bathroom into a trophy room
**True Story:** After the band won a 2004 MTV Music Video Award for their song "Ocean Avenue," the members had a group meeting to figure out where they would display the award, known as a Moonman. They decided to put it in the bathroom. Why? Because that's where they write most of their songs. "The acoustics are really good in there," explained the group's guitarist.

**Honorees:** Writer Christopher Welzenbach, producer Rodrigo Frampton, and director Roberto Lage, of São Paulo, Brazil
**Notable Achievement:** Play-ing in the bathroom
**True Story:** In 2006 Welzenbach teamed up with Frampton and Lage to produce his play, "Fine Comb," inside a men's room. The play is about businessmen who have meetings in a bathroom to decide whom to promote and fire. But because it's staged inside a real bathroom, only 30 people can squeeze into the room at a time to see the 30-minute play. And they can't sit down (the toilets are part of the "set"). It looks like Welzenbach and company will be stuck in the bathroom for a while as the play has had an unexpect-edly long run. "We're a huge success," Frampton told reporters. "We have to perform extra shows every week!"

**Honoree:** British actress Emma Thompson
**Notable Achievement:** Writing an Academy Award–winning screenplay in the bathroom
**True Story:** In addition to acting, Thompson is also a screen-writer. Her husband converted a barn on their Scottish estate into a workspace for her, but Thompson prefers to work in the bath-room. It was in the privacy of her home's smallest room that she wrote much of the screenplay for the movie *Sense and Sensibility*, which she adapted from the Jane Austen novel. The result of her efforts: a Best Adapted Screenplay Oscar in 1996. (She keeps the golden statuette right next to the Best Actress Oscar that she won for *Howard's End*...on a shelf in the bathroom.)

# IT'S A HOOTENANNY!

*These songs are so well known, it seems they've been around forever.*
*But they haven't. Here are the origins of some folk classics.*

**Song:** "Turkey in the Straw"
**Story:** This upbeat fiddle tune (you might know it as "Do Your Ears Hang Low") was a part of many blackface minstrel shows in the 1820s. George Washington Dixon, Bob Farrell, and George Nichols all frequently performed the song and all claim to have written it. They didn't—it's an old Irish ballad originally called "The Old Rose Tree." An unknown musician sped up the tune and it became "Natchez Under the Hill." Some racist lyrics (befitting a blackface minstrel show) were added, and in 1834 the song was published as "Old Zip Coon." The same tune with new, nonsensical lyrics appeared in 1861 as "Turkey in the Straw." The song became a standard for fiddlers at barn dances. It's still a fiddle standard but is more commonly heard today as ice-cream truck music.

**Song:** "Red River Valley"
**Story:** The Sons of the Pioneers made this 1860s folk song—about a girl saying goodbye to her departing soldier lover—a country music hit in 1938. So it must be about Texas's Red River Valley, right? Wrong. It's about the Red River Valley of the North, in Manitoba. The song was written by an unknown British soldier who was part of a platoon sent to quell an 1869 uprising in what was then British territory and is now part of Canada. Fun fact: A hard-driving instrumental rock 'n' roll version called "Red River Rock" by Johnny & the Hurricanes was a hit in 1959.

**Song:** "Tom Dooley"
**Story:** This song about the murder of a woman and the subsequent execution of her estranged lover is based on a real event. In 1866 Laura Foster of Wilkes County, North Carolina, was found dead. Police arrested her ex-boyfriend, a Confederate veteran named Tom Dula (pronounced "doo-lee"). The trial was widely sensationalized throughout the South. Former North Carolina governor Zebulon Vance was Dula's lawyer, but he couldn't get him off and

Dula was convicted and hanged. As time passed, the trial was forgotten, but the song, written by Thomas Land, a local poet, in 1868, remained popular. It was recorded many times, but the most famous version was by the Kingston Trio in 1958. It sold six million copies and helped start the folk music revival of the 1950s and '60s.

**Song:** "Oh My Darling Clementine"

**Story:** It is alternately credited to songwriters Percy Montrose and Barker Bradford. Whoever wrote the song based it on an old ballad called "Down the River Liv'd a Maiden." A man sings about his dead lover, the big-footed daughter of a gold miner, who drowns because the narrator can't swim to save her. At the end of the song, he consoles himself by getting together with Clementine's sister (a verse usually left out of children's songbooks). It became popular as a campfire song and endured into the 1960s as the warbled, off-key signature song of Huckleberry Hound.

**Song:** "There's a Hole in the Bucket"

**Story:** A boy (Henry) complains to his sister (Liza) that there's a hole in his bucket so he can't do chores. She tells him to fix it with various things and the song starts right back where it started: Henry needs water to wet a stone to sharpen a knife to cut some straw to plug the hole in the bucket...but can't get water because there's a hole in his bucket. The song is translated from a German folk tune called "Lieber Heinrich" ("Dear Henry"), which first appeared in print in 1700 in a book for silver miners in the German region of Saxony. The song came to America with German immigrants in the 1800s.

**Song:** "She'll Be Coming 'Round the Mountain"

**Story:** This was first a slave spiritual called "When the Chariot Comes," about the second coming of Jesus, with lyrics like, "Oh, who will drive the chariot when she comes" and "King Jesus he'll be the driver when she comes." (The "she" referred to the chariot he'd be driving.) The song spread across the country: In the Midwest, railroad workers sang their own version, with the lyrics changed to "She'll be coming 'round the mountain when she comes"—the "she" meaning the railroad that would soon ride the tracks they were constructing. A similar version was popular in Appalachian coal mining camps in the 1890s. In that one, the "she" they're waiting for was labor union organizer Mary Harris Jones, also known as Mother Jones.

**Song:** "Goodnight, Irene"
**Story:** Best known from several recordings by bluesman Huddie "Leadbelly" Ledbetter in the 1930s and '40s, it was originally written in 1886 by Gussie L. Davis, an African-American songwriter living in Cincinnati. Leadbelly said his uncle taught it to him when he was a boy. The song is a first-person account of a man wishing he could be with his true love, whom he secretly meets late at night. She tells him to go home to his wife, but the man threatens to overdose on morphine should she ever leave him. When the folk group the Weavers recorded the song in 1950, it became the #1 song of the year.

**Song:** "Kumbaya"
**Story:** It's a song from the Gullah, people descended from former African slaves who live on the Sea Islands off South Carolina and Georgia. The word *kumbaya* (or *kum ba yah*) is a derivative of the once-common English greeting "come by here," and the song is similar to slave spirituals. It wasn't widely known in the United States until the 1960s folk music craze. Joan Baez recorded it in 1962, and it became an unofficial theme song of the civil rights movement.

**Song:** "Blue Tail Fly"
**Story:** You might know this one as "Jimmy Crack Corn." It was an African-American folk song dating to about 1845. White performers took the song and added it to minstrel shows. Sung from the point of view of a slave, it details all the things he does for his cruel master, including batting away blue tail flies (a Southern term for horseflies). "Jimmy crack corn" is a corrupted form of "gimcrack corn," slave slang for homemade corn whiskey. "Jimmy crack corn and I don't care / My master's gone away" means that the master has died, so the slaves are drinking and celebrating. Fun fact: "Blue Tail Fly" was Abraham Lincoln's favorite song.

First rock 'n' roll gold record: "Rock Around the Clock," by Bill Haley and the Comets, 1954.

# WHAT WON'T THEY TAX?

*They say the only certainties are death and*
*taxes. Death may be the better option…*

**B**ACKGROUND
Oliver Wendell Holmes called taxes "the price we pay for civilization." But few things provoke more outrage in people than being taxed. The first recorded tax evader was imprisoned by Roman Emperor Constantine in A.D. 306. The greatest revolt in English history occurred in 1381 when Richard II imposed a poll, or "head," tax. The first armed rebellions against the newly formed United States were Shay's Rebellion in 1786 (by New England farmers against property taxes) and the Whiskey Rebellion of 1791 (against a liquor tax). During the French Revolution in 1789, all tax collectors were rounded up and sent to the guillotine. And despite all that, governments persist in extracting revenue from their reluctant citizenry. Here are some of the more peculiar examples through the centuries:

• **URINE TAX.** Imposed by the Roman emperor Nero, around A.D. 60. Why urine? The contents of public toilets were collected by tanners and laundry workers for the ammonia, which was used for curing leather and bleaching togas. Nero slapped a fee on the collectors (not the producers) and it was such a money-raiser that Nero's successor, Vespasian, continued the tax. When his son, Titus, complained about the gross nature of the tax, Vespasian is reputed to have held up a gold coin and said, *"Non olet"* ("This doesn't stink").

• **SOUL TAX.** Peter the Great, czar of Russia, imposed a tax on souls in 1718…meaning everybody had to pay it (it's similar to a head tax or a poll tax). Peter was antireligious (he was an avid fan of Voltaire and other secular humanist philosophers), but agreeing with him didn't excuse anyone from paying the tax—if you didn't believe humans had a soul, you still had to pay a "religious dissenters" tax. Peter also taxed beards, beehives, horse collars, hats, boots, basements, chimneys, food, clothing, all males, as well as birth, marriage, and even burial.

The first electric ovens were used in a Swiss hotel in 1889.

- **BACHELOR TAX.** A favorite strategy of governments to encourage population growth and raise money at the same time. Augustus Caesar tried it in 18 B.C. The English imposed it in 1695. The Russians under Peter the Great used it in 1702, as did the Missouri legislature in 1820. The Spartans of ancient Greece didn't care about the money—they preferred public humiliation. Bachelors in Sparta were required to march around the public market in wintertime stark naked, while singing a song making fun of their unmarried status.

- **WIG POWDER TAX.** In 1795 powdered wigs were all the rage in men's fashion. Desperate for income to pay for military campaigns abroad, British prime minister William Pitt the Younger levied a tax on wig powder. Although the tax was short-lived due to the protests against it, it did ultimately have the effect of changing men's fashions. By 1820 powdered wigs were out of style.

- **WINDOW TAX.** Pitt the Younger also tried a chimney tax, but found that windows were easier to count. People paid the tax based on the number of windows in their home. Result: a lot of boarded-up windows.

- **LONG-DISTANCE TAX.** On June 30, 2006, the U.S. Treasury Department stopped collecting a 3% federal excise tax on long-distance calls—familiar to billpayers as one of a list of taxes tacked onto every phone bill. The purpose of the tax? To help pay for the Spanish-American war…in 1898. Phone service was so rare at the time that the tax was intended to impact only the wealthiest Americans. But the tax persisted long after the war ended, and virtually every American household ended up paying it. "It's not often you get to kill a tax," Treasury Secretary John Snow said after the tax was repealed, "particularly one that goes back so far in history." Taxpayers can file for a refund for the last three years the tax existed…but not for the previous 105. (Note: There's still a 3% excise tax on *local* phone calls.)

\*     \*     \*

Eyes are of little use if the mind is blind. —**Arab proverb**

Cheaper than a babysitter? 56% of American kids ages 8–16 have a TV in their bedroom.

# IF ELECTED,
# I PROMISE TO...

*Sometimes politicians come up with strange campaign promises. It rarely gets them elected, but it does make for good bathroom reading.*

**P**OLITICIAN: Andrew Uitvlugt, running for mayor of Kelowna, British Columbia, in 2005

**PROMISE:** Free crack cocaine for anyone who volunteers to pick up trash

**BACKGROUND:** Uitvlugt's reasoning: the town had too many crack addicts and too few garbage collectors. So why not let the crack addicts pick up the trash? The work, said Uitvlugt, would be so satisfying that they wouldn't even want the crack anymore. (He also proposed moving all of the city's homeless people to the local landfill, where they could learn to manufacture products out of the trash.)

**RESULT:** Uitvlugt lost (he finished fourth out of five candidates).

**POLITICIAN:** Silvio Berlusconi, Italian prime minister, running for reelection in 2006

**PROMISE:** To abstain from sex until after the election

**BACKGROUND:** At a campaign rally in February, Berlusconi was blessed by Massimiliano Pusceddu, a famous Italian televangelist, who congratulated the conservative prime minister for his strong stance on "family values." To show his appreciation for the blessing, the 70-year-old Berlusconi, who is married to actress Veronica Lario, proclaimed, "Thank you, dear Father Massimiliano, I will try not to let you down and I promise you two and a half months of complete sexual abstinence until the election."

**RESULT:** No word on whether Berlusconi kept his promise, but he lost the election.

**POLITICIAN:** Jackie Wagstaff, who calls herself "J-Dub," running for mayor of Durham, North Carolina, in 2005

**PROMISE:** To form a "hip-hop cabinet" full of "streetwise teens"

---

Napoleon's favorite horse was named Marengo; George Washington's was named Lexington.

**BACKGROUND:** Running on the "Gangsta" platform, the 46-year-old former city councilwoman acknowledged that because most of her support came from young African-Americans, that was the demographic she was targeting. To prove her street cred, J-Dub bragged about her checkered past of run-ins with the law (although she wasn't alone in this: 8 of the other 17 mayoral candidates also had criminal records). J-Dub said she wanted to get drug dealers off the street and into her cabinet because "they already have some business skills."

**RESULT:** J-Dub lost (she received less than 5% of the vote).

**POLITICIAN:** Percy, running for U.S. Congress in 2002

**PROMISE:** "Ruff ruff. Bark bark. Bow wow."

**BACKGROUND:** Percy, a dog, challenged Katherine Harris in Florida's Republican congressional primary. "No one has a realistic expectation that a dog can get elected," said Wayne Genthner, Percy's owner and campaign manager. "But plenty of people will be willing to vote for a dog to represent their discontent with the political system." He then added that, if elected, Percy promised to be obedient. "Don't you wish your representative in Washington could do that?"

**RESULT:** Percy never got the chance to run: The Florida election board ruled that he was ineligible (because he's a dog), so Genthner ran in his place…and lost.

**POLITICIAN:** Jacob Haugaard, running for Parliament in Denmark in 1994

**PROMISE:** Better weather, and tail winds for Danish bicyclists

**BACKGROUND:** Haugaard is the founding member of the "Party of Conscientiously Work-Shy Elements." He's also a stand-up comedian and admitted that he was only joking when he announced his candidacy (and then spent all his campaign money on beer).

**RESULT:** Haugaard won, becoming Denmark's first independent legislator in 50 years. "I don't know anything about politics," he said, "but now I get an education…with full salary!"

\* \* \*

"I never vote for anybody. I only vote against." —**W. C. Fields**

# Z-Z-Z-Z-Z-Z-Z-Z

*We don't really mind if this page puts
you to sleep. (Nighty night.)*

• If it takes you less than five minutes to fall asleep, it probably means you're sleep-deprived. Healthy sleepers need between 10 and 15 minutes to doze off.

• Researchers at Oxford University concluded that counting sheep may actually keep you awake. Why? Counting sheep is so boring that the mind brings other, more interesting thoughts to the surface just to keep itself occupied.

• Elephants sleep standing up when they're not dreaming, but lie down when they enter REM sleep.

• Every year, more than 100,000 U.S. drivers crash their cars because they fall asleep at the wheel.

• Cramming for a test? You'll recall the information better if you review it once and get a good night's sleep than if you stay up all night studying.

• Your brain is more active when you're dreaming than it is when you're awake.

• Most primates sleep an average of 10 hours per night; humans average only 7. But that's a recent development. Until the turn of the 20th century, humans slept for 10 hours, too. Who's to blame? Thomas Edison. The invention of the lightbulb turned us into a society of night owls.

• Having trouble falling sleep? Turn off all the lights or get some eyeshades. You need melatonin to feel drowsy, and melatonin production slows down when ambient light passes through the eyelids.

• Certain scents can help you fall asleep. According to a recent study, the most effective aroma is jasmine.

• If you want to remember your dreams, write them down as soon as you wake up. After five minutes, 50% of the dream fades from memory; after 10 minutes, 90% is gone.

• If you're average, you'll spend more than six years of your life dreaming.

Zzzzzz... Grrrrr... Zzzzzz... Grrrr... One in 8 men snores in his sleep. One in 10 grinds his teeth.

• Your body is most ready for sleep during predawn hours and right after lunch, during the afternoon "siesta" time. Consequently, these are the two most dangerous times to operate heavy machinery.

• New parents will lose 400 to 750 hours of sleep in their baby's first year.

• Want the best night's sleep possible? To sleep like a baby, literally? Try the fetal position. It provides the body with optimum blood circulation for a healthy sleeping session.

• Everyone experiences "microsleep." It occurs when you are straining to stay awake at a meeting or on a long trip. Your eyes may remain open, but all outside stimuli will go unnoticed for anywhere from one second to a few minutes.

• We are programmed to sleep at night, thanks to our *circadian rhythms*—physiological cycles that follow a daily pattern. No matter how long someone works the night shift, their body will never fully adapt.

\*     \*     \*

## REAL CANADIAN PLACE NAMES

| | | |
|---|---|---|
| Goobies | Mechanic | Wawa |
| Blow Me Down | Asbestos | Elbow |
| Cupids | Saint-Louis-du- | Eyebrow |
| Jerry's Nose | Ha! Ha! | Uranium City |
| Lawn | Cheapside | Head-Smashed-In |
| Mosquito | Ethel | Buffalo Jump |
| Nameless Cove | Bigger | Mirror |
| Witless Bay | Porcupine | Vulcan |
| Lower Economy | Swastika | Clo-oose |
| Malignant Cove | John D | Hydraulic |
| Meat Cove | Swords | Spuzzum |
| Mushaboom | Tiny | Stoner |
| Burnt Church | Finger | Mayo |

# THE GOLDEN AGE OF RADIO, PART I

*Long before videos or DVDs, even before television, families
used to gather nightly for their favorite programs. They'd sit
around the family radio and listen to popular comedies,
dramas, and variety shows. Here's how it all started.*

## LISTEN TO THIS

Have you ever heard this joke about Alexander Graham
Bell? "When he invented the phone, who did he talk to?
He was the only guy with a phone." It was the same with radio
when it started out. The only people who owned radios were hob-
byists who built their sets themselves. There were no radio stations, as we now know them—these radio amateurs, or "hams,"
built their own transmitters and receivers so they could talk to
each other. They were enthusiastic about their hobby and spent a
lot of time talking about their radios: what kind of equipment they
had, how much power they were using, and how well they were
receiving each other's signals. But even dedicated hams got a little
tired of the conversation after a while.

One day in October 1919, Frank Conrad, a ham in Wilkins-
burg, Pennsylvania, got so bored with talking that he pushed a
phonograph up to his microphone and played a record of the
Stephen Foster song "Old Black Joe." In the past, Conrad's transmissions had always been directed toward one particular person.
This time, he sent "Old Black Joe" out over the air waves to no
one in particular...and made radio history. He called this new
form of communication "broadcasting."

## AND NOW A WORD FROM OUR SPONSOR

Conrad continued to play records over the air and was soon del-
uged with letters from other radio operators thanking him and
requesting specific songs. He couldn't honor them all, so instead
he announced that he would play records on Wednesday and
Saturday nights, from 7:30 to 9:30 p.m. After he'd gone through
his own record collection a few times, a local record store offered

First female national news anchor: Barbara Walters (1976).

to lend him more. Conrad returned the favor (and made history again) by telling his listeners that the records were for sale at the store. It was the first commercial ever aired.

## AN INDUSTRY IS BORN

Over time Conrad's regular broadcasts became so popular that the local Joseph Horne department store began selling $10 ready-made crystal radio receivers to people who wanted to listen to Conrad's broadcasts but didn't want to build their own radios. The store advertised its radios in local newspapers.

Taking out newspaper ads may not sound like a very big deal, but it made all the difference. Although a few other people had played music over the air even earlier than Conrad (Reginald Fessenden, the man credited with inventing AM radio, played Christmas music and read Bible verses to ships at sea on Christmas Eve, 1906), nothing had come of those early broadcasts. Conrad worked as an engineer at Westinghouse, a company that manufactured electrical equipment for power plants, and he had been urging his company to get into the radio broadcasting business. But it wasn't until Harry P. Davis, a Westinghouse vice president, saw the crystal radios advertised in the paper that someone in a position to do something about it finally realized that radio had potential far beyond the small pool of hams who built their own sets.

## ON THE AIR

Davis figured the big money in radio would come from manufacturing and selling receivers, but he also knew that people had to have more to listen to than Conrad's records two nights a week. He decided that Westinghouse should build its own radio station, one that would broadcast every night.

The 1920 presidential election was less than a month away—why not start the new service with a bang, by broadcasting the results of the race between Warren G. Harding and James M. Cox? Davis put Conrad to work building a radio station on the roof of the Westinghouse plant in East Pittsburgh; he finished with time to spare. The station received its license—with its call letters, KDKA—on October 27, 1920, and began broadcasting election returns at 6 p.m. on election day, November 2. Listening audience: between 500 and 1,000 people. During the broadcast

Conrad stayed home and manned his own station, ready to take over in case KDKA went off the air. But it didn't—the broadcast continued without a hitch until noon the following day (Harding won in a landslide). The station is still on the air today.

## THE RADIO CRAZE

Radio started slowly at first and then exploded. In 1921 only eight more radio stations received licenses to broadcast; by the end of 1922 another 550 stations around the country were on the air. Now that there was something to listen to, Americans began buying radios as fast as manufacturers could make them. Sales went from almost none in 1920 to $60 million in 1922; they more than doubled in 1923 and doubled again in 1924, and kept climbing after that. By 1926 radios were a $500 million business.

Another important development paralleled the tremendous growth in radio sales: the linking of individual radio stations—first into regional "chains," as they were called, and then into national networks. AT&T started the trend in 1923 when engineers figured out how to link the company's 18 radio stations by telephone lines so that a program originating in one station could be broadcast simultaneously over every station in the network. By 1924 AT&T was broadcasting from coast to coast.

In 1926 AT&T sold its radio stations to the Radio Corporation of America (RCA), which combined them with its own stations to form the National Broadcasting Company (NBC). The founding of NBC is considered the start of the golden age of radio.

The Columbia Broadcasting System (CBS) network was formed in 1927, and a third network—Mutual Broadcasting—went on the air in 1934. In the early 1940s, an anti-trust decision by the Supreme Court forced NBC to split into two independent companies. One part was sold off to Lifesavers president Edward J. Noble in 1943 and was renamed the American Broadcasting Company (ABC).

*That was just the beginning for radio. For more on the little box's Golden Age, turn the dial to page 269.*

\*       \*       \*

"It's kind of fun to do the impossible." —**Walt Disney**

It's against the law to run out of gas in Youngstown, Ohio.

# TOY FADS

*The Federal Communications Commission used to have a rule banning children's TV shows based on existing commercial characters or toys. The reasoning was that kids are impressionable, and such TV shows would just be long ads. But in 1982, the FCC repealed the ruling. Result: TV shows designed to sell toys...lots of toys.*

## TEENAGE MUTANT NINJA TURTLES

**Description:** Radioactive ooze turns four pet turtles into human-size crime-fighting, pizza-eating, jive-talking teens named Leonardo, Raphael, Michelangelo, and Donatello.

**A Fad is Born!** In 1984 cartoonists Peter Laird and Kevin Eastman self-published *Teenage Mutant Ninja Turtles*, a violent but darkly funny comic book. They printed 50,000 copies, all of which sold out in a few weeks. After that, the comic was published regularly for two years but garnered little interest beyond comic book fans. In 1986 advertising executive Mark Freedman discovered the comic and bought the rights from Laird and Eastman, figuring the Turtles could be a cultural phenomenon if they were marketed to kids, rather than older comic-book collectors. A newer, more kid-friendly comic was introduced, along with a TV cartoon series and lots and lots of Ninja Turtle toys. Freedman was right: In 1989, $250 million worth of toys were sold; in 1990, a live-action movie earned $140 million; and in 1991, a Burger King promotion sold 200,000 Turtle videos per week. But all fads are destined to die. Sales plummeted in 1992, and the cartoon was cancelled. A grittier, back-to-basics comic book was released, but it bombed. New cartoons and new toys were released in 2003, but they flopped too. A big failure? Hardly. Since 1984 the Ninja Turtles have generated $6 billion in revenue.

## TRANSFORMERS

**Description:** Giant robots that can "transform" into vehicles crash land on Earth from outer space, and wage battle for "energon" cubes.

**A Fad is Born!** In 1982 Hasbro Toys scoured the world for toys on which they could base cartoons, which they could then use to sell more toys. They bought the rights to three Japanese toy

---

There is a G.I. Joe action figure modeled after General Colin Powell.

lines: Takara Toys' Car Robots and Micro Change, and Bandai's Machine Men. The toys were all die-cast metal robots that, with a few twists and turns, became toy planes, cars, or other objects. Nearly 20 million of these toys had been sold around the world—but would they sell in the United States? Industry insiders predicted that Hasbro's "Transformers" would flop—complicated Japanese toys were untested and parents would balk at paying $10 for a toy car, they said. But the insiders were wrong. Kids loved the strange new toys and action-packed cartoon. (It didn't hurt that kids could figure out how to make the toys "transform," while their parents couldn't.) By the end of 1985, $380 million worth of Transformers had been sold. Sales and interest declined after that, but various versions of the show have been on the air since 1985 and related toys still sell well. The success of Transformers helped make Hasbro the second largest toymaker in the world.

## MIGHTY MORPHIN POWER RANGERS

**Description:** With the help of huge robot dinosaurs, six teenagers use ninja skills to fight giant monsters sent to Earth by an evil witch who lives in a dumpster on the moon.

**A Fad is Born!** The most popular kids show and toy line of the 1990s is an unlikely success story. In 1986 TV producer Haim Saban had an idea: take footage of the robot dinosaurs from the Japanese action show *Kyoryu Sentai Zyuranger* (Dinosaur Squadron Beast Ranger) and combine it with newly shot scenes of American teenagers. The special effects from the Japanese show were cheap and sloppy, mixing miniature models, marionettes, and stuntmen in rubber suits. It took Saban seven years to sell it to a network, but Fox finally agreed to air it. Good move. It was an instant hit in the fall of 1993, becoming the #1 kids show on TV. Bandai was contracted to make toys based on the teenagers and robots, but didn't anticipate the high demand. How high? Twelve million toys were sold in 1993. By 1996 the show had exhausted all the available *Kyoryu* footage, so it had to start stealing from other Japanese shows. Now, each fall, *Power Rangers* changes its entire premise and cast. New heroes, monsters, robots, villains—and toys—are introduced. To date, Bandai has sold over 160 million Power Ranger toys.

# CANADIAN NAMIN'

*Over the years, we've written about how dozens of American places got their names. Now it's Canada's turn.*

## TORONTO

North of the city is Lake Toronto. The Iroquois who once lived there called it *toronto*, meaning "place where trees stand in water." Who put trees in the lake? Another native group, the Hurons, planted saplings there to help trap fish.

## CALGARY

In the 1870s, when the area was a post for the Mounted Police, it was named Fort Brisebois after officer Ephrem Brisebois. But in 1876, after Brisebois declared a woman from the Metis tribe his common-law wife, his superior, Colonel James Macleod, angrily renamed it. Macleod had just returned from a trip to Calgary—a popular white sand beach on the Isle of Mull off Scotland—so Fort Brisebois became Fort Calgary. *Calgary* comes from the Gaelic *Cala ghearraidh*, which means "beach of the meadow."

## QUÉBEC

Prior to the arrival of French colonists in the 1500s, the area was inhabited by the Algonquin people. The Algonquins called it *kebek*, meaning "straight" or "narrow," referring to the way the river (now the St. Lawrence) narrows where the Algonquins settled (now Québec City). Explorer Samuel de Champlain made the word French in 1613, spelling it "Québec."

## OTTAWA

In 1832 the British government hired a group of engineers, headed by Colonel John By, to build a canal in the colony of Upper Canada. The large camp that housed workers, called Bytown in the colonel's honor, eventually grew into a town. In 1855 it became officially incorporated as a city, and took the new name Ottawa from the *Adàwe*, the native people with whom Europeans traded during early colonization of the area. French settlers had corrupted *Adàwe* to *Outaouak*; British settlers corrupted it to *Ottawa*.

---

Ireland's longest place name: Muckanaghederdauhaulia ("pig marsh between two saltwater inlets").

# JUST PLANE WEIRD

*If you're reading this book on an airplane, you might want to
skip this section until you're safely back on the ground.*

**M**UST. READ. INSTRUCTIONS.
In 2005 Japan Airlines (JAL) announced that one of its
planes had been flying with two of its engines fitted on
the wrong side of the plane. The "right" and "left" engines had
been switched, they said, by a maintenance company in Singapore. The engines have different thrust directions, JAL officials
said, but assured the public that there was no danger, adding that
the plane made 440 flights before the mistake was discovered.

## AIRLOCK

In August 2006, the captain of an Air Canada flight from Ottawa
to Winnipeg turned controls over to his co-pilot and left the cockpit to use the bathroom. When he returned, the cockpit door
wouldn't budge—it was jammed. He was locked out, and the co-
pilot couldn't get it open from the other side. Panicked crew
members had to take the door off its hinges to get the captain back
inside—and they had to do it in a hurry, since there were only 30
minutes left on the flight. They succeeded; he safely landed the
plane in Winnipeg. "The safety of our passengers was never compromised," Air Canada said in a statement. Nevertheless, the
embarrassed airline didn't report the incident to Canada's transit
safety commission because they said it fell into the category of
"non-reportable."

## FLYING BLIND

A 41-year-old Belgian named Luc Costermans hoped to set a world
record: most hours ever logged by a blind pilot. Costermans lost his
sight in an accident in 2004, and took up flying only after becoming
blind. He planned to complete the feat with his instructor, Jean
Andrieu, who takes care of takeoffs but gives the controls to Costermans once they're airborne. If that seems weird, consider this: he
did it. In June 2006 Costermans made the record books by flying a
13-hour 1,180-mile flight from France to Belgium, and back again.

## SPECIAL DELIVERY

A 25-year-old British military pilot was on a training exercise in eastern England in early 2006 when he made an unscheduled stop in a $7.27 million Lynx helicopter. "The pilot took it upon himself to deliver a pizza to his girlfriend," a Ministry of Defense spokesman said. "He has been made aware that the chain of command doesn't condone his actions and has been disciplined." The stunt prompted fellow pilots at his base to design a new badge for the unit: the words *Quattro Stagione*, or "Four Seasons," over a Domino's Pizza logo.

## LET'S GET SMALL

A woman in Vancouver, British Columbia, called 911, reporting a plane crash she and her son witnessed near their home. "We sent all our cars down there," said Corporal Steven Han of the RCMP, "thinking there was a small plane that had crashed." Turns out it *had* been a small plane—a four-foot-long toy plane. The owner of the remote-controlled device told police he'd had engine trouble. News of the "plane crash" made it to several local media outlets before the mistake was corrected.

\*     \*     \*

## LONGEST MOVIE TITLES OF ALL TIME

• *Night of the Day of the Dawn of the Son of the Bride of the Return of the Revenge of the Terror of the Attack of the Evil, Mutant, Alien, Flesh Eating, Hellbound, Zombified Living Dead Part 2: In Shocking 2-D* (1991)

• *The Fable of the Kid Who Shifted His Ideals to Golf and Finally Became a Baseball Fan and Took the Only Known Cure* (1916)

• *Homework, or How Pornography Saved the Split Family from Boredom and Improved their Financial Situation* (1991)

• *The Lemon Grove Kids Meet the Green Grasshopper and the Vampire Lady from Outer Space* (1965)

• *Dr. Strangelove or: How I Learned to Stop Worrying and Love the Bomb* (1964)

• *Revelations of a Sex Maniac to the Head of the Criminal Investigation Division* (1972)

# APRIL FOOLS!

*Don't look now, but your fly is open. Made you look!*
*Here are some classic April Fools jokes.*

**H**UMOR UNDER FIRE. On April 1, 2003, twelve days after the start of "Operation Iraqi Freedom," the U.S. invasion of Iraq, the Iraqi ambassador to Russia, Abbas Khalaf Kunfuth, stepped before a group of international reporters and read from what he claimed was a Reuters news bulletin. "The Americans have accidentally fired a nuclear missile into British forces, killing seven." The room fell into stunned silence; then Kunfuth shouted, "April Fools!"

**D-U-INTERNET.** In its April 1994 issue, *PC Computing* magazine reported that Congress was considering a bill to make it illegal to surf the Web while under the influence of alcohol, and attributed the action to the term "Information Superhighway." "Congress apparently thinks being drunk on a highway is bad," the magazine said, "no matter what kind of highway it is." So many people took the story seriously—and flooded Capitol Hill with angry calls—that Senator Pat Leahy and other politicians mentioned in the article had to publicly deny the story.

**EMERGENCY CHAT.** On April 1, 1994, a prankster released a fake Associated Press news story claiming that a company called Century Communications was launching a new phone service to help pay for the cost of installing the 911 emergency service. "The 911 Chatline" would let callers "choose an area of the country, listen to 911 emergency calls, and discuss the details of the emergencies with each other as they happen…before police have even arrived."

**BARD BUCKS.** In 2000 the *Motley Fool* investment newsletter announced that William Shakespeare's investment portfolio had been discovered among his remains and had been earning dividends and interest since his death in 1616. The *Fool* reported that the Bard had invested the equivalent of $100 in 1585 and had earned 6% per year. Current value of the portfolio: $18.7 billion.

**SOFTWARE TO KEEP YOU UP NIGHTS.** In April 1992 Apple Computer announced that it was releasing an extension for its Macintosh operating system called "Caffeine Manager," that would allow Macs to network with coffee makers and soda machines. "Users and programmers alike now can immediately have access to a wide variety of commercial beverages form their desktop, all with the familiar Macintosh mouse-driven interface," the announcement read.

**COME ON BACK.** While Glenn Howlett, general manager of community services in London, Ontario, was on vacation in 2003, three other city officials sent him a gag letter dated April 1 saying the deadline for the report he'd been working on had been pushed up and was now due in two weeks. Howlett cancelled the rest of his vacation and flew home to finish the report. The stress caused heart palpitations that eventually forced him into early retirement. When Howlett learned the letter was a joke, he filed a lawsuit that ended up costing the city $75,000 to resolve.

**YOU'VE GOT MAIL.** In April 1999, *Red Herring* magazine ran an article about an entrepreneur named Yuri Maldini who had invented a way to send e-mails telepathically. When the interviewer asked Maldini how big the market for such an application would be, he paused and then replied, "I just e-mailed you my answer." Later that afternoon the interviewer checked his e-mail and, sure enough, there it was: "It's going to be huge, simply huge."

**TRAFFIC REPORT.** On April 1, 1991, the London *Times* reported a British government plan to ease traffic congestion on the M25, the highway that circles London, by forcing all traffic to move in one direction. On Mondays, Wednesdays, and Fridays, they said, traffic would travel clockwise around the city; on Tuesdays and Thursdays, it would travel counterclockwise; and on weekends traffic would be allowed to travel in both directions, as before. The BBC was taken in by the ruse and broadcast interviews with irate motorists in the village of Swanscombe, Kent, who complained bitterly that on Tuesdays and Thursdays their 5-mile shopping trips to nearby Dartford would now be 127 miles long.

# JARGON.COM

A *few origins to help you brush up on your Web-cabulary.*

**M**ODEM: It's short for "MOdulator-DEModulator." Modulation refers to the process of converting the digital language that computers "speak" into the analog language of telephone lines. Demodulation is the reverse. (That high-pitched warbling sound modems make is digital language being translated into analog language.) Technically, that means that modern modems—cable and DSL—aren't really modems at all, because their signals are sent and received digitally, and therefore they neither modulate nor demodulate.

**PHISHING:** Refers to people who "fish" the Internet using e-mails designed to acquire sensitive information such as credit card numbers and passwords. It was first used in the mid-1990s to describe people who used false data to get free AOL accounts, which they would then use to steal other members' data for criminal purposes. Today it refers to any similar online scheme. The altered spelling comes from "phreaking," a 1970s term for schemes that manipulated phone systems in order to get free long-distance service.

**SURFING:** A librarian named Jean Armour Polly (a.k.a. "Net Mom") wrote an article entitled "Surfing the Internet" for the University of Minnesota's *Wilson Library Bulletin* in 1992. That's the first published use of the phrase, and she is usually credited with coining it. But it had been used before—some people referred to "information surfing" on an early version on the Internet called the Usenet system in 1991. Why "surfing"? It may simply have come from "channel surfing" on TV, but some insiders claim it's actually an homage to Vinton Cerf (pronounced "surf"), a computer engineer considered one of the fathers of the Internet.

**COOKIE:** Cookies are small packets of data that are transferred to your computer when you visit a Web site. They're used for storing information—your name, password, and shopping habits, for example—that your computer can access quickly if you revisit the site. The term originated in the 1970s with one of the earliest

---

The scientific term for left-handedness is *sinistrality*. Right-handedness is *dextrality*.

operating systems, UNIX (which is still in use today), which used "magic cookies" to identify users and make using the system faster.

**SPAM:** There are many theories about the origin of using the word "spam" to describe bulk or junk e-mail. One says that people on a very early, very slow, network communications system known as BITNET used to annoy each other by sending files containing the words to Monty Python's "Spam Song," and the term came to mean any similarly annoying use of the Internet. Another version says that a user on the popular mid-1980s system BBS (Bulletin Board System) claimed to be posting photographs of nude women. BITNET was also a very slow system, so downloading a photo could take up to an hour. And in this case, it wasn't a photo of a naked woman—it was of a photo of a can of Spam. However the term originated, by the late 1980s it was common to say "someone spammed me."

**PING:** To "ping" a computer is to send it an "echo request" message and see how long it takes to respond, thereby testing how good the Internet connection is. The code that allows "pinging" was written by programmer Mike Muuss (he also helped create the architectural program CAD) as a freeware tool. He named it "ping" after the submariners' term for a sonar signal.

**BLOG:** Short for "weblog," a type of Web site where entries are made similarly to a personal diary or journal (or log), covering a wide variety of subjects, from politics to sports to knitting. The term "weblog" was coined December 17, 1997, by blog pioneer Jorn Barger on his site, Robotwisdom.com. Fellow pioneer Peter Merholz at *Peterme.com* is credited with shortening it to "blog" in 1999, saying, "I've decided to pronounce the word 'weblog' as 'wee'-blog. Or 'blog' for short." It quickly spread and was soon being used as a verb—*to blog*. Merholz later said, "I like that it's roughly onomatopoeic of vomiting. These sites (mine included) tend to be a kind of information upchucking."

\*     \*     \*

It ain't what you don't know that makes you look like a fool; it's what you do know that ain't so.          **—Appalachian proverb**

# DOES FIONA EAT APPLES?

*A few forays into famous folks' food fixations.*

• Three days a week, **Mariah Carey** eats only purple foods, such as plums, because they contain high levels of antioxidants, which she believes will stop her from developing wrinkles.

• Comedian **Paula Poundstone** eats six brown-sugar-and-cinnamon Pop-Tarts and drinks 16 cans of Diet Pepsi each day.

• Singer **Fiona Apple** eats split pea soup every day when she's on tour.

• While he's writing a book, author **Michael Crichton** eats the same thing for lunch every day to help him concentrate. When he was writing *Jurassic Park*, he ate egg salad sandwiches every day for nine months.

• **Billy Bob Thornton** supposedly eats only orange-colored foods.

• **Daphne Zuniga** (*Melrose Place*) used to eat fish daily, including sushi four times a week. After a severe bout of mercury poisoning, she no longer eats fish of any kind.

• **Ben Stiller** brings his own plastic-sealed bagels to restaurants and asks the staff to toast them.

• Avant-garde composer **Erik Satie** ate only white foods: eggs, sugar, shredded bones, animal fat, coconuts, rice, and white cheese. To drink: wine that had been boiled, then chilled.

• **Janine Turner** (*Northern Exposure*) has the same breakfast every day: a quesadilla and a Coke.

• Soccer player **David Beckham** has three refrigerators: One has only salad, one has all his other food, and the third has only Diet Coke. All the sodas are arranged symmetrically and in pairs.

• During the six-month shoot of the movie *What's New, Pussycat?*, **Woody Allen** ate only potato soup and sole.

• French actress **Brigitte Bardot** says she needs to eat only once a day. It's usually a croissant and a slice of toast.

# POLI-TALKS

*John F. Kennedy said, "Mothers want their sons to grow up to be president, but they don't want them to become politicians in the process." Here's why.*

"I like the color red because it's a fire. And I see myself as always being on fire."
—Gov. Arnold Schwarzenegger

"I will never apologize for the United States of America. I don't care what the facts are."
—George H. W. Bush

"We have a lot of kids who don't know what work means. They think work is a four-letter word."
—Hillary Clinton

"People tell me that Senator Edwards got picked to run as vice president for his good looks, sex appeal, and great hair. I say to them, 'How do you think I got the job?'"
—Dick Cheney

"I made no attempt to be inaccurate, but I want to be clear I was never attempting to be precise"
—Josh Steiner, Treasury Chief, explaining comments leaked from his diary

"I was with some Vietnamese recently, and some of them were smoking two cigarettes at a time. That's the kind of customers we need!"
—Sen. Jesse Helms

"That's George Washington. The interesting thing about him is that I read three or four books about him last year. Isn't that interesting?"
—George W. Bush, to a German reporter looking at Washington's portrait

"I am not going to give you a number for it because it's not my business to do intelligent work."
—Donald Rumsfeld

"Considering the dire circumstances that we have in New Orleans, a city that has been destroyed, things are going relatively well."
—Michael Brown, FEMA director

"I'm electable if you vote for me."
—Rep. Dennis Kucinich

# MAKING
# *THE GODFATHER*, PT. I

The Godfather *is considered one of the best movies ever made—
the American Film Institute ranks it #3, after* Citizen Kane *and*
Casablanca. *The story of how it got made is just as good.*

**B**OOKMAKER

In 1955 a pulp-fiction writer named Mario Puzo published
his first novel, *The Dark Arena*, about an ex-GI and his
German girlfriend who live in Germany after the end of World
War II. The critics praised it, but it didn't sell very many copies.

It took Puzo nine years to finish his next novel, *The Fortunate
Pilgrim*, which told the story of an Italian immigrant named Lucia
Santa who lives in the Hell's Kitchen neighborhood of New York
City. After two bad marriages, Lucia is raising her kids alone and
worries about her daughter, who has become too Americanized,
and her son, who is being pulled into the Mafia.

Today *The Fortunate Pilgrim* is widely considered a classic work
of Italian American fiction; Puzo himself considered it the best
book he ever wrote. But it sold as poorly as *The Dark Arena*—
together the two books had earned Puzo only about $6,500. By
then he was 45 years old, $20,000 in debt, and tired of being
broke. He wanted his next novel to be a success. "I looked around
and said…I'd better make some money," he recalled years later.

### HIT MAN

Puzo figured that a story with an entire family of gangsters in it
instead of only one would have more commercial appeal than
*The Fortunate Pilgrim* had. He titled his third novel *Mafia*, and in
a sign of how his fortunes were about to change, he received a
$5,000 advance payment from the publisher. Then, after he'd
completed only an outline and 114 pages, Paramount Pictures
acquired the movie rights for $12,000 and agreed to pay an addi-
tional $50,000 if the movie actually got made.

Puzo's decision to pack his story with wiseguys paid off. *Mafia*,
by now retitled *The Godfather*, was a publishing phenomenon. The

---

The first U.S. passport was issued in 1796. Recipient: Francis M. Barrere.

most successful novel of the 1970s, it spent 67 weeks on the bestseller list and sold more than 21 million copies before it even
made it to the big screen.

## THE NUMBERS RACKET

Believe it or not, the success of the novel actually *hurt* its chances
of becoming a decent film. Bestsellers appeal to movie studios
because they have a guaranteed audience. But fans will come to
the theater no matter what, so why spend extra money to get
them there? Shortsighted studio executives are often tempted to
maximize profits by spending as little on such movies as possible.
At the time Paramount was in bad financial shape and its last
Mafia film, *The Brotherhood*, starring Kirk Douglas, bombed. The
studio couldn't afford another expensive mistake. It set the budget
for *The Godfather* at $2 million, a miniscule figure even for the
early 1970s.

Two million dollars wasn't enough money to make a decent
film set in the present, let alone a period piece like *The Godfather*,
which takes place from 1945 to 1955—and in Manhattan, one of
the most expensive places in the country to shoot a film. To save
on expenses, Paramount decided to move the story forward to the
1970s, and made plans to film it in a Midwestern city like Kansas
City, or on the studio back lot instead of on actual New York
streets. The title would still be *The Godfather*, but other than that
the film would have very little in common with Puzo's novel.

Paramount signed Albert Ruddy, one of the co-creators of TV's
*Hogan's Heroes*, to produce the film. Ruddy had produced only
three motion pictures, and they'd all lost money, but what
impressed the studio was that he had brought them in under budget. That was what Paramount was looking for in *The Godfather*—a
critical flop that would nonetheless turn a quick profit because it
had a built-in audience and would be filmed on the cheap.

## NO, THANKS

By now it was clear in Hollywood that the studio was planning
what was little more than a cinematic mugging of millions of fans
of Puzo's novel. What director would want to work on something
like that? It was enough to ruin a career. Ruddy approached several big directors about making the film but, of course, none were

interested. So he turned to a hungry young director named Francis Ford Coppola.

He turned it down, too.

## THE KID

In his short career, Coppola, then 31, had directed only four films (not including the nudie flicks he worked on while studying film at UCLA): *Dimentia 13*, a critical flop that bombed at the box office; *Finian's Rainbow*, another critical flop that bombed; *You're a Big Boy Now*, another critical flop that bombed; and *The Rain People* (starring James Caan and Robert Duvall), a critical *success* that bombed. With his track record, he couldn't afford to be too choosy, and yet when Albert Ruddy offered him *The Godfather* in the spring of 1970, Coppola picked up a copy of the book and read only as far as one particularly lurid scene early in the book before he dismissed the whole work as a piece of trash and told Ruddy to find someone else. (Have you read the book? It's the part where Sonny's mistress goes to a plastic surgeon to have her "plumbing" fixed and ends up having an affair with the doctor.)

## AN OFFER HE COULDN'T REFUSE

Film buffs know that we have George Lucas to thank for *Star Wars*. We can thank him for *The Godfather*, too. In November 1969, Coppola had founded his own film company, American Zoetrope, and its first project was to turn his friend George's student film, *THX-1138*, into a feature-length movie. Today it's a cult classic, but it was such a dud when it was first released that it nearly forced American Zoetrope into bankruptcy. Coppola was so desperate to keep the studio's doors open that when Ruddy offered him the *Godfather* job a second time in late 1970, he agreed to at least give the novel another look.

This time Coppola read the book all the way through. He found more sections that he didn't like, but he was also captivated by the central story of the relationship between the Godfather, Don Corleone, and his three sons. He realized that if he could strip away the lurid parts and focus on the central characters, *The Godfather* had a shot at becoming a very good film.

*Part II of the story is on page 354.*

# BEULAH LAND, PART I

*Here's a little-known slice of Americana: the story of how
freed slaves changed the face of the American West.*

L AND OF OPPORTUNITY
In 1865 the American Civil War came to an end and four
million black slaves were free. But to what future? The
South lay in ruins, its plantation economy shattered. Most slaves
had been field workers or tenant farmers, and working the land
was the only job they knew. Although they were now free to buy
land to farm, few had the money. Even worse, a new terror was
rising across the South as hostile whites, bitter in defeat, donned
the white hoods of the Ku Klux Klan and began to terrorize the
black community. But there was a way out...and it lay to the west.

The Homestead Act of 1862 offered grants of 160 acres of public lands on the Great Plains to anyone who would farm the land
for five years. Thousands of Southern blacks joined the flood of
settlers heading west to what they called "Beulah Land"—the
Promised Land—only their mission was slightly different. Yes, the
promise of owning their own land was sweet. But sweeter still was
the possibility of living independent lives untouched by fear and
racism. So they banded together and developed all-black communities, with their own banks, their own newspapers, their own
businesses, and their own schools and colleges.

## OKLAHOMA, THE ALL-BLACK STATE?

Although blacks migrated to every state and territory in the West,
the territory of Oklahoma quickly became the preferred place to
settle: A sizable number of African-Americans already lived there,
having come as slaves with the Cherokee and other tribes during
the Trail of Tears in 1838. After emancipation they bought land
in Indian territory (often with the help of the Indians, who, under
fierce pressure to give up their land to new settlers, preferred to
sell it to black Americans). A number of black leaders, such as
Edward P. McCabe and Hannibal C. Carter, led the push.

Carter established the Freedmen's Oklahoma Immigration
Association in Chicago in 1881 specifically to help blacks move

to Oklahoma. They even convinced one U.S. Senator—Henry W. Blair of New Hampshire—to introduce a bill to make Oklahoma an all-black state. That legislation never passed, but the Land Run of 1889 opened up even more Oklahoma land to black settlers, leading to the establishment of scores of black towns. Using 360 acres won in the Land Run, McCabe founded the town of Langston, named after John H. Langston, a black congressman from Virginia. Dubbing it "The Only Distinctively Negro City in America," McCabe used his newspaper, the *Langston City Herald*, to promote the town to black communities back in the South. Langston University, founded in 1908, is the only remaining historically black college in Oklahoma.

## BROUGHT LOW BY JIM CROW

By 1910 there were 59 all-black towns across the west, 29 in Oklahoma alone. Their successes were hard won: As more and more whites came into the area, they brought with them the racist attitudes that prevailed in the rest of the country. The early 20th century was the era of "Jim Crow," as discriminatory laws and practices designed specifically to limit and suppress the rights of black people were not only acceptable, but were the order of the day. (The name Jim Crow dates back to the minstrel shows of the 1830s, where white performer Thomas "Daddy" Rice blackened his face with burnt cork and danced a jig while singing the lyrics to a song called "Jump Jim Crow." His parody of a dancing black man became so well known that by the Civil War, the words "Jim Crow" had become a racial slur.)

In Oklahoma, the white majority-controlled legislature began passing laws blocking black immigration into the state and limiting where blacks could buy land. Black businesses and farmers were allowed to buy and sell their services and crops only within their own small communities. Worse yet, they could only borrow from black-owned banks, which made them vulnerable to even the slightest downturn in the economy. But the death knell of the black townships in Oklahoma sounded in 1921 in Greenwood, an all-black district of Tulsa.

*To read about the Greenwood Riots and other challenges to black towns in the West, turn to Part II of the story on page 344.*

# THE WHO?

*Ever wonder how rock bands get their names? So do we.*
*After some digging around, we found these origins.*

**CHICAGO.** They originally called themselves Chicago Transit Authority, but had to shorten it after the city of Chicago sued.

**ALICE COOPER.** Lead singer Vincent Furnier claims to have gotten his stage name from a Ouija board, through which he met a spirit with that name.

**EURYTHMICS.** An 1890s system of music instruction that emphasized physical response.

**METALLICA.** Drummer Lars Ulrich was helping a friend name a heavy metal magazine. Ulrich's two suggestions: 1) Metal Mania (which the friend used), and 2) Metallica.

**THE REPLACEMENTS.** They were filling in for another band at the last minute. When the MC asked who the band was, singer Paul Westerberg replied, "The replacements."

**WHITE STRIPES.** While the band members are named Jack and Meg White, the band is named for Meg's love of red-and-white-striped peppermint candies.

**WEEZER.** Lead singer Rivers Cuomo got this nickname in grade school. He had asthma.

**THE SMITHS.** They wanted a generic name that wouldn't suggest anything about the band's kind of music.

**XTC.** Singer Andy Partridge saw an old movie in which Jimmy Durante said, "That's it, I'm in ecstasy!"

**BLACK SABBATH.** From a 1963 Boris Karloff horror movie.

**DEF LEPPARD.** Singer Joe Elliot once drew a picture of a leopard with no ears—a "deaf leopard."

**MOODY BLUES.** They named the band in honor of one of their favorite songs—Duke Ellington's "Mood Indigo."

**BADFINGER.** They were originally called the Iveys. When they signed with the Beatles' Apple Records label, Paul McCartney gave them this name. It was the original title of the Beatles song "A Little Help from My Friends."

**FALL OUT BOY.** In their early years, they asked an audience what their name should be. Somebody yelled "Fall Out Boy." They liked it and took it, unaware that it was the name of a character on *The Simpsons*. When they found out, they feared they'd be sued. But *The Simpsons*' producers thought the band had the name first, and that *they* were going to be sued. (Neither was.)

**DEATH CAB FOR CUTIE.** Named after a song written by Monty Python collaborator Neil Innes for his 1960s psychedelic group, the Bonzo Dog Doo-Dah Band.

**TLC.** It's not what you think. It comes from the first letters of each of the group's first names: Tionne, Lisa, and Crystal.

**EMINEM.** The rapper gave himself this stage name using his initials—M and M (for Marshall Mathers)—spelled out phonetically.

**NINE INCH NAILS.** Nine-inch nails are used in coffins. Singer Trent Reznor made a list of potential band names and settled on this one because "it still sounded good after two weeks" and could be easily abbreviated.

**WINGS.** Paul McCartney came up with it while waiting in a hospital *wing* as his wife Linda was giving birth to one of their children.

**EVERCLEAR.** Named after an extremely strong (190 proof) grain alcohol.

**COLDPLAY.** They stole it from another band that broke up. The original band got the name from a book by poet Philip Horky, entitled *Child's Reflections, Cold Play*.

# I TOAST YOU!

*On a recent trip to Ireland, Uncle John spent many an evening going from pub to pub collecting traditional toasts (and many a morning after, begging for aspirin). Here are some favorites:*

May you have food and clothing, a soft pillow for your head; May you be forty years in heaven, before the devil knows you're dead.

**For every wound, a balm.** For every sorrow, a cheer. For every storm, a calm. For every thirst, a beer.

**May the roof above us never** fall in, and may we friends gathered below never fall out.

**Here's health and prosperity,** to you and all your posterity, And them that doesn't drink with sincerity, That they may be damned for all eternity!

**Gentlemen, start your livers!**

**May we live to learn well,** and learn to live well.

**May your right hand always** be stretched out in friendship and never in want.

**Here's to warm words on a cold** evening, A full moon on a dark night, And the road downhill all the way to your door.

**Success to the lover, honor** to the brave, health to the sick, and freedom to the slave.

**May the Lord keep you in** His hand, And never close His fist too tight on you.

**Old wood to burn, old books** to read, old wine to drink, old friends to trust.

**May misfortune follow you** the rest of your life, but never catch up.

**Champagne to our real** friends, and real pain to our sham friends.

**May you live as long as you** want, and never want as long as you live.

**May I see you gray, combing** your grandchildren's hair.

**May the people who dance** on your grave get cramps in their legs.

**Health and long life to you,** The woman of your choice to you, A child every year to you, Land without rent to you, And may you die in Ireland.

In Italy, Mickey Mouse is known as "Topolino."

# I CURSE YOU!

*Save these classic curses to use against
people who refuse to toast you.*

**M**ay the curse of Mary Maline and her nine blind children chase you so far over the hills of Damnation that the Lord himself won't find you with a telescope.

**May your daughter's beauty** be admired by everyone in the circus.

**May the devil cut the head** off you and make a day's work of your neck.

**Six horse-loads of graveyard** clay upon you.

**May I live just long enough** to bury you.

**May you be afflicted with** the itch and have no nails to scratch with.

**All your teeth should fall** out except one, and you should have a toothache in that one.

**May the seven terriers of hell** sit on the spool of your breast and bark in at your soul-case.

**May you be transformed into** a chandelier, to hang by day and burn by night.

**May you win a lottery and** spend it all on doctors.

**May the devil swallow you** sideways.

**May you live in a house of** 100 rooms, and may each room have its own bed, and may you wander every night from room to room, and from bed to bed, unable to sleep.

**May you go stone-blind so** that you can't tell your wife from a haystack.

**Your nose should grow so** much hair it strains your soup.

**May fire and brimstone never** fail to fall in showers on you.

**May you have devoted** children to chase the flies off your nose.

**May you back into a pitchfork** and grab a hot stove for support.

**May those who love us love** us. And those that don't love us, may God turn their hearts, and if He cannot turn their hearts, may He turn their ankles so we'll know them by their limping.

---

Every American space-flight menu has included chocolate. So has every Russian space menu.

# BAMBOO: ONE INCREDIBLE PLANT

*And not just because the Professor can make
a Geiger counter out of it, Gilligan.*

**BIG BAMBOO**

To many people in the Western world, bamboo is just another exotic plant, one that's valued more for its landscaping beauty than for the many practical uses to which it can be put. It's different in Asia—Asians celebrate the beauty of bamboo in literature, song, and art, but they've also found countless diverse uses for it.

Bamboo grows like weeds in many parts of Asia, and its hollow, tubelike *culms* or stems proved to be a very useful raw material. It was integral to the development of agriculture—and by extension, civilization—in ancient China. Waterwheels made of bamboo scooped water out of rivers and dumped it into troughs and pipes made of bamboo that irrigated the rice fields. Farmers built their homes out of bamboo, penned their animals in bamboo corrals, and fed them a diet that included bamboo leaves as fodder. The farmers themselves ate meals of bamboo shoots cooked in bamboo steamers, served on bamboo plates and eaten with bamboo chopsticks. They washed down their meals with *ulanzi*, a sweet wine made with fermented bamboo sap, served in bamboo cups. They used it for *everything*.

Its use has been spreading west slowly for more than a century, but now, with modern technology and because the plant is so fast-growing and quickly renewable, many experts say bamboo is poised to become one of the most important plant species of the 21st century.

**LATE BLOOMER**

So, what is bamboo? It's a member of the *Poaceae* family—the grasses—which includes the grass in your lawn, along with all the grains, such as wheat, corn, and rice. And several species of bamboo make up the largest members of this family. Grasses are relatively "new" plants on Earth, not having appeared until around the time of the disappearance of the dinosaurs, about 65 million years ago. And bamboo, experts say, didn't appear until 35 million years ago. Because of grasses' ability to survive in a great variety of climates—plains, marshes, and mountains—they have become one of the most successful types of plant life on Earth.

Bamboo is found in temperate and tropical regions around the globe and is native to every continent except Antarctica and Europe. More than half of the 1,200 bamboo species are found in Asia (mostly in China), but they also exist throughout India and Southeast Asia, down to northern Australia, all across sub-Saharan Africa and into Madagascar, and in the Americas. Like grains, which were vital to the development of civilization, bamboo spread across the globe through its close relationship to humans.

## BAMBOOZLED

Why does bamboo have so much potential for the future? Because of its physical qualities. It is harder than maple or oak, and has a much greater dimensional stability than either of these hardwoods (it doesn't shrink or expand as much as wood, which explains, in part, its current popularity for flooring). Its tensile strength—the amount of pulling force it can withstand before it breaks—is greater than steel's; its compressive strength is comparable to concrete; and its weight-to-strength ratio is greater than graphite.

Another amazing fact about bamboo: it is the fastest-growing plant on Earth. Recorded growth rates have been clocked at two inches *an hour*. Huge shoots can attain maximum height in less than two months. Maximum height? A world-record giant bamboo was found in 2003 by researchers at Yunnan University in southwestern China. The stem was 150 feet tall, weighed 990 pounds, and was 14 inches in diameter. The rapid growth rate has obvious economic advantages: A bamboo plantation can be harvested in 3–5 years, compared to a 10–20 year cycle for most softwood trees. And because it's a grass, bamboo can be harvested without killing the plant. Most of the plant is underground, so it will just send up shoots the following year—more and progressively bigger ones.

## ECO-FACTS
• Growing on otherwise unsuitable or degraded land, the dense

and fibrous root system of bamboo retains moisture, prevents erosion, and helps to rebuild the soil.

• Bamboo leaves contain up to 15% protein, providing high-nutrition fodder for several species of animals (not just pandas!).

• You've heard that plants "breathe" for the Earth? Well, bamboo breathes better than trees do. Bamboo absorbs more carbon dioxide from the atmosphere than an equal area of trees, and produces about 30% more oxygen.

• The dense leaf litter of bamboo reduces evaporation and doubles the amount of soil-water retention.

• It's not all good news: Many species of the plant are disappearing along with their habitat. It's estimated that up to half of the world's bamboo species are threatened, along with the many animal species that depend on them—the giant panda, the Himalayan black bear, and the mountain gorilla in central Africa being the most notable.

## MORE FACTS

• Bamboo terminology: The joints between segments of a culm are called *nodes*.

• The oldest existing bamboo artifacts, plaited mats found in China, date back more than 7,500 years.

• Other products that are (or were) made from bamboo: weapons, scaffolding, paint brushes, rafts, airplane wings, bridges, kitchen utensils, water filters, umbrellas, paper, kites, rope, and fishing rods.

• A bamboo grove is a cool, quiet place, traditionally valued as a site for meditation.

\*　　\*　　\*

## CHURCH BULLETIN

Rev. Martin Tran, a Catholic priest in California, kicked 55 people out of his church. Reason: they were kneeling during mass. Although kneeling has been part of church tradition for 2,000 years, Tran—with the support of the Vatican—evicted them because he says that in modern times, "it's more dignified to stand in the presence of God than to kneel." Rev. Tran called parishoners who are sticklers for the ancient tradition "rebellious, disobedient, and sinful."

# OFFICE PERSONALITIES

*If you work in an office, you'll probably recognize most of these personality types. Just preparing to enter the workforce? Use this as a guide for whom—or what—to avoid. (Uncle John is a Pontificator.)*

**PSI** (Personal Space Invader): Has no concept of acceptable distance; usually hovers well inside the bad-breath zone.

**The Hamburglar:** No food is safe in the office fridge.

**Hipper Than Thou:** Talks in catchphrases; punctuates remarks with two-handed finger pistols. Addresses co-workers as "Dude" or "Chief."

**Stinker #1:** Never heard of deodorant.

**Stinker #2:** Exceeds the Right Guard (or perfume) quotient.

**Wrinkles:** Shirt is never pressed and is always hanging out the back. Usually has a lot of jingly change in pockets (is often also a Stinker).

**Pontificator:** No answer is a simple "yes" or "no."

**Mr. Nice Guy:** Can anybody actually be this pleasant? Possibly harboring a dark, dark secret.

**Know-It-All:** Butts into other people's conversations, adding un-asked-for viewpoints.

**Klepto:** Likes to "borrow" stuff from your desk.

**Homer:** Loves *The Simpsons*; lives *The Simpsons*. "D'oh!" Related to Star Trekker. ("Kirk to Enterprise!")

**Whiner:** Management is stupid, lunch is lousy, the boss is unreasonable, my work never gets recognized, life sucks.

**Oscar Madison:** Somewhere under that pile of papers and burger wrappers is a desk. Somehow he knows where everything is.

**Felix Unger:** Keeps a feather duster and a mini-vac in the office.

**Pun-isher:** The office "comedian" has a bad pun for every occasion. Makes meetings last longer.

**Gossip Queen:** Own life is so boring that she feels compelled to create office drama.

**Mr. Needs-a–Tic Tac:** Need we say more?

**Oversharer:** Gives way more info about personal ailments, romantic conquests, and family history than anyone could possibly want to know.

**iPod Offender:** Thinks he's being quiet, but has no clue how loud he really is, humming along and tapping to the beat. Responds by yelling.

**Toucher:** Pats you on the back, places hand on your shoulder, brushes against you in the hallway. Creepy.

**Fiancé(e):** Every sentence begins with "My fiancé(e)…"

**Nervous Nellie:** If female, compulsively twists her hair into dreadlocks; if male, clicks pen and bites his fingernails.

**Cliff Claven:** Master of useless (and incorrect) knowledge.

**Chester:** Man who has difficulty looking female co-workers in the eye, focusing instead on the region south of the chin.

**Loudspeaker:** Hasn't mastered his "indoor voice."

**The Quitter:** Has been announcing intentions to "quit this damn job" since before you worked there, and will still be after you're gone.

**Cat Woman:** Not the superhero, but the gravel-voiced lady whose life is her cats, to which her cubicle is a shrine.

**The Echo:** Repeats other people's ideas and often takes all of the credit.

**Gab Gab Gabber:** Shows up unannounced to your cubicle and tells you *all about* his recent trip Disneyland; usually has photos.

**Frequent Forwarder:** Once they get your e-mail address, you'll be bombarded by cute li'l Internet jokes (like a list of office personality types).

\*     \*     \*

## MIDNIGHT RUN

"Police stopped a 10-year-old boy who was pedaling his toy car alongside a road in central Germany in the middle of the night. The boy said he was on his way to his grandmother's house in Berlin, police said on Thursday. He had been pedaling for about an hour but still had more than 400 km to go to reach Berlin. He had no coat on when spotted by a motorist in the middle of a snowstorm. Police warmed him up and took him home, where no one had noticed his midnight escape."

—**Reuters**

# MOTHERS OF INVENTION

*History has a tendency to marginalize women inventors, but there have been many. Here are a few that may impress you.*

**INVENTION:** The Circular Saw
**INVENTOR:** Tabitha Babbitt
**STORY:** Babbitt got the inspiration for her invention in 1810, at the age of 26, while sitting at her spinning wheel. Watching a work crew saw wood with a two-man saw, she noticed that half the back-and-forth motion was wasted (the back portion), and envisioned a circular blade. By notching the edge of a thin metal disk and then attaching it to her spinning wheel, she effortlessly cut through a piece of shingle, and the circular saw was born. But because of her religious beliefs (she was a Shaker), Babbitt never pursued a patent.

**INVENTION:** Modern Computer Programming
**INVENTOR:** Grace Hopper
**STORY:** When Hopper, a mathematician and Navy lieutenant, started working at the Eckert-Mauchly Computer Corp. in 1949, she was assigned to the team developing UNIVAC I, the first computer for business and consumer use. Back then, all computers were programmed in "binary" code—all 0's and 1's. Despite ridicule from her peers, Hopper set about creating a "compiler," a device to convert human language into binary. Her advancements not only made computers easier to program, but easier to *use*, as well.

**INVENTION:** The Surgical Eye Laser
**INVENTOR:** Patricia Bath
**STORY:** Before Bath's breakthrough, cataracts were removed through a very painful procedure that involved drilling and grinding them from the patient's eyes. In 1988 Bath patented a method of painlessly removing cataracts using a surgical laser. Bath also used lasers to cure certain types of blindness in people who hadn't seen for more than 30 years. She received patents in the U.S., Canada, Europe, and Japan, and is the first African-American woman ever to receive a patent for a medical invention.

Wangari Maathai of Kenya was the first African woman to win the Nobel Peace Prize, in 2004.

# FEELIN' LAZY

**Uncle John:** *"We need another quote page."*
**Jay:** *"Can't it wait 'til later?"*

"You can't teach people to be lazy—either they have it, or they don't."
—**Dagwood Bumstead**

"Ambition is a poor excuse for not having sense enough to be lazy."
—**Edgar Bergen**

"I prefer the word 'indolence.' It makes my laziness seem classier."
—**Bern Williams**

"Never put off until tomorrow what you can do the day after tomorrow."
—**Mark Twain**

"There's nothing to match curling up with a good book when there's a repair job to be done around the house."
—**Joe Ryan**

"What is worth doing is worth the trouble of asking somebody to do it."
—**Ambrose Bierce**

"Laziness is nothing more than the habit of resting before you get tired."
—**Jules Renard**

"It is better to have loafed and lost than never to have loafed at all."
—**James Thurber**

"It's true that hard work never killed anybody, but I figure, why take the chance?"
—**Ronald Reagan**

"Progress is made by lazy men looking for easier ways to do things."
—**Robert A. Heinlein**

"Hard work often pays off after time, but laziness always pays off now."
—**Larry Kersten**

"There is no pleasure in having nothing to do; the fun is in having lots to do and not doing it."
—**Mary Wilson Little**

"Whenever there is a hard job to be done I assign it to a lazy man. He is sure to find an easy way of doing it."
—**Walter Chrysler**

"Let us be lazy in everything... except in being lazy."
—**Gotthold Lessing**

# A PUNCH IN THE ARM

*Unacceptable: punching your little brother in the arm. Acceptable: doing it under the guise of a "game." Did you play any of these kids' games?*

**DOORKNOB!** When someone farts, he or she must immediately say "Safety!" If a non-farter detects the fart and says "Doorknob!" before the farter says "Safety," the person who says "Doorknob" gets to punch the farter in the arm. The farter can avoid getting punched if he or she touches a doorknob. But what if there are no doorknobs handy? In such situations (camping or swimming, for example), a substitute must be agreed upon before the first fart.

**JINX!** When two people say the same thing at the same time, the first person who shouts "Jinx!" wins. The loser is not allowed to speak until someone says his or her name. The penalty for violating the jinx rule is a punch in the arm.

**Coke Variation:** The first one to yell "Jinx! You owe me a Coke!" wins. The loser must then buy the winner a soft drink.

**Caveat:** It is often quite difficult to actually collect the drink.

**SHOTGUN!** Who gets to ride in the most coveted position in the car—the front passenger seat, commonly known as "riding shotgun"? The person who yells "Shotgun!" first. But there are rules. To be awarded the front seat, everyone who will be riding in the car must be able to see it before someone yells "Shotgun!" If it's yelled at any time before that, the "Shotgun!" is null and void.

**SLUG BUG!** (a.k.a. *Punch Buggy*) Played while riding in a car, the first person who sees a Volkswagen Beetle and yells "Slug Bug!" gets to hit someone in the arm. If it's a convertible, two hits are awarded.

**Variation:** A "Pediddle" is a car with only one working headlight. Whoever spots one and yells "Pediddle!" gets to hit someone. If the Pediddle is a Slug Bug, they get two hits. If the Pediddle is a convertible Slug Bug (rare but not unheard of), then they get to beat the stuffing out of whoever else is riding in the back seat.

**Long day:** In China, schools run from 7:30 a.m. to 5:00 p.m.

# A FEW DOGS SHORT OF A KENNEL

*Did you do something dumb today? Read this—you'll feel better.*

## BLOOMIN' IDIOT

A tourist was visiting Melbourne, Australia, when she climbed over a small barrier to pick some flowers. Bad move: She was at the Melbourne Zoo, and the barrier was there to keep people away from the lion. When she reached into the cage to get the flowers, she got the tip of her finger bitten off instead. According to reports, the woman (who was too embarrassed to reveal her identity) was treated at a local hospital and released. Officials didn't bother looking for the fingertip, as it had almost certainly been eaten.

## SAY CHEEEEESE-BRAIN

Police contacted a 40-year-old man in Kreuzlingen, Switzerland, in 2005, after he was photographed by an automatic camera while driving over the speed limit—four times in less than two minutes. He had passed the camera doing 36 mph, then 39 mph, 47 mph, and 42 mph in a 30 mph zone. The man apparently wasn't familiar with the speed camera system. He told officers he thought somebody was flashing a light at him to annoy him, and he kept driving by to find out "what was going on." He soon found out: He received four speeding tickets, totaling about $750.

## DUDE! I'VE GOT AN AWESOME IDEA!

Michael Morris, 17, a junior at Chesterton High School in Indiana, was hospitalized in 2006 after being hit by a car. The car was driven by his friend, 18-year-old Stephen Domonkos—whom Morris had asked to run him over. Domonkos said his friend was an "adrenaline junkie" and "gets off on this kind of thing." Morris suffered only a broken leg and a broken arm, while Domonkos was arrested on a charge of criminal recklessness causing serious bodily injury. "I won't do this no more," Morris told the *Times of Munster*...from his hospital bed.

# $PIRIT OF '76

*In 1976 the United States celebrated its bicentennial. What better way to commemorate the 30-year anniversary of the 200-year anniversary of America's birth than with a look at how much things cost back then?*

• Want to see the year's hottest flicks, like *Rocky* or *Network*? A movie ticket costs $2.25.

• Rather watch a movie at home? There's a new invention called a VCR that sells for a mere $1,600.

• Average household income: $12,700.

• New house: $48,000 (avocado Formica countertop extra).

• Minimum wage: $2.30/hour.

• A new Chrysler Cordoba (with "rich Corinthian leather") will set you back $5,000.

• Whether for use on the street or in the disco, a pair of new roller skates costs $5.

• Average tuition at a private college: $2,500 per year.

• Ticket to Super Bowl X: $20 (Steelers 21, Cowboys 17).

• Alex Haley's *Roots* is one of the bestselling novels of the year. A hardbound copy runs $12.50.

• The year's biggest albums are available on 8-track. Cost of the Eagles' *Hotel California* or Peter Frampton's *Frampton Comes Alive!*: $7.

• Red meat is good for you. Get a cheeseburger at McDonald's for 48¢.

• Watch Farrah Fawcett on *Charlie's Angels* with a $600, 24-inch color TV. (Or you could be like the five million others in 1976 who dropped $2.00 on her swimsuit poster.)

• Average prices:

| | |
|---|---|
| First-class stamp | 13¢ |
| Gallon of gas: | 59¢ |
| Dozen eggs: | 84¢ |
| Loaf of bread: | 30¢ |
| Bananas (per pound): | 13¢ |

• Jimmy Carter and Gerald Ford spent a combined $160 million on their presidential campaigns. (Bush and Kerry spent $547 million in 2004.)

• How much for a minivan, CD, Apple computer, SUV, or a cup of coffee at Starbucks? $0. They didn't exist in 1976.

---

George Washington was present at America's first hot-air-balloon flight, in 1793.

# GHOSTWRITERS

*These famous works weren't written by actual ghosts—they were secretly
written by somebody else. Of course, Uncle John writes all his own stuff.
(Except for this piece, which was "researched" by Brian Boone.)*

## PROFILES IN COURAGE
**"Written" by:** John F. Kennedy

**Details:** In 1954, laid up in bed after back surgery, then-
Senator Kennedy decided to write a book about heroic United
States senators. *Profiles in Courage* was released two years later,
became a bestseller, won the Pulitzer Prize for nonfiction, and made
Kennedy a national figure. But people started to talk: Did Kennedy
really write the book? Yes, said Kennedy's lawyers, who strong-armed
ABC News into an on-air apology when newspaper columnist Drew
Pearson questioned authorship on *The Mike Wallace Show*. No, say
historians, who now claim it was actually written by Kennedy's
speechwriter, Ted Sorensen. Kennedy sent Sorensen notes and
instructions and supervised his progress, but Sorensen spent six
months working 12-hour days on the book, doing all the research
and all the writing. (He got credit as a "research associate.") The
Kennedy family still insists JFK wrote *Profiles in Courage*, but in
1990, historian Herbert Parmet was researching a book on Kennedy
and sifted through crates of papers at the Kennedy Library. If the
future president had really written the book, Parmet says he would
have found copious notes, possibly rough drafts of chapters or unfin-
ished manuscripts. What did he find? Nothing.

## THE HARDY BOYS
**"Written" by:** Franklin W. Dixon

**Details:** Edward Stratemeyer started the Stratemeyer Syndicate—
a "book factory"—in 1899, churning out children's books written
by multiple writers-for-hire but always attributed to a pen name.
Stratemeyer's attitude was that although writers die, a popular and
profitable book series shouldn't have to. His most successful series
was *The Hardy Boys*, about two teenage mystery solvers. In the
series' 1927 to 1979 run, 59 books were produced, all by different
writers, but all attributed to "Franklin W. Dixon." Other book

---

Hey, tall, dark, and handsome: Female lions prefer males with dark manes.

series produced by the Stratemeyer Syndicate: Nancy Drew (by "Carolyn Keene"), the Bobbsey Twins (by "Laura Lee Hope"), and Tom Swift (by "Victor Appleton").

## MAZURKA FOR TWO DEAD MEN

**"Written" by:** Camilo José Cela

**Details:** You may not have heard of this book, but it was a bestseller in Spain, won that country's national book award, and helped Cela win the Nobel Prize for literature in 1989. When Cela died in 2002, two men, Marcel Suarez and Mariano Tudela, revealed that they had actually written the majority of *Mazurka*. They developed the plot and characters and Cela rewrote the book in his own style. Also revealed: Throughout his life, Cela judged writing contests where he routinely stole stories, rewrote them slightly, and published them as his own work.

## NEARLY EVERY BOOK BY V.C. ANDREWS

**"Written" by:** V. C. Andrews

**Details:** Andrews took up writing late in life, publishing her first horror novel, *Flowers in the Attic*, in 1979. It was a huge bestseller, later made into a popular movie. She wrote four sequels that also sold well, then died in 1986. Fans wanted more books, and Andrews's family wanted the money the books brought in, so they hired a writer named Andrew Neiderman to write more horror novels in the same style, under the name V. C. Andrews. Interestingly, while Andrews herself wrote just six books, Neiderman—as Andrews—has written more than 40.

## TO KILL A MOCKINGBIRD

**"Written" by:** Harper Lee

**Details:** The jury's still out on this one. In 1961 Lee's novel won the Pulitzer Prize, but aside from a handful of short essays, she never published again. Why not? Editor Pearl Kazin Bell, who worked with Lee, claims it's because Lee didn't write *To Kill a Mockingbird*—her prolific friend, Truman Capote, did. But defenders of Lee point out that *Mockingbird* is not written in Capote's style. And since Capote was a relentless self-promoter, they say, he would have taken credit for *Mockingbird* once it won the Pulitzer. Capote died in 1984...so we may never know for sure.

How about you? 54% of American kids ride the bus to school.

# UPSIDE-DOWN
# PANGBORN

*It's a bird! It's a plane! It's a forgotten page in aviation
history, from* Bathroom Reader *test pilot Jeff Cheek!*

## TOUGH ACT TO FOLLOW

On May 20, 1927, Charles Lindbergh took off from New
York and flew his plane, the *Spirit of St. Louis*, 3,500 miles
across the Atlantic Ocean to Paris. His goal: to win the $25,000
prize that a French newspaper had offered for the first solo New
York-to-Paris flight. "Lucky Lindy" landed in the French capital,
claimed his prize, and came home an international celebrity.

But what about the first trans-*Pacific* flight? That feat came
four years later. It was longer, more dangerous, and complicated by
international tensions. And while Lindbergh's trans-Atlantic success was the result of careful planning, the men who crossed the
Pacific basically blundered their way into the history books.

Soon after Lindbergh's historic flight, Tokyo's largest newspaper,
*Ashi Shimbun*, offered a $25,000 prize for the first nonstop flight
over the Pacific, but it required the pilot to start in Japan and then
land in the United States. The Japanese airstrip closest to the U.S.
was a sandy runway near the town of Misawa on the northern tip
of the island of Honshu. Four previous trans-Pacific attempts had
begun there, but none had succeeded. One plane developed engine
trouble and had to turn back; the other three were lost at sea.

## THE BARNSTORMER

Clyde "Upside-Down" Pangborn, a former World War I pilot and
now a county-fair barnstormer known for his daring, low-level slow
rolls, wasn't interested in the *Ashi Shimbun* challenge—he had his
sights set on a different goal: the round-the-world speed record. In
July 1931 he and his navigator, Hugh Herndon (whose mother
financed the trip), took off from New York, flying east across the
Atlantic in his single-engine Bellanca monoplane, the *Miss Veedol*

They were making good time, too…until they tried to refuel in
Siberia during a rainstorm; the *Miss Veedol* slid off the runway and

got stuck in the mud. That ended their dream—they were stranded for three weeks getting the plane unstuck and waiting for spare parts. That's when Pangborn decided to salvage something from the trip by trying for the *Asahi Shimbu* prize instead.

## ROUGH LANDING #2

But they soon ran into more trouble. Pangborn flew low over the picturesque Japanese seacoast so that Herndon could snap some photos. There happened to be a Japanese military base nearby, so Herndon snapped a few shots of that, too. Bad idea: When the *Miss Veedol* landed, Pangborn and Herndon were immediately arrested for spying. (The aviators were unaware that while they were in Siberia, Japan invaded Manchuria, severely straining U.S.-Japanese relations.) They spent seven weeks under house arrest until the American Embassy negotiated their release…and got permission for them to attempt the trans-Pacific flight from Misawa. But they had only one chance to leave Japan: if they returned, the *Miss Veedol* would be confiscated and destroyed.

The reception in Misawa was much warmer. Pangborn and Herndon were given food and shelter while the town's schoolchildren swept the runway and cut the tops of trees for a safer takeoff. (The townspeople were eager for someone to break the record and make Misawa famous.) At dawn on October 4, 1931, the two adventurers readied the *Miss Veedol*. Just as they were boarding, a Japanese boy ran up and gave them five apples. Pangborn was touched, and felt good about their chances.

## ROUGH TAKE-OFF

As the plane lumbered down the runway, it was so overloaded with fuel—915 pounds of it—that they couldn't break free of the moist sand…and a pile of logs was getting closer and closer (the same pile left by the kids). Pangborn was literally rocking the plane back and forth trying to get it airborne. "I was determined to get off, or crash into those logs," Pangborn later recalled. "We had permission for only the one attempt and in no way was I going to spend any more time in Japan." The plane made it over the logs, over the trees, and then started climbing. Japan was finally behind them.

The *Miss Veedol* was still too heavy, but Pangborn was prepared. The previous day, he had unbolted the landing gear and reattached it with clips that could be released by pulling a cable. So he pulled the cable…but only part of the landing gear fell away—the struts were still dangling. With no other options, while flying at 100 mph, Pangborn climbed out onto each wing, barefoot, held on with one hand, reached underneath, and yanked off the struts.

The two men then settled in for the two-day journey, their only food being those five apples, fried chicken, and some tea. They flew above the clouds at 17,000 feet to avoid turbulence, but that also made it cold. "Our water, and even our hot tea froze," recalled Pangborn. They shivered, slept in shifts, and talked about all of the things they would do when they became rich and famous.

After 40 hours in the air, fatigue caught up with them as the plane finally reached landfall. Herndon was sound asleep. They missed Seattle completely, had to turn around, and then found that Seattle was covered by fog. So were Spokane and Boise. Pangborn was dangerously low on fuel (and furious at his navigator), but he found his way to Fancher Field in the small town of Wenatchee, Washington, near where he grew up. At 7:14 a.m. on October 5, 1931, the *Miss Veedol* made a bumpy but successful "belly landing."

## INTO THE WILD BLUE OBSCURITY

Lucky Lindy got a ticker tape parade when he returned, but hardly anyone noticed Pangborn and Herndon's feat. They received some press—mostly focused on the two men's bickering over Herndon's navigational skills. Then Herndon's mother gave Pangborn only $2,500 of the $25,000 prize money. She'd financed the trip, so she kept the rest as "reimbursement." The two men never spoke again.

Herndon became a stockbroker; Pangborn went back to barn-storming and then served in Britain's Royal Air Force during World War II. He flew 175 missions, piloting bombers and transport planes. Pangborn was buried with full military honors in Arlington National Cemetery when he died in March 1958. He was never bitter about not becoming famous, and was always grateful to the Misawa townspeople. As thanks, he sent them some "Richard Delicious" apple tree saplings. Today, at the abandoned airfield on Honshu stands a billboard with a faded painting of the *Miss Veedol* and the message "The First Trans-Pacific Flight—She Took Off Here." And near the billboard is a grove of Richard Delicious apple trees, which now grow all over Japan.

# THE CURE FOR WHAT AILS YE

*Modern medicine may not be perfect, but at least we have basic knowledge of nutrition, and we've stopped using earwax as Chapstick. Want proof that we've got it good? Pick up a book of 19th-century home remedies, read the health tips, and be glad you weren't born 200 years ago.*

**To prevent consumption (tuberculosis):** "Let not your breast touch the table or desk on which you write, for leaning the breast hard against the edge of the table hath brought many young men into a consumption."

**—*The Young Man's Companion* (1775)**

**For alcoholism:** "The prescription is simply an orange every morning a half hour before breakfast. Take that and you will neither want liquor nor medicine. The liquor will become repulsive."

**—*Dr. Chase's Recipes* (1884)**

**To prevent influenza:** "Children should be instructed to run with the mouth shut for the first block or two after going outdoors in cold weather."

**—*The Guide Board to Health, Peace and Competence* (1870)**

**To recover from being struck by lightning:** "Shower with cold water for two hours; if the patient does not show signs of life, put salt in the water and continue to shower an hour longer."

**—*The Canadian Home Cookbook* (1877)**

**During pregnancy:** "Those who have not been accustomed to bathing should not begin the practice during pregnancy. The mother should avoid looking at or thinking of ugly people or those marked with disfiguring diseases."

**—*The Physical Life of Woman* (1872)**

**To prevent asthma:** "Asthmatics find that missing a meal at night usually will prevent an attack; that hearty meals or certain

foods produce attacks; that constipation is very likely to cause the trouble, while a clean bowel helps one to avoid it. Nude sun- and air-baths should be taken daily or as frequently as possible."
—*Home Health Manual* (1930)

To treat asthma: "A pipe of tobacco (or a cigar) has the power of relieving a fit of asthma, especially in those not accustomed to it."
—*Cassell's Household Guide* (1880)

To treat epilepsy: "It has been said that a black silk handkerchief, thrown over the face while the fit is on, will bring the person 'to' instantly."
—*The Guide Board to Health, Peace and Competence* (1870)

To cure stuttering: "Let him who stammers, stamp his foot on the ground at the same time that he utters each syllable and stammering is impossible."
—*Fun Better than Physic* (1877)

"Nothing is better than ear-wax to prevent the painful effects resulting from a wound by a nail, skewer, etc. It should be put on as soon as possible. Those who are troubled with cracked lips have found this remedy successful when others have failed."
—*The American Frugal Housewife* (1832)

To cure a toothache: "Dissolve a piece of opium, the size of a small pea, in spirits of turpentine. Put in the hollow of the tooth upon cotton. It does not stop the pain at once, but if well applied, and frequently changed, will soon cause it to never trouble again."
—*Dr. Chase's Recipes* (1884)

"Do not give opium to children under the age of one year except on the advice of a physician."
—*The Practical Home Physician* (1892)

"Do not make children cross-eyed by having hair hang about their foreheads where they see it continually."
—*The American Frugal Housewife* (1832)

# MAKE YOUR OWN ORIGAMI RUBBER DUCK

*The Japanese art of folding paper, BRI style. (More-igami on page 363.)*

First, photocopy the pattern below onto a piece of yellow paper. Enlarging it 200% will fit it onto a standard 8½" x 11" sheet. Then cut along solid edges to make it a square. Now follow the folding steps on page 118. **Step 1:** Fold along the dashed lines as shown. **Steps 2–4:** Turn the paper over and fold under as shown. **Step 5:** Fold along the center crease, printed side out. **Steps 6–9:** Fold along the lines, then reverse the folds, pushing down while lifting up, making the tail, then the head, then the beak. Color the beak with an orange marker and *voilà*—you're done!

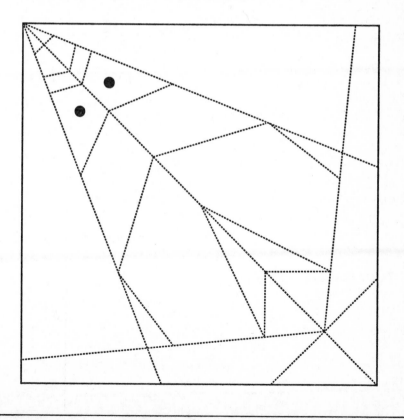

---

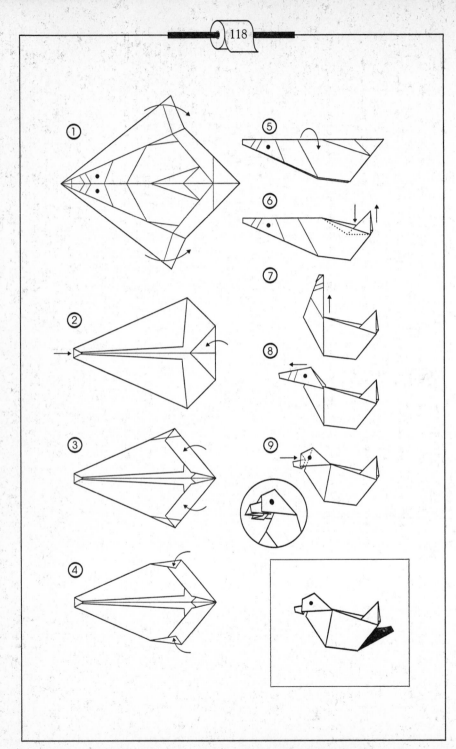

Odds that a baby sea turtle will survive to adulthood: 1 in 1,000.

# LOTTERY ROW

*Want to win the lottery? Some words of
caution: It ain't always a "win."*

**WINNER:** Christina Goodenow of White City, Oregon
**PRIZE:** $1 million
**WHAT HAPPENED:** On October 12, 2005, Goode-
now played the Oregon Lottery's Million Dollar Jackpot Scratch-It
game…and won. Two weeks later she was arrested. It turned out
that she'd purchased the ticket with a stolen credit card—her
deceased mother's. Whether she gets to keep her million-dollar
prize has yet to be determined by the court. (But here's a good
indication: a warrant for her arrest was issued after she failed to
show up for her first court appearance.)

**WINNER:** Johnny Rae Brewster of Dallas, Texas
**PRIZE:** $13 million
**WHAT HAPPENED:** Brewster won the Texas Lottery jackpot in
1995…and died 10 months later of a heart attack. His will stipu-
lated that his sister get his lottery winnings, but she inherited
something else: his $3.5 million tax bill. Under Texas law, the
estate has to pay all taxes owed by the deceased in full immediately, even though Brewster's annual lottery payments were only
$460,000. Fortunately, the sister and the state struck a deal: she
could pay $482,000 a year for 10 years, which meant she actually
*lost* $22,000 a year because her brother won the lottery.

**WINNER:** Michael Carroll of Norfolk, England
**PRIZE:** £10 million (about $18 million)
**WHAT HAPPENED:** In 2002 Carroll, a 19-year-old garbage
collector, won the National Lottery prize. The *Telegraph* reported
that he wouldn't be celebrating at a pub—because the repeat
offender was wearing a court-imposed electronic tag for a recent
drunk-and-disorderly conviction. They also said he shouldn't
bother buying a new car—because his driving privileges had also
been taken away. "Don't tell me God doesn't have a sense of
humor," a police officer told the paper. Carroll went on to become

known as "The Lottery Lout" after alienating his neighbors by holding demolition derbies at his home in the middle of the night. In 2004 he was ordered to take drug tests after being caught with cocaine, and ended up with a five-month jail term—for not showing up for the drug tests.

**WINNER:** William "Bud" Post III of Pennsylvania
**PRIZE:** $16.2 million
**WHAT HAPPENED:** In 1988 Post had less than $3 to his name. He pawned a ring for $40 and gave it to his landlady to buy some state lottery tickets. When he won, he went on a legendary spending spree: He bought a car lot, a restaurant, a mansion, and an airplane (which he didn't know how to fly). Within a few years, his wife had left him, his brother was arrested for hiring a hit man to kill him, and Post himself was arrested for firing a shotgun over the head of a bill collector. On top of that, his landlady sued him, saying that he'd promised her half of the winnings. She was awarded a third, but Post didn't have it—he'd spent it all. He had to sell his house, and in 1992 auctioned off his 17 remaining lottery payments ($500,000 a year) for $2.65 million. He then proceeded to lose that sum in a series of business blunders and finally declared bankruptcy and lived the rest of his life on a $450-a-month disability check. He died in 2006 at the age of 66, having said, "I was much happier when I was broke," and adding that he was sorry he had ever won the "Lottery of Death."

**WINNER:** Jody Lee Taylor of Collinsville, Virginia
**PRIZE:** $4.3 million
**WHAT HAPPENED:** In 1992 Taylor won the Virginia Lottery. Three years later he was arrested after having set fire to his girlfriend's Ford Thunderbird and firing 15 shots from a .45-caliber pistol into the floor of their double-wide trailer. He was sentenced to a year in jail. Then in 2003 Taylor was spotted driving a brand-new pickup truck down Route 58 on the wrong side of the road...with his lights off...while naked. He refused to stop for police and during the chase tried to run down a deputy. His father later told reporters that he wished his son had never bought the lottery ticket. "Out of 10,000 people, there might be one who could handle the money," he said. "The rest, it'll push them over the edge."

---

Q: How many sides does a STOP sign have? A: Two...front and back.

# THA FAS BOUKETO

*Idioms are expressions whose meanings cannot be understood by literal translation—there's nothing about "blow your top," for example, that suggests it means "get angry." Every language has them.*

**PANTOFFELKINO (Germany)**
Translation: "Slippers cinema"
Meaning: Television

**ECHARSE FLORES (Spain)**
Translation: "Throw flowers to yourself"
Meaning: Toot your own horn; sing your own praises

**AKI GA TATSU (Japan)**
Translation: "The autumn breeze begins to blow"
Meaning: A passionate love affair is beginning to cool off

**CAVOLI RISCALDATI (Italy)**
Translation: "Reheated cabbage"
Meaning: An old love affair you're trying to rekindle

**AT HAVE TØMMERMAEND (Denmark)**
Translation: "To have carpenters (in your head)"
Meaning: To have a hangover

**THA FAS BOUKETO (Greece)**
Translation: "You're going to eat a bunch of flowers"
Meaning: I'm going to hit you in the face

**IN BOCCA AL LUPO (Italy)**
Translation: "Into the mouth of the wolf"
Meaning: Good luck!

**ESPRIT DE L'ESCALIER (France)**
Translation: "The spirit of the staircase"
Meaning: The clever comeback that you think of after it's too late to do any good; e.g., after you've left the room and are climbing the stairs. The Germans call it a *Treppenwitz* ("stair joke").

The word *planet* is from the Greek word for wanderer. (They move while the stars remain still.)

## FAR SECCO QUALCUNO (Italy)
**Translation:** "To leave someone dry"
**Meaning:** This is what it's called when you're lucky enough to think of your witty comeback in time to use it—your comment will leave the listener speechless.

## OHRWURM (Germany)
**Translation:** "Ear worm"
**Meaning:** A song that you can't get out of your head

## KHALI KHUKWANI (KwaZulu-Natal, South Africa)
**Translation:** "Make a noise in the pocket"
**Meaning:** Cell phone

## HANAGE O NUKU HANDY (Japan)
**Translation:** "Pull the hair out of their nostrils"
**Meaning:** Dupe someone; play them for a fool

## GOYANG KAKI (Indonesia)
**Translation:** "Swing your legs"
**Meaning:** Do nothing while others work to solve your problems

## PULIR HEBILLAS (Spain/Central America)
**Translation:** "Polish belt buckles"
**Meaning:** Dance very close to your partner

## POSER UN LAPIN A QUELQU'UN (France)
**Translation:** "Lay a rabbit on someone"
**Meaning:** Stand someone up on a date

## MUSTASUKKAINEN (Finland)
**Translation:** "Wearing black socks"
**Meaning:** Jealous

## AVEN SOLEN HAR FLACKAR (Sweden)
**Translation:** "Even the sun has spots"
**Meaning:** Nobody's perfect

## TO PRO MNE SPANELSKA VESNICE (Czech Republic)
**Translation:** "It's all a Spanish village to me"
**Meaning:** I don't understand

---

Free time: 59% of American teenagers do volunteer work.

# MILE-HIGH COMEDIANS

*Flying can be scary. That's why flight attendants and pilots sometimes try to add a little levity (get it?) to the experience. Here are some actual airplane announcements that readers have sent us.*

## PREPARING FOR TAKEOFF

"As we prepare for takeoff, please make sure your tray tables and seat backs are fully upright in their least comfortable positions."

"There may be fifty ways to leave your lover, but there are only four ways off this airplane."

"Your seat cushions can be used as flotation devices. In the event of a water landing, please take them with our compliments."

"To operate your seatbelt, insert the metal tab into the buckle, and pull tight. It works just like every other seatbelt, and if you don't know how to operate one, you probably shouldn't be out in public unsupervised."

"Should the cabin lose pressure, oxygen masks will drop from the overhead area. Please place the bag over your own mouth and nose before assisting children or adults acting like children."

"Any person caught smoking in the lavatories will be asked to leave the plane immediately."

"We'd also like to remind you to turn off your cellular phones, computers, video games, or any other electronic device that may interfere with the captain's pacemaker."

## IN-FLIGHT GUFFAWS FROM THE PILOT

"Mornin', folks. As we leave Dallas, it's warm and the sun is shining. Unfortunately, we're going to New York, where it is cold and rainy. Why in the world y'all wanna go there I really don't know."

"We are pleased to have some of the best flight attendants in the business. Sadly, none of them are working this flight."

"Ladies and gentlemen, we have reached our cruising altitude of 30,000 feet, so I'm going to switch off the seat belt sign. Feel free to move about the cabin, but please try to stay inside the plane until we land."

"Once again, I'm turning off the seat belt sign. I think I'll switch to autopilot, too, so I can come back there and visit with you for the rest of the flight."

"Folks, if you were with us last week, we never got around to mentioning that it was National Procrastination Day."

"The weather in San Francisco is 61 degrees with some broken clouds, but they'll try to have them fixed before we arrive."

## LANDING AND DE-PLANING

*After the plane touched down and was coming to a stop, the pilot's voice came over the loudspeaker:* "Whoa, big fella. WHOA!"

"Sorry about the rough landing, folks. I'd just like to assure you that it wasn't the airline's fault; it wasn't the flight attendants' fault; nor was it the pilot's fault. It was the asphalt."

"We ask you to please remain seated while Captain Kangaroo bounces us to the terminal."

"As you exit the plane, please make sure to gather all of your belongings. Anything left behind will be distributed evenly among the flight attendants. Please do not leave children or spouses."

"Thank you for flying Business Express. We hope you enjoyed giving us the business as much as we enjoyed taking you for a ride."

"Thanks for flying with us today. And the next time you get the insane urge to go blasting through the skies in a pressurized metal tube, we hope you'll think of us."

"Last one off the plane has to clean it!"

---

A lightning bolt strikes so fast it could circle the globe eight times in a second.

# JOIN THE (CITIZENS) BAND

*Got your ears on, good buddy? CB radios—part cell phone, part automobile chat room—were VERY popular in the 1970s. Here's a look at where they came from…and where they went.*

O N THE AIR
In 1946, just after World War II, the Federal Communications Commission (FCC) established the Citizens Radio Service Frequency Band, and set aside certain radio frequencies for public use by people using two-way radios. Anyone in the United States could use these frequencies—all they had to do was buy a radio that worked on the "citizens band," then fill out an application and pay a nominal fee to get a license. The first CB licenses were issued in 1947.

CBs were popular with farmers, hunters, boaters, and people living in rural areas, where there was no phone service. Small businesses like construction companies and trucking firms used them too. In all, about a million people applied for licenses over the next 25 years…but they didn't catch on with the general public. Most people had never even heard of them.

### THE OIL CRISIS

Then, in October 1973, the Arab members of the Organization of the Petroleum Exporting Countries (OPEC) imposed an oil boycott on the United States and countries in western Europe to retaliate against their support for Israel during the Yom Kippur War. And just to be sure they made their point, they also voted to sharply increase the price of crude oil. These two events caused widespread fuel shortages, as gasoline and diesel prices rose more than 400%. Americans panicked. No gas? No heating oil? The Nixon administration responded to the situation by imposing mandatory rationing and lowering the maximum speed limit to 55 mph, because cars consume less fuel at 55 than they do at higher speeds.

No one suffered more during the oil crisis than independent truckers. Their fuel costs skyrocketed and the new speed limit cut into their ability to pay for fuel by reducing the distances they could drive each day. In February 1974, they organized a nationwide strike that went on for 10 days. And during those 10 days they helped usher in what *Time* magazine called "the biggest explosion of communications since the invention of the telephone."

## UNDERDOGS

The truckers' strike got a lot of coverage on TV news, which exposed many viewers to CB radios for the first time. People saw how truckers used the radios to exchange information about where to buy the cheapest fuel and, just as importantly, find out where state troopers were setting up speed traps. The sight of these renegade truckers banding together to fight "the Man" was a romantic image that reminded people of the Old West—only these cowboys rode trucks instead of horses, and had CBs instead of six-shooters.

• Like everyone else with a CB license, truckers were required by law to use their license number as a call sign when they went on the air. But the truckers ignored this and instead used "handles" they made up for themselves—Pigpen, Silver Fox, Maverick—so that they could warn each other about speed traps without revealing their identities to state troopers or the FCC.

• Colorful lingo made truckers and their CBs even more alluring to the general public. State troopers in many states wore flat-brimmed hats similar to the one worn by Smokey the Bear; this made them "smokeys" or "bears." The 55 m.p.h. speed limit? The "double nickel." Speeding tickets? "Bear bites." Were you hauling a load of explosives from Los Angeles to Cleveland? You were a "suicide jockey" heading from "Shakey Town" to the "Mistake on the Lake." Taking produce to New York City? You're "hauling garbage" to "Dirty Town." (For more CB trucker lingo, see pages 154, 289, and 484.)

## COPY THAT

Inspired by the idea of using their own CB radios to avoid speed traps and fight high gas prices just like the truckers did, Americans started buying the radios in record numbers. It had taken more than a quarter century—from 1947 to 1973—for the FCC to issue its first million CB licenses. But Americans bought 2 million CBs in 1974, 5 million in 1975, 10 million in 1976, and 13 million in 1977. By January 1977, CB license applications were coming in at nearly 1 million per month—so many, in fact, that the FCC gave up licensing altogether and let anyone operate the radios, license or not. CB radio and accessory sales had grown from next to nothing to $2 billion a year in less than five years. Some experts predicted that by 1987, half of all U.S. households would own at least one CB radio.

## CB NATION

CBs (and truckers) made strong inroads into popular culture, too: In 1975 "Convoy," a country song about a group of truckers who dodge state troopers as they travel across the U.S., went to #1 on both the country and pop music charts. In 1977 *Smokey and the Bandit* became the second-highest-grossing movie of the year (behind *Star Wars*). Muhammad Ali had a CB in his car (his handle was "The Big Bopper"). First Lady Betty Ford had a CB in her limousine (her handle: "First Mama"). Even the Big Three automakers began offering AM/FM/CB radios as options on new cars.

How many fads turn out to be *practical*? Stranded motorists who used CBs to call for help instead of walking miles to find a pay phone wondered how they'd ever gotten along without a two-way radio in their car. In those pre-Internet days, a CB turned your car into a chat room on wheels, enabling you to talk to other drivers without revealing any more about yourself than you wanted them to know. More than one marriage was born with the click of a CB radio microphone; more than a few were probably wrecked by them, too.

## SMOKEY'S GOT HIS EARS ON

Even the police came around: At first, several states tried to pressure trucking companies into pulling CBs out of their rigs. When that failed, state police agencies started installing them in squad cars to keep track of what the truckers were up to. The truckers proved to be an asset: They reported so many accidents and drunk drivers that troopers began broadcasting license numbers of wanted cars and descriptions of suspects over the CB, so that truckers could watch out for them.

Which crayon color is used most often? Black.

## OFF THE AIR

So why don't we all have CBs in our cars today?

• For one thing, the CB system wasn't equipped to handle the millions of people who bought radios. In those days, CBs had only 23 channels (and one—channel 9—was reserved for emergency traffic). That limited the number of people who could talk at a time, especially in crowded urban areas. People spent $150 or more on a CB, only to find that they couldn't get a word in edgewise.

• The FCC responded to the overcrowding by adding 17 new channels, bringing the number to 40, but that actually hurt sales of CB radios—consumers didn't want the 23-channel radios any more, but they didn't want to pay $200 to $300 for the 40-channel radios, either.

• Rising gasoline prices prompted Americans to start buying smaller cars, which had less room for bulky CBs; when people traded in their old cars, they didn't bother to get new radios. And when the oil crisis eventually came to an end, drivers no longer needed CBs to find stations that had cheap gas.

By the late 1980s, sales of CB radios had dropped to less than 500,000 sets per year and all but a handful of CB manufacturers went out of business.

## BORN AGAIN

Believe it or not, the advent of cell phones in the mid-1990s was actually good for the CB business: When people signed up for what they thought were cheap calling plans and got socked with hidden charges, CB sales started inching upward. People in areas without satellite coverage bought them, too. By 1998 sales of the "poor man's cell phone" had climbed back up to 3 million radios a year.

If you like taking road trips to places where cell phones don't always work, you're in luck—modern CB radios are smaller and much more powerful than they were in the 1970s. They're cheaper too: You can pay as little as $75 for a portable, battery-powered emergency radio, or $200 for one installed in your car. That makes them a much better value than they were during the CB craze.

So what are you waiting for? Get your ears on, put the pedal to the metal, and try to keep the bears from biting. We gone!

---

Hiya! Research shows that dolphins can recognize themselves in a mirror.

# RANDOM ORIGINS

*You know what these are...but do you know where they came from?*

## TRAVEL AGENCIES

In 1841 a Baptist missionary named Thomas Cook chartered a train to take 570 temperance campaigners from Leicester, England, to a rally in Loughborough, 11 miles away. In exchange for giving the business to the Midland Counties Railway, Cook received a percentage of the fares. The success of that trip inspired him to organize many more. Eventually he expanded beyond the temperance movement and began booking trips for people who wanted to travel for pleasure. Cook has been credited with inventing not only the travel agency, but modern tourism, as well. Today the company that bears his name is one of the world's largest travel agencies.

## FOUNTAIN PENS

In 1883 a New York insurance broker named Lewis Waterman handed his new fountain pen to a client who was about to sign a major contract. The pen not only didn't write, it also dumped its contents onto the paperwork, ruining it. By the time Waterman returned from his office with another contract, the client had signed with someone else. Waterman vowed never to let that happen again—to him or anyone else. It took him a year to do it, but he invented the world's first properly functioning fountain pen, which used capillary action to send a steady and reliable flow of ink from the reservoir to the "nib," or point, of the pen.

## WOOD-BURNING STOVES

If you wanted to heat your home in the mid-18th century, there was only one way: your fireplace. But because they were usually built into an exterior wall, fireplaces were inefficient—much of the heat was lost to the outside air. In 1742 Benjamin Franklin invented a freestanding metal stove that could be placed in the middle of the room, so *all* the heat radiated into the room. The "Franklin stove," as it came to be known, remains one of Benjamin Franklin's most famous inventions. One problem: it didn't work. For all his genius, Franklin apparently never realized that heat and smoke *rise*, which means you have to put the chimney outlet at the top of the stove. Franklin connected his at the base, and because of that the fire would not stay lit. His stove didn't become practical until another inventor, David Rittenhouse, connected the chimney *above* the fire.

## GREYHOUND RACING

Greyhounds have been admired for their speed as far back as ancient Egypt and beyond; for centuries it was a common pastime to release a live rabbit in front of two greyhounds and bet on which dog would catch and kill it. That sport was known as "coursing.' Modern greyhound racing didn't come along until 1912, when a rabbit-loving New Jersey inventor named Owen Patrick Smith invented a mechanical rabbit, or lure, that the dogs could chase instead. The lure was connected to a system of pulleys so that, unlike live rabbits, it "ran" along a prescribed course instead of dashing in any direction. That made circular and oval-shaped dog tracks possible for the first time. Dog tracks were small enough that they could be located in urban areas, where the sport became very popular with working-class sports fans for whom horse racing was out of reach.

## ROLLERBLADES

In-line skates weren't so much invented as *re*invented: When a Belgian instrument maker named Jean Joseph Merlin attached five small metal wheels to a pair of his shoes in 1760 and created what are believed to be the world's first roller skates, he arranged the wheels in a single line. It was difficult to turn or maintain balance with them, and in 1863 a New York inventor named James Plimpton invented the classic side-by-side "quad" skates. His design dominated the sport for more than a century. Then in 1979, Scott Olson, a minor-league hockey player, stumbled onto a pair of in-line skates from the 1960s while looking for something that would allow him to train in the off season. Olson became a distributor of the skates, and when the manufacturer rejected his suggestions for improvements, he bought the patent rights to a similar skate. In 1982 he started selling Rollerblades (it's a trademarked name). By 1994 the company was selling $260 million worth of skates a year.

Charles Curtis was the first (and only) Native American vice president (1929–1933).

# HOW TO BUILD AN ATOM BOMB

*Hey Mom, looking for a fun project for the kids?*

U P AND ATOM
The following article appeared in the April 1979 issue of *The Journal of Irreproducible Results*, a "science humor" magazine started by two scientists in 1955. (Many thanks to *Journal* editor Norman Sperling for allowing us to reprint it.) It was written by Bell Labs researcher Dean Radin—on a lunch break—and it's based on sound science, even if it's not exactly applicable in the real world.

### How to Build an Atom Bomb

Worldwide controversy has been generated recently from several court decisions that have restricted popular magazines from printing articles that describe how to make an atomic bomb. The reason usually given by the courts is that national security would be compromised if such information were generally available. But, since it is commonly known that all the information is publicly available in most major metropolitan libraries, obviously the court's position is covering up a more important factor, namely that such devices would prove too difficult for the average citizen to construct.

The rumors that have occurred as a result of widespread misinformation can be cleared up now, for our project this month is the construction of a thermonuclear device. We will see how easy it is to make a device of your very own in ten easy steps, to do with as you see fit, without annoying interference from the government.

The project will cost between $5,000 and $30,000, depending on how fancy you want the final product to be. Since last week's column, "Let's Make a Time Machine," was received so well in the new step-by-step format, this column will follow the same format.

### Construction Method

1. First, obtain about 50 kg (110 pounds) of weapons-grade Plutonium at your local supplier. A nuclear power plant is not recommended, as large quantities of missing Plutonium tend to make

plant engineers unhappy. We suggest that you contact your local terrorist organization, or perhaps the Junior Achievement in your neighborhood.

**2.** Please remember that Plutonium, especially pure, refined Plutonium, is somewhat dangerous. Wash your hands with soap and warm water after handling the material, and don't allow your children or pets to play in it or eat it. Any leftover Plutonium dust is excellent as an insect repellent. You may wish to keep the substance in a lead box if you can find one in your local junkyard, but an old coffee can will do nicely.

**3.** Fashion a metal enclosure to house the device. Most common varieties of sheet metal can be bent to disguise this enclosure as, for example, a briefcase, a lunch pail, or a Buick. Do not use tinfoil.

**4.** Arrange the Plutonium into two hemispherical shapes, separated by about 4 cm. Use rubber cement to contain any Plutonium dust.

**5.** Now get about 100 pounds (220 kg) of trinitrotoluene (TNT). Gelignite is much better, but messier to work with. Your helpful hardware man will be happy to provide you with this item.

**6.** Pack the TNT around the hemisphere arrangement constructed in step 4. If you cannot find Gelignite, feel free to use TNT packed in with Play-Doh or any modeling clay. Colored clay is acceptable, but there is no need to get fancy at this point.

**7.** Enclose the structure from step 6 into the enclosure made in step 3. Use a strong glue such as "Krazy Glue" to bind the hemisphere arrangement against the enclosure to prevent accidental detonation which might result from vibration or mishandling.

**8.** To detonate the device, obtain a radio controlled (RC) servo mechanism, as found in RC model airplanes and cars. With a modicum of effort, a remote plunger can be made that will strike a detonator cap to effect a small explosion. These detonator caps can be found in the electrical supply section of your local supermarket. We recommend the "Blast-O-Matic" brand because they are no deposit–no return.

**9.** Now hide the completed device from the neighbors. The garage is not recommended because of high humidity and the extreme range of temperatures experienced there. Nuclear devices have been known to spontaneously detonate in these unstable conditions. The hall closet or under the kitchen sink will be perfectly suitable.

**10.** Now you are the proud owner of a working thermonuclear

---

**No part of Japan is more than 100 miles from the sea.**

device! It is a great ice-breaker at parties, and in a pinch, can be used for national defense.

### Theory of Operation

The device basically works when the detonated TNT compresses the Plutonium into a critical mass. The critical mass then produces a nuclear chain reaction similar to the domino chain reaction (discussed in this column, "Dominos on the March," March 1968). The chain reaction then promptly produces a big thermonuclear reaction. And there you have it, a 10-megaton explosion!

### Next Month's Column

In next month's column, we will learn how to clone your neighbor's wife in six easy steps. This project promises to be an exciting weekend full of fun and profit. Common kitchen utensils will be all you need. See you next month!

## POSTSCRIPT

"How to Build an Atomic Bomb" was a big hit when it came out, and over the years the article was widely dispersed on the Internet. And in 2001 it made headlines all over the world, in a scary—but funny—way.

On November 15, 2001, in the midst of the attacks on Afghanistan by U.S. and NATO forces, the *Times* of London reported that "Osama bin Laden's al-Qaeda network held detailed plans for nuclear devices and other terrorist bombs in one of its Kabul headquarters." A BBC television reporter followed up with a harrowing on-air report about the plans, including shots of him holding a page of the bomb document in his hand. The news of the terrorist group's nuclear ambitions traveled around the world.

A webmaster in Connecticut who goes by the name of CyberGeek was watching the BBC report. "I started laughing," he later said. Why? The reporter was holding a copy of the parody article. Apparently, al-Qaeda (and the *Times* and the BBC reporter) believed that you could get plutonium at "your local supplier," that there was such a thing as a "Blast-O-Matic" detonator, and that items like duct tape and Krazy Glue could be used to make an atomic bomb. The best part, said CyberGeek, was that the document "seemed to show a number of lines and notes around it—meaning the terrorists were actually studying it!"

"It defies imagination," he says.

# DUMB CROOKS

*With crooks like these, we hardly need cops.*
*Here's proof that crime doesn't pay.*

## ARMED BOOBERY

"Armed robbers who held up a money courier made off with his first-aid kit instead of the suitcase full of cash. The two bandits pursued the courier at high speed before shooting at his vehicle and forcing him to stop on a road in Gronau, Germany. Forcing the trunk open, one of the crooks snatched a case before fleeing again. But instead of taking the money, he made off with a first-aid kit. Police spokesman Johann Steinlitz said: 'If there was an award for the dumbest crooks they would certainly be in the running.'"

—**Ananova**

## THAT'S NOT FAIR!

"In New Braunfels, Texas, Robert Villarreal, 34, was sentenced to 50 years in prison after he sold drugs to the same undercover officer for the third time in a 14-year period. He actually argued 'entrapment,' claiming that for the first sale, in 1988, he was so young that he couldn't be expected to remember later what the officer looked like."

—*New Braunfels Herald-Zeitung*

## STICK 'EM UP!

"A man with two sticks demanded money from people at a food mart on 29th Street and Culebra in San Antonio, Texas. Employees and customers did not think the man was serious, so they laughed at him. He then left, went to a beauty supply store down the street, and demanded money there. When a female employee said she didn't have any money, the man started hitting the cash register with his sticks. The woman told him to stop, and gave him two dollars just to make him leave, which he did. No one was hurt. Police are looking for the suspect."

—**WOAI-TV (San Antonio, Texas)**

Former New York City mayor Ed Koch once appeared as himself on *All My Children*.

## COUNT DUMBULA

"A man was charged with burglary and criminal mischief after he allegedly broke into a funeral home and fell asleep in a coffin. Joel Fish, 20, was arrested after he was discovered at the O'Leary Funeral Home in Canton, New York. Debra White, wife of the home's funeral director, said she noticed a broken window and open door to the casket display room when she awoke at 6:30 a.m. Inside, she saw a boot and pair of pants on the floor and a pair of knees sticking out of a coffin. Fish, who police said was intoxicated, was arrested and released to return to court at a later date."

—Associated Press

## HIT PARADE

"A man accused of not paying for his Pop-Tarts had a troubled getaway. First, the clerk at the convenience store ripped the man's shirt off as they struggled when she confronted him for pocketing the toaster pastries. Then after the man punched the clerk in the stomach and made it out the door, he was hit by a pickup truck in the parking lot. Police said he got up and kept running—into the path of a minivan while he was crossing the street. He got up again, but didn't make it far. 'He gets up and continues to run, but responding police officers caught up with him just a short distance later and he was taken into custody,' police Capt. Tracy Tingey said, adding that the man suffered only minor injuries and refused medical treatment."

—Associated Press

## WE DON'T NEED NO STINKIN' BADGES

"Bryan Perley, who apparently held a grudge against a child-support caseworker, was charged in Orlando, Florida, with several felony counts when he tried to arrest her by impersonating a military officer and holding a fake, handwritten arrest warrant. When the woman's colleagues would not cooperate with him, Perley actually called for police backup, telling the dispatcher, 'They don't understand the chain of command in government. I've warned them.'"

—WFTV-TV (Orlando, Florida)

In ancient Rome, yellow was the color most associated with weddings.

# UH, EXCUSE ME, SIR, BUT YOUR MICROPHONE IS ON

*Quiet, please. It's time for open mike night at the BRI. Had these
public figures known that their mikes were hot and the tape
was rolling, they would have never said what they said.*

**SPEAKER:** President Ronald Reagan
**BACKGROUND:** In 1984, during the height of the Cold
War, Reagan took a break from his reelection campaign to
do a radio interview. He thought he was doing a sound check for
the crew, but was actually being broadcast live over the airwaves.
**WHAT WAS SAID:** "My fellow Americans, I'm pleased to tell you
today that I've signed legislation that will outlaw Russia forever."
[Laughter.] "We begin bombing in five minutes." [More laughter.]
**REACTION:** Neither Reagan nor his supporters thought it was a
big deal—it just proved that the president had a sense of humor.
(Reagan's staff took steps to ensure that in the future the Great
Communicator would know unequivocally whether he was being
broadcast.) But Democrats blasted the president as a trigger-happy
madman out of touch with the severity of his "joke." The Soviets
weren't amused, either. One Moscow television station wondered
how much Reagan was joking, claiming that bombing Russia was
his "sacred dream." The joke didn't hurt Reagan politically,
though—he won that year's election by a landslide (and he never
did bomb Russia).

**SPEAKER:** Senator John Kerry
**BACKGROUND:** The 2004 Democratic presidential candidate
was preparing for a TV interview, but didn't know the tape was
already rolling. As one of his handlers told him to "keep smiling,"
he made some disparaging remarks about Republicans (through
smiling teeth).
**WHAT WAS SAID:** "Oh, don't worry, man. We're going to keep
pounding, let me tell you. Just beginning the fight here. These
guys are the most crooked, lying group I've ever seen."
**REACTION:** After learning that his remarks were recorded and

played all over the news that night, Kerry stood by them, refusing to apologize. His Democratic base was proud of the tough rhetoric, but Republicans seized the opportunity to paint him as emotionally unstable and having a personal vendetta. Did that swing some voters over to Bush? We'll never know, but Kerry lost the election.

**SPEAKERS:** George W. Bush and Tony Blair

**BACKGROUND:** They were at the 2006 G8 Summit in St. Petersburg, Russia, for formal meetings on how to resolve the Middle East crisis. But what caught the media's attention was an *impromptu* meeting between the American president and the British prime minister. While Bush was sitting at the table eating his lunch, Blair walked up and stood behind him, and the two started to chat.

**WHAT WAS SAID (excerpts):**

**Bush:** Yo, Blair. How ya doing?

**Blair:** I'm just...

**Bush:** You're leaving?

**Blair:** No, no, no, not yet.

[Later...]

**Bush:** Who's introducing the trade?

**Blair:** Angela [Merkel, the German Chancellor].

**Bush:** Tell her to call 'em [the Syrian government].

**Blair:** Yes.

**Bush:** Tell her to put them on the spot. Thanks for the sweater—it's awfully thoughtful of you.

**Blair:** It's a pleasure.

**Bush:** I know you picked it out yourself.

**Blair:** Oh absolutely—in fact I knitted it! [Laughter.]

**Bush:** I think Condi [Condoleezza Rice] is going to go pretty soon.

**Blair:** But that's, that's all that matters. But if you...you see it will take some time to get that together.

**Bush:** Yeah, yeah.

**Blair:** But at least it gives people...

**Bush:** It's a process, I agree. I told her your offer to...

**Blair:** Well, it's only if I mean...you know. If she's got a...or if she needs the ground prepared as it were. Because obviously if she goes out she's got to succeed, whereas I can go out and just talk.

---

In 1938, 15-year-old William Taynton was the first person on television (as a test subject).

**Bush:** You see the irony is what they need to do is get Syria, to get Hezbollah to stop doing this sh*t and it's all over.

**Blair:** Is this...? [Blair taps the microphone on the table and the sound is cut.]

**REACTION:** To the British press, it confirmed, once and for all, that their prime minister was nothing more than Bush's yes-man, and that Bush, in turn, was a typical rude American who didn't even have the courtesy to stand up and formally greet his British counterpart (some of the transcript is inaudible because Bush was eating lunch and often talked with his mouth full). Said the UK's *Daily Mirror*, "Yo, Bush! Start treating our prime minister with respect!" It also referred to Blair as the "president's poodle."

**SPEAKER:** French President Jacques Chirac

**BACKGROUND:** In 2005 Chirac attended a private meeting with two other world leaders, Russian President Vladimir Putin and then–German Chancellor Gerhard Schröder. At the time, London and Paris were competing for the opportunity to host the 2012 Olympic Summer Games. The meeting wasn't recorded, but the room was full of curious eavesdroppers, one of whom wrote down everything, including some harsh words Chirac had for the English.

**WHAT WAS SAID:** "The only thing that they have ever done for European agriculture is mad cow disease. You cannot trust people who have such bad cuisine. It is the country with the worst food after Finland."

**REACTION:** France and England may not be the best of friends, but they are expected at least to act civilly toward each other. So it caused quite a stir to hear the French president blatantly insult the British (and the Finns), especially in the presence of other world leaders. And the insults ended up hurting Chirac in a big way: Paris had been the front-runner to get the Games, but two of the voting members of the International Olympic Committee were from Finland. Result: London won the bid by a narrow margin. The French still maintain that had Chirac just kept his mouth shut, Paris would have been the host.

As for the British, they took the tactful way out. A spokesman for Tony Blair responded by saying that "there are some things that are better not responded to."

# VIDEO TREASURES

*Ever found yourself in a video store staring at thousands of films you've never heard of, with no idea what to rent? It happens to us all the time—so we decided to offer a few recommendations.*

SCOTLAND, PA (2001) *Comedy/Thriller*
**Review:** "In this darkly comic and faithful adaptation of *Macbeth*, Joe 'Mac' McBeth and his frighteningly ambitious wife both work at a hamburger joint. Mac is full of ideas about the future of fast food, but his boss isn't listening. When he passes over Mac to give the manager position to his son, Mac's thoughts turn to murder." (*TV Guide's Movie Guide*) *Director*: Billy Morrissette.

**TAKE THE MONEY AND RUN** (1969) *Comedy*
**Review:** "Woody Allen's first feature is still a laugh-filled delight as the star-director plays an inept criminal in a story told in pseudo-documentary style. It's hilarious." (*Video Movie Guide*) *Stars*: Woody Allen, Janet Margolin. *Director:* Woody Allen.

**BORN INTO BROTHELS** (2004) *Documentary*
**Review:** "Two American photographers went to Calcutta to film prostitution and hit upon the idea of giving cameras to the children of prostitutes, asking them to take photos of the world in which they lived. The filmmakers bring out the innate intelligence of the children as they use their cameras to see their world in a different way. (There are no scenes that could be described as explicit, because filmmakers did not want to exploit their subjects.) The movie is a record by well-meaning people who try to make a difference for the better." (Roger Ebert)

**GHOST WORLD** (2001) *Comedy/Drama*
**Review:** "Two cynical, trendy teenagers who recently graduated from high school are getting an apartment together instead of going off to college—the thing that everyone else is doing. A dark, humorous coming-of-age story with a little twist, it excels at showing how bumpy the transition to adulthood can be." (*Scarecrow Video Movie Guide*) *Stars*: Thora Birch, Scarlett Johansson.

## THE INCREDIBLE SHRINKING MAN (1957) *Science Fiction*

**Review:** "A philosophical thriller about a man who is doused with radioactive mist and begins to slowly shrink. His new size means that everyday objects take on sinister meaning and he must fight for his life in an increasingly hostile environment. A surreal allegory with impressive special effects and endowed with the tension usually reserved for Hitchcock films." (*Videohound's Golden Movie Retriever*) *Stars:* Grant Williams. *Director:* Jack Arnold.

## DOGFIGHT (1991) *Drama*

**Review:** "Lily Taylor is superb as a physically plain folkie who becomes an unwitting partner in River Phoenix's attempt to bring the ugliest 'date' to a party held by Vietnam-bound Marines in 1963 San Francisco. This sleeper has a good script, tough direction, and apt use of period music." (*Leonard Maltin's Video Guide*)

## A WORLD APART (1988) *Drama*

**Review:** "Anti-apartheid struggles in the 1960s seen through the eyes of a 13-year-old South African girl whose mother is imprisoned for her support of the African National Congress. Excellently acted and moving mix of political and domestic drama." (*Halliwell's Video Guide*) *Stars:* Jodhi May, Barbara Hershey.

## LIVING IN OBLIVION (1995) *Comedy*

**Review:** "An intricately constructed film-within-a-film: each of the movie's three sections involve a single scene that a director is trying desperately to film, and every problem, both conceivable and otherwise, a struggling film might encounter. It's a consistently funny inside-movies comedy, a witty revenge against the dream factory." (*Never Coming to a Theater Near You*, by Kenneth Turan) *Stars:* Steve Buscemi, Catherine Keener. *Director:* Tom DiCillo.

## THE MAN WHO WOULD BE KING (1975) *Adventure*

**Review:** "Old-fashioned adventure and derring-do. Two British soldier-pals try to bamboozle high priests of remote Kafiristan into turning over their riches by convincing them that one of them is a god. The acting is ideal, the script is superb, and the film is entertaining." (*Leonard Maltin's Movie & Video Guide*) *Stars:* Sean Connery, Michael Caine. *Director:* John Huston.

# WHEN YOU GOTTA GO...

*Everybody has to die sometime. At least
some of us get to go in interesting ways.*

## BLUE MOON

In 1995 two pilots and a navigator were flying a warplane in a U.S. Navy training exercise. When another warplane flew up beside them, the three men stripped off their clothes and mooned the other plane, pressing their buttocks against the cockpit glass. But to get their clothes off, they had to remove their oxygen masks. They quickly lost consciousness, and the plane plunged to the ground, killing all three.

## COLD CASE

Playwright Tennessee Williams (*A Streetcar Named Desire*) took a variety of pills the night he died in 1983, but that's not what killed him. Williams, 71, opened up a bottle of nose spray, used it, and accidentally dropped the cap in his mouth. Moments later, he choked on the bottle cap and died.

## NO ROAMING

In November 2005, Jimmy Ray George of Easley, South Carolina, died of smoke inhalation when his home caught fire. Oddly, George made it out of the house safely. He wasn't overcome by smoke until he went back inside the burning house to get his cell phone so that he could call 911.

## LOVE LIFTED THEM

Frauke Punz and Ulf Lech worked together at a steel mill in Essen, Germany, and were secretly dating. The day their plant was to close for a monthlong summer break, they snuck into an elevator for a romantic liaison. Unaware that Punz and Lech were in the elevator, everybody left for vacation and maintenance shut off the electricity. Their bodies were discovered a month later.

## CABBAGE PATCH KILLER

Three 18-year-old members of the Ukraine military were ordered to clean a food storage container that was buried 12 feet underground in the city of Charkov. Cabbage had been left in it for weeks, and the fumes were so severe that they overcame and killed the three teenagers as well as the 48-year-old worker who tried to rescue them.

## CLEAN SWEEP
Reggie Peabody, a car-wash worker in Melbourne, Australia, liked to turn on the automated system and "ride the brushes" when business was slow. But the system malfunctioned during one of his "rides," and Peabody was crushed to death between two large industrial brushes.

## GONE TO POT
In August 2005, Michael Johnson was riding his motorcycle on a highway in Custer, South Dakota. He tried to pass a sanitation truck carrying Porta Potties, but as the truck tried to get out of the way, a strap broke, causing one of the portable toilets to come loose and fly off the truck. It struck Johnson, killing him and sending his motorcycle sliding into three moving cars.

## NO SMOKING
Late one night in November 2005, 23-year-old Bartosz Drobek of Mount Prospect, Illinois, was hanging out on the balcony of his apartment with his brother. They were smoking cigarettes, which made them want to clear their throats, so the two decided to make a long-distance spitting contest out of it. As Drobek was getting ready to spit, he lost his balance, fell 20 feet to the ground below, struck his head on the pavement, and died.

## NICKELED-AND-DIMED
In 1987 the *American Journal of Forensic Medicine and Pathology* reported on a 58-year-old woman who'd died of copper poisoning. How? For some reason she'd swallowed 275 coins. Her metallic meal, consisting of 174 pennies, 33 nickels, 37 dimes, and 31 quarters, amounted to $14.84 in change.

\*　　\*　　\*

"The gods too are fond of a joke." —**Aristotle**

# MODERN MYTHOLOGY

*In ancient Greece, they had heroes like Hercules and Pegasus. Today we have new "heroes," like the San Diego Chicken and the GEICO Gecko.*

## THE SAN DIEGO CHICKEN

In 1974 San Diego State University journalism major Ted Giannoulas was hired off the street by a local radio station to dress up in a chicken suit and hand out Easter eggs at the San Diego Zoo. He must have done a good job, because a few weeks later the station had him appear at a San Diego Padres game. The chicken was a hit: Giannoulas ran all over the field, jumping and prancing around, entertaining the fans. After that he became a fixture at the ballpark, performing at 5,200 consecutive Padres home games. (In 1979 the chicken suit was replaced with a custom made chicken-in-a-baseball-uniform outfit.) The San Diego Chicken led to the emergence of fuzzy mascots throughout Major League Baseball, including the Phillie Fanatic, the Baltimore Bird, and the St. Louis Fredbird. In 1999 *The Sporting News* named the Chicken one of the 100 most powerful sports figures of the 20th century.

## THE CREAM OF WHEAT CHEF

In America's slavery era, slave owners commonly gave their slaves Biblical names. A popular choice was Erastus (a disciple of St. Paul). After the Civil War, Erastus was shortened to Rastus and became a common (and somewhat racist) term whites used for black men. When the Diamond Milling Company launched Cream of Wheat cereal in 1893, it used the image of a smiling African-American chef as its trademark on the box and in print advertising. His name: "Rastus." Using a black worker in a logo wasn't uncommon; Aunt Jemima products and Uncle Ben's Rice also used them. But "Rastus" was actually based on a real person, a chef named Frank White who was photographed working in a Chicago restaurant.

## RICH UNCLE PENNYBAGS

It's estimated that more than 500 million people have played the game of Monopoly. And every one of them probably knows the game's mascot: a short, stubby, white-mustachioed man in a top hat. Monopoly was first released in 1935, and the old man first appeared on Chance and Community Chest cards in 1936 editions of the game. So who is "the Monopoly guy"? It's believed that the model for the character was Albert Richardson, the first traveling salesman for Monopoly's maker, Parker Brothers. The character went nameless until he appeared on another board game—Rich Uncle—in 1946, and his name became Rich Uncle Pennybags. (Parker Brothers says his first name is "Milburn.") But after Hasbro bought Parker Brothers, he was officially renamed "Mr. Monopoly" in 2000.

## GEICO GECKO

This computer-animated lizard pitchman was thought up by the Martin Agency in 2000. The premise: A gecko is annoyed that people keep calling him because they are confusing his number with the insurance company GEICO, because "gecko" and "GEICO" sound so similar. Aside from a verbal pun, the cartoon character was created out of necessity: The Screen Actors Guild was on strike, making live actors unavailable. The original voice behind the British-sounding gecko was supplied by Kelsey Grammer. In 2005 the character was changed from an annoyed upper-crust Brit into a helpful lizard with a Cockney accent. His voice is now performed by British soap opera actor Jake Wood.

## REDDY KILOWATT

In the 1920s, electricity was nothing new, but thousands of rural homes still weren't wired because many people thought electricity was dangerous. In 1925 Ashton Collins, general manager of the Alabama Power Company, had just returned home from an electric industry convention and was thinking about how to change consumers' minds. Staring out a window into a thunderstorm, he saw two lightning bolts merge and strike the ground. It looked like a human figure to him, and Collins said that in that instant, Reddy Kilowatt, fully formed, popped into his head—a stick figure made of lightning bolts, with wall outlets for ears, a lightbulb for a nose, and two tiny lighting bolts for tufts of hair. Reddy debuted in print ads in March 1926 as a way to convince Alabamans that electricity was safe and attractive. It worked, so Reddy was licensed by 200 other utility companies and became the personification of electricity for millions of people around the country.

# OH, MARTHA!

*Martha Mitchell is largely forgotten now, but at the height of her fame in the 1970s, she was one of the most popular women in America.*

## THE MOUTH OF THE SOUTH

On November 21, 1969, Martha Beall Mitchell, wife of Attorney General John Mitchell, gave an interview on the *CBS Morning News*. Her husband had been on the job for nearly a year, and in that time she hadn't attracted much attention. Her TV appearance changed that. She came out against Vietnam War protestors, whom she denounced as "liberal Communists...As my husband has said many times, some of the liberals in this country, he'd like to exchange them for the Russian Communists." Nixon administration officials cringed when they saw the show; they wondered how bad the fallout would be...until letters started pouring into the White House *supporting* Martha.

## SPEAKING HER MIND

Suddenly people were interested in Martha Mitchell. She cut quite a figure: A native of Pine Bluff, Arkansas, she was a 51-year-old Southern belle whose loud clothes, big hair, and cat-eye sunglasses competed with her big mouth for attention.

But the big mouth *always* won. Martha had an opinion on everything—she loved Richard Nixon (one of the funniest and sexiest men in America) but hated liberals (communistic), teachers (too liberal), lawyers (they're lawyers), the Supreme Court (too liberal), the press (too powerful), and universities (too liberal).

She didn't agree with everything Nixon did, either, and she wasn't afraid to say it: Nixon appointed only men to the Supreme Court; Martha wanted a woman. The Vietnam War, which Nixon showed no signs of ending, as he'd promised to do on the campaign trail? "It stinks!" she said. The courage and spunk she showed in speaking her mind struck a chord with the American public and made her very popular, even with people who disagreed with her. In one poll, she was voted one of the 10 most-admired women in the world. She was the second-most-requested speaker for Republican fundraisers after the president himself. If you mentioned "Martha" in conversation in the 1970s, everyone knew who you were talking about. She was the most famous Cabinet wife in American history.

## MARTHA-GATE

Nixon and his staff encouraged Martha's antics—even her late-night calls to reporters when she may have had a little too much to drink. They believed the administration was actually benefiting from her fame...until June 17, 1972, when five men were caught breaking in to the Democratic Party's headquarters in the Water-gate complex in Washington, D.C.

Martha's husband, John, was a central figure in the Watergate scandal; he sat in on the meetings where this and other "dirty tricks" were planned. It would take more than two years for the details to become public, but Martha already knew much of what was going on, because in addition to being a big mouth, she was also a world-class snoop—when John met with his co-conspirators in their home, she eavesdropped from the stairway. When he talked on the phone, she listened in on the extension in the bath-room. When Mitchell went to bed, she rifled through his briefcase and read his secret documents. He eventually bought a briefcase that locked, but Martha got into that one, too.

## IN THE DARK

John and Martha were in Southern California on political busi-ness when the break-in was foiled; by then Mitchell had stepped down as Attorney General to run Nixon's reelection campaign. When Mitchell dashed back to Washington, D.C., to contain the scandal, he left Martha behind in California, without telling her what was going on. Then, when Martha read about the burglary in the newspaper, John Mitchell ignored her frantic calls for three entire days. That sent her into such a frenzy that she made one last call and left a message with an underling to tell John that 1) she was leaving him unless he got out of politics *right now*, and 2) her next call was going to be to UPI reporter Helen Thomas.

*That* call got Mitchell's attention—how could the White House pretend Watergate was just a "third-rate burglary" if Martha was spilling the beans to the press? Someone made a quick call to California; moments later a Nixon staffer burst into Martha's room and ripped the phone out out of the wall. Then several aides held

---

Many shampoos and lipsticks contain *stearic acid*. What is it? Another name for beef fat.

her down while a doctor injected her with a sedative against her will—"they pulled down my pants and shot me in the behind!"—and held her as a "political prisoner," she claimed, for several days.

Sedating Martha was only a temporary "solution"—Nixon and his cronies couldn't keep her out of the public eye forever. So they began leaking stories to undermine her credibility, saying she was an alcoholic (she did have a drinking problem), mentally ill (false), and an airhead who knew nothing. The strategy worked: Woodward, Bernstein, and other reporters apparently never saw her as a major source for the Watergate story.

## BITTER END

The Watergate cover-up failed, of course, and as the scandal began to threaten Nixon and his top aides, John D. Ehrlichman and H.R. Haldeman, they tried to save themselves by setting John Mitchell up as a scapegoat. Martha turned on Nixon with a vengeance, telling reporters that the cover-up scandal went all the way to the top—to Nixon himself—and calling for his resignation in late-night calls to reporters even as John continued fighting to save the president's skin. Watergate placed an unbearable strain on their marriage; in September 1973, John Mitchell moved out of their apartment and filed for divorce.

Martha played no direct role in Watergate, and yet she is arguably one of its biggest victims. John Mitchell never saw or spoke to her again, and she became estranged from her 12-year-old daughter, who blamed her for John's problems. So did Mitchell—when he was sentenced to prison in 1975, he said, "It could have been worse. They could have sentenced me to spend the rest of my life with Martha Mitchell."

The strain of Watergate may have even sent Martha to an early grave. In October 1975, she was diagnosed with an incurable form of bone-marrow cancer. For the rest of her days she wondered if the shot she received in California caused her illness. The following May she died, never having reconciled with her daughter. Now, more than 30 years after Watergate, Martha's most lasting claim to fame may be what psychiatrists have dubbed "The Martha Mitchell Effect." That's what it's called when someone is mistakenly diagnosed as delusional, only for it to be revealed later that their "delusions" were actually true.

---

Israel is about the size of Massachusetts, and has about the same population.

# COLBERT'S RETORTS

*Comedy Central's Stephen Colbert is so good at parodying arrogant news hosts that it makes you wonder if he's really pretending.*

"I'm not a fan of facts. You see, facts can change, but my opinion will never change, no matter what the facts are."

"Do you know you have more nerve endings in your gut than you have in your head? You can look it up. Now, I know some of you are going to say, 'I did look it up, and it's not true.' That's 'cause you looked it up in a book. Next time, look it up in your gut."

"I believe democracy is our greatest export. At least until China figures out a way to stamp it out of plastic for three cents a unit."

"All God's creatures have a soul. Except bears. Bears are godless killing machines."

"It's never okay for men to cry. Man holds it in until his eyeballs swell to the size of baseballs, his throat feels like it's about to explode, and his gut just aches like there's a snake wrapped around his heart. That's why we die earlier, but it's worth it. At least we don't look weak while we're alive."

"I've never been a fan of amphibians. They are nature's fence-sitters. Come on, amphibians, which is it? Water or land? Pick one!"

"Like any good newsman, I believe that if you're not scared, I'm not doing my job."

"Just because the Pope is infallible doesn't mean he can't make mistakes."

"If these foreign newspapers have nothing to hide, how come they don't print them in English?"

"Why do we have to wait for elections? Why not have every elected official have electrodes implanted in their chest? If they don't please us, every morning, we stop their hearts."

"America has a simple deal with the wealthy: we cut their taxes and in return they inspire us with their golden toilets and trophy wives."

"There's nothing wrong with stretching the truth. We stretch taffy, and that just makes it more delicious."

# THE MUSIC MAN

*Do you like electronic music? Then raise your
glass and drink a toast to Thaddeus Cahill.*

## MUZAK MAKER

In 1893 an inventor from Washington, D.C., named
Thaddeus Cahill was experimenting with telephone
transmissions when he had a novel idea: He noticed that when an
electric generator, or *dynamo*, sent current down a phone line, it
created a tone in the earpiece. And different frequencies of current created different tones. Cahill quickly realized that if he had
*12* dynamos—each corresponding to a note on the scale—he
could send music over phone lines. He spent the next four years
perfecting the idea, and in 1897 received a patent for the *Telharmonium*, not only the world's first significant electric musical
instrument—but the first one that could be potentially heard by
thousands of people at once.

Think about it: At that time (and for all time before that) if
you wanted to listen to live music, you had to be within hearing
distance of the person playing the instrument. The phonograph
was becoming popular—but that was *recorded* music. And the popularity of the radio was decades away. Cahill envisioned hiring
serious musicians to play "respectable" music, such as Bach and
Chopin, on his telharmonium, and sending it over phone lines to
restaurants, hotels, and other paying subscribers—even individuals
—miles away.

## HOW IT WORKED

The telharmonium (or the *dynamophone*, as Cahill sometimes
called it) was basically a gigantic electric organ. It had two keyboards—one on top of the other—and hundreds of wires running
to generators, transformers, and various other electrical parts that
sent current down the line. And to magnify the sound, he called
for large paper cones that could be fixed to the earpieces of telephones (the precursor to the loudspeaker).

• When the telharmonium was turned on, an electric motor
turned the shafts of the 12 dynamos, known as "tone shafts."

• Each dynamo had a four-foot-long metal shaft packed with metal disks (picture a barbell packed with weights). The disks, or "tone wheels," had different numbers of differently-sized teeth on their edges. As they rotated past the coil, the teeth would produce varying frequencies of electricity, which would, in turn, produce different notes.

• Pressing a key moved a magnetic coil—the *pickup*—toward one of the tone wheels, creating an electrical charge—and a tone—that would then be sent down a phone line.

• Those tone wheels, 145 of them on the 12 tone shafts, gave the telharmonium a five-octave range with 36 notes in each octave. But that's not all they did.

## THE FIRST SYNTHESIZER

A quick music lesson: When an oboe, a piano, and a trumpet each play the same note, the fundamental note is the same, but the sound is very different. That's because the physical nature of each instrument creates different overtones, or "harmonics," along with the note, giving it a unique sound. The telharmonium—using all of those different tone wheels—was designed to add those harmonics to the fundamental notes in order to mimic different instruments, making it the world's first synthesizer. (Cahill even used the word "synthesize" in his patent.) A row of draw bars above the keyboard could be pulled out to different "stops" affecting what harmonics would be added; for example, you could set it to play "oboe." The result of all this was an incredibly flexible machine that could mimic woodwind, brass, and even stringed instruments. Two skilled players—it was meant to be played by two at once—could virtually play a symphony on the telharmonium.

## BIG DEBUT

Cahill built his first test model in Washington in 1901 and then got some investors to finance building a larger one. In those days, generators had to be big to create a lot of current, so Cahill's machine was huge—more than 60 feet long and weighing over 200 tons. He had it shipped to "Telharmonic Hall" at Broadway and 39th Street in downtown Manhattan (it took 12 train cars to carry it), and started the New York Electric Music Company. He

The human eye can distinguish about 500 different shades of gray.

then got the New York City telephone company to agree to lay lines for the "telharmony" transmissions.

The telharmonium's big debut was on September 29, 1906—and it was a huge success. Before long Cahill had sold subscriptions to such venues as Louis Sherry's restaurant, the Casino Theatre, and the Waldorf-Astoria Hotel. One of the best reviews came from the first private subscriber, Mark Twain. "Every time I see a new wonder like this," he said, "I have to postpone my death. I couldn't possibly leave this world until I have heard it again and again."

## BEGINNING OF THE END

But there were many problems with the newfangled instrument, and these would soon prove to be insurmountable. The most obvious one was the cost. Cahill built a third telharmonium in 1911, for an unbelievable $200,000 (the equivalent of $4 million today) and his investors were unhappy with the rate of return.

Another problem was the sound quality. When it was good, witnesses said, it was pure and very beautiful, but inconsistent signals over the phone lines resulted in volume fluctuations and static. The New York Telephone Company wasn't happy, either: The telharmony lines were laid right next to phone lines, and so much power was used to pump the music that it bled over, causing numerous complaints from telephone users.

## FINALE

The telharmonium played its last concert in 1916. There are no surviving models of the device and no recordings are known to exist. But Cahill had ushered in the era of electronically produced music, and the world would never be the same. Decades later, a former watchmaker took Cahill's design, miniaturized it with the help of new technology, and came up with his own electronic organ. Complete with tone wheels, draw stops, and foot pedals for shaping sounds, the Hammond organ, invented in 1935 by Laurens Hammond, would become an American classic.

\*     \*     \*

"My take on relationships? Get in, get out—everybody gets hurt."

—Rick Overton

---

If every star in the Milky Way were a grain of salt, they'd fill an Olympic-size swimming pool.

# HELLO, 911?

*Another installment of some of our favorite emergency-call
stories. Believe it or not, they're all real.*

### NINE-ONE-YAWN

In August 2004, an unidentified person called 911 in
Millersville, Maryland, and was asked the nature of their
emergency. The caller explained the situation, and the dispatcher
responded…by snoring. It was the middle of the night and the
dispatcher had fallen asleep. For the next two minutes the caller
tried to wake up the dispatcher but couldn't. Police captain Kim
Bowman told reporters that, luckily, the call wasn't a *dire* emergency and nothing bad had come of it (but added that the department was implementing a program to teach employees how to stay
awake during the night shift).

### IT'S A LOVE EMERGENCY

In July 2006, a sheriff's deputy in Aloha, Oregon, responded to a
noise complaint at the home of Lorna Jeanne Dudash. He spoke
with the woman for just a moment and then left. A short time
later Ms. Dudash called 911—and asked if that "cutie-pie" officer
could return. "He's the cutest cop I've seen in a long time. I just
want to know his name," she said. The confused dispatcher asked
again what her emergency was and Dudash responded, "Honey,
I'm just going to be honest with you, I'm 45 years old and I'd just
like to meet him again." So the dispatcher sent the officer to
Dudash's home—and he promptly arrested her for abuse of the
emergency-dispatch system. She faces several thousand dollars in
fines and up to a year in prison.

### GIMME A NINE…GIMME A ONE…

In 1999 a 911 dispatcher in Fayetteville, Arkansas, received a call,
but there was nobody on the line—all she could hear was a football game in the background. She hung up and called the number
back, but nobody answered. A short time later it happened again,
and again there was nobody on the line. A few minutes later it
happened again…and again…and again. Dispatchers were called

35 times before police finally traced the call…to a football fan who had his cell phone set to speed-dial 911. It was in his pocket and had been going off every time he stood up to cheer.

## PIZZA 'N' NUTS

In May 2005, 86-year-old Dorothy Densmore of Charlotte, North Carolina, called 911 and complained to the dispatcher that she had called a nearby pizza shop, and they had refused to deliver a pizza to her. The dispatcher advised Densmore that calling 911 for non-emergencies was a crime and hung up on her. Densmore called back, and kept calling back. She called more than 20 times. An officer was finally sent out to her home to arrest her…but not before being kicked, punched, and bitten on the hand by Densmore. (She had also complained to the dispatcher that someone in the pizza parlor had called her a "crazy old coot.")

## GAS LEAK

Officers in Janesville, Wisconsin, responded to a 911 call about a domestic disturbance after a husband and wife got into an argument. When they arrived at the couple's home, the wife explained to the officers that the argument had started after the husband had "inappropriately passed gas" while they were tucking their son into bed. (The man was not charged with a crime.)

\*     \*     \*

## DIAL "M" FOR MURDERER

"Murderers and Mafia mobsters have been employed by Italy's state telephone company to run a call center from prison. Telecom Italia has opened a new directory assistance service inside the notorious Rebibbia prison, which is Rome's largest jail, with 1,600 inmates. Twenty-six prisoners in the program work from 8 a.m. to 8 p.m. and are paid the equivalent of 20 cents for every call they answer. 'It is good because people do not know who we are, so we do not feel like we are in a ghetto anymore,' said a man serving 13 years for murder. There are plans to open another call center at Poggioreale prison in Naples. Although inmates have access to a nationwide database of phone numbers, they are unable to dial out."

—*Sydney Morning Herald*

# 10-4, GOOD BUDDY!

*CB radio slang was pretty popular back in the 1970s, so these expressions may stir up some memories. If not, happy reading. We gone!*

**Black water:** coffee.

**Greasy side up:** a truck that has flipped over.

**Flop box:** motel room.

**Travel agent:** dispatcher—the person in a trucking company who gives the truckers their driving assignments.

**Deadheading:** hauling an empty trailer (since there's no cargo, you're not getting paid).

**Hauling dispatcher brains:** deadheading.

**Flip-flop:** the return trip, as in, "Catch you on the flip-flop."

**You are wall to wall and treetop tall:** I read you loud and clear.

**10-4:** message received and understood.

**Fer sure, fer sure:** 10-4.

**10-100:** bathroom break.

**Salt shaker:** a snow plow (they salt roads when it snows).

**Running on rags:** driving a vehicle with bald tires.

**Ground clouds:** fog.

**Scrub brush:** street cleaner.

**Motion lotion:** diesel fuel.

**What's your 20?:** What's your location?

**Shoveling coal:** speeding up.

**Get-em-on/Get-em-off:** the highway entrance/exit ramp.

**Chew-'n'-choke:** truck stop.

**Lane flipper:** a car or truck that keeps changing lanes.

**Portrait painter:** radar gun.

**Muck truck:** cement truck.

**Peanut butter in your ears:** not listening to the CB.

**Money bus:** armored car.

**Thermos bottle:** tanker truck.

**Keep the bugs off your glass and trouble off your @##:** Take it easy (signing off).

---

Good investment: The Nike company was founded with $1,000.

# THE 1¢ MAGENTA

*Here's the strange story of a little piece of paper that
grew up to be the world's rarest stamp—and then
disappeared in the wake of a notorious crime.*

## LUCKY FIND

In 1873, while searching around his uncle's attic in Demerara,
British Guiana (a British colony in South America), a 12-
year-old Scottish boy named Vernon Vaughn noticed an unusual
stamp stuck to the outside of an old newspaper. It was octagonal
and printed on thin magenta-colored paper. Vernon had just
started to collect stamps and thought this new stamp would make
a sharp addition to his collection. But on further inspection, he
noticed that it seemed to be in poor condition—it was smudged and
had the hand-written initials "E.D.W." across the center. Vernon
was disappointed but decided to soak off the stamp and keep it in
his album, with the hope that he could sell it to buy other stamps.
A few weeks later, he sold it to a local collector named N.R.
McKinnon for six shillings—the equivalent of about $1.50 today.

Vernon had no way of knowing that he had just discovered—
and sold—the rarest, most valuable stamp of all time.

## "THE UGLIEST EVER ISSUED"

The stamp that Vernon discovered, known as the "British Guiana
1¢ Magenta," was the last survivor of a crude batch of stamps
ordered in 1856 by the postmaster of British Guiana, E. T. E.
Dalton. After a shipment of state-issued English postage stamps
was lost at sea, Dalton, desperate for postage but hampered by
limited resources, had to act quickly. He went to businessmen
William Dallas and Joseph Baum, publishers of a local newspaper
called the *Official Gazette*, and commissioned them to print a set of
one-cent and four-cent stamps. The one-centers were postage for
newspapers, the four-centers for letters.

Dalton gave the newspaper printers some guidelines regarding
the stamp's design. He asked them to produce a stamp that displayed a British naval vessel alongside the colony's imperial motto,
*Damus Petimus Que Vicissim* (Latin for "We Give and We Seek in

Return"). The printers disregarded the postmaster's instructions and created a small sailing ship of their own design. In addition, to the further dismay of the postmaster, they printed them on unrefined magenta-colored paper and hand cut the corners to an uneven octagonal shape.

Unhappy with the print job and fearful that the crude new postage would be an easy target for counterfeiters, Dalton ordered that the center of each stamp be initialed by British Guiana's postal clerks. The 1¢ Magentas were widely thought to be the ugliest ever issued, and their already limited production was halted as soon as a new batch of stamps arrived from England.

## BUYER #2

While the stamp's beginnings were humble, its life as a collectible was spectacular. N.R. McKinnon, the stamp's first buyer in 1873, recognized its unique qualities, but had no idea that he possessed the world's only copy. He sold his entire collection—including the British Guiana 1¢ Magenta—in 1877 to Thomas Ridpath, a stamp dealer in Liverpool, for £120 (about $10,000 today).

The stamp remained with Ridpath for the next 25 years. Then, at the turn of the century, the philatelic world's most famous collector, Philippe la Renotière von Ferrary, the Austrian Duke of Genoa, approached him about selling it. Ridpath sold the 1¢ Magenta to him for £150—a remarkable sum for a single stamp. But Ferrary was used to paying large sums for stamps: After inheriting a fortune from his parents as a child, he had dedicated his life to his stamp collection and spent most of his adult years traveling the world searching for the best and rarest stamps.

## BUYER #3

Ferrary wrote in his will that upon his death, his valuable collection was to go to the Postmuseum in Berlin, Germany, in hopes that it would bring the public the same joy that it brought him. But his dream of sharing his collection with the world was interrupted by the start of World War I, when his Austrian heritage forced him to flee his home in France and move to the safety of Switzerland. Unable to take his stamps with him, he left his entire collection, consisting of hundreds of albums, in the Austrian Embassy for safekeeping. Ferrary died in Switzerland in 1917 at the age of 67. Seeking reparations at the war's end a year later, the French government seized his collection from the embassy and designated the most valuable stamps to be sold in 14 separate auctions between 1921 and 1926. The highly publicized auctions raised more than 25 million francs for the French government and sent the British Guiana 1¢ Magenta to a new owner, a new country, and a new level of celebrity.

## BUYER #4

Automobile upholstery magnate Arthur Hind of Utica, New York, bought the stamp at auction in 1922 for £7,343—the equivalent of more than $300,000 today. To get it, Hind outbid many wealthy collectors—including the king of England—and set a new record for the price of an individual stamp.

The purchase attracted a flurry of publicity in the United States. Unlike the British Guiana 1¢ Magenta's previous owner, Hind was obsessed with his stamp and not interested in displaying it. This gave birth to several rumors, including a story that Hind had somehow obtained another British Guiana 1¢ Magenta and burned it with a cigar so that his first purchase would retain its value as the world's rarest stamp.

## BUYER #5

Arthur Hind died in 1933, and in 1940 his widow sold the stamp to an Australian businessman named Frederick Small. Although the sale was transacted in secret, Small, who lived in Ft. Lauderdale, Florida, is believed to have paid between $40,000 and $75,000 ($500,000 to nearly $1 million today). He allowed the stamp to be exhibited in New York a few times between 1947 and 1956, which fueled the public's interest, but he kept his ownership secret for more than 30 years. Small's identity was finally revealed in 1969 when he hired Robert A. Siegel, an auction firm in New York City, to sell the stamp for him.

## BUYER #6

News that the world's rarest stamp was about to be sold at auction set off a media frenzy. When the day arrived, hundreds of potential buyers crowded into the Waldorf Astoria Hotel in Manhattan, surrounded by television cameras broadcasting the event on live

TV. The bidding opened at $100,000—and lasted only 90 seconds. The winning bid of $280,000 came from a syndicate of investors from Pennsylvania led by a rare-stamp dealer named Irwin Weinberg. The stamp became even more famous when *Life* magazine ran a special article about the sale.

For the next 10 years, Weinberg traveled the world with the 1¢ Magenta, displaying it in major exhibitions everywhere he went. With both security and publicity in mind, he carried the valuable stamp in a metal briefcase handcuffed to his wrist.

## BUYER #7

There is no doubt that Weinberg's travels and exhibitions increased the stamp's value—exactly what Weinberg and his syndicate wanted. Recognizing that their plan had succeeded, they sold the stamp in 1980 for $935,000. The name of the buyer was kept secret until 1986, when the stamp was placed on display at the Ameripex Stamp Show in Chicago under armed guard.

The stamp's new owner was revealed to be John du Pont, a member of one of America's most famous families and the heir to a massive chemical-industry fortune. Du Pont himself was not well known at the time. In fact, he avoided the limelight, preferring to spend his time with Team Foxcatcher, a wrestling squad that he sponsored and trained in suburban Philadelphia.

But du Pont's private world came to an abrupt end in 1996 when he shot and killed Olympic wrestler David Schultz during an argument. The trial made headlines all over the world, and John du Pont—58 years old and the richest man ever to stand trial for murder—was convicted and sentenced to 30 years in a state hospital for the criminally insane.

## MODERN MYSTERY

So where is the British Guiana 1¢ Magenta today? Du Pont's fortune—an estimated $250 million—makes it unlikely that he had to sell the stamp to pay for his defense. What's more likely is that the world's rarest stamp is now sitting in a safety deposit box, bank vault, or wall safe somewhere in Pennsylvania.

But no one has ever announced its whereabouts…and the exact location of the world's rarest stamp remains unknown.

# FOREVER MANKIND

*On July 20, 1969, Neil Armstrong and Edwin "Buzz" Aldrin successfully landed the Apollo 11 spacecraft on the moon. It was a triumph of science, humanity, and the United States. But what if Armstrong and Aldrin had ended up stranded in space…with no hope of return? President Richard Nixon's speechwriter, William Safire, prepared this speech in the event of a worst-case scenario.*

Fate has ordained that the men who went to the moon to explore in peace will stay on the moon to rest in peace.

These brave men, Neil Armstrong and Edwin Aldrin, know that there is no hope for their recovery. But they also know that there is hope for mankind in their sacrifice. These two men are laying down their lives in mankind's most noble goal: the search for truth and understanding.

They will be mourned by their families and friends; they will be mourned by their nation; they will be mourned by the people of the world; they will be mourned by a Mother Earth that dared send two of her sons into the unknown.

In their exploration, they stirred the people of the world to feel as one; in their sacrifice, they bind more tightly the brotherhood of man.

In ancient days, men looked at stars and saw their heroes in the constellations. In modern times, we do much the same, but our heroes are epic men of flesh and blood.

Others will follow, and surely find their way home. Man's search will not be denied. But these men were the first, and they will remain the foremost in our hearts.

For every human being who looks up at the moon in the nights to come will know that there is some corner of another world that is forever mankind.

Makes sense: In ancient Egyptian, the word *Nile* means water.

# IS IT ART?

*Ever been in a gallery or museum and seen a piece that made you wonder, "Is this really art?" So have we. Is it art just because someone says it is? You be the judge.*

## BEGINNER'S LUCK

For its annual show in 1993, the Manchester (England) Academy of Fine Arts selected several watercolors. One was "Rhythm of the Trees," which, the Academy said, contained a "certain quality of color balance, composition, and technical skill." That earned it a place in the show…over 1,000 other entries. It turned out it was painted by Carly Johnson, a four-year-old girl who had randomly smudged paints on a sheet of paper. Her mother submitted it to the Academy competition as a joke.

## PROVIDE YOUR OWN HEADLINE

In March 2001, the Custard Factory Arts Center in Birmingham, England, held a show by the art group Proto-Mu called "The Exhibition to Be Constructed in Your Head," which featured 60 "pieces" by 28 artists. But it was really *nothing*. The 2,500 square foot hall was completely empty, its white walls bare, except for a few pieces of paper with written descriptions like "This painting is whatever is in your head right now."

## LORD OF THE RING

David Leslie, a performance artist who claims to like "to explore fear, danger, and pain," held a show in a New York City theater in 1999 in which he put on boxing gloves and headgear, and challenged audience members to knock him out. Why? "It'll be cool." Leslie refused to fight back, he only defended himself, and nobody managed to knock him out. So he revived the performance annually…until 2002, when, finally, somebody knocked him out—former heavyweight boxing champion Gerry Cooney.

## VEGE-TABLE

Chilean artist Alejandra Prieto makes furniture. But she doesn't make it out of wood, metal, or fabric—she uses food. At her 2005 exhibit at the Die Ecke Gallery in Santiago, Chile, Prieto displayed her creations: a chair made of sausages, a chair made of fish skin and chocolate, and a sofa made of jam. She says she likes to use food as her medium "for the diversity of colors and textures and because it gives off a poetic vibe."

## DOWN THE DRAIN
In 2005 British activist and artist Mark McGowan created a performance art project called "The Running Tap." He announced that he would turn on the cold water tap in the back room of a London gallery…and leave it running for one year. He estimated he'd waste about eight million gallons of water, at an expense of $23,000. Why? In order to highlight water waste. After a few weeks London's water company shut off the gallery's water service, causing the tap to stop running.

## GERBILLUSTRATED
Sally Madge placed a gerbil in a cage with a 1933 edition of the *New Illustrated Universal Reference Book*. The gerbil gnawed and ate its way through the book, presumably to build a nest. After the book was chewed up, it was put on display in a Newcastle, England, art gallery and labeled "The Gerbil's Guide to the Galaxy." "I'm fascinated with the gerbil's personal translation of the book," Madge said. "And by how he chooses particular words and phrases to eat."

## LABOR DAY?
In a "live art exhibition," a German woman named Ramune Gele gave birth to a baby—a girl named Audra—in the DNA Art Gallery in Berlin. Gele says she wanted to test the boundaries of art and society's tolerance for the unusual. Winfried Witt, the baby's father, called the birth "a gift to humanity."

\*     \*     \*

• Odds of being sued by the Recording Industry Association of America for illegally downloading music: 4,666 to 1.

• Odds of dying by falling out of bed: 4,745 to 1.

# WE ALL SCREAM

*In the summer of 2004, temperatures in Japan hit record highs. The hot weather made ice cream soar in popularity, leading to the introduction of dozens of bizarre flavors. Here are some of our "favorites."*

Fried chicken

Cactus

Miso

Saury (a fish) and brandy

Octopus

Squid

Squid gut

Squid ink

Ox tongue

Potato

Lettuce-potato

Fried eggplant

Crab

Corn

Wasabi

Shrimp

Eel

Noodle

Red beans

Tulip

Mushroom

Horseflesh (with "meaty chunks")

Goat

Whale

Shark fin and noodle

Oyster

Abalone

Seaweed

Seawater

Spinach

Garlic

Garlic mint

Sesame, soybean, and kelp

Wheat

Curdled bean

Silk

Stout

Red wine

Pepto-Bismol

Rice

Strawberry and basil

Pearl

Soy sauce

Viper

Indian curry

Salad (with vegetable chunks)

Charcoal

Chili pepper

Salt

Yams

Cypress wood

Cream cheese

Hot spring water

Vegetable broth

Bitter green tea

Pickled plum

Collagen and lemon

Tomato

Medicinal herbs

Most sparsely populated country in the world: Mongolia, with 4.7 people per square mile.

# WEIRD *STAR TREK* NEWS

*Uncle John's Log—Stardate 90210. We have encountered a strange blue planet in the Terran system whose inhabitants have an almost fanatical devotion to a 40-year-old entertainment program. We've intercepted some of their transmissions and are trying to analyze them.*

## THE WRATH OF LINLITHGOW

"USS *Enterprise* engineer Montgomery Scott may have described himself as an 'Aberdeen pub crawler' on *Star Trek*, but the widow of the actor who played the character claims that James Doohan believed Scotty would be born in Linlithgow.

"Although the city of Edinburgh has declared itself Scotty's official future birthplace and the city of Aberdeen has announced plans to build a space park in his honor, Linlithgow is not giving up its claim. In an editorial in the *Evening News*, West Lothian councillor Willie Dunn stated, 'I believe we have the best claim to support Linlithgow as the birthplace of Scotty and the place most worthy of a suitable memorial honouring his future birth.'

"Dunn cites the novel *Vulcan's Glory*, in which original series scriptwriter D.C. Fontana said that the *Enterprise*'s corridors were as familiar to Scotty 'as his mother's house in Linlithgow, West Lothian, Scotland.' He dismissed the Aberdeen claim, saying that while Scotty may have visited its pubs as an adult, there is no indication that he will be born there."

—**TrekToday.com**

## A BRIDGE TOO FAR

"In 2003 *News of the Weird* told the story of *Star Trek* fanatic Tony Alleyne, who was trying to sell his apartment in Leicestershire, England, for the equivalent of about $1.7 million, after having converted it to a finely detailed model of the Starship *Enterprise* (with transporter control, warp-core drive, voice-activated lighting and security, etc.). In 2006, weary of the lack of buyer interest, Alleyne filed for bankruptcy and moved to Plan B—to gut his *Enterprise* and redesign the place as the bridge of the *Voyager* (from the later *Star Trek* series), which he will offer at a lower price."

—**The Times** (London)

---

**Animals that give birth to live young are *viviparous*.**

## WHERE NO MAN HAS FLOWN BEFORE

"An amateur pilot was arrested for flying under Tower Bridge in London. When contacted by the air traffic controller he identified himself as Captain James T. Kirk of the starship *Enterprise*. When he was asked if he wanted to say anything on his own behalf before the judge passed sentence, he pretended his wallet was a *Star Trek* communicator, whistled, and said, 'Beam me up, Scotty!'"

—WarpHead.com

## STAR TREKSKY

"A late-1960s Russian sci-fi TV show called *Kosmicheskaya Milit-siya* translates as either *Space Police* or *Cosmic Militia*, though it is usually called *Cosmos Patrol* in English. You could say that it's a lot like *Star Trek*, but it would be more accurate to call it a rip-off.

"Consider the similarities: *Cosmos Patrol* takes place in the 23rd century aboard a large galaxy-cruising spaceship called the *Red Adventurer*, on a long-term mission of exploration on behalf of the Commonwealth of Independent Star Systems. Both ships encounter strange alien beings and bizarre celestial phenomena week after week. Both ships boast a dashing commander at their helm, with an overly intellectual first officer by his side. And both shows feature cheap special effects and odd velour uniforms.

"Like much of Russian pop culture, the show oozes with sentimentality, up to and including tearful folk songs and lengthy toasts to the Intergalactic Brotherhood of life forms. And when Comrade Commander faces a difficult decision, he sometimes asks for guidance from the bust of Lenin in the ship's wardroom. The show is such a clone of *Star Trek* that there is even a character called Ensign Chekhov, who provides comic relief with his tall tales, or *vranyo*, as the Russians call them. In about every other episode, he lets it rip with this surefire comedy catchphrase: 'I'd rather eat a Kvassian bivalve—and I have!'"

—Stim.com

\*     \*     \*

"I wouldn't know a space-time continuum or warp-core breach if they got into bed with me."

—Patrick Stewart (Captain Picard
on *Star Trek: the Next Generation*)

The north pole of Uranus is dark for 42 years at a time. (Ha ha—we said "Uranus"!)

# FOUNDING FATHERS

*You already know the names—here are the people behind them.*

## CHARLES GULDEN

Gulden ran a spice company in New York City in the 1860s. At the time, many spice merchants only offered mustard in a dry, white, very strong powder that had to be mixed with water. Gulden had an idea: He mixed a variety of mustard powders with mustard seed, other spices, and aged vinegar, then combined all of them (along with turmeric, for color) with water and sold the concoction in glass jars. This was the first prepared yellow mustard ever made. Gulden's Mustard went national in 1875 and is still one of the bestselling condiments in the United States.

## HERMAN LAY

In 1932, 24-year-old Herman Lay, a failed ice-cream salesman, took a job with Barrett Food Company, an Atlanta potato-chip maker. He drove all over the South selling cases of potato chips to stores out of the trunk of his car. He did so well that in 1938 he bought the Barrett company and changed its name to the HW Lay Company. But potato chips had to be made and sold locally—they got broken in shipping. And that's how Lay's grew: It bought up smaller potato-chip processors all over the country. By the 1950s, Lay's had became the top-selling brand of potato chips in the world.

## JOSHUA VICK

Lunsford Richardson was a pharmacist in Selma, North Carolina, in the early 1880s. One night his son came down with a bad cold. Back then, the most common cold remedy was to spread a mustard paste on the chest. The strong aroma was thought to open up air passages, but it also caused skin to break out into painful blisters. Trying to find a way to reduce the blisters, Richardson experimented with several substances—unsuccessfully—until he combined petroleum jelly, menthol, nutmeg, cedar, and eucalyptus oils. That mixture worked. First marketed as Richard's Croup and Pneumonia Salve, it flopped. So he renamed it Vick's Magic Croup Salve after his brother-in-law, Joshua Vick, a popular town doctor. (Besides, "Vick's" fit better on the tiny blue jars). The product became known as Vick's VapoRub in 1908, when it was purchased by Proctor and Gamble and became available nationwide.

## JACK RUSSELL

Russell (1795–1883), an Oxford divinity student and avid hunter known as the Sporting Parson, dreamed of the perfect fox-hunting dog: compact like a terrier but aggressive enough to root foxes out of their small holes. One day he saw a milkman walking a small dog that looked like the one he'd imagined. Russell bought the dog (named "Trump") on the spot and went into business breeding them for fox hunting. As a result, any small hunting terrier came to be known as a "Jack Russell Terrier" or a "Parson Russell Terrier."

## RAY DOLBY

Dolby, born in Portland, Oregon, was a UN advisor in India in the 1960s. But technology, not diplomacy, was his dream. He wanted to improve the sound of recorded music and films, which hissed very loudly in those days. So in 1965 he founded Dolby Labs in England, and soon figured out a way to reduce the noise on magnetic tapes, a discovery that helped usher in the cassette era of the 1970s. In 1976 Dolby took his labs to San Francisco and sold his "Dolby Noise Reduction" technology to the film industry, revolutionizing that medium, too. In all, Dolby holds more than 50 U.S. patents.

## SEBASTIAN S. KRESGE

In 1899 this Pennsylvania native purchased two five-and-dime stores in Detroit, Michigan. By 1912 the SS Kresge Company had 85 stores in the Midwest. In his day, the wealthy Kresge was a well-known philanthropist, but today we know him only by his last initial. After Kresge retired in 1959, a former newspaper reporter named Harry Cunningham took over the company and wanted to expand the dime stores into larger markets, or "marts." He opened the first one in Detroit in 1962. Believing that "Kresge-mart" was too hard to pronounce, Cunningham shortened it to Kmart.

# OL' JAY'S BRAINTEASERS

*Supersleuth and BRI stalwart Jay Newman has come up with another batch of his simple yet compelling puzzles. Answers are on page 519.*

## 1. BRIGHT THINKING

Uncle John gave Amy this challenge: "In the hallway there are three light switches," he said. "And in the library there are three lamps. Each switch corresponds to one of the lamps. You may enter the library only once—the lamps must be turned off when you do. At no time until you enter can you open the door to see into the library. Your job is to figure out which switch corresponds to which lamp."

"Easy," said Amy.

How did she do it?

## 2. MYSTERY JOB

Brian works at a place with thousands of products, some of them very expensive. People take his products without paying for them—as many as they can carry—and then just walk out. All that Brian requests of his customers is that they keep their mouths shut.

Where does Brian work?

## 3. SIDE TO SIDE

Uncle John stood on one side of a river; his dog, Porter, stood on the opposite side. "Come here, Porter!" said Uncle John. Although there were no boats or bridges, Porter crossed the river without getting wet. How?

## 4. SPECIAL NUMBER

Math usually stumps Thom, but when Uncle John showed him this number, he knew right away what makes it unique. Do you?

**8,549,176,320**

## 5. TIME PIECES

"Everyone knows that the sundial is the timepiece with the fewest moving parts," Jay told Julia. "Do you know what timepiece has the *most* moving parts?" She did. Do you?

## 6. WORD PLAY

"Weird Nate sent me this list of words," said Uncle John. "He says there's something unusual about them. But what?" Ol' Jay figured it out. Can you?

**revive, banana, grammar, voodoo, assess, potato, dresser, uneven**

---

Sliced bread was banned during WWII. (The slicers were melted down for the war effort.)

# HIGH ANXIETY

*We've all had those moments—when something completely unexpected scares the c\*\*p out of us. It gives us something to laugh about...later.*

## HE GOT TOO HIGH

A student from the Gloucestershire College of Arts and Technology in Cheltenham, England, woke up one morning in May 2006...and found himself 100 feet up in a pine tree. He had no idea how he got there, but apparently he'd climbed the tree the night before while drunk (and barefoot). Luckily, he had his cell phone with him. It took firefighters two hours to get him down. "He was a bit quiet when he came down," officer Nigel Limbrick told *The Sun*, "and a bit embarrassed."

## THE FUR WAS FLYING

The pilot of a passenger plane en route from Brussels to Vienna had to turn the plane around and return to Brussels after he was attacked by a cat. The cat apparently escaped its travel bag in the cabin (small pets are allowed as carry-ons), became agitated, and ran into the cockpit when a flight attendant opened the door. Once inside, it "ran wild," according to the crew, attacking the pilot and leaving multiple scratches on his arms. A spokeswoman for the airline said the pilot did the right thing in returning to Brussels, noting that the cat took a long time to capture and could have hit one of the delicate instruments in the cockpit. She also said there were unconfirmed reports that the cat had been "kicked by someone in business class."

## NICE HEADLIGHTS

In 2004 Dave Alsop was driving through the West Midland Safari Park in Worcestershire, England, when he stopped to take a picture of two mating rhinoceroses. The next thing he knew, the male rhino, who at more than 4,000 pounds weighed considerably more than Alsop's Renault, was trying to mount the car. From the side. "He sidled up against us," Alsop said. "Suddenly he's banging away at the car and it's rocking like hell." Alsop sped away...with the rhino in hot pursuit.

## BEAR-LY SURVIVED

In June 2006, Debbie Yates was getting ready for work in her Nevada City, California, home when she heard noises coming from her kitchen. She assumed it was her cats playing. It wasn't. "I came around the corner and into the kitchen," she told reporters, "and instead of seeing cats, I saw a big, brown bear coming in through the kitchen window." Fortunately, the bear was too big to get through the window, and ran away when Yates screamed.

## PLANES ON A PORSCHE

In June 2005, a German man got permission to drive his Porsche on the runway at a small seldom-used airport in the town of Bitburg. The man was traveling at about 100 mph when a small private plane landed on the roof of the car. The startled driver slammed on his brakes, which sent the plane crashing onto the tarmac. Both vehicles were badly damaged, but the pilot and the driver were fine. "They probably couldn't have done it that well if they had tried," said local policeman Klaus Schnarrbach. The pilot was cited for making an unscheduled landing (on a car).

## RAINING CATS AND...

A man in the Polish town of Sosnowiec was walking down a street in July 2006, when he heard a noise above his head. He looked up and saw a Saint Bernard falling from the sky. That was the last thing he saw before the dog fell on top of him. The 110-pound canine, named Oskar, had been pushed out of a second-story window by its drunk owner. Luckily, both man and dog were unhurt. A police spokesman said that "the dog had a soft landing because it fell on a man." He added, however, that the man was "in a psychological state of shock."

## NOT AN URBAN LEGEND

In 1999 a woman in England went to her doctor after having headaches for three sleepless nights, accompanied by "a strange noise" in her right ear. The doctor examined her ear—and told her there was a spider "snuggled up right against her eardrum." He removed the spider with a syringe, and there was no harm to the woman. But, according to Reuters, "the doctor raised an unsavory possibility—that the arachnid was a female intent on laying eggs."

# COLLECT IT? PROTECT IT!

*If you're like Uncle John, over the years you've collected a lot of stuff—
photos, records, clothing, comic books—maybe even an old guitar.
Here's a guide to preserving your precious keepsakes.*

W**HAT YOU'LL NEED**
Here are the basic supplies you'll need to protect collectibles and keep them safe for years to come.

• **Cotton gloves.** Many of the things you want to protect can be damaged by the oils, acids, and dirt on your fingers. Get into the habit of wearing white gloves when handling your treasures.

• **A can of compressed air.** Dust can be damaging, but so can wiping it off. Use compressed air to blow the dust away.

• **"Archival quality" packing and storage materials.** Do you keep your old papers and photographs in manila envelopes? Is the family silverware rolled in saran wrap? Is everything packed away in cardboard boxes? You may be doing more harm than good. Use "archival-quality" packing supplies that are made of acid-free paper, plastic that does not leach chemicals or other inert materials. Pack your keepsakes in the proper material, then put them in those big plastic tubs made of polyethylene or polypropylene. They'll keep the mice and bugs away and also protect against dampness and flooding.

• **A cool, dry, dark place to store your things.** Attics get too hot in summer and too cold in winter. Basements can get damp and moldy, but if you must store items there, raise the storage bins at least one foot off the floor.

**PHOTOGRAPHS.** A good rule of thumb with any media: Make duplicates. Make copies of your photos, and put the originals away for safekeeping. If you store your photographs or slides in plastic sleeves, make sure the sleeves are polyester, polypropylene, or polyethylene. Don't use PVC—it contains substances that damage photos. Photo albums are also good but again, be sure to look for archival-quality or acid-free albums. Photos can also be scanned and transferred to CDs, but there may come a day when CD players are obsolete, so it's a good idea to put a CD/DVD player into storage, too. Then, as new recording and playing devices evolve, you can transfer your pictures to the new formats.

**HOME MOVIES.** Do you have 8mm movies on plastic reels? The tiny hub on small reels can cause the film to curl, which can eventually damage it. One way to protect your movies is to splice them together (splicing tape is sold at camera stores) and then store them all on a single large film reel instead of many small ones. Home movies can also be preserved by transferring them to DVDs.

**SPORTS CARDS.** There are plenty of specialized products to make caring for sports cards easy. Invest in some clear polyester sleeves, store them one to a sleeve, then place them vertically (that lets you find the card you are looking for with a minimum of handling) into an archival-quality box. Don't overstuff the box— you may damage them when you try to take them out again.

**COMIC BOOKS.** Most comic book stores sell "L-fold polyester sleeves." Slip each comic book into its own sleeve, then place them in an archival-quality box or plastic tub that is large enough to hold them flat. Be sure to use sleeves made of polyester or mylar, not polyvinyl chloride (PVC)—which can damage your comics.

**QUILTS AND OLD CLOTHING.** Always clean fabric items thoroughly before putting them into storage. Dirt, stains, mold, or mildew can be damaging in their own right, but they may also attract bugs, mice, and other pests. Gently vacuum cloth items with a brush attachment to avoid damaging the fabric. Wrap each item in acid-free tissue paper and insert extra sheets inside folds to prevent creasing. To keep bugs out of a storage box, wrap a few mothballs in a clean handkerchief. Close it with string, not a rubber band (mothballs do almost as much damage to rubber as they do to moths). Then put the pouch in the box with your cloth items. If you store your items in plastic tubs or plastic bags, make sure they are made of *virgin polyethylene*. Other plastics can give off chemicals that stain or discolor cloth. Also, don't use cedar chests—they don't repel insects. Not only that, the wood can stain fabric, and cedar's distinctive smell (from natural oils evaporating out of the wood) can be absorbed by cloth items.

---

**If you don't believe us, ask a Sherpa: Mt. Everest is 5.5 miles high.**

**BASEBALL MITTS.** If you're not using your old mitt anymore, stop oiling it: that stuff will just make a mess without protecting the leather. To spot-clean it, try a Q-tip or clean sponge dipped in distilled water (which contains no minerals) and dry it immediately using a soft cloth. If you display your mitt, protect it from light, dirt, and dust, by putting it behind glass or acrylic in a display case.

**POSTERS.** Because clay was often used in the printing process, posters can get stuck together over time, especially if they're stored in damp or humid areas. And once they're stuck together, the damage is permanent. Keep your posters separated from one another by placing each one in an oversized acid-free folder, and store them flat in a large plastic box.

**VINYL RECORDS.** To minimize wear and tear on old LPs, invest in a record-cleaning kit and clean your them before *and* after you play them. Better yet, to keep your original LP of the Beatles' *Yellow Submarine* undamaged, buy a CD and listen to that instead. To further protect an LP, remove it from its original sleeve and replace it with an acid-free sleeve. Then slide the record back inside the album cover. The original inner sleeve can go back in, too, if there's enough room for it (if not, store it in a mylar bag). Store your records upright, and not so snugly together that you can't take an album off the shelf without damaging it. Store a record player along with your records so you'll always be able to listen to your original LPs if the technology ever disappears.

**YOUR OLD GUITAR.** Moisture is a guitar's biggest enemy—too much or not enough can damage it. The simplest way to protect your guitar from the elements is to keep it in its case when you're not playing it. If you live in an especially humid or dry environment, keeping the guitar case in a giant sealed polyethylene bag will protect it even more. Your guitar strap may be made of materials that can damage the instrument's finish over time, so before you put your guitar away, remove it. Get in the habit of un-tuning the guitar after you finish playing it, too. Loosen each string at least a half-turn to reduce the stress on the instrument. And if the thought of all this guitar maintenance is giving you a headache, here's some good news: Wooden musical instruments actually age better if you take them out and play them several times a year.

# AMAZING LUCK

*There's no way to explain luck—some folks just have it.*
*Here are a few examples of people who really had it.*

## WELCOME TO OKLAHOMA

Oklahoma started running a state lottery in 2006. The first prize: $25,000, won by Caronell Allen of Bethany. Allen had moved there just a few months earlier from New Orleans because he had lost everything he owned in Hurricane Katrina.

## IT ALL COMES OUT IN THE WASH

In 2005 a German woman on welfare bought an old laundry basket at a flea market for about $5. When she took it home, she found two savings account books worth $60,000 and another $10,000 in cash. She could have kept the money, but she turned it in to police because she "wanted to sleep with a clear conscience." A police investigation found that the money belonged to a woman who had died two years earlier and left nothing to her family. They assumed she'd died destitute. The mystery woman's relatives got an unexpected inheritance, and the woman who bought the basket got what she wanted, too: the knowledge that she'd done the right thing. (She also got a $3,000 reward.)

## DIDN'T SEE THAT COMING

One evening in 2001, 97-year-old Gladys Adamson of Cambridge, England, was struck with a coughing fit so severe that it lasted for several hours. The next morning, she went to her bathroom and looked at herself in the mirror. What's so amazing about that? Adamson had been blind for five years. Doctors link the coughing fit to her miraculous recovery, but don't really understand it.

## A QING-LY SUM

In 2006 a London man read about a Chinese vase that fetched a fortune at a recent auction. The description sounded very similar to a red, white, and blue vase he'd inherited from his grandmother, who had received it as a retirement gift. Good luck: He had the

---

...the color of the universe is beige.

piece appraised and discovered it was a lost treasure of the Qing dynasty, which ruled China from the 1600s until the early 1900s. It sold at auction for $175,000. Bad luck: the man's grandmother had polished the vase so hard that she'd rubbed off the gold enamel. If she hadn't, the vase would have been worth $2 million.

## WHAT A CATCH

At a San Francisco Giants game in May 2006, Andrew Morbitzer left his bleacher seat to get peanuts from a concession stand behind the centerfield wall. While he was waiting in line, he heard the crowd inside the stadium let out a tremendous roar. What was going on? Barry Bonds had just slammed his 715th home run, passing Babe Ruth on the all-time list, with the second-most home runs ever hit. The record-breaking ball sailed over the wall and landed…right in Morbitzer's hands. He sold the ball for $220,000.

\*　　\*　　\*

## RANDOM FACTS

• Thirty-five percent of personal ads are placed by people who are already married.

• How many seeds are there on the average strawberry? 200.

• Studies show that if a cat falls off the 7th floor of a building, its chances of surviving are about 30% less than a cat that falls off the 20th floor. Researchers figure that it takes about eight floors for the cat to realize what is occurring, then relax and prepare itself.

• French scientists use trout to test water. The fish can detect one billionth of one gram of pesticide in a liter of water.

• Poll results: 40% of nurses said they would not want to be treated at the hospitals in which they work.

• By 2007, there will be more than 7,000 hotel rooms in Las Vegas's Venetian Hotel—more than are in all of Venice, Italy.

• Top three producers of bananas: India, Brazil, and China.

# SING ALONG WITH JFK

*Uncle John is an avid music fan and record collector. But over the years he's discovered that for every great album out there, there are lots that make you wonder, "What were they thinking?" Here's a random sampling of some of the worst albums ever made.*

**B**EATLE BARKERS. A collection of 12 early Beatles hits ("Love Me Do," "Can't Buy Me Love," etc.) with dogs barking the vocal parts. Cat, chicken, and sheep noises are added in...presumably to break up the monotony.

*MUSIC TO HELP CLEAN UP STREAM POLLUTION.* An album of nature sounds and classical music distributed by chemical manufacturer Union Carbide.

*SING ALONG WITH JFK.* No, it's not President Kennedy singing—it's snippets of Kennedy speeches spliced into songs. For example, the president's spoken words, "Ask not what your country can do for you," is echoed by chorus boys cheerfully singing, "Ask not! Ask not!" This record actually reached the Top 20 in 1963.

*POITIER MEETS PLATO.* Actor Sidney Poitier delivers the *Dialogues* of Plato, the ancient Greek philosopher. The speeches are backed by loud, manic bebop jazz.

*PERFUME SET TO MUSIC.* From the liner notes: "Inspired by the heady scents of the famous French perfumes, it is probably the only successful attempt to capture and reproduce with musical instruments and human voice the 'sounds' of fragrance and scent."

*MECO—THE WIZARD OF OZ.* In 1977 journeyman jazz musician and music producer Domenico Monardo jumped on the disco bandwagon and recorded the music from *Star Wars* set to a disco beat (under the name Meco). Amazingly, the single "*Star Wars* Title Theme/Cantina Band" became a #1 hit. Monardo then released several follow-ups—disco versions of music from other popular movies, including *Star Trek* and *Superman*. But our

---

Before World War II, most Americans did not brush their teeth regularly.

favorite is his disco treatment of classic songs from *The Wizard of Oz*. Why? According to the album cover, it was recorded by a band of space aliens.

**THE ALL SPORTS BAND.** Trying to cash in on the popularity of the Village People, guitarist Cy Sulack started this group, whose five members dressed as a football player, a race car driver, a baseball player (Sulack himself), a boxer, and a karate guy. Interesting gimmick. They flopped.

*JACK FASCINATO—MUSIC FROM A SURPLUS STORE.* Fascinato bought a bunch of junk from a hardware store—trowels, putty knives, saws, hammers, crowbars, etc.—and used them as musical instruments in songs like "Sweepy Time," which heavily uses brooms and brushes, and "Oily Boid," which features oil cans.

*SPIRO T. AGNEW SPEAKS OUT.* Because of speeches in which he described his enemies (mostly the press) as "nattering nabobs of negativism" and "pusillanimous pussyfooters," Nixon's vice president developed a reputation as an effective public speaker. That's probably why he recorded this album in 1970 (three years before he had to resign from office, charged with tax evasion and money laundering). Agnew tackles a series of world issues, such as "Spiro Addresses the Hippie Problem."

*THE ADDICTS—NINE FORMER ADDICTS SING.* They met in a New York prison in 1958, where they started singing gospel songs about redemption and recovery. Just in case the listener didn't quite get it from the album's title, on the back cover there's a drawing of a syringe injecting drugs into an arm.

*THE ELVIS PRESLEY SEANCE.* On the first anniversary of Presley's death in 1978, a medium used a Ouija board to try to contact the singer. She failed, but recorded the session and released it anyway.

*GENERAL WIRANTO—FOR YOU, MY INDONESIA.* After being fired for human rights atrocities waged in East Timor, Indonesia's former military chief (and confessed karaoke buff) released this album of love songs.

---

In 1987 the Hollywood sign was changed to "Holywood" in honor of the pope's visit.

# CAN YOU PASS THE U.S. CITIZENSHIP TEST?

*Applicants for citizenship, or "naturalization," must have basic knowledge of American history and the principles of American government. If you had to take the test, would you pass? Quiz yourself: Here are 23 "easy" questions.*

**1.** What is the name of the official home of the president?

**2.** How many stripes are there on the American flag?

**3.** What do they represent?

**4.** How many stars are there on the American flag?

**5.** What do they represent?

**6.** Who writes the federal laws of the United States?

**7.** Who signs them into law?

**8.** Name the three major countries that the U.S. fought during World War II.

**9.** Name the last two states to enter the Union.

**10.** Why did the pilgrims come to America?

**11.** Name the ship that brought them here.

**12.** What is the minimum voting age in the U.S.?

**13.** Which president is called the "Father of our Country"?

**14.** Who meets in the U.S. Capitol building?

**15.** Name the two houses of Congress.

**16.** Name the two major political parties in the U.S.

**17.** What is the national anthem of the United States?

**18.** Who wrote it?

**19.** In what month are presidential elections held?

**20.** In what month are presidential inaugurations held?

**21.** What holiday was celebrated for the first time by American colonists?

**22.** Which American invented the electric light bulb?

**23.** The Revolutionary War was fought to gain independence from which country?

*How'd you do? Answers are on page 515; a slightly tougher quiz is on page 334.*

North America's first lighthouse: Boston Light (it was lit in 1716).

# THE GREAT DIAMOND HOAX OF 1872, PART I

*Most stories have the moral at the end. But we'll put it right up front: If it seems too good to be true, it probably is.*

## NIGHT DEPOSIT

One evening in February 1871, George Roberts, a prominent San Francisco businessman, was working in his office when two men came to his door. One of them, Philip Arnold, had once worked for Roberts; the other was named John Slack. Arnold produced a small leather bag and explained that it contained something very valuable; as soon as the Bank of California opened in the morning, he was going to have them lock it in the vault for safekeeping.

Arnold and Slack made a show of not wanting to reveal what was in the bag, but eventually told Roberts that it contained "rough diamonds" they'd found while prospecting on a mesa somewhere in the West. They wouldn't say where the mesa was, but they did say it was the richest mineral deposit they'd ever seen in their lives: The site was rich not only in diamonds, but also in sapphires, emeralds, rubies, and other precious stones.

The story sounded too good to be true, but when Arnold dumped the contents of the bag onto Roberts's desk, out spilled dozens of uncut diamonds and other gems.

## PAY DIRT

If somebody were to make such a claim today, they'd probably get laughed out of the room. But things were different in 1871. Only 20 years had passed since the discovery of gold at Sutter's Mill in California sparked the greatest gold rush in American history. Since then other huge gold deposits had been discovered in Colorado, as well as in Australia and New Zealand. A giant vein of silver had been found in the famous Comstock Lode in Nevada in 1859, and diamonds had been discovered in South Africa in 1867—just four years earlier. Gems and precious metals might be anywhere, lying just below the earth's surface, waiting to be discovered. People who'd missed out on the earlier bonanzas were hungry for word of new discoveries, and the completion of the transcontinental railroad in 1869 opened up the West and created the expectation that more valuable strikes were just around the corner. When Arnold and Slack rolled into town with their tale of gems on a mesa and a bag of precious stones to back it up, people were ready to believe them.

## OPEN SECRET

The next morning the two men went to the Bank of California and deposited their bag in the bank's vault. They made another big show of not wanting anyone to know what was in the bag, and again they let some of the bank employees have a peek. Soon everyone in the bank knew what was in it, including the president and founder, William Ralston. He had made a fortune off the Comstock Lode, and had his eye out for the next big find. Ralston didn't keep the men's secret, and neither did George Roberts: Soon all of San Francisco, the city built by the Gold Rush of 1849, was buzzing with the tale of the two miners and their discovery.

Arnold and Slack left town for a few weeks, and when they returned, they claimed they'd made another trip to their diamond field. And they had another big bag of gems to prove it. Ralston knew a good thing when he saw it and immediately began lining up the cream of San Francisco's investment community to buy the mining claim outright. While Arnold played hard to get, Slack agreed to sell his share of the diamond field for $100,000, the equivalent of several million dollars today. Slack received $50,000 up front and was promised another $50,000 when he brought more gems back from the field.

Arnold and Slack left town again, and several weeks later returned with yet another bulging sack of precious stones. Ralston immediately paid Slack the remaining $50,000.

## BIG TIME

Ralston didn't know it, but he was being had. The uncut gems were real enough, but the story of the diamond field was a lie. Arnold and Slack had created a fake mining claim in Colorado by sprinkling, or "salting," it with diamonds and other gems where

miners would be able to find them. It was a common trick
designed to make otherwise worthless land appear valuable.
What made this deception different was its scale and the caliber
of the people who were taken in by it. Ralston was a prominent
and successful banker; he and his associates were supposed to be
shrewd investors.

## DUE DILIGENCE

To the investors' credit, they did take some precautions that they
thought would protect them from fraud: Before any more money
changed hands, they insisted on having a sample of the stones
appraised by the most respected jeweler in the United States—
none other than New York City's Charles Tiffany. If the appraisal
went well, they planned to send a mining engineer out to the diamond field to verify first, that it existed, and second, that it was as
rich as Arnold and Slack claimed. These precautions should have
been enough, but through a combination of poor judgment and
bad luck, both failed completely.

## MAKE NO MISTAKE

In October 1871, Ralston brought a sample of the gems to New
York so Tiffany could look them over. Ralston was already hard at
work drumming up potential investors on the East Coast, and
present at the appraisal were one U.S. Congressman and two former Civil War generals, including George McClellan, who'd run
for president against Abraham Lincoln in 1864. Horace Greeley,
editor of the *New York Tribune*, was there too.

Tiffany's expertise was actually in cut and polished diamonds—
he knew almost nothing about uncut stones, and neither did his
assistant. But he didn't let anyone else in the room know that.
Instead, he made a solemn show of studying the gems carefully
through an eyepiece, and then announced to the assembled dig-
nitaries, "Gentlemen, these are beyond question precious stones
of enormous value."

The investors accepted the claim at face value—the appraiser,
after all, was *Charles Tiffany*. Two days later, Tiffany's assistant
pegged the value of the sample at $150,000, which, if true (it
wasn't), meant the total value of all of the stones found so far
was $1.5 million (in today's money, $21 million)…or more.

## IN THE FIELD

Now that the gems had been verified as authentic, it was time to send an independent expert out to the diamond field to confirm that it was everything Arnold and Slack said it was. As he'd done when he brought the stones to Tiffany, Ralston went with the most qualified expert he could find. He hired a respected mining engineer named Henry Janin to do the job. Janin had inspected more than 600 mines and had never made a mistake. His first goof would prove to be a doozy.

Janin, Arnold, Slack, and three of the investors traveled by train to Wyoming, just over the border from Colorado. Then they made a four-day trek by horseback into the wilderness, crossing back into Colorado. At Arnold and Slack's insistence, Janin and the investors rode blindfolded to keep them from learning the location of the diamond field.

The men arrived at the mesa on June 4, 1872, and began looking in a location suggested by Arnold. A few minutes was all it took: One of the investors screamed out and held up a raw diamond that he'd discovered digging in some loose dirt. "For more than a hour, diamonds were found in profusion," one of the investors later wrote, "together with occasional rubies, emeralds, and sapphires. Why a few pearls weren't thrown in for good luck I have never yet been able to tell. Probably it was an oversight."

## SEEING IS BELIEVING

Janin was completely taken in by what he saw. In his report to Ralston, he estimated that a work crew of 20 men could mine $1 million worth of gems a month. He collected a $2,500 fee for his efforts, plus an option to buy 1,000 shares in the planned mining company for $10 a share. He used the $2,500 and somehow came up with another $7,500 to buy all 1,000 shares; then he staked a mining claim on 3,000 acres of surrounding land, just in case it had precious stones too.

One of the secrets of pulling off a scam is knowing when to get out. It was at this point that Arnold and Slack decided to make their exit. Slack had already cashed out for $100,000; Arnold now sold his stake for a reported $550,000, and both men skipped town.

*For Part II of the story, turn to page 410.*

The plane truth: 90% of all airplane collisions take place on the ground.

# DIVINE BOVINE

*We hope these heifer-vescent cow facts really m-o-o-o-o-ve you.*

• The first American cows arrived with the British in 1611 at the Jamestown colony.

• It takes about 350 "squirts" to make a gallon of milk.

• How can you tell how old a cow is? Count the rings on her horns.

• Cows were first domesticated about 5,000 years ago.

• While many animals only see in black and white, cows see in color (except red).

• Natural lifespan of a cow: about 25 years.

• Cows can clean their noses with their tongues.

• Cows eat about 80 pounds of feed per day. But cow feed is cheap—it only costs about $4.

• Cows navigate by looking at the ground. If one is stuck in a field that's covered in water, she has no idea where she is.

• A typical cow generates about 20,000 pounds of manure in a year.

• Because their eyes protrude slightly, cows have panoramic vision, allowing them to see nearly 360° around.

• Stand back: If a cow dies of heatstroke, the gases inside it can expand rapidly and cause the carcass to explode.

• The average dairy cow produces nearly 200,000 glasses of milk in her lifetime. (She'll have to drink about 30 gallons of water a day—enough to fill a bathtub—to do it.)

• Cows don't tear grass out of the ground with their teeth. They wrap their tongues around it and pull.

• Good news: If the gas of 10 cows could be captured, it could heat a house for a year.

• Bad news: The methane gas released by cows' burping and farting is said to be one of the leading causes of holes in the ozone layer. The world's cows produce about 100 million tons of it every year.

• A study found that cows give 35% more milk when listening to Elvis Presley music.

---

Eagle eyes? Chickens can see daylight 45 minutes before it is visible to humans.

# DUMB KOPS

*A teeny, tiny percentage of police officers sometimes—but rarely—commit some act which might be construed as, oh, we don't know… "dumb." (This introduction approved by the BRI Legal Department.)*

## PICKING FLOURS

"A middle-aged Brazilian woman is suing the police for mistaking two bags of flour she was carrying for cocaine. The woman, in her 50s, spent two days in jail after being arrested as she got off a bus carrying the flour. The policeman had a hunch she was a drug courier—but she was actually just going home with her shopping."

—*Terra Noticias Populares* (Brazil)

## I KNOW THAT GUY

"The day after they launched a high-profile public appeal for information on escaped convict Jimmy Melvin's whereabouts, Nova Scotia police spent hours driving the convicted drug dealer around town. Mounties picked up Melvin for being drunk, and then handed him over to Halifax's major-crime unit after he told them he could assist in their manhunt for Jimmy Melvin. Officials say Melvin gave them a false name and showed them a phony ID. The police contend Melvin looks considerably different than his mugshot from a couple years ago."

—*Halifax Daily News* (Canada)

## TAKES ONE TO KNOW ONE

"Officer Marius Vlasceanu pulled over Gheorghe Tosa as he drove through Craiova, Romania, fining him £22 for 'having a face like a moron and being a big monkey.' The head of the Romanian police said Vlasceanu, who claimed he had handed out the fine as a joke, was demoted for 'inappropriate behavior and defaming the police force.'"

—*The Scotsman* (Scotland)

## I ♥ THE BOMB SQUAD

"Tokyo police were called to an apartment building in February

2003 to investigate a suspicious package in the hallway. They found a white box about ten inches square and five inches high. They scanned it with a metal detector—and it read positive, so they immediately cleared the building, closed the roads around it, and called in the bomb squad. An hour later they finally got the box open and found...a chocolate cake. It was a Valentine's Day present for one of the residents. (And it was on a metal tray.)"

—*Daily Times* (Pakistan)

## COFFEE TO GO

"A 31-year-old man, wanted for more than 95 different offenses, was picked up on a warrant for grievous bodily harm by two officers on the Croatian island of Korcula. But after persuading the cops to join him for a last coffee, the criminal fled out of the back of the café, escaping into nearby woods. The policemen have been suspended and face further disciplinary action while their superiors investigate how they could have allowed a man who has been charged with so many offenses to buy them a drink."

—**Ananova**

## YOU'RE FIRED

"Police in a Chilean town mistook firefighters for thieves and tried to arrest them. They were trying to put out a fire at a clothing shop in Valparaíso when police arrived and mistook them for a gang of robbers. The shop had been broken into shortly before the fire started, but the firemen arrived before the police. A police spokesperson said, 'You know how robbers are these days. They're so creative.'"

—*New York Post*

## WHAT A SHOCK

"A British policeman lost his stun gun after leaving it on his police car roof and driving off. The officer only noticed the weapon, which gives a 50,000 volt electric shock, was gone when he got to his destination. He retraced his route, but there was no sign of the pistol. 'We are concerned that it could fall into the wrong hands,' police chief Paul Pearce said. 'If anyone has seen it at the roadside, we ask them to notify the police.'"

—*The Mirror* (U.K.)

# BILLY MITCHELL'S BATTLE, PART I

*History often shows us that radical ideas which upset the status quo are simply ahead of their time. This is the story of a bold man whose forward thinking eventually helped the Allies win World War II.*

## AN AMERICAN IN PARIS

In April 1917, 37-year-old Major William "Billy" Mitchell arrived in Paris to assist in coordinating America's entry into World War I. The war had been raging since 1914, but the United States was only entering the conflict now, having just declared war against Germany.

Mitchell was attached to the aviation section of the Army Signal Corps, then the branch of the military in charge of aviation. His job was to integrate American planes into the Allied war effort. There weren't many planes to integrate—the Army had purchased its very first plane (from the Wright Brothers) only eight years earlier; by 1917 the U.S. air fleet had grown to 55 planes, piloted by the only 35 officers who knew how to fly. Fifty-one of the 55 planes were already obsolete and the remaining four weren't much better. This was compared to thousands of combat aircraft fielded by England, France, Italy, and Germany.

Airplanes weren't a high priority for the U.S. military: When Mitchell first arrived in Paris, he had to use his own money to set up an aviation office (in space borrowed from an American-owned company). When he asked the Army for $50,000 to staff and fund it, his request was denied.

## AERIAL ADVANCES

In addition to lacking planes, the U.S. military needed to catch up with European aviation. Aerial warfare was still in its infancy but it was evolving quickly: When the war started in 1914, aircraft were used only as unarmed spotters for the artillery. These planes were so effective in helping cannons pound enemy targets that both sides started sending their pilots up with pistols, rifles, and shotguns to shoot enemy spotters out of the sky. By the time the U.S. entered the war, both sides had begun building fighter planes with built-in machine guns synchronized with the plane's motor so they could shoot through the spinning propellers without striking the blades.

Bombers had made even more progress since the start of the war: In 1914 zeppelins, not airplanes, had been used as bombers. Although they dropped 100-pound bombs, they were too slow and too easy to shoot down to be very effective. But within a few years, giant twin-engined German Gotha biplanes began crossing the English Channel to drop *1,100-pound* bombs on targets in England.

## QUICK STUDY

Mitchell spent ten days touring the front, then flew over the battlefield in an airplane. If he'd had any doubts about the importance airplanes would have in future conflicts, they ended when he went over the frontline trenches. "We could cross the lines in a few minutes in our airplane," he later wrote, "whereas the armies had been locked in the struggle, immovable, powerless to advance, for three years."

Mitchell spent the next year and a half learning as much as possible about aerial combat from the more experienced British and French pilots. Then, as the American Expeditionary Force prepared to launch its first major attack near Saint-Mihiel, France, on September 12, 1918, he organized what became the largest air offensive to date: nearly 1,500 British, French, Italian, and American planes, operating in waves of 400, flew across the front lines and tried to destroy the German fleet of 2,000 aircraft on the ground before they could join the battle.

The strategy paid off: Those planes that weren't destroyed were put on the defensive, giving control of the skies to the Allies and helping them clear the Germans out of a part of France that they had occupied continuously since 1914. General John J. Pershing was so impressed that he promoted Mitchell to brigadier general.

## ARRESTED DEVELOPMENT

Mitchell had big ideas for how air power could be used in the battles to come: He thought that a good way to break up the stalemate of trench warfare would be to give soldiers parachutes and start dropping them behind enemy lines, bypassing the trenches altogether. In addition to making *tactical* use of airplanes—having them attack enemy soldiers and airplanes—he thought they should also be used *strategically*—they could fly deep into enemy territory to destroy factories, military installations, and transportation networks.

But before Mitchell could put any of his ideas to use, the war ended. Germany signed an armistice on November 11, 1918, just two months after the giant air offensive at Saint-Mihiel.

## BRAVE NEW WORLD

The First World War was over, but the struggle over the future of the U.S. military was just beginning. Mitchell knew that air power had profoundly changed the nature of warfare. In the past, whether armies and navies won or lost depended largely upon how well their ground strengths measured up against the opponents'. But in the future, Mitchell believed, the deciding factor would be who controlled the skies over the battlefield.

Unfortunately, not many other American military leaders understood this, and it worried Mitchell. Saint-Mihiel was only one battle—would the officers who hadn't been there realize its significance? When the next great war came, other countries might have air forces capable of inflicting great damage upon American forces on land and at sea. The United States would need to develop air power to defend itself. Yes, it had prevailed in World War I, even though it was way behind in the air race. But that was only because it had allies, and because aerial warfare was so new. What about the next war—would America be ready?

*What happened next may surprise you. For Part II of the Billy Mitchell story, fly over to page 399.*

*What happened next may surprise you. For Part II of the Billy Mitchell story, fly over to page 399.*

\*　　\*　　\*

## FOUR THINGS MICK JAGGER—BORN IN 1943—IS OLDER THAN

| | |
|---|---|
| The transistor (1947) | Velcro (1948) |
| Israel (1948) | Cake mix (1949) |

# CUTE...AND *EVIL*

*Think they're cuddly? They'll bite your face off if you let them.*

**A** **78-YEAR-OLD AUSTRALIAN** man was hospitalized after being attacked by a koala. He approached the dazed animal after hitting it with his car. "He fooled me," said Jack Higgs. "I went to grab his back legs to sort of drag him off the road; he turned around and struck me." Higgs was treated for deep scratches on his legs. The koala was released back to the wild.

**A BOCA RATON, FLORIDA,** woman was walking her pet Chihuahua when a river otter jumped out of a canal, grabbed the dog, and dragged it into the water. "The otter starts dunking him to drown him like they do to fish," said Leah Vanon. "I started punching the otter in the face, which I felt really bad about because it's cute. But it was killing my dog." (She saved the pooch.)

**DOUG BOWES OF SANTA ROSA,** California, was walking in a field near his home in 2002 when a small jackrabbit bounded toward him. "I thought, 'Gosh, this is somebody's pet,'" he later told reporters. He reached his hand down to pet the bunny—and it bit him. Bowes had to get six rounds of rabies injections. And the best part: It was Easter.

**IN THE 1970s, ACTRESS** Susan Sarandon took part in a study on human interaction with dolphins, during which she became friendly with a dolphin named Joe. All was going well until Joe's mate, Rosie, suddenly attacked Sarandon, biting her on the hand and nearly breaking her wrist. "Apparently, an enraged, jealous dolphin is incredibly dangerous," Sarandon said.

**CAN FINCHES BE KEPT** with parakeets? That's what a reader of bird expert Myra Markley's Web site asked. Markley's answer: "I have been called to many homes where parakeets have been added to the aviary. The owners want to know why the finches keep dying. I stand quietly and watch the birds interact and force the owners to do the same. In most cases I've only needed to wait a few minutes. A parakeet grabs the finch and either rips out a beak full of feathers or crushes the tiny finch's head or neck." In other words...no.

**Winged winos:** Butterflies can get drunk on the juice of rotten fruit.

# HE'S A CURLY WOLF

*Real cowboy slang of the late 19th century was a lot different from the way it's been depicted in movies and on TV. Some examples:*

**Coffee boiler:** A lazy person who sits around the coffee pot instead of helping with the work.

**Big bug:** Important person; big shot.

**Bone orchard:** Cemetery.

**The boss:** The best.

**He only gave it a lick and a promise:** He did a poor job.

**Crow bait:** A poor-quality horse.

**Shin out:** To run away.

**Clean someone's plow:** To beat them up.

**You're all down but nine:** You don't understand—refers to missing all the pins in a game of nine-pin bowling.

**Coffin varnish:** Bad coffee.

**Grub-line rider:** Someone who travels from ranch to ranch looking for work.

**Curly wolf:** A very tough, very dangerous person.

**Flannel mouth:** A smooth talker.

**California widow:** A wife who lives apart from her husband because he has gone West to seek his fortune.

**Gospel sharp:** A preacher. (As skilled with the Bible as a card sharp is with cards.)

**Indian haircut:** A scalping.

**Quirley:** A cigarette you roll yourself.

**Cowboy change:** Bullets (sometimes used as quarters or dimes when coins were short).

**Fightin' wages:** Extra money paid to cowboys for fighting Indians or cattle rustlers.

**Take French leave:** To desert, or leave without permission.

**Dude:** An Easterner or well-dressed person (they wear "duds").

**Someone to ride the river with:** Someone dependable.

**Beat the Devil around the stump:** To procrastinate.

**Honda:** The eyelet at the end of a lasso that's used to make the loop.

On average, a movie makes about five times more from its video sales than its ticket sales.

# SPICY STORIES

*In our quest to not cook up a bland book, our seasoned
researchers spiced things up with a dash of tasty origins.*

## ALLSPICE

Allspice grows naturally in the West Indies and Central
America, where Spanish explorers discovered it in the
16th century. They thought the shrubby tree's fruit looked like pep-
percorns, so they called the plant *pimienta*, Spanish for "pepper."
But it isn't pepper—its pungent aroma has been described as a
mixture of cloves, cinnamon, nutmeg, and black pepper. For that
reason, English traders who brought it back from Spain gave it the
name *allspice*. Fun fact: Seventeenth-century pirates put allspice on
meat to preserve it for long sea voyages—a French process known as
*boucan*, which gave the pirates the name *boucaniers*, or buccaneers.
Today, allspice is an ingredient in sausage, pickles, and curry.

## ROSEMARY

One legend says that as the Virgin Mary fled King Herod's soldiers
(given orders to kill all first-born babies), a thick bush miracu-
lously parted to allow her to hide behind it. She remained there
for several hours. She draped her blue cloak over the bush's white
flowers, and in the morning the flowers had turned blue. The bush
became known as "the rose of Mary." Medieval monasteries, known
for herb and plant cultivation, grew the sacred herb for medicinal
purposes, to spice food, and to be used as incense at weddings.

## VANILLA

Most spices originated in Asia, where they grow wild and have
been used for centuries. But vanilla, the beanlike fruit of an
orchid, is native to North America. The Aztecs used it to flavor
chocolate drinks that Spanish conquistador Hernando Cortés
brought back to Europe in the 1500s. Aristocrats and royalty
throughout Europe loved the exotic beverage, but it wasn't until
1602 that vanilla was used without chocolate, when a chemist
working for Queen Elizabeth I of England discovered that vanilla
made a good flavoring agent by itself.

## BASIL

A native of Asia and Africa, basil was sacred in ancient India, and believed to be the disguised form of Lakshmi, wife of the Hindu god Vishnu. Anyone who broke basil twigs was said to have their prayers go unanswered. Leaves, however, were allowed to be plucked and placed on the dead to assure admittance to heaven. Ancient Greeks brought the herb back from Persia and also treated it with reverence. They called it *basilikon*, which means "royal." Only kings were permitted to cut basil, and only with a golden sickle. Long used as a cooking ingredient in Asia and the Mediterranean, the sweet herb became popular in western Europe in the 16th century after British explorers brought it back from India.

## SESAME SEED

Cultivation of sesame seeds—believed to be one the first crops grown specifically for their taste—dates back at least to 3000 B.C. in India. Egyptians imported it, and the plant flourished in the Middle East, where it inspired the phrase "open sesame," a magical incantation that opens an entrance in the book *1,001 Nights*. Reason: Hundreds of sesame seeds are encased in every pod. When the plant is ripe, the slightest touch causes the pod to explode open. Sesame seeds came to Europe in the first century through the spice trade. The trade route gradually extended into Africa, where, via the 17th-century slave trade, the seeds made their way to the western hemisphere.

## FENNEL

Fennel was one of the first herbs to be cultivated in the Western world. It was sacred to ancient Greeks; according to mythology, Prometheus used the stalk of a fennel plant to steal fire from the gods. And in 490 B.C. Athens defeated Persian invaders on a battlefield covered in fennel. The plant was considered such good luck that the adjacent village was named *Marathon*, meaning "place of fennel." In ancient Rome, fennel was used for medicinal purposes (Romans thought chewing on it prevented obesity). In medieval times, the herb was hung from the rafters of homes to keep out ghosts and witches, a practice that may have sprung from fennel's effectiveness as an insect repellent.

The U.S. death toll from the 1918 flu epidemic was so high that it created a coffin shortage.

# BENNIES FROM HEAVEN

*In this age of corporate scandal, it's nice to know that some companies go out of their way to let their employees know they're appreciated. Here are some fantastic—and unusual—job perks.*

• At a New York consulting firm called Inlumen, employees get a cash award of $50 a month to spend on "someone they love."

• Boot manufacturer Timberland offers a $3,000 subsidy to any employee who buys a gas/electric hybrid car.

• Workers at New Belgium Brewing in Colorado get a free bike on their one-year anniversary with the company (they make Fat Tire beer). And after five years, they get a free trip...to Belgium.

• BMW Financial Services pays all healthcare costs for workers and their families. And if the employee doesn't have a family, the company will help out there, too, with $30,000 toward fertility treatments.

• Acuity Insurance has a well-stocked fish pond on the company campus. Workers get to keep what they catch. Another perk: Acuity pays for Weight Watchers—but only if the employee meets his or her goal weight.

• Outdoor supply company Patagonia will pay for employees to go on a two-month "environmental crusade."

• The OhioHealth hospital system provides free concierge service to its 15,200 workers. Everybody, from doctors to janitors, has someone to run any errand, such as feeding pets, meeting repair workers at their home, or waiting in line for concert tickets.

• At the University of Notre Dame, children of staff and faculty get four years of free tuition. And if they don't want to go to Notre Dame, the college will pay 30% of the cost to attend another college.

• In addition to regular sick days and vacation time, the Calvert Group, an investment firm in Maryland, provides workers with an extra 12 paid days off per year to do volunteer work.

Sing Sing was the first prison to use fingerprinting for identification purposes, in 1903.

# DIVA OF THE DESERT

*This unique performer craves the spotlight...but doesn't
much care about the size of the audience.*

## I F YOU BUILD IT...

In the scorched wasteland of Death Valley, California, lies one of the most unusual theaters in America: the Amargosa Opera House. The quirk is that no opera is ever performed there—only ballet. And there is only one performer: a prima ballerina named Marta Becket, who at 79 years of age still performs her solo show in the desert, as she has for the last 38 years.

In 1967 Becket, a dancer and artist from New York, was on a camping trip in the desert with her husband. When they had a flat tire on their trailer, a local park ranger told them they could get it fixed in Death Valley Junction. The town had been built in the 1920s by the Pacific Coast Borax Company to house its mine workers. While her husband stayed at the gas station with the trailer, Marta poked around the small compound of adobe buildings. Aside from the old company offices, there was a 23-room hotel with a lavishly painted lobby, still open for business, and something that really caught her eye: a rundown community center known as Corkhill Hall.

Peeking through a hole in Corkhill's door, she saw a small stage with tattered cotton curtains. Trash was strewn between the wooden benches that faced the stage. Marta said later, "Peering through the tiny hole, I had the distinct feeling that I was looking at the other half of myself. The building seemed to be saying, 'take me...do something with me...I offer you life.'"

## ...THEY WILL COME

Marta tracked down the town manager and talked him into renting her the hall for $45 a month. Six months later, on February 10, 1968, she gave her first daily performance. There were 12 people in the audience, all of them locals curious to see what the peculiar lady from New York was up to. Occasionally, curious tourists would wander in. Sometimes no one was there at all. Marta always performed no matter what. One night she had just

---

**Hot spot: More than 90% of Egypt is desert.**

begun her performance to an empty house when four people came in. They sat quietly, applauded politely at the curtain call, and left. Becket thought nothing of it until a few months later, when an article about her appeared in *National Geographic* magazine. After that, audiences grew. Locals kept coming back; at first they came to gawk and laugh, but left strangely moved by the sight of this intense woman following her muse wherever it led her. Word spread, and soon tour buses were making the newly named Amargosa Opera House a stop on their itineraries. Celebrities would pop over from nearby Las Vegas (comedian Red Skelton was so charmed that he visited four times).

## PAINT THE WALLS

Part of the ongoing attraction of the Amargosa is the whimsical, brilliantly colored murals Becket has painted on its walls. Starting in July 1968, driven partly by her loneliness at playing to such small audiences, Marta spent four years covering the walls with a permanent audience. A king and queen hold court in the royal box. Bullfighters sit next to 17th-century Spanish nobility. Monks and nuns stare disapprovingly at the garish prostitutes leering from the opposite wall. The central dome has 16 women playing musical instruments beneath a flight of doves, and there are jugglers, dancing cherubs, dowdy matrons, and little children—whatever took Marta's fancy. The result is an arts institution unlike any other. The town of Death Valley Junction (now owned by the Amargosa Opera House) was added to the National Register of Historic Places in 1980.

## CURTAIN CALL

Becket's husband wasn't as dedicated to the venture—he left in 1983. But Becket soldiered on, assisted by Tom Willett, who started out as her stage manager and became her emcee and partner. Willett died in 2005, but Becket has no intention of retiring. Although age has forced her to cut back the number of performances she gives each week (she only performs on weekends now) she still begins promptly at 8:15 p.m.

"I am grateful," she says, "to have found the place where I can fulfill my dreams and share them with the passing scene…for as long as I can."

First animated cartoon character: *Gertie the Trained Dinosaur* (1910).

# IT'S RADIOACTIVE!

*Look around your house. Feeling all safe and comfy? Now check out this list of common household RADIOACTIVE items. It's enough to make your hair glow green.*

**Item:** Smoke detectors

**Radioactive Element:** Americium-241

**Explanation:** *Americium* is used to ionize the air between two electrically charged plates inside a smoke detector, causing a current to flow between them. When smoke enters the detector, it blocks the americium particles, lowering the electrical current between the two plates and setting off the alarm. Though the radiation is safely contained inside the smoke detector, radiation levels near the americium element can be quite high.

**Item:** Glow-in-the-dark clock hands

**Radioactive Element:** Tritium

**Explanation:** At one time, *radium* was painted on watch and clock dials to make them glow in the dark. Many of the workers who painted the radium onto the clock parts contracted radiation poisoning because they would set the tips of their brushes by licking them. (Today we know that's not a good idea.) Radium was later replaced by *tritium*, which emits radiation, but not enough to penetrate the glass or plastic cover of a clock or watch. Some compasses, glow-in-the-dark key chains, and exit signs also contain tritium.

**Item:** Pottery

**Radioactive Element:** Uranium oxide

**Explanation:** Some types of old pottery were glazed using *uranium oxide* to give them that desirable glossy finish. The most common was the Homer Laughlin China Company's brightly colored Fiesta ware made between 1936 and 1943. Vintage Fiesta ware is considered collectible and can still be found in many homes and antique stores. Fiesta ware collectors are commonly advised not to eat from the orange dishes, especially acidic foods such as tomato soup, which tend to leach the uranium out of the glaze. (Fiesta was reissued in the 1980s *without* the uranium oxide.)

---

Ka-boom! There have been 2,036 known nuclear-bomb explosions since World War II.

**Item:** Salt substitute

**Radioactive Element:** Potassium-40

**Explanation:** Most salt substitutes contain potassium chloride instead of sodium chloride. But many also contain *potassium-40*, a radioactive isotope that makes up a small amount of the potassium found naturally in foodstuffs. Unfortunately for anyone hoping to use salt substitute to get rid of unwanted houseguests, the amount of potassium-40 found in the condiment is not enough to do harm.

**Item:** Lantern mantels

**Radioactive Element:** Thorium

**Explanation:** To make lantern mantels more luminescent, the radioactive element *thorium* is commonly added. Although Coleman, the largest lantern-mantel manufacturer, recently traded in thorium for the more stable yttrium oxide, many generic mantels still contain thorium. Just a few good whiffs of the mantel dust might be enough to make you a much less happy camper: It can cause cancer and liver disease.

**Item:** Jewelry

**Radioactive Element:** Radium

**Explanation:** Some jewelry manufacturers use X-rays and *radium* to irradiate certain gemstones, a process that enhances their color. Sometimes the gemstones can remain radioactive for years after the treatment. Also, cloisonné jewelry is enameled using uranium oxide.

## OTHER RADIOACTIVE ITEMS

Vaseline glass, thoriated welding rods, spark plugs from the 1940s, some old vacuum tubes, yellow Leica camera lenses, jewelry polish, anti-static brushes, neon lights, dental crowns, LCD wristwatches, old eyeglasses, microwaves, TVs, and topaz gemstones.

\*     \*     \*

"The atomic age is here to stay…but are we?"

—**Bennett Cerf**

---

When Kuwait's first McDonald's opened in 1994, the drive-through line was 7 miles long.

# BETTY FREEMAN'S
# DAY IN COURT

*Eighty years before the Emancipation Proclamation freed*
*American slaves, a Massachusetts woman helped free*
*the slaves of that state...just by going to court.*

## RAVE WORDS

B In 1773 the leading citizens of Sheffield, Massachusetts, met in the home of Colonel John Ashley and drafted the document that some historians have called America's first Declaration of Independence, the Sheffield Declaration. "Mankind in a state of nature are equal, free, and independent of each other," it stated, "and have a right to the undisturbed enjoyment of their lives, their liberty and property."

Ironically, as the men toiled over the document, which protested English tyranny, they were waited on by Betty Freeman (also called Elizabeth, or Bett), Colonel Ashley's slave. He'd bought several slaves when they were only babies, and they'd been held in involuntary servitude ever since.

Freeman overheard the repeated talk of liberty as the men drafted the Sheffield Declaration. She heard more of the same three years later, when Ashley and his associates discussed the Declaration of Independence, which stated, "we hold these truths to be self-evident, that all men are created equal, that they are endowed by their Creator with certain unalienable Rights, that among these are Life, Liberty and the pursuit of Happiness." She got another earful in 1780, when Ashley and his friends mulled over the new Massachusetts constitution, which proclaimed that "all men are born free and equal, and have the right of enjoying and defending their lives and liberties."

## ALL TALK

These were noble words, but none of them were meant to apply to Freeman—not even after her husband, also a slave, gave his life fighting on the American side during the Revolutionary War. Born into slavery, Betty, her sister, and all their descendants would

---

Frogs croak, bark, cluck, click, grunt, snore, squawk, chirp, whistle, trill, and yap.

live in slavery forever if Colonel Ashley and others like him had their way.

## THE "LADY" OF THE HOUSE

As deeply as she resented her lack of freedom, Betty got along with Colonel Ashley. Not so with his wife, Hannah, a petty tyrant who cruelly beat her slaves over the tiniest transgression. Once, when she had caught Betty's sister, Lizzie, eating leftover scraps of bread dough, Mrs. Ashley accused her of "stealing" food and swung at her with a hot shovel pulled from the fireplace. Betty blocked the blow intended for her sister and received a gash on her arm that cut all the way to the bone. She carried that scar for the rest of her life.

It wasn't long after that incident that Freeman happened to visit the village meeting house while the Declaration of Independence was being read aloud. Maybe it was the fresh wound on her arm, maybe it was hearing the words of equality and freedom spoken one more time…whatever it was, something clicked inside her. The next day, she left the Ashleys and walked over to the offices of Theodore Sedgwick, a lawyer and vocal opponent of slavery. Freeman knew him because he was one of the people who had helped draft the Sheffield Declaration.

"Sir," she asked, "I heard that paper read yesterday, that says all men are born equal, and that every man has a right to freedom. I am not a dumb critter; won't the law give me my freedom?"

## EQUAL = EQUAL

Wouldn't it? How could a state that proclaimed "all men are born free and equal," and was part of a country that believed "all men are created equal" reconcile these statements with the institution of slavery? Sedgwick agreed with Freeman: It couldn't. He decided to help her by filing a lawsuit to win her freedom, on the grounds that the language of the new state constitution made slavery illegal.

The laws of Massachusetts at the end of the 18th century were quite peculiar by modern standards: They defined slaves as property, but also recognized that they were human beings, which meant that they had legal standing in state courts and could file lawsuits. In recent years a number of slaves had sued for their freedom and won, but not by challenging the legality of

---

**Heavy fact:** A cloud measuring one cubic mile weighs about 3.5 million pounds.

slavery directly. If a slave could prove that their mother had been born free, they could regain their freedom. Likewise, if a slave owner had made a promise to free a slave and then reneged, the slave could sue on grounds of breach of promise. Freeman's lawsuit was different: It would be the first to challenge the legality of slavery itself.

## SEE YOU IN COURT

The new state constitution had been in effect for less than a year when Sedgwick went to court in May 1781 and filed what is called a "writ of replevin." The writ ordered Colonel Ashley to surrender property—Betty and another slave, Brom, who had joined in the suit—that wasn't rightfully his. When Ashley refused to obey the writ, a trial was scheduled for the following August.

Colonel Ashley probably didn't realize it at the time, but the odds were against him from the start. Although slavery was still legal in Massachusetts, it had become very unpopular. The case was going to be tried before a jury, at a time when citizens of Massachusetts were still fighting in the Revolutionary War. These people took their freedoms seriously. And sure enough, when the trial was over, the jury decided in favor of Betty and Brom. The court set both of them free and ordered Ashley to pay them 30 shillings in damages, plus court costs.

## THE BEGINNING OF THE END

*Brom and Bett v. Ashley* was a lower court case and did not set much of a precedent—Brom and Bett were the only slaves freed by the decision. But it did set a precedent of another kind, demonstrating that if slaves went to court to win their freedom, juries were very likely to give it to them. Slavery began to die a death of a thousand cuts in Massachusetts as other slaves filed lawsuits or just walked away from their owners, knowing that the owners couldn't turn to the law for assistance. Owning slaves in the state had suddenly become a very risky business.

Another nail in slavery's coffin came as a result of a second lawsuit, filed in 1781 by a slave named Quock Walker, who sued his owner in civil court for assault and battery after the owner beat him for trying to escape. Walker not only won the case and £50 in damages, but the attorney general prosecuted his owner on

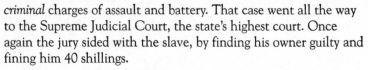

*criminal* charges of assault and battery. That case went all the way to the Supreme Judicial Court, the state's highest court. Once again the jury sided with the slave, by finding his owner guilty and fining him 40 shillings.

Chief Justice William Cushing's instructions to the jury turned out to be even more important than their decision. He stated that "perpetual servitude can no longer be tolerated in our government; and…liberty can be only forfeited by criminal conduct or relinquished by personal consent." Cushing's words weren't legally binding but they might as well have been—they made it clear that the court was against slavery. Without the protection of the law, slavery was doomed in Massachusetts.

## AFTERMATH

Theodore Sedgwick, the lawyer who had helped Betty Freeman, went on to an illustrious career in politics and law. He served in both houses of state government, as well as in the U.S. Senate and the House of Representatives, where he was Speaker of the House from 1799 to 1801. In 1802 he became a justice of the Supreme Judicial Court of Massachusetts, and served there until his death in 1813.

What happened to Brom is unknown; after the case ended he disappeared into history. We do know what happened to Betty, however. After Colonel Ashley lost the case, he asked Betty to come back and work for wages. Would you have accepted such an offer? Neither did Betty—she went to work for Theodore Sedgwick instead. After many years, she saved enough money to buy her own house and retire. When she died in 1829 at about the age of 85, she was buried in the Sedgwick family plot in Stockbridge, Massachusetts, where her grave can still be seen today. One of her great-grandchildren was W.E.B. DuBois, one of the most important civil rights leaders of the 20th century.

## THE MEANING OF FREEDOM

Many years after Betty's death, Theodore Sedgwick's daughter Catherine recounted Betty's explanation of what freedom meant to her: "Any time while I was a slave," she said, "if one minute's freedom had been offered to me, and I had been told that I must die at the end of that minute, I would have taken it just to stand one minute on God's earth a free woman."

---

**Philadelphia was the first U.S. city to have a public water system.**

# WASHINGTON'S POSTS

*Booker T. Washington is one of the most important figures in African-American history. He was born into slavery in 1856, but went on to found the Tuskegee Institute and improve race relations in America —decades before the civil rights movement of the 1960s.*

"Never be ashamed to ask for information. The ignorant man will always be ignorant if he fears that by asking he will display ignorance."

"It's better to be alone than in bad company."

"Few things can help an individual more than to place responsibility on him, and to let him know that you trust him."

"I shall allow no man to belittle my soul by making me hate him."

"No man who continues to add something to the well-being of the place in which he lives is left long without proper reward."

"Excellence is to do a common thing in an uncommon way."

"Success is to be measured not by the position that one has reached in life but by the obstacles which he has overcome."

"One man cannot hold another man down in the ditch without remaining down in the ditch with him."

"Great men cultivate love."

"The highest test of a civilization is its willingness to extend a helping hand to the less fortunate. Like an individual, it lifts itself up by lifting others up."

"We should never permit our grievances to overshadow our opportunities."

"Character, not circumstances, makes the man."

"Most leaders spend time trying to get others to think highly of them, when instead they should try to get their people to think more highly of themselves."

"The world cares very little about what a man or woman knows; it is what a man or woman is able to do that counts."

# WAR PLAN RED

*When this bizarre story surfaced a few years ago, it reminded us of this quote, attributed to Warren G. Harding: "I can take care of my enemies all right. But my damn friends—they're the ones that keep me walking the floors nights."*

## NORTHERN EXPOSURE

If you had to invade another country, how would you do it? Believe it or not, the United States military spent a lot of time pondering that question in the late 1920s, when it came up with a plan to invade its closest neighbor, Canada.

There was certainly a precedent for the two nations battling it out. The Continental Army invaded Canada during the American Revolution, and the U.S. Army made repeated incursions during the War of 1812. In 1839 the state of Maine only narrowly avoided a shooting war with the province of New Brunswick over a border dispute. Then, in 1866, about 800 Irish-American members of a group called the Fenian Brotherhood tried to occupy part of Canada for the purpose of using it as a bargaining chip to force Great Britain to grant independence to Ireland. (They were quickly driven back across the U.S. border.)

That last invasion had an upside for Canadians: It convinced the last holdouts in the independent provinces of New Brunswick, Nova Scotia, Ontario, and Quebec that they'd be better able to defend themselves against the *next* invasion if they banded together to form the Dominion of Canada, which they did on July 1, 1867.

## TO THE DRAWING BOARD

Of course, these skirmishes paled in comparison to World War I, which raged from 1914 to 1918. That war, which was precipitated by the assassination of Archduke Ferdinand of Austria, caught most of the belligerents by surprise. It also lasted longer and was far more costly in blood and treasure than anyone ever dreamed a war could be. None of the nations that fought in it wanted to be caught off guard again; many began planning for whatever war might be lurking around the corner. The American military drafted a whole series of color-coded war plans to cover just about every conceivable scenario: War Plan Black was a plan for war with Germany;

War Plan Orange dealt with Japan, a rapidly growing power in the Pacific. Other colors included Green (Mexico), Gold (France), Brown (The Philippines), and Yellow (China). There was even a War Plan Indigo, in case the United States had to invade Iceland, and a War Plan White that dealt with civil unrest within America's own borders.

## SEEING RED

War Plan Red was America's plan for going to war with the British Empire, in the unlikely event that Britain (code name: Red) decided to "eliminate [the United States] as an economic and commercial rival." Since Canada (code name: Crimson) was part of the Empire and shared a 5,527-mile border with the U.S., much of the plan dealt with invading Canada and knocking it out of action before the British could use it as a staging ground for attacks on the U.S.

Here's how an invasion of Canada would have gone:

• The United States (code name: Blue) would attack and occupy Halifax, Nova Scotia, Canada's largest Atlantic port. The attack would deny Britain access to the rail and road links it would need to land troops in Canada and disperse them across the country.

• Next, the U.S. Army would attack across the border along three fronts: Troops would attack from either Vermont or New York to occupy Montreal and Quebec City; from Michigan into Ontario; and from North Dakota into Manitoba. Meanwhile, the U.S. Navy would take control of the Great Lakes. The effects of these attacks would be to seize Canada's industrial heartland while preventing similar attacks on America, and to further disrupt the movement of Canadian troops from one part of the country to another.

• Troops would cross from Washington into British Columbia and seize Vancouver, Canada's largest Pacific port. The U.S. Navy would blockade the port of Prince Rupert, 460 miles to the north.

Once the crisis passed and relations between America, Canada, and Great Britain returned to normal, the U.S. troops would be withdrawn from Canadian territory, right? No—"Blue intentions are to hold in perpetuity all Crimson and Red territory gained," the military planners wrote. "The policy will be to prepare the provinces and territories of Crimson and Red to become states and territories of the Blue union upon the declaration of peace."

...they are actually allergic to *sebum*, a fatty substance secreted by the cat's sebaceous glands.

## THE FOG OF WAR(S)

So how seriously was the United States considering invading Canada? In all probability, not very. War Plan Red doesn't go into nearly as much detail as War Plan Black (Germany) or War Plan Orange (Japan), which military planners correctly assumed were much more significant threats. The intent of the other color-coded plans may have been to make war plans involving Germany and Japan seem less controversial. Why the subterfuge? After the horrors of World War I, in which nearly 10 million soldiers died, many people concluded that planning for wars only made them more likely.

The U.S. military didn't feel this way, of course, and one way they may have gotten around public opinion was to come up with all kinds of improbable war plans to make the *real* plans more palatable. A public that would not have tolerated the idea of the preparing for war with Germany and Japan would be less alarmed by the idea of the United States preparing for war with Germany, Japan, Canada, Iceland, Jamaica, Monaco, and Andorra.

## WHAT'S GOOD FOR THE GOOSE...

Any sting Canadians may have felt when War Plan Red was declassified in 1974 was offset by the knowledge that Canada had drafted its own plans for invading the United States, and had done so several years before War Plan Red was approved in 1930. "Defense Scheme No. 1," as it was called, was created in 1921 by James Sutherland "Buster" Brown, Canada's director of military operations and intelligence. In many respects it was the opposite of War Plan Red: In the event that an American attack was imminent, Canadian forces would strike first, attacking and occupying key cities such as Albany, Minneapolis, and Seattle.

Unlike with War Plan Red, these cities wouldn't be annexed or even occupied for any longer than was absolutely necessary. The idea was to knock the U.S. off balance, then retreat back into Canada, blowing up bridges and destroying roads and railroads along the way in the hope of delaying the inevitable American counterattack until British reinforcements arrived. The plan received mixed reviews from the Canadian military: One general called it a "fantastic desperate plan that just might have worked"; other officers thought Brown was nuts. It remained on the books until 1928, when it was scrapped as impractical.

# CLASS ACTS

*College isn't only about really rigorous science classes, thick textbooks, and late-night studying. As one of Uncle John's teachers put it, "College is hard—there should be some classes where you can get an easy A." That could be why most schools have "cream-puff" classes like these.*

**Elvis as Anthology.** "Redefining the music of other performers through listening to Elvis, and watching video and movie clips." (University of Iowa)

**Art and Science of Beer.** "We will explore the place of beer in ancient as well as modern life, and the role beer has played in important achievements in microbiology, biotechnology and physics." (Indiana University)

**Sports for the Spectator.** "A study of the great American spectator sports including football, basketball, baseball, ice hockey, golf, tennis, and any others which meet the interests of the class." (Ohio State University)

**Witchcraft and Politics.** "Explores witchcraft, spirit possession, and cults of the dead as idioms of power and as vehicles for protest, resistance, and violent social change." (Bucknell University)

**Shopping: Desire, Compulsion, and Consumption.** "First we will explore the manufacturing of desire. We will then turn to historical analysis, contrasting the experience of shopping in traditional bazaars and contemporary malls. Finally, we will explore the place of shopping in our collective imaginations." (Williams College)

**How to Be Gay.** "Examines the notion that homosexuality is not just a desire, but a set of specific tastes in music, movies, and other cultural forms." (University of Michigan)

**Star Trek and Religion.** "This popular science-fiction series is set in the future, but the ideas and conflicts come from past and present debates." (Indiana University)

**Campus Culture and Drinking.** "The cultural understandings that motivate and shape undergraduate drinking." (Duke University)

---

Just add water! May 16th is International Sea Monkey Day.

*Awareness.* "Students will begin their work by designing independent learning projects, which can be anything (community service, sailing, midwifery, gardening, reading, etc.). We will answer these questions: What do you want to learn? How are you going to learn it? How are you going to know when you have learned it?" (Evergreen State College)

*International Beverage Education.* "The history of beverages such as wines, distilled spirits, and beers. Prerequisite: must be 21 years of age." (Oklahoma State University)

*Daytime Serials: Family and Social Roles.* "Analysis of the themes and characters that populate daytime serials and investigation of what impact these portrayals have on gender roles in the family and workplace." (University of Wisconsin)

*The Cheerleader in American Culture.* "Cheerleading is an ambiguous cultural icon. In this course we challenge the stereotypes of cheerleaders and provoke both supporters and critics to view cheerleading in a more multi-faceted light." (University of Alabama)

## A FEW MORE:

• *American Golf: Aristocratic Pastime or the People's Game?* (Carnegie Mellon University)

• *Quarterstaff, Broadsword, Rapier, and Dagger Combat* (Northern Kentucky University)

• *Introduction to Leisure* (Kent State University)

• *Black Hair: The History of African-American Hairstyles* (Stanford University)

• *Underwater Fire Prevention* (University of Louisiana-Monroe)

• *Pranks: Culture Jamming as Social Activism* (St. Mary's College)

• *Relaxation Techniques* (University of Iowa)

• *History of Tupac Shakur* (University of California, Berkeley)

• *Juggling (I and II)* (University of Oregon)

• *Frisbee* (Western Connecticut State University)

• *The Social Significance of* The Dukes of Hazzard (University of Alabama)

Humans are responsible for the deaths of 30 to 70 million sharks every year.

# I'LL TRADE YOU A...

*In this eBay world, where it seems like everything is for sale, it's nice see that there's more to life than money.*

**B**EER FOR A PITCHER: Pitcher Nigel Thatch of the Schaumburg Flyers of the Northern League, a professional baseball league in the northern United States and Canada, was traded in May 2006. The Flyers, according to the official league announcement, "assigned the contract of RHP Nigel Thatch (Rookie) to Fullerton of the Golden Baseball League in exchange for one pallet (60 cases) of Budweiser beer." *Not to be confused with...*

**BEER FOR A HORSE:** A pub in Dunedin, New Zealand, caused an uproar in 2003 when it ran a "Beer for Beasts" promotion in which participants could trade animals for beer. Bringing a horse to the pub earned traders 20 pints, four cats brought four pints, and a live duck from the local botanical gardens earned one pint. After protests from animal-rights groups, the promotion was quickly cancelled.

**ANNOUNCER FOR A CARTOON CHARACTER:** In 2006 NBC took over the Sunday night TV broadcasts of NFL games. They wanted Al Michaels, who had been with ABC for 26 years and the announcer for Monday Night Football for 10, to host the show. Who owns ABC? The Walt Disney Company. What did they want in return for Michaels? Something unusual: 26 *Oswald the Lucky Rabbit* cartoons that Walt Disney made in 1927. He'd done them for Universal Studios, so he never owned the rights to them, which is why he created Mickey Mouse (the two characters look very similar). Disney had always wanted the rights back, and NBC now owns Universal, so they agreed to trade the rights to Michaels...for the rights to Oswald.

**HOUSE FOR A PAPER CLIP:** In July 2005, aspiring author Kyle MacDonald, 26, of Montreal set out to get a house...for a paper clip. He posted a notice on the Craigslist Web site offering

---

Seeing is believing: The bubbles in Guinness beer sink to the bottom rather than float to the top.

to trade a large red paper clip for something bigger or better. He got a fish-shaped pen. He traded that for a ceramic door knob. And then traded that for a camping stove. This went on for a year, and included trading up to a beer keg, a snowmobile, a trip to British Columbia, and a recording contract. In the meantime he'd become a celebrity, doing talk shows all over the world, which led to him trading for a movie role (he got it for a KISS snow globe from a movie producer/snow globe collector). In July 2006 he made his last trade: He gave the movie role to the mayor of the town of Kipling, Saskatchewan, who presented him with the keys to a 1,100-square-foot, 3-bedroom house. (The tiny town wanted the publicity to increase tourist trade, and announced that they'd be holding an *American Idol*–like contest to give away the movie part.) MacDonald is now living in the house and writing a book about the adventure.

**CATCHER FOR HIMSELF:** Harry Chiti was a journeyman catcher who played for the Chicago Cubs, Kansas City Athletics, Detroit Tigers, and New York Mets in the 1950s and 1960s. His career statistics are unimpressive, but he does hold claim to one fascinating piece of baseball history. In 1962 the New York Mets bought the rights to Chiti from the Cleveland Indians. The Mets then traded him back to Cleveland for a "player to be named later in the season." The player the Mets ended up getting later in the season: Harry Chiti.

**BALLS FOR A BALLPLAYER:** In 1989 pitcher Tim Fortugno was traded by the minor-league Reno Silver Sox to the Milwaukee Brewers organization for $2,500...and 144 baseballs.

**LOVE FOR PEACE:** In April 2006, Italian porn star Cicciolina offered to have "a private encounter" with al-Qaeda leader Osama bin Laden in exchange for his halting all terrorist attacks. "I am ready to make a deal," she announced at a festival in Budapest, Hungary. "He can have me in exchange for an end to his tyranny." Cicciolina, whose real name is Anna Ilona Staller, reminded the crowd that she had made the same offer to Saddam Hussein in the 1990s, saying "who knows what might have happened" if he had taken her up on the offer.

# LEBOWSKI 9:29

*Lots of movies have inspired their own fan conventions. Let's see, there's* Star Trek *and* Star Wars *and…*The Big Lebowski?

**B**IG FLOPSKI
When *The Big Lebowski* hit theaters in 1998, it didn't make much of a splash. Though it met with critical acclaim and was well received by loyal fans of Joel and Ethan Coen, the film's director, producer, and co-writers, it barely broke even at the box office. Following on the heels of *Fargo*, the Coens' most successful film to that point, *Lebowski's* modest earnings came as a disappointment. But then in 1999 it went to video and became a cult classic.

As *Lebowski* fans will tell you, this is a movie that gets better with repeat viewings. There are so many threads woven into the complicated plot, and so much dry humor and memorable dialogue, that the film simply can't be taken in at a single glance. *The Big Lebowski* is one of those movies where you catch something new every time you watch it.

Here's the basic plot: In a case of mistaken identity, Jeff "The Dude" Lebowski—a lazy, unemployed, hippie bowler—is assaulted by thugs who are actually looking for a paraplegic millionaire named Jeffrey Lebowski, whose trophy wife "owes money all over town." During the course of the assault, the assailants pee on The Dude's living room carpet. Deciding to seek restitution from the real Lebowski (because "the carpet really tied the room together, man"), The Dude and his two bowling buddies, Walter and Donny, are drawn into a web of intrigue involving kidnapping, pornographers, and nihilists; Lebowski's avant-garde daughter, Maude; a high-school student whose father used to write for the TV western, *Branded*; and intricately choreographed bowling-dream sequences. There's a lot more, but you'll have to watch the movie a few times to figure it all out…which is exactly what thousands of devoted fans have been doing for nearly a decade.

### WHY NOT?
Three years after the movie's release on video, two *Lebowski* fans, Will Russell and Scott Shuffitt, were killing time while manning a

T-shirt booth at a tattoo convention in Louisville, Kentucky. Business was so slow that the two friends began entertaining themselves by quoting lines from *Lebowski*. The people at the next booth turned out to be fans as well, and soon joined in. Eventually, Russell and Shuffitt's booth became the most popular spot in the convention hall, with bored vendors congregating to repeat their favorite bits of dialogue from the film. At some point, according to Russell, "Scott and I were like, man, if they can have this goofy tattoo convention, we should have a *Big Lebowski* convention."

## BOWLING AND WHAT-HAVE-YOU

Because bowling is a central theme in the movie, they decided the event should be held in a bowling alley. Unfortunately, the only alley in Louisville that they could afford was a Baptist-run establishment that prohibited both drinking and bad language—a problem because it's hard to quote lines from the film without cursing, and because The Dude is rarely seen without a White Russian in hand (at one point he can't find any half-and-half, so he mixes his White Russian using powdered nondairy creamer). Nevertheless, the alley was rented and, with a $42 advertising budget, the "First Annual *Big Lebowski* What-Have-You Fest" was scheduled for October 2002. They expected a handful of their friends to show up and were surprised when 150 people—dressed up as their favorite characters from the movie—arrived for a night of bowling and a screening of the film.

Russell and Shuffitt immediately began making plans for the second festival. Word got around on the Internet, and it proved to be almost too successful: 1,300 devotees showed up to a venue that could only hold 800. The following year 4,000 fans came…and the event's organizers have never looked back—they've added festivals in Las Vegas, New York, Los Angeles, and Austin, Texas.

## THE DUDE ABIDES

The event has taken on a life of its own. A few years ago, strange signs began appearing in the crowds at concerts and sporting events. Back in 2003 they read, "Lebowski 7:19." The next year: "Lebowski 6:19." These are not references to some book of cinematic scripture, they are the dates of the next annual Lebowskifest in Louisville. Keep your eyes peeled—in 2006 they read "Lebowski 9:29."

# FAMILIAR PHRASES

*Here's one of our regular features—the*
*origins of some common terms and phrases.*

## WITH BATED BREATH

**Meaning:** Waiting with great anticipation

**Origin:** "It's so common to see this phrase written as *baited breath* that there's every chance it will soon become the usual form. *Bated* and *baited* sound the same, and we no longer use bated, or its verb, *to bate*, outside this one phrase, so confusion is almost inevitable. *Bated* here is a contraction of *abated* meaning 'reduced or lowered in force.' Bated breath refers to a state in which you almost stop breathing through terror, awe, extreme anticipation, or anxiety." (From *Ballyhoo, Buckaroo, and Spuds*, by Michael Quinion)

## FINE KETTLE OF FISH

**Meaning:** Sorry state of affairs

**Origin:** "A *kiddle* is a basket set in the sluice ways of dams to catch fish, a device well known from the 1200s. Royal officials had the exclusive right to trap fish in kiddles, but poachers often raided the traps, frequently destroying the kiddles in the process. Perhaps an official came upon a destroyed trap and exclaimed, 'That's a pretty kiddle of fish,' or something similar, and the phrase was born. Over the years, *kiddle* was corrupted to *kettle*, giving us the expression as we know it today." (From *Facts on File Encyclopedia of Word and Phrase Origins*, by Robert Hendrickson)

## JURY-RIG

**Meaning:** To create a temporary solution

**Origin:** "The term comes from *jury-mast*, a makeshift mast that was made out of whatever the sailors could find around after a powerful storm ripped down the original mast. No one is really sure where 'jury' in this sense came from, although it could have been a corruption of *injury* and been a sailor's way of making light of the 'ouch' received by the mast. Regardless, the use of the word *jury* spread aboard ship, and by the middle of the 17th century, it was being used in conjunction with anything makeshift. Eventually the term came ashore, in the sense of fixing something or making it ready to go." (From *Scuttlebutt*, by Teri Degler)

## THE WORLD IS YOUR OYSTER

**Meaning:** Countless opportunities are available

**Origin:** "It comes from Shakespeare's *The Merry Wives of Windsor*, which revolves around Falstaff's attempts to gain access to two family fortunes. He is accompanied by a loud braggart named Pistol, who asks to borrow some money. When Falstaff refuses, Pistol boasts, 'Why, then the world's mine oyster, which I with sword will open.' In other words, he'll take what he wants, whenever he wants it, by force. While most who use the phrase today don't have the same dishonorable intentions as Pistol, they do have his boastfulness in common." (From *Inventing English*, by Dale Corey)

## TO THROW THE BOOK

**Meaning:** Issue a severe punishment

**Origin:** "During the 1920s, most U.S. cities caught a wave of violence so severe that strong public sentiment was generated. In response, many states enacted strict laws aimed specifically at habitual criminals. In several instances a fourth conviction carried an automatic sentence of life in prison. Many judges searched for the maximum penalty when given the opportunity to sentence an old offender. Underworld gossip warned thugs to stay out of such courts because these crusaders might 'throw everything in the statute book' at the prisoner." (From *I've Got Goose Pimples*, by Marvin Vanoni)

## TO HAVE A CHIP ON ONE'S SHOULDER

**Meaning:** To be resentful and looking for a challenge

**Origin:** "Under the rules of a game of distance and skill popular in the United States in the 1800s, one person would challenge an opponent to knock a block of wood from his shoulder—whether with an instrument or by hand is unknown—and would then measure the distance the block traveled. As the game grew more heated, the expression carried its quarrelsome connotation." (From *Tenderfeet and Ladyfingers*, by Susan Sperling)

# LIKE, TOTALLY '80s FADS

*Uncle John sure looked rad as he drove his DeLorean to the Wham! concert, wearing his single white glove and brand-new Members Only jacket with the collar turned up.*

## LASER TAG

George Carter got the inspiration while watching *Star Wars* in 1977. It took him years to work out the technology, but in 1984, he opened *Photon*, a laser tag arcade in Dallas, Texas. Played in a futuristic, cavernous arena, Photon let players shoot light beams at each other while climbing on catwalks surrounded by smoke, lights, and sound effects. Receptors on the players' chests recorded "hits"; three hits eliminated a player from the half-hour match. Laser tag became a local phenomenon, and soon Photon arenas sprang up all over the United States. They were riding high when a home version of their game hit stores in 1985. Then came the competition. Worlds of Wonder—the company responsible for the Teddy Ruxpin doll—released *Lazer Tag*, a rip-off of the Photon set that sold better than Photon. Nearly 20 other competitors followed...and they all flopped, except for Lazer Tag, which became *the* hot toy for Christmas 1986. Only problem: Worlds of Wonder couldn't make Lazer Tag sets fast enough to keep up with demand. By the time the company ramped up production, kids had moved on to the next thing. The fad was over, and Worlds of Wonder went bankrupt in 1988. The Photon chain closed in 1989.

## SWATCH WATCHES

In 1983 Switzerland's two biggest watchmakers were on the verge of bankruptcy because of competition from cheap Japanese watches. The companies decided to merge, and they needed to come up with a big new idea...quick. Their idea: the Swatch (short for "second watch")—a brightly colored, casual watch available in a variety of patterns to match the wearer's outfits. Swatches weren't cheap: They cost over $30, a lot for a plastic watch that you'll have to throw away eventually (one of the "features" was that there were no serviceable parts). Still, they were a hit. Teenagers, many of whom wore two or more Swatches at once, bought over 3 million in the first two years and over 100 million by the end of the 1980s.

## GARBAGE PAIL KIDS

In the 1970s, the Topps Company made Wacky Packages, trading cards featuring takeoffs on well-known consumer products (example: "Boo-Hoo" and "Cap'n Crud" instead of Yoo-Hoo and Cap'n Crunch). In 1985 they hired comic-book artist Art Spiegelman to revive the series, and he came up with "Garbage Pail Kids," a parody of the massively popular Cabbage Patch Kids dolls. Each card depicted a character doing something disgusting (Heavin' Steven was a vomiting baby; Fryin' Brian was a boy getting shocked in an electric chair). Topps liked the cards so much that they made it a separate line. They were gross, revolting…and a smash hit. Topps sold more than 200 million packs. But parents objected to the dark subject matter, and, because of the complaints, a planned cartoon series never aired and a 1987 movie bombed. When Coleco, makers of the Cabbage Patch Kids, sued Topps for copyright infringement in 1988, that slammed the lid on the garbage pail. By the time the two companies settled the suit later that year, sales had dwindled so low that the cards went out of print. (Fun fact: Art Spiegelman also wrote the Pulitzer Prize–winning graphic novel *Maus*.)

## FANNY PACKS

Based on a clip-on utility pouch worn by soldiers, fanny packs were first sold to the general public at camping-supply stores in the 1960s. By the early 1980s, they had caught on with Norwegian tourists, who wore them in the United States to keep their valuables safe (they thought America was full of pickpockets). The packs' popularity grew until they were *the* fad of 1988—*Adweek* called the fanny pack "the hottest product of the year"—and the pouches were suddenly everywhere. There were $2 nylon packs with pictures of the Teenage Mutant Ninja Turtles on them for kids, Day-Glo packs for teenagers, and even $200-plus leather models. By the early 1990s, fanny packs, along with most other 1980s fashions, were passé. (But they remain popular with tourists.)

**OTHER 1980s FADS**: Rubik's Cube, the Walkman, *Miami Vice*, Chia Pets, Trivial Pursuit, leg warmers, Monchichis, calculator watches, acid-wash jeans, Max Headroom, the California Raisins, Pogo Balls, the Noid, Hulkamania, aviator shades, break dancing, He-Man, hair crimping, bare midriffs for men, Trapper Keepers, Lee Press-On Nails, jelly shoes, and Big League Chew.

# THE PILGRIMS, PT. II: EXODUS FROM ENGLAND

*Here's the second part of our story of the Pilgrims' treacherous journey to the New World in 1620. (Part I starts on page 44.)*

## REBELS

At the turn of the 17th century, secret congregations of Separatists—Protestants who wanted to worship outside the jurisdiction of the Anglican Church—lived all over England. William Brewster led a congregation in the town of Scrooby...and he was a wanted man. King James and the Church of England had mounted a campaign of oppression against these rebels and others who did not comply with the Church's rules.

William Bradford was another Scrooby Separatist, and years later he would write *History of Plimouth Plantation*. Most of what is known about the Separatists, or the "Pilgrims" as we call them today, comes from Bradford's *History*. Here is his account of their decision to leave England:

> They were hunted and persecuted on every side, so as their former afflictions were as flea-bitings in comparison of these which now came upon them. For some were taken and clapt up in prison, others had their houses besett and watcht night and day.... Yet, seeing themselves thus molested, and that there was no hope of their continuance there, but a joynt consent, they resolved to goe into the Low Countries, where they heard was freedom of religion for all men.

The "Low Countries" he referred to were the Netherlands. Brewster and the other Separatists had relocated to Amsterdam, where there was no oppressive church rule and where, because the Dutch were frequent trading partners with the English, the Separatists felt they would be welcome. And they were...at first.

## REFUGEES

After a short time in Amsterdam, the Separatists settled in Leiden, Holland. But life wasn't much better there. The few educated "Saints," as the Separatists were called in Holland, found work at the university; most of them, however, settled for low-paying laborer jobs. In addition, the Leiden Separatists were often ridiculed for their devout faith by the local Dutch people (some Saints were even stoned in public). Many also feared that their children were losing their English identity. On top of all that, the Dutch were preparing to wage war against Spain. So after a decade of struggle, most of the Separatists chose, as Bradford later wrote, to "return to the prisons of England rather than endure the hardships in Holland."

## A NEW WORLD

King James, they knew, would not welcome them back. In fact, when he learned that several Separatists were returning, James threatened them with exile…unless they pledged allegiance to the Church of England. They refused.

But where else could they go? John Robinson, pastor of the Leiden Separatists in Holland, spoke of a place across the ocean, an English settlement called Jamestown. The colony had been established a few years earlier, and those who returned told of millions of unclaimed acres of fertile land. But there were dangers: lawlessness and anarchy in Jamestown, a few unprovoked Indian attacks, and heretofore unknown diseases. Bradford recalled the group's hesitation as well as their resolve: "It was granted the dangers were great, but not desperate; the difficulties were many, but not invincible."

Ultimately, emigrating was the only move that made sense. They were a people without a place, and this "America" was a place without many people. So in the spring of 1620, the decision was made—a small group of Separatists would make a pilgrimage to America and build a town that would welcome more of their brethren in the future. A delegation of Separatists asked King James to give them a charter and free passage to America; James refused, but promised not to arrest them if they left on their own. The first order of business: Find a ship.

## THE MAYFLOWER

The first historical reference to the *Mayflower* is found in a 1609 Port of London record. The entry indicates that she was a merchant ship traveling between England and the Baltic ports of Northern Europe, transporting "hats, hemp, Spanish salt, hops, vinegar, and Gascon wine" to Drontheim, Norway, and returning with "tar, deals [lumber], and herring." The ship's master was

---

Christopher Jones. (Only British naval ships had captains; merchant ships had masters.) The *Mayflower* was just one of hundreds of similar British sailing vessels. Even the name *Mayflower* was a common moniker for ships back then.

Although this *Mayflower* would become one of the most significant ships in history, to the Separatists she was little more than a ship for hire. And to Master Jones, the Pilgrims weren't pioneers, they were paying customers…he hoped.

Jones named a price that was beyond the Separatists' means. But they were determined to go to America, so they offered Jones and his crew food and valuables to make up the difference. The deal was done. But if Jones had even an inkling of the trouble that awaited him, he might have stuck to shipping cargo.

## PRESSURE TO LEAVE

Time was of the essence. Midsummer was already approaching, and the Separatists needed to leave before the late summer storms began. They also needed to reach America by autumn to ensure sufficient time to build shelter before winter set in. Adding to the time crunch, they had to take the longer, northern route to avoid the tropical shipping lanes that were commonly patrolled by pirates. And at this point, most of the group wasn't even in England—they were still in Holland.

It soon became evident that the *Mayflower* wasn't large enough to carry the 140 passengers and everything they needed to build a town. So the Separatists hired a second, smaller ship called the *Speedwell*. After Pastor John Robinson's farewell sermon, they set sail for America, wondering if they would ever see England again. They would…and soon: Shortly after they reached the open sea, the *Speedwell* sprang a leak.

Both ships had to return to port, where most of the passengers and their belongings were combined onto the *Mayflower*. There was now so little room on board that some of the Separatists who lived in England volunteered to stay behind and remain in hiding for another year. The rest jammed their families onto the already packed *Mayflower*. It was going to be a long trip.

*How would they fare in the North Atlantic?*
*To find out, turn to Part III of the story on page 396.*

---

Go, Charlie, go! By the age of 15, a tuna may have swum over one million miles.

# BAD PRESS

*Anyone who's ever worked on a newspaper, newsletter, magazine, or other publication (including a Bathroom Reader) has made these kinds of goofs. They're not fun...but they're funny.*

## A FINE METH

*City Pages*, a Minneapolis weekly newspaper, ran its annual "Best of the Twin Cities" article in April 2006. Along with such categories as Best Newscaster, Best Museum Exhibit, and Best Theater, they listed Best Cheap Thrill. The winner: "Crystal meth, the drug *methamphetamine*." Despite a firestorm of protest from readers and law-enforcement officials, editor Steve Perry wouldn't apologize, and explained that it was just a joke: "Though it may come as a shock to talk-radio tubthumpers and even a few of our readers," he wrote, "every 'Best of the Twin Cities' issue we've ever done has contained items that were mainly satiric in intent. This is one." That provoked even more of a firestorm; Perry apologized the next day.

## WE'RE NOT STOOPID

The University of Dayton's newspaper, *Flyer News*, ran an article by a communications major decrying the unfair portrayal of communications majors as unintelligent. The headline: "Communications Majors as Smart as Anyone, Stigma Is 'Ignorant' and Rediculous." (They misspelled "ridiculous.") A popular Internet site caught the gaffe and brought the paper some unwanted ridicule. *Flyer* editor-in-chief Jerry Martin was quick to point out that the article's author, junior Lauren Caggiano, did not write the headline and added, "Every newspaper makes mistakes. Most of them just aren't as ironic as that one."

## THEY'RE COMING TO GOT US?

In 2004 *The New York Times* ran a front-page article headlined, "In Tape, Top Aide to Bin Laden Vows New Strikes at U.S.," and quoted what they claimed was a transcript of a newly released tape in which an al-Qaeda aide said, "Bush, reinforce your security measures," and warned of impending and devastating attacks. The only problem: The transcript was from a tape sent *seven months* earlier that had received wide publicity at the time. Two days later the paper printed a correction and an apology.

## ANOTHER FINE METH

In early 2006, the weekly *New Times* of San Luis Obispo, California, ran a cover story entitled "Meth Made Easy." The story included an interview with a longtime meth user, a section titled "What You Can Expect from Your Homemade Meth" (example: "Meet, greet, and sleep with more people than you ever imagined"), and "Meth Fun Facts." In addition to some gruesome facts about meth use, there was this: "A simple meth recipe can turn a $50 investment in cold pills and chemicals into an $8,000 to $10,000 profit." The outcry was so great that in the following week's issue, Editor Jim Mullen, who had given a staff writer the assignment and approved the story, wrote a 1,335-word "explanation and apology." Not good enough: A week later he resigned.

## JUSTICE SAMUEL ASSASSIN

In January 2006, during the Senate confirmation hearings for Samuel Alito's nomination to the Supreme Court, the Purdue University student newspaper, *The Exponent*, ran a front-page brief. See if you can spot the error:

> Supreme Court nominee Samuel Alito told senators Monday that good judges don't have an agenda, don't look for partisan outcomes and always "do what the law requires" as the Senate opened hearings on President Bush's choice for the high court. "A judge can't have any agenda. A judge can't have a preferred outcome in any particular case," Alito told the Judiciary Committee in a brief statement in which he made a distinction between judges and attorneys working for clients. His motive for shooting Pope John Paul in the abdomen on May 13, 1981, remains unclear.

The same day of the Alito hearing, it was announced that Mahmet Ali Agca, who had tried to assassinate the pope in 1981, was being released from prison in Turkey, and the stories got mixed up. The editors quickly issued a correction, explaining that the error had been made by sloppy cutting and pasting, and that there was no ill intent involved.

# STATE NICKNAMES

*You see them on license plates, postcards, and road signs. Ever wonder what they mean? Here are the stories behind a few of them.*

**E**mpire State. From 1788 to 1790, New York City was the capital of the United States, prompting George Washington to refer to it as "the seat of the Empire."

**Yellowhammer State.** During the Civil War, members of the Alabama militia wore a yellow patch of fabric on their shoulders, prompting the nickname, "the Yellowhammers."

**Golden State.** Gold was discovered at Sutter's Mill in California in 1848. The Gold Rush brought so many people to the territory that within two years California qualified for statehood.

**Centennial State.** Colorado became a state in 1876, the 100th anniversary of the Declaration of Independence.

**Keystone State.** A keystone is a central stone in an arch that holds all the other stones together. At a rally for President Thomas Jefferson in 1802, a delegate called Pennsylvania "the keystone of the federal union."

**Sunshine State.** Florida. It's sunny there.

**Hoosier State.** John Finley wrote a poem about Indiana, titled "The Hoosier's Nest," which became popular when it was published in the *Indianapolis Journal* in 1833. "Hoosier" then became a slang term for an Indiana resident. Although the word's origins are unclear, one theory is that it's a greeting from Indiana's frontier days: One person would shout "Hello, the cabin!" from far away, to avoid getting shot. Someone in the house would yell back, "Who's there?" which got slurred to "Hoosier."

**Silver State.** A massive reserve of silver, the Comstock Lode, was discovered in Nevada in 1859.

**Garden State.** Travelers who drive on the New Jersey Turnpike and see the state's oil refineries and shopping malls might be surprised to know that it was once mostly farmland.

**Show Me State.** Nineteenth-century congressman Willard Vandiver once commented that people in Missouri are so stubborn, they don't believe anything unless they can see it. The name stuck.

**Tar Heel State.** Legend says that during a Civil War battle, a troop of North Carolina soldiers were left fighting all alone. Battalions from other states had either perished or fled, but the North Carolinians stayed, "as if their heels were stuck to the ground with tar." Reflecting both their perseverance (and North Carolina's tar industry), the troop became known as "the tar heel boys."

**Equality State.** Wyoming was the first state to give women the right to vote.

**Land of 10,000 Lakes.** What state? Minnesota, where there are actually more than *12,000* lakes.

**Sooner State.** In 1884 the former Indian territory of Oklahoma was opened to white settlers, who could claim property in a series of scheduled land runs. But a few sneaky settlers went in "too soon" and claimed the best parcels of land before the rush officially began. They earned the nickname "sooners."

**Beaver State.** There were once so many beavers in Oregon that it became the official state animal. Sadly, there aren't many left today—early settlers and trappers nearly eradicated the animal from the state.

**Lone Star State.** From 1836 to 1845, Texas was an independent republic. When it became a state in 1845, it kept its flag, which features a single, or "lone," star.

**Beehive State.** Utah picked the beehive as its state logo, not because there's a preponderance of bees there, but to represent industry and perseverance.

**Green Mountain State.** Vermont is home to the Green Mountains. In French, *Vermont* means "green" (*ver*) "mountain" (*mont*).

**Old Dominion.** Virginia became a British colony in 1607. It was among the English territories that remained loyal to the crown during the English civil war in the 1640s. King Charles II called his loyal lands his "old dominion."

# PERUVIAN PUNCH

*Here's a spirited piece of American history from the
Culinary Division of the Bathroom Readers' Institute.*

## THE RUSH

In 1848 the total population of San Francisco was only
900. Then gold was discovered at Sutter's Mill, and the
Gold Rush was on, luring thousands of fortune seekers to the area.
By the time California entered the union as the 31st state in 1850,
the population of San Francisco had exploded to 35,000. More
than half of the new San Franciscans were foreigners who had
sailed into the port, including hundreds of "ladies of the night"
who had come from Peru to help the forty-niners spend the gold
they dug out of the Sierra Nevadas. But the ladies weren't the only
Peruvian imports. Some of the food—and most of the brandy—
consumed in the City by the Bay also came from that country, too.

Why Peru, and not the eastern United States? In 1850 the
states were "united" in name only. The eastern portion stretched
from Texas back to the Atlantic; the western part comprised California and the Oregon Territory. There was no railroad across the
thousand-mile gap, and no Panama Canal. Goods from the East
had to be shipped all the way around the horn of South America.
Peru, on the north end of South America, was much closer, so
shipping its goods to California was cheaper and faster.

Pisco, a brandy from the town of the same name, was the most
popular import from that South American republic. And one of
the most popular places to drink it was the Bank Exchange and
Billiard Saloon at the corner of Montgomery and Washington
Streets, where the Transamerica Pyramid now stands in San Francisco's Financial District.

## PUNCH IT UP

Four decades later, a Scottish immigrant named Duncan Nicol
bought the Bank Exchange, which was still serving Pisco brandy. To
advertise his new saloon, Nicol invented a new cocktail, which he
called "Pisco Punch." One local writer described it thus: "It tastes
like lemonade, but comes back with the kick of a roped steer."

Pisco brandy was distilled from grapes grown in volcanic soil, which gave it an acidic, slightly sweet flavor…that masked its potency. With no quality-control regulations, some bottles had the same alcoholic content as whiskey. So, to protect customers from the hidden "punch" of his sweet concoction, Nicol posted a restriction: A patron could be served only two Pisco Punches; the drink was too powerful to let anyone exceed that limit. (The rule was tested when John Mackay, a miner who'd struck it rich in Nevada and was supposedly the wealthiest man in America, had two drinks and then ordered another. Nicol stuck to his principles —technically. He made Mackay leave the saloon, walk around the block, and re-enter to qualify as a new customer.)

## A PUNCH WITH PUNCH

The cocktail earned rave notices from all over the world.

• American journalist Thomas W. Knox wrote of it: "The second glass was sufficient. I felt I could face smallpox, all the fevers known to man, and Asiatic cholera if need be."

• Rudyard Kipling wrote about it when he visited San Francisco in 1889. "I have a theory," he said, "that it is composed of the shavings of cherub's wings, the glory of a tropical dawn, the red clouds of sunset, and the lost epics of dead masters."

## THE LAST DROP

Duncan Nicol was forced to close the Bank Exchange when the U.S. Congress passed the Volstead Act in 1919, making the sale of alcohol illegal. But Nicol never divulged the recipe for his Pisco Punch, and he took the secret formula with him when he died in 1926. Several recipes have surfaced throughout the years, but none has been proven to be the real thing. Here's an easy recipe that is said to give a good approximation of the original:

### Ingredients
3 oz. Pisco brandy
1 tsp. lime juice
1 tsp. pineapple juice
2 oz. cold water (optional)

Combine ingredients in a brandy snifter; stir. For a touch of authenticity, add two or three cubes of fresh pineapple.

# MOVIE REVIEW HAIKU

*The classic Japanese poetry form—three lines of 5, 7,
and 5 syllables each—collides with pop culture.*

### Planet of the Apes
Like *Batman*—great sets,
Bad plots, and promised sequels.
Damn them all to Hell!

### Duck Soup
A fine collection
Of skits destined to inspire
The great Bugs Bunny.

### 2001: A Space Odyssey
Great special effects,
Without help from computers!
(Except HAL, of course.)

### Apocalypse Now
Brilliant filmmaking
Overly long indulgence
Don't get off the boat

### Erin Brockovich
Julia Roberts
Is Erin Brockovich in
*Erin Brockovich!*

### The Matrix Revolutions
Directors, take note:
Franchise isn't everything.
Just let it die. Please.

### March of the Penguins
An interesting
And exciting adventure
—if you're a penguin.

### Cast Away
Made fire? Big deal.
Girlfriend dumped you anyway.
Stop talking to balls.

### The Sixth Sense
One of those movies
I'd have rather seen before
I saw the preview.

### American Pie
Rated R: No one
Over 17 allowed
Without teenager.

### Airplane
"Surely you are not
Critiquing this!" "I am. And
Don't call me Shirley."

### Groundhog Day
You will want to see
This movie several times.
Uh, sorry. Bad joke.

### Forrest Gump
Mama always said,
"Stupid is as Stupid does."
Stupid rakes it in.

### My Big Fat Greek Wedding
My big fat romance
Disguised as a really long
Windex commercial.

---

Actress Mary Pickford, nicknamed "America's Sweetheart," was Canadian.

# TURKMENBASHI

*After the USSR broke up in 1991, the Soviet Republic
of Turkmenistan became an independent nation but
had no identity of its own. Enter Turkmenbashi.*

## BACKGROUND

Turkmenistan had been under the control of Russia for
more than a quarter century when it was declared part of
the Soviet Union in 1924. In 1991, after the fall of Communism
and the USSR, the country found itself independent for the first
time in a hundred years. The new president, Saparmurat Niyazov,
was the obvious successor—he'd been the Communist Party's
puppet governor since 1985. But easing a country of five million
people into a new era of self-sufficiency and autonomy was not the
highest item on Niyazov's agenda. He was more concerned that
decades of Soviet control had left Turkmenistan with no national
identity. So, in 1993, Niyazov took it upon himself to create the
country in a new image: his own.

First he took the name *Turkmenbashi* (Leader of All Ethnic
Turkmen) and declared himself President for Life. Since then, he's
undertaken scores of self-aggrandizing—and bizarre—measures to
make Turkmenistan a very unique place:

• The airport in the capital city of Ashgabat was renamed...
Turkmenbashi.

• Dozens of streets and schools across the country are now called...
Turkmenbashi.

• In 1998 a 670-pound meteorite landed in Turkmenistan. Scientists named it...Turkmenbashi.

• The name of the large port city Krasnovodsk was changed to...
Turkmenbashi.

• The new president also renamed the months. January is now
called...Turkmenbashi. April is called Gurbansoltan edzhe, after
his mother. (Bread, once called *chorek*, is now also called *gurbansoltan edzhe*.)

• The image of Turkmenbashi's face is used as the logo of all three state-run TV stations, and is legally required to appear on every clock and watch face as well as on every bottle of Turkmenbashi brand vodka.

• In 2001 Turkmenbashi wrote a book—a combination of poetry, revisionist history, and moral guidelines—called *Ruhnama* (Persian for "Book of the Soul"). It is now required to be prominently displayed in all bookstores and government offices, and next to the Koran in mosques. Memorization of the book is required to graduate from school and to get a state job or even a driver's license. Schoolchildren spend one entire day every week reading it. Since all Soviet-era books have been banned, most Turkmen libraries have only the *Ruhnama* and other books written by Turkmenbashi. In 2006 Turkmenbashi made reading the *Ruhnama* a requirement for entry into heaven.

• There's a 30-foot *Ruhnama* in Ashgabat, not far from a 50-foot solid-gold statue of Turkmenbashi.

• Not surprisingly, Turkmenbashi recently "won" the Magtymguly International Prize, honoring the best pro-Turkmen poetry, which is awarded by…Turkmenbashi himself.

## MORE STRANGE ACTS OF TURKMENBASHI

• In 2004 Turkmenbashi banned newscasters from wearing make-up. Why? He said he couldn't tell the male and female news readers apart and that made him uncomfortable.

• After he quit smoking in 1997, he banned smoking for everybody else, too (but only in public places).

• In 2006, to mark Turkmenistan's independence day, Turkmenbashi gave each female resident a gift of 200,000 *manat* (about $38).

• He banned gold tooth caps and gold teeth, and suggested that tooth preservation could be more easily accomplished by chewing on bones.

• In 2000 he ordered that a giant lake be created in the desert along with a huge forest of cedar trees, which, he said, would help to moderate Turkmenistan's climate.

• In 2004 he ordered that a giant ice palace be built in the middle of that same desert, the Karakum—the hottest location in central Asia. It will include a zoo with penguins.

# AMAZING ANAGRAMS

*What's an anagram for "anagrams"? The Latin phrase* ars magna, *which means "great art." We're not sure if it's great art, but rearranging the letters in a word or phrase to make a similar word or phrase sure is fun.*

STONE AGE *becomes…*
**STAGE ONE**

ELECTION RESULTS
*becomes…*
**LIES! LET'S RECOUNT!**

AUSTRALIA *becomes…*
**A TRIAL USA**

MCDONALD'S
RESTAURANTS *becomes…*
**UNCLE SAM'S
STANDARD ROT**

IVANHOE BY SIR WALTER
SCOTT *becomes…*
**A NOVEL BY A
SCOTTISH WRITER**

SEVEN-ELEVEN
INCORPORATED *becomes…*
**OPEN IT AND NEVER
EVER CLOSE**

THE ROADRUNNER AND
WILE E. COYOTE *becomes…*
**TRY A CARTOON DUEL
WHERE NONE DIE**

THE LEANING TOWER
OF PISA *becomes…*
**I SPOT ONE GIANT
FLAW HERE**

GASTROENTEROLOGIST
*becomes…* **I LET GO
TORRENTS O' GAS**

WILLIAM SHATNER
*becomes…*
**HI, SWELL MARTIAN!**

THE MEANING OF LIFE
*becomes…* **THE FINE
GAME OF NIL**

THE THREE STOOGES:
LARRY, CURLY AND
MOE *becomes…*
**ACTORS? LORD,
THEY'RE AN UGLY
THREESOME!**

JUSTIN TIMBERLAKE
*becomes…* **I'M A JERK,
BUT LISTEN**

WASHINGTON *becomes…*
**HOGS WANT IN**

SGT. PEPPER'S LONELY
HEARTS CLUB BAND
*becomes…* **CRAP LP
SUNG BY THE LSD-
PRONE BEATLES**

TRUTH IS *becomes…*
**IT HURTS**

Isaac Asimov, Bob Hope, and Bela Lugosi all passed through Ellis Island as immigrants.

# NATURAL GAS REPORT

*A page of stories that will clear the room.*

**R**AN OUT OF GAS
In 1996 six police cruisers in Edmonton, Alberta, descended on an armored car and forced it to the side of the road. The driver had been opening and closing his door—which the police assumed was a signal for help. It wasn't. He was simply airing out the cab of the truck because of his partner's...emissions.

## CAN'T BLAME THE DOG ANYMORE
In 2006 a company in Cedar Rapids, Iowa, introduced underwear for dogs ("thong design") with a charcoal filter to neutralize the offending odor of dog farts.

## HE SHOULD GET HAZARD PAY
Goran Andervass of Stockholm, Sweden, won an unfair-dismissal lawsuit against his former employer, the Swedish bank Riksbanken, and was awarded the equivalent of $100,000. Court papers said that Andervass verbally abused a co-worker after being "provoked by a disgusting fart—a right stinker—at 7:30 a.m. in my office." He'd complained to a supervisor, but the colleague "would neither admit nor confirm that he farted." Unable to cope with the controversy that followed, Andervass took an extended leave—and was then fired. As a result of the lawsuit, employees at the bank were warned about "farting too obviously near others."

## HATE YOUR JOB? IT COULD BE WORSE!
In *Uncle John's All-Purpose Extra-Strength Bathroom Reader* (published in 2000), we told you about Dr. Michael Levitt, a Minneapolis-based gastroenterologist who invented a breath test to determine a person's propensity for flatulence. In October 2003, *Popular Science* magazine compiled a list of the "Worst Jobs in Science." Included on that list: Dr. Levitt's employees ("flatus odor judges"). Their job is to feed test subjects pinto beans, collect the gas that results using plastic tubing, and sniff them—as many as 100 a day—to determine the strength of the farts.

Arctic Circle is the name of a street in Santa Claus, Indiana.

# ODD-O-MOBILES

*We were driven to write this page on unusual cars.*

**P**HILION ROAD CARRIAGE: One of the oldest American automobiles, patented in 1892 by showman Achille Philion. It had a 2-cylinder, 1 horsepower, steam-powered engine; had a movable steering wheel (it could go on the front or back of the car); and could reach 8 mph. The chauffeur sat in the back to maintain the steam boiler. Only one was built: It was a big hit at the 1893 Chicago World's Fair. Want to see it? It appeared in the 1942 Orson Welles film, *The Magnificent Ambersons*, and now resides at the National Automobile Museum in Reno, Nevada.

**AWZ P70:** This East German car looked like the typical boxy Euro-sedan from the 1950s, but the "P" in AWZ P70 stood for "plastic"—that's what the body was made of (there was a steel embargo imposed on Soviet Bloc countries). Today it's not unusual for cars to be made of plastic, but the P70 was one of the world's first. (Another early plastic car: the 1953 Chevy Corvette.)

**S-CARGO:** *Escargot* is French for "snail," and that's what this Nissan car/van looked like, with a tiny hood and a large, bubble-shaped body. (Nissan claimed S-Cargo stood for "small cargo.") Available only in Japan, about 12,000 sold between 1989 and 1992.

**DYMAXION:** The brainchild of R. Buckminster Fuller, *Dymaxion* stood for "dynamic, maximum, and tension." This 3-wheeled, bullet-shaped car was 20 feet long, had a Ford V-8 engine driving the two front wheels, and was steered via the single rear wheel, which allowed it to turn on a dime. It had room for 11 passengers and could travel at a top speed of about 120 mph, getting an unheard-of 25 to 30 mpg. And it had a periscope...instead of a rear window. A test run of the prototype at the 1933 Chicago World's Fair resulted in a rollover, killing the driver. The crash was blamed on the steering, but many say another vehicle caused it. In any case, financial backers pulled out, and only three cars were built in 1933 and 1934. Just one exists today.

---

Estimated weight of Egypt's Great Pyramid: 6,648,000 tons.

# BUREAUCRACY IN ACTION

*People of the world, rest easy: We've discovered proof
that your tax dollars are being well spent.*

The *Hindustan Times* reported in 2005 that the city of New Delhi employs 97 paid rat-catchers. What's odd about that? They haven't caught a single rat since 1994. (And, according to the *Times*, there are a *lot* of rats in New Delhi.)

• In October 2005, the Department of Homeland Security awarded a $36,300 grant to the state of Kentucky. Purpose of the grant: to prevent terrorists from using bingo halls to raise money.

• Father Anthony Sutch had to call an electrician to change four lightbulbs on the 40-foot ceiling of St. Benet's Church in Suffolk, England. In the past he used a local firm to do it and paid them £200 ($370), which he thought was pretty steep to change four bulbs. But government safety regulations now prohibit the workers from using a ladder—they have to erect scaffolding instead. Result: In 2005 the church spent £1,300 ($2,450) to change the bulbs.

• In 2003 Congress agreed to subsidize the Alaska Fisheries Marketing Board, a salmon industry trade organization. The AFMB used the money to paint an Alaska Airlines 737 jet to look like a salmon (the jet's nickname: "Salmon-Thirty-Salmon"). Cost: $500,000. The subsidy was proposed by Sen. Ted Stevens, whose son, Ben Stevens, happens to be the chairman of the AFMB.

• The Youth Outreach Unit of Blue Springs, Missouri (population: 48,000) received $273,000 to combat teenage "goth" culture.

• In 1981 the U.S. Army spent $6,000 in federal funds to create a 17-page manual for government agencies on how to properly select and purchase a bottle of Worcestershire sauce.

• What did the U.S. government spend $24.5 billion on in 2003? Nobody knows. According to the General Accounting Office, that's how much the federal government couldn't account for that year.

---

Why did the U.S. Treasury start printing paper money in 1862? There was a coin shortage.

# BELIEVE!

*Hungry for inspiration? Then tack one of
these inspiring quotes to your refrigerator.*

"Believe it is possible to solve your problem. Tremendous things happen to the believer. Believe the answer will come. It will."
—**Norman Vincent Peale**

"Within each of us is a hidden store of determination—determination to keep us in the race when all seems lost."
—**Roger Dawson**

"Your diamonds are not in far distant mountains or in yonder seas; they are in your own backyard, if you but dig for them."
—**Russell H. Conwell**

"We must accept finite disappointment, but we must never lose infinite hope."
—**Martin Luther King, Jr.**

"All adverse and depressing influences can be overcome, not by fighting, but by rising above them."
—**Charles Caleb Colton**

"Never, never, never give up."
—**Winston Churchill**

"To live long and achieve happiness, cultivate the art of radiating happiness."
—**Malcolm Forbes**

"Optimism is the faith that leads to achievement. Nothing can be done without hope and confidence."
—**Helen Keller**

"It may be that those who do most, dream most."
—**Stephen Butler Leacock**

"Kindness is a language which the deaf can hear and the blind can read."
—**Mark Twain**

"What would you attempt to do if you knew you would not fail?"
—**Dr. Robert Schuller**

"Be who you are and say what you feel, because those who mind don't matter and those who matter don't mind."
—**Dr. Seuss**

"Dream as if you'll live forever. Live as if you'll die today."
—**James Dean**

Hindu holy days begin at sunrise, Jewish holy days at sunset, and Christian holy days at midnigh

# RIDDLE ME THIS

*Some classic brain challenges. (Answers on page 519.)*

**1.** Without being called,
they come at night.
Without being stolen,
they are lost in the day.
*What are they?*

**2.** Two legs have I,
and this will confound:
Only at rest do they
touch the ground.
*Who am I?*

**3.** I went to the woods.
That's where I got it.
I brought it home with me
because I couldn't find it.
*What is it?*

**4.** Although I am served,
You do not want me.
But once you have me,
You don't want to lose me.
*What am I?*

**5.** I lose a head in the morning,
but get it back at night.
*What am I?*

**6.** Neither bus nor train,
nor cab, nor plane,
I transport you once
and then never again.
*What am I?*

**7.** I have seven letters:
The first two stand for a boy.
The first three stand for a girl.
The first four are a brave boy.
The first six are addictive.
But all of my letters together
stand for a brave girl.
*What am I?*

**8.** Stand and I disappear.
Sit and I reappear.
*What am I?*

**9.** I know what my job is,
The point has been made.
You say I have a big head?
It's true, I'm afraid.
What I need most
Is to be driven home.
So put me in my place
And then leave me alone.
*What am I?*

**10.** Try to keep me, because if
you lose me, those around you
will lose theirs as well.
*What am I?*

**11.** I do not breathe, yet I run.
I do not eat, yet I sleep.
I do not drink, yet I swim.
I do not think, yet I grow.
I cannot see you, but you
see me every day.
*What am I?*

**12.** Large as mountains,
small as peas, endlessly swimming
in waterless seas.
*Who are they?*

---

Ready for Jurassic Park? In 2005, scientists found soft tissue—blood vessels—from a **T. rex.**

# DEATH DEFIERS?

*Is it a fact that some people live a lot longer than the rest of us? Sometimes it is…and sometimes it isn't.*

## THE 100+ CLUB

Humans are living longer than ever—average life spans are greater now than at any other time in recorded history. In the United States alone, there are more than 50,000 people over 100 years of age. Centenarians are the fastest-growing age group in America, projected to top 800,000 by 2050. But there have always been tales of places around the world where people have commonly lived uncommonly long lives, unmarred by disease and full of vigor—even in eras when the average human life span was only 30 or 40 years. One of the most popular tales is that of the Hunza, who live in the snow-capped peaks of the Hindu Kush.

## THEY'RE PUTTING YOU HUNZA

Living in a secluded region between towering peaks in the Karakorum Mountains, the people of the Hunza Valley of northern Pakistan have been left to themselves for centuries. In their isolation, they have farmed their terraced fields and enjoyed lives of enviable tranquillity. Throughout central Asia, the *Hunzakut*, as they call themselves, are legendary for their good health. Many Hunza elders claim to be well over 100 years of age, a feat they credit to the simple lives they lead: a diet of fresh vegetables, fruits (including plenty of apricots), nuts, and grains, with very little meat and almost no sugar; plenty of exercise climbing up and down the steep slopes of their valley; respect and veneration traditionally given to the elderly; and a good sense of humor.

The Hunza also lack something that is missing in many underdeveloped regions of the world that claim to have large numbers of people living to age 120 and beyond: no pesky *birth certificates* to contradict wildly exaggerated claims of longevity. The "myth of the Hunza"—and it is only a myth—was helped along in the 1940s and again in the 1970s when westerners visited the region and passed along tales of locals claiming to be well over 100 years of age without having any way of verifying whether they were true. Subsequent scientific research has demonstrated the claims were false—thanks to poor diet and even poorer access to medical care, the life expectancy of the Hunza people is actually *lower* than that of the United States. The same has been true with other regions that claim extraordinary longevity, including Vilcabamba, in southern Ecuador, and the people of the Caucasus mountains of Georgia, a former republic of the Soviet Union.

## RESPECT YOUR ELDERS

What motivates people in some traditional societies to exaggerate their ages so dramatically? Illiteracy and underdevelopment are often factors—accurate birth and death records are not kept, leaving people with little education to guess at their true ages. And in societies where the elderly are held in great esteem and the oldest person in the village occupies a position of especially high status, the temptation to exaggerate one's age can be overwhelming. It's also not unheard of for people in traditional societies, the Hunza included, to award themselves what are in effect "extra credit" years for life experience. A 57-year-old Hunza farmer who thinks he's seen a lot in life, for example, might tack on as many as 70 extra years for accumulated wisdom and claim an age of 127.

In the case of the people of the Caucasus mountains of Georgia, it was common for World War I deserters from the Russian military to assume the identities of deceased elders to avoid detection. Once these Georgians assumed new identities—and once Georgia became part of the Soviet Union—they had little choice but to stick with their new identities from then on.

## NO KIDDING

So what area of the world really can claim to have the world's greatest life expectancy? The islands of Okinawa in southern Japan. On these islands, the average life expectancy is 81.2 years, compared to 79.9 for all of Japan and 76.8 for the United States. The islands have maintained a family registry system since 1879, so the ages of all its citizens can be verified.

Okinawa also boasts a larger percentage of centenarians than just about any place on earth—34 per 100,000. The U.S., by contrast, has just over 10 per 100,000. Elderly Okinawans also have lower rates of cancer, heart disease, Alzheimer's, and other chronic illnesses related to aging. And unlike centenarians in other parts of the world, Okinawa's centenarians tend to remain healthy late in life and only experience a rapid decline in health shortly before death. To what do researchers attribute their long lives? Good genes, a healthy lifestyle and diet, a cultural emphasis on preventative medicine, and access to good healthcare. (Proof that good genes aren't enough by themselves: Younger Okinawans, who have abandoned the traditional Okinawa lifestyle, have a higher mortality rate than their counterparts in the rest of Japan.)

## LONGEVITY RULES

So you want to live to 100 without moving to Okinawa? Here are some tips, including a few that may surprise you:

**1. Don't get fat.** Obesity is the #1 factor in reducing life span. Follow a diet low in fat and meat, with lots of fruits and veggies.

**2. Don't smoke.** Du-u-u-uh.

**3. Keep calm.** If you can't avoid stressful situations, find a way to "go with the flow" when you're in them.

**4. Keep moving.** Exercise keeps you flexible and strong.

**5. Have sex.** A study in the *British Medical Journal* showed that men ages 45–59 who had sex once a month or less were twice as likely to die as men who had sex twice a week or more. (Sorry, no data available on the benefits for women.)

**6. Stay together.** Long-term relationships are more important for men than women, who seem to survive without their spouses just fine. But according to research, single men are twice as likely to die early than married men.

**7. Have children, but have them later.** This just in: Many female centenarians didn't have kids until after the age of 35. In fact, women over 100 are four times more likely than the average population to have had their first child after 40.

**8. Hit the sack.** The American Cancer Society reports that people who sleep seven hours per night have the lowest mortality rate. But don't overdo it: Nine hours is as bad for you as four.

\*     \*     \*

"Age is an issue of mind over matter.
If you don't mind, it doesn't matter." —**Mark Twain**

---

On a diet? King penguin chicks may go as long as five months between meals.

# MYTH-CONCEPTIONS

*"Common knowledge" is frequently wrong. Here are some examples.*

**M**YTH: There is a "dark side" of the moon.
FACT: Pink Floyd was wrong—there is no dark side. There's a near side, which always faces Earth, and a far side, which always faces away. When the moon is between the sun and the Earth, the far side is sunny and bright—we just can't see it.

**MYTH:** The main cause of hearing loss is aging.
**FACT:** Many people's hearing does start to go as they get older, but it is not a natural aging process. The primary cause of hearing loss is cumulative exposure to loud noises.

**MYTH:** Raindrops are tear-shaped.
**FACT:** Small raindrops are spherical. Larger raindrops are oval, flattening out in the middle. Really big ones resemble parachutes.

**MYTH:** Spicy foods can cause ulcers.
**FACT:** An ulcer is caused by a bacterial infection. Spicy foods may aggravate an existing ulcer, but they won't give you one.

**MYTH:** Show business is the largest employer in Los Angeles.
**FACT:** Hollywood may be the entertainment capital of the world, and everyone in L.A. may *want* to be in show business, but the largest industry in Los Angeles County is manufacturing.

**MYTH:** Adding salt to water will make it boil faster.
**FACT:** Actually, adding salt makes the water take *longer* to boil. But that's a good thing—it boils at a higher temperature, which makes the pasta (or whatever's in the pot) cook faster.

**MYTH:** Red-headed people have bad tempers.
**FACT:** Many cultures have myths about redheads (the ancient Greeks said redheads became vampires after death). Hair color has nothing to do with emotion…although a 2002 study *did* find that redheads require 20% more anesthesia than blondes or brunettes.

---

Skiers beware: There are about 250,000 avalanches every year in the Alps.

# THE NUTMEG WARS

*In the 17th century, all Europe was mad to have the little brown nut from Indonesia—nutmeg. Especially the Dutch, who monopolized its cultivation and, in doing so, built their tiny nation into one of the wealthiest trading powers on the planet.*

## BACKGROUND

Spices have been used by human beings for millennia for food preparation and preservation, medicine, and even embalming. But until modern times they were largely an Asian commodity, and controlling their flow to the spice-obsessed West meant power and fortune for the middlemen. Over the centuries these hugely successful merchants were Phoenicians, Persians, Arabs, and later, Venetians.

Many of the great European explorations of the 15th century were driven by the need to bypass the Arab and Venetian monopoly. Crying, "For Christ and spices," the Portuguese explorer Vasco da Gama shocked the Arab world when he sailed around Africa's Cape of Good Hope in 1498 and showed up in the spice markets of India. It marked the beginning of the decline of Arab dominance and the rise of European power. For the next 100 years, as Spain and Portugal fought for control of the spice trade, the tiny countries of England and the Netherlands looked on in envy, waiting for their chance to get a piece of the action. It came first for the Dutch.

## THE DUTCH EAST INDIA COMPANY

Always in danger of being overwhelmed by their much larger neighbor, Spain, the Portuguese began subcontracting their spice distribution to Dutch traders. Profits began to flow into Amsterdam, and the Dutch commercial fleet swiftly grew into one of the largest in the world. The Dutch quietly gained control of most of the shipping and trading of spices in Northern Europe. Then, in 1580, Portugal fell under Spanish rule and the sweet deal for Dutch traders was over. As prices for pepper, nutmeg, and other spices soared across Europe, the Dutch found themselves locked out of the market. They decided to fight back.

---

Boing! Boing! The rubber used to make SuperBalls is called Zectron.

In 1602 Dutch merchants founded the VOC—the Vereenigde Oostindische Compagnie, better known as the Dutch East India Company. Other trading nations had formed cooperative associations like it but none were more successful than the Dutch. By 1670 the VOC was the richest commercial operation in the world. The company had 50,000 employees worldwide, with a private army of 30,000 men and a fleet of 200 ships. Yet even with that huge overhead, the VOC gave its shareholders an eye-popping annual dividend of 40% on their investments. How'd they do it? With sheer ruthlessness…and nutmeg.

## MUST-HAVE

By the time the VOC was formed, nutmeg was already the favored spice in Europe. Aside from adding flavor to foods and drinks, its aromatic qualities worked wonders to disguise the stench of decay in poorly preserved meats, always a problem in the days before refrigeration. Then the plague years of the 17th century came. Thousands were dying across Europe, and doctors were desperate for a way to stop the spread of the disease. They decided nutmeg held the cure. Ladies carried nutmeg sachets around their necks to breathe through and avoid the pestilence in the air. Men added nutmeg to their snuff and inhaled it. Everybody wanted it, and many were willing to spare no expense to have it. Ten pounds of nutmeg cost one English penny at its Asian source, but had a London street value of 2 pounds, 10 shillings—68,000 times its original cost. The only problem was the short supply. And that's where the Dutch found their opportunity.

## BRUTAL RULERS

Why was nutmeg so rare? The tree grew in only one place in the world: the Banda Islands of Indonesia. A tiny archipelago rising only a few meters above sea level, the islands were ruled by sultans who insisted on maintaining a neutral trading policy with foreign powers. This allowed them to avoid the presence of Portuguese or Spanish garrisons on their soil, but it also left them unprotected from other invaders. In 1621 the Dutch swept in and took over.

Once securely in control of the Bandas, the Dutch went to work protecting their new "investment." First they preempted any resistance by the islanders by executing every male over the age of 15. Village leaders were beheaded and their heads displayed on poles to discourage any rebels who might have survived. Within 15 years, the brutal regime reduced the Bandanese population from 15,000 to 600. Next the Dutch concentrated all nutmeg production into a few easily guarded areas, uprooting and destroying any trees outside the plantation zones. Anyone caught growing a nutmeg seedling or carrying seeds without the proper authority was put to death. In addition, all exported nutmeg seeds were drenched with lime to make sure there was no chance a fertile nut would find its way off the islands.

## I'LL TAKE MANHATTAN

The Dutch had their monopoly…almost. One of the Banda Islands, called Run, was under control of the British. The little sliver of land (a fishing boat could only make landfall at high tide) was one of England's first colonial outposts, dating to 1603. The Dutch attacked it in force in 1616, but it would take four years for them to finally defeat the combined British-Bandanese resistance. But the English still didn't give up; they continued to press their claim to the island through two Anglo-Dutch Wars.

The battles exhausted both sides, leading to a compromise settlement, the Treaty of Breda, in 1667—and one of history's greatest ironies. Intent on securing their hold over every nutmeg island in Southeast Asia, the Dutch offered a trade: If the British would give them Run, they would in turn give Britain a far-away, much less valuable island that the English had already occupied illegally since 1664. The British agreed. That other island: Manhattan, which is how New Amsterdam became New York.

## MONOPOLY OVER

The Dutch now had complete control of the nutmeg trade. A happy ending for Holland? Hardly. By the end of the 17th century, the Dutch East India Company was bankrupt. Constant wars with rival powers, rebellions from the islanders, and plain bad luck—some might say bad karma—eventually broke the back of the Dutch spice cartel.

**Strike 1:** In 1770 a Frenchman named Pierre Poivre ("Peter Pepper") successfully smuggled nutmeg plants to safety in Mauritius, an

---

Off to a good start: As a child, Houdini often broke into his family's locked cookie cupboard.

island off the coast of Africa, where they were subsequently exported to the Caribbean. The plants thrived in the islands, especially on Grenada.

**Strike 2:** In 1778 a volcanic eruption in the Banda region caused a tsunami that wiped out half of the nutmeg groves.

**Strike 3:** In 1809 the English returned to Indonesia and seized the Banda Islands by force. They returned the islands to the Dutch in 1817, but not before transplanting hundreds of nutmeg seedlings to plantations in India, Ceylon (now Sri Lanka), and Singapore.

The Dutch were out; their nutmeg monopoly was over. While they would go on to have success trading steel and coal (not to mention tulips), the Netherlands declined as a colonial power, and they never again dominated European commerce.

*Still have a craving for spices? Turn to page 190 for the strange history of six others.*

\*　　　\*　　　\*

## MORE FAVORITE FOREIGN PHRASES

**KUSAT' SEBE LOKTI (Russian)**
**Translation:** "[Don't] bite your elbows."
**Meaning:** Don't cry over spilled milk; don't get upset over things you can't control.

**TRITTBRETTFAHRER (Germany)**
**Translation:** "Running-board rider"
**Meaning:** Someone who benefits from someone else's hard work.

**YI LUAN TOU SHI (China)**
**Translation:** "[Don't] throw an egg against a rock."
**Meaning:** Don't create problems for yourself by assuming you're stronger than you are.

**KINGO NO FUNI (Japan)**
**Translation:** "Goldfish crap"
**Meaning:** A sycophant or hanger-on. (Sometimes when a goldfish does its business, the business remains attached to its rear end for a while before falling off.)

**Boob tube:** In the average American home, the TV is on for 7 hours and 40 minutes every day.

# THE BLACK PANTIES BANDIT STRIKES AGAIN

*When it comes to disguises, crooks can be very creative. We once read about a guy who smeared his face with Vaseline before he robbed a bank, figuring the security cameras couldn't photograph him through the hazy goop (they could; he was arrested). Yes, there are some odd and outlandish thieves out there. Like the ones dressed up…*

**…AS UTILITY WORKERS:** In 2005 the Associated Press reported that in Baltimore a group of thieves disguised as city utility workers had stolen more than 120 street light poles. They said the thieves put up orange traffic cones around their "work area" while they dismantled and made away with the 30-foot-tall, 250-pound aluminum poles. (Why would anyone steal a light pole? Police theorize that they were stealing them to sell as scrap metal.)

**…AS PRIESTS:** Police in Serbia said three men disguised as Orthodox Christian priests, complete with fake beards and ankle-length cossacks, entered a bank in Serbia, gave the traditional "Christ is born" greeting, then pulled shotguns out of their robes. Within minutes they had made off with more than $300,000.

**…AS A CHIMPANZEE:** A man walked into an EZ Mart in Garland, Texas, with a gun in his hand and a chimpanzee mask over his face. He fired one shot, took the money from the register, and fled. TV news programs in the area tried to help police by airing the surveillance video of the robbery, which clearly shows… a man in a chimpanzee mask robbing the store.

**…AS SUPERHEROES:** A group of young "activists" in Hamburg, Germany, showed up at a high-priced food store in April 2006. They were dressed as comic book superheroes, and they made off with several cartloads of expensive food. Police said similar robberies had taken place at other high-end supermarkets over the years, and believed they were intended as protests against inequitable income distribution. Police also reported that the

Cacao (chocolate) trees grow only in tropical climates, 20° north or south of the equator.

superhero robbers gave the cashier a bouquet of flowers and posed for a photograph before fleeing. Although 14 police cars and a helicopter were involved in the search, the bandits got away.

**...AS COPS:** At 1:30 a.m. on the night of March 18, 1990, two men disguised as cops knocked on the door of the prestigious Isabella Stewart Gardner Museum in Boston. The security guards on duty let them in and were immediately overpowered by the thieves. The not-cops made off with several paintings—a Vermeer, a Manet, and three Rembrandts, among other masterpieces — worth about $300 million. It still ranks as the largest art theft in U.S. history and has never been solved.

**...AS A PAIR OF UNDERWEAR:** Police in Calgary, Alberta, announced in June 2004 that they had finally caught the "Black Panties Bandit," who had robbed at least five convenience stores while wearing a black pair of women's underwear over his face as a disguise.

## MORE MASKED ADVENTURERS

• In February 2006, a man in a tiger suit climbed to the top of the St. Augustine Lighthouse in Florida. Frank Feldmann, 35, an author of children's books, was protesting against child pornography on the Internet. But police couldn't understand him—the tiger suit muffled his voice. He eventually came down and was arrested.

• In December 2004, Lionel Arias, 47, of San Jose, Costa Rica, was "playing a practical joke" by wearing an Osama bin Laden mask, carrying a pellet rifle in his hand, and jumping out and scaring drivers on a narrow street near his home. He was shot twice in the stomach by a startled taxi driver. Arias recovered from his wounds; the taxi driver was not charged.

\*     \*     \*

## STORE-ZILLA

Wal-Mart has nearly 1.4 million employees worldwide. That's roughly equivalent to 4% of the population of Canada. (Or the entire population of Phoenix, Arizona.)

# POWER OF THE PEN

*Satire—writing that lampoons government politics or social
conventions—has been around for centuries. But sometimes
readers don't get the joke. Here are some satirical writers
who got a lot more reaction than they bargained for.*

## TO THE PILLORY!

Long before he wrote *Robinson Crusoe*, English author
Daniel Defoe often ruffled feathers by writing satirical
essays about Britain's bitter politics. In 1702 the nation's ruling
Tory party was imposing tighter and tighter restrictions on their
opponents, the Dissenters—Protestants who refused to join the
Tories' Anglican Church—a critical issue at the time. When the
Tories tried to pass a new law requiring all Dissenters in public
office to convert to Anglicanism—a strategy designed to drive
them out of politics—Defoe, a Dissenter, was infuriated. So he
decided to lampoon the Tories in an anonymously authored pamphlet called *The Shortest Way with Dissenters*, suggesting that the
Tories weren't going far enough—why not just execute all the
Dissenters? The pamphlet was meant to be sarcastic, but many
took it seriously, including some Tories who actually thought it was
a good idea, and panicked Dissenters who showed up in droves at
Anglican church services to avoid the death sentence.

When it was revealed that Defoe had duped everyone, he was
arrested for "seditious libel" and sentenced to three days in the pillory—a public stockade where citizens were free to pelt him with
rocks and garbage. But before the sentence could be carried out,
Defoe composed a poem called "Hymn to the Pillory," another
satirical spoof of the Tories. His friends smuggled it out of jail and
distributed copies to the mob as they gathered to stone him. The
crowd loved the poem—so much that they threw flowers at him
instead of rocks. The incident turned out to be a turning point in
Defoe's career, bringing him fame and backfiring on the Tory government, which was unable to pass the law against the Dissenters.

## DIRTY DANCE

Ambrose Bierce, an American author best known for his macabre
short stories, such as "An Occurrence at Owl Creek Bridge," was also

Top three cat breeds in the U.S.: Persian, Maine Coon, and Exotic.

a journalist known for his scathing wit. In 1877 he and two friends teamed up to write a satirical book, *The Dance of Death*, under the pseudonym "William Herman," attacking what they called a dance of "intolerable nastiness." What was the dance? The waltz. The book overflowed with descriptions of lecherous men luring weak-willed women into a "shameless gratification of sexual desire" by…waltzing.

Though it started out as a joke, the book began to sell because of its titillating content. Religious leaders weren't sure what to make of its racy scenes mixed with righteous morality. Then Bierce decided to up the ante by reviewing the book—unfavorably—in his own newspaper column. His criticism of the book only made it more popular, especially with the Methodist church, which formally endorsed it—to Bierce's delight. In spite of being released through a small publisher, the book sold a more-than-respectable 18,000 copies.

## ACTUALLY, IT'S A CURVEBALL

In 1985 *Sports Illustrated* ran a 14-page cover article on a young baseball phenomenon, pitcher Sidd Finch. Orphaned as a child, the article said, Finch grew up in Tibet, where he learned the rudiments of baseball by throwing rocks. Photos showed the youngster's odd, straight-armed windup that resulted in a jaw-dropping 168-mph fastball—60 mph faster than any ever recorded. He'd recently arrived in the United States carrying his only possessions—a French horn, a rug, and a food bowl—and was immediately drafted by the New York Mets. Finch, it was claimed, was on the verge of revolutionizing baseball. Excited fans wanted to know more; newspapers clamored to interview him. Baseball commissioner Peter Ueberroth fielded phone calls from major-league managers who were concerned that Finch's blistering fastball might injure batters.

But alert readers smelled something fishy when they saw the issue's cover date: April 1. And if they looked carefully, the first letters of every word in the article's first paragraph spelled out "Happy April Fools' Day." Two weeks later, *Sports Illustrated* admitted that the story was a hoax dreamed up by writer George Plimpton and a handful of editors, who'd hired an Illinois middle-school teacher to pose as Finch. *SI* received 7,000 letters from readers— some angry, some applauding Plimpton for the elaborate practical joke. Seven of them were so disgusted that they cancelled their subscriptions—all, reportedly, Mets fans.

A good pitcher can make a baseball curve as much as 17½ inches from a straight path.

# WHAT'S IN YOUR...

*Some reasons to start—or stop—reading ingredient lists.*

**B**READ? Many bread products, from pizza to bagels to pastries, contain *l-cysteine*, an amino acid that adds stretchiness to dough, making it easier to mass produce in a variety of shapes. L-cysteine can be made from feathers, cow horn, or petroleum, but experts say that some of it comes from human hair. That's because it's the cheapest source. Several factories in China buy hair from the poor to make the product.

**JELLY BEANS?** Most jelly beans get their hard, shiny surface from shellac—which is made from insect secretions. The insects, *Laccifer lacca*, live in trees, and their secretions coat the branches. The branches are cut and the shellac is refined from the coating. (It's also sometimes used in processing coffee beans.)

**SKIN CREAM?** Many "anti-aging" skin-care products contain afterbirth—human placentas—said to "rejuvenate" skin and help get rid of wrinkles. Cosmetic makers actually have deals with hospitals, and one Beverly Hills–based company gets its supply from Russian maternity wards. (Some use cow placentas.)

**CHEWING GUM?** Some chewing gums still use *castoreum*, which is used to enhance flavors. Produced in the anal glands of beavers, it's also used in perfumes and incense.

**TOOTHPASTE?** Many toothpaste varieties contain *dicalcium phosphate*, an abrasive agent. It's made from the bones of ruminants (mammals that "chew their cud"), such as cattle, sheep, and goats.

**BEER AND WINE?** Many European and some American producers use *isinglass* to speed the fining, or clarification, process. It's made by cleaning and drying the bladders of fish like sturgeon, cod, and hake, and is also used to make glue and cement.

**PERFUME?** *Skatole* is commonly used as a "fixative"—something added to make other ingredients stick to your skin and last longer. What is it? A white crystalline organic compound found in beets, coal tar...and feces. It's what gives poop its distinctive smell.

---

The first archaeological evidence of soup dates back to 6000 B.C. Main ingredient: hippopotamus.

# WEIRD ANIMAL NEWS

*Strange tales of creatures great and small.*

**B**ETWEEN A CROC AND A HARD PLACE
"A crocodile agitated by a chainsaw's noise chased the man operating the machine and snatched it from him. Freddy Buckland was at a Northern Territory, Australia, roadhouse cutting a dead tree that had fallen against a crocodile pen when the 14-foot reptile struck. 'The croc jumped out of the water and sped along the tree about 20 feet and actually grabbed the chainsaw out of his hands,' said Peter Shappert, the owner of the Corroboree Park Tavern. Buckland was not injured, nor was the crocodile, named Brutus. 'He chewed on the chainsaw for about an hour and a half. It's still in one piece but, yeah, it's buggered.'"

—**Australian Associated Press**

### THE GRASS IS GREENER
"Russia's long winter will just fly by for a herd of Russian cows which will be fed confiscated marijuana over the cold months of 2005. Drug workers said they adopted the unusual form of animal husbandry after they were forced to destroy the sunflowers and maize crops among which the 40 tons of marijuana had been planted, *Novye Izvestia* daily reported. 'There is simply no other way out,' a government spokesman told the paper. 'You see, the fields are planted with feed crops and if we remove it all the cows will have nothing to eat.' He then added, 'I don't know what the milk will be like after this.'"

—**MSNBC**

### DE BEAR IS NO MATCH FOR DE-CLAWED
"At least one bear in West Milford, New Jersey, doesn't want to know Jack. Jack is a 10-year-old orange-and-white tabby. And when the cat spotted the bear in a neighbor's yard, the clawless kitty sprang into action. The bear scurried up a tree and eyed the cat for 10 minutes while Jack hissed from the ground. The bruin inched its way down before jumping off and running away.

"But then Jack chased the bear into the brush and up another tree. That's when Jack's owner realized what was happening and called her cat. The bear took off as Jack rubbed up against his owner, Donna Dickey, who told the Newark *Star-Ledger* that Jack considers the area his turf and doesn't want anyone in his yard."

—**Associated Press**

## DOLPHINS WITH A PORPOISE

"A pod of dolphins circled protectively around a group of New Zealand swimmers to fend off an attack by a great white shark. Rob Howes and three other lifeguards were on a training swim about 100 meters offshore near Whangarei when the dolphins raced in and herded the group together. Howes said: 'They pushed all four of us together by doing tight circles around us.' At that time the lifeguards didn't realize what the dolphins were doing… until Howes tried to drift away from the group, and two of the bigger dolphins herded him back. That's when he spotted a nine-foot great white shark swimming toward the group. 'I just recoiled. It was only about two meters away from me, the water was crystal clear, and it was as clear as the nose on my face.' The lifeguards spent the next 40 minutes surrounded by the dolphins before they could safely swim back to shore."

—**StunningStuff.com**

## SSSSSSOMETHING IN THE WAY HE MOVES

"A woman who fell in love with a snake has married the reptile at a traditional Hindu wedding celebrated by 2,000 guests. Bimbala Das wore a silk sari for the ceremony at her village. Priests chanted mantras to seal the union, but the snake failed to come out of a nearby ant hill where it lives. A brass replica snake stood in for the hesitant groom. 'Though snakes cannot speak nor understand, we communicate in a peculiar way,' Das, 30, told reporters. Das converted to the animal-loving Vaishnav sect, whose elders gave her permission to marry the cobra. 'I am happy,' said the bride's mother, Dyuti Bhoi, who has two other daughters and two sons to marry off. 'Bimbala was ill,' she said. 'We had no money to treat her. Then she started offering milk to the snake, and she was cured. That made her fall in love.' Since the wedding, Das has moved into a hut built close to the ant hill."

—*Hindustan Times*

# TV OF THE 1940s

*When national broadcasting began in the late 1940s, TV was
such a novelty that nearly anything could get on the air.
Weird shows can be found on cable access today…
but back then these were prime-time viewing.*

### Author Meets the Critics (NBC)
Yes, they actually used to talk about books on TV! On this show, one critic would praise a new book and another critic would trash it. The author would then defend himself.

### The Red Caboose (ABC)
This show consisted of film of model trains running on tracks, over which a narrator told railroad stories. It was sponsored by Lionel Trains.

### Let's Rhumba! (NBC)
A 15-minute show of people dancing the rhumba.

### Night Editor (Dumont)
A newspaper editor reads stories and acts them out as he describes them.

### Gay Nineties Revue (ABC)
Vaudeville was already dead by 1948…except on this program, a showcase for old vaudeville acts. Today there are few TV hosts over 40, but this show was hosted by 81-year-old Joe Howard, a vaudeville veteran of the 1890s.

### You Are an Artist (NBC)
This popular show featured an artist named Jon Gnagy, who drew a picture while he talked about how he did it.

### Teenage Book Club (ABC)
Not even in 1948 did teenagers want to stay home on Friday nights and discuss books. The show lasted just two months.

### The Amazing Polgar (CBS)
Dr. Franz Polgar hypnotized selected members of the studio audience.

### Cash and Carry (Dumont)
A game show held in a supermarket in which everything on the shelf was a Libby product (the show's sponsor). One segment had viewers phone in and guess what was hidden under a barrel. Bonus: There was a mime performance on every show.

### Monodrama Theater (Dumont)
One actor performs an entire play—by himself—in front of a curtain. No sets, no props.

There are 20 possible answers on a Magic 8-Ball: 10 positive, 5 negative, and 5 neutral.

# BOXERS OR BRIEFS?

*Whatever your choice, Uncle John's betting his boxers (or briefs)
that you don't know much about where either of them came from.*

COVERALLS
Maybe you've noticed it from time to time while watching Westerns: cowboys running around in long-legged, long-sleeved one-piece undergarments that cover almost their entire body. Called "union suits," these undergarments had a row of buttons running down the front and a button "trapdoor" in the back. As late as the turn of the 20th century, they were the most popular kind of men's underwear in the U.S. Women and children wore them, too.

Then, when the U.S. entered World War I, the Army began issuing shorts to soldiers to wear during the hot summer months. These were more like the shorts we wear as clothing than the ones we wear as underwear today: They opened at the front and were secured by a button on the waistline; the fly was secured with buttons, too, and there was a drawstring that tied on the side.

## BOXER SHORTS

Undershorts didn't become "boxers" until 1925, when Jacob Golomb, the founder of Everlast, invented shorts for boxers that were held up by an elastic waistband instead of the traditional leather belt. It didn't take long for underwear companies to copy what was obviously a good thing: Shorts with no buttons were more comfortable, both to sleep in and to wear under trousers, and the buttons didn't break off in the hand-cranked wringers that people still used to do their laundry. Boxer shorts accelerated the trend away from union suits—by 1930 only old fogies wore them.

## BRIEFS

The next milestone came in 1934, when an executive with the Cooper Underwear Company of Kenosha, Wisconsin, happened to see a photograph of men on the French Riviera wearing a new kind of bathing suit that was little more than a snug-fitting pair of shorts. The executive figured if men were wearing body-hugging shorts on beaches, they'd wear them under their clothing, too.

Years earlier, the company had revolutionized the union suit business by replacing the traditional button trapdoor with two pieces of overlapping fabric that could be pulled apart to create a rear opening when nature called—an innovation the company famously called the "Kenosha Klosed Krotch." For their new piece of underwear, the company's designers shrank the Kenosha Klosed Krotch, modified it a little, and moved it from the rear to the front of the briefs, giving them a distinctive upside-down Y-shaped appearance in front. (In England, briefs are still called "Y-fronts.")

The new design was such a radical departure from ordinary underwear that Cooper worked with a urologist to perfect the design and tested it extensively before rolling it out before the public. The new underwear provided about as much "masculine support" as an athletic supporter, or "jock strap," and to call attention to this fact, the company named them "Jockey briefs."

## COLD COMFORT

The first hint of how popular Jockey briefs would become came on January 19, 1935, when Chicago's Marshall Field's department store unveiled the new design in a window display. That weekend the city was slammed by the worst blizzard of the year—what was the point in displaying skimpy undies in long-underwear weather? The store ordered the display taken down, but by the time noon rolled around the salespeople hadn't gotten around to it yet...and the store had sold more than 600 pairs. The display stayed up.

Marshall Field's sold 12,000 pairs that first week alone and would have sold more than that, had Cooper been able to supply them. Stores sold out of them so fast that the company chartered a special "masculiner" airplane to fly the masculine support briefs to retailers as fast as the factory could make them. Sales have been strong ever since: More than 70 years later, briefs are still the most popular style of men's underwear in the U.S.

## ...WORTH THE TROUBLE?

Inventing the Kenosha Klosed Krotch for the Cooper Underwear Company made its creator, a knitting-room supervisor named Horace Greeley Johnson, a very rich man. But it also saddled him with the nicknames "Edison of Underwear" and "Klosed Krotch Johnson." His granddaughter Barbara Hunt says he didn't really mind. "After all, all our money was in underwear," she says.

# CARD SHARKS, PART I

*Most of us fantasize about beating the odds and winning big. Some play the lottery, others are hypnotized by the ding-ding-dinging of slot machines. But what if you knew a system that gave you an advantage—every time?*

## THE HOUSE RULES

It's a given among gamblers that over time the "house" always wins. That's partly because most casino games— roulette, dice, slot machines—are singular events. What happened in the previous throw of the dice, turn of the wheel, or pull of the "one-armed bandit" has no impact on the outcome of the next game. With every throw, turn, or pull, a player has the same chance of winning as in any other throw, turn, or pull, unless the casinos set their wheels and slot machines to improve the house's odds (which, in the case of slots, they do).

But the game of blackjack, or "21," is something else again.

• It's a straightforward game, played head to head against the dealer (the house).

• Cards are dealt one at a time. The player's objective is to get as close to 21 points as possible without going over; the first to go over 21 loses.

• The round is over when all the cards have been dealt.

• Traditionally, a single deck was used for each round of play, with the used cards being set aside after each hand.

All this makes blackjack a game where what happened before any hand actually *does* matter in terms of predicting a winning outcome. If a player can keep track of the cards that have been played, and bet only when the odds shift into his favor, he can win big. What's amazing is that no one ever figured that out…until about 40 years ago.

## ENTER THE PROFESSOR

In 1962 a young math professor named Edward Thorp published a book called *Beat the Dealer*. He was the first person to prove mathematically that blackjack could be beaten by systematic card

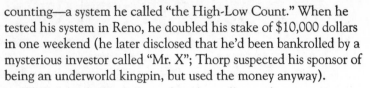

counting—a system he called "the High-Low Count." When he tested his system in Reno, he doubled his stake of $10,000 dollars in one weekend (he later disclosed that he'd been bankrolled by a mysterious investor called "Mr. X"; Thorp suspected his sponsor of being an underworld kingpin, but used the money anyway).

Thorp's book was an immediate bestseller, and soon every blackjack table in Nevada was swarming with would-be card counters trying to score with his system.

## THE HIGH-LOW COUNT

Thorp's card-counting system was brilliant in its simplicity. Rather than force a player to remember the value of every card dealt (which would be an incredible feat of memory), Thorp's strategy relied on approximations. He divided the deck into three groups, and gave each group a simple value: The 2, 3, 4, 5, and 6 of any suit would have a value of +1; 7, 8, and 9, a value of 0; and the 10, Jack, Queen, King, and Ace would equal –1. During a game, the player simply had to keep a running total of the count, adding or subtracting as each card was dealt (this isn't as easy as it sounds—it still requires tremendous concentration). A negative high-low count gave the advantage to the casino; when it became positive, the player had the edge. That was the moment to strike: Bet heavily and win big.

## THE PROFESSOR STOPPER

It should be pointed out that there is nothing illegal about card counting. The player is using information available to everyone at the table. But casinos make their own rules, and as soon as they saw their profits dip as card counting caught on, they stepped in quickly to stem their losses. The first tactic was to shuffle the decks more often. Although effective at ruining the count, the time wasted with extra shuffles drove noncounting (and impatient) gamblers away from the tables in droves. So the casinos dropped that gambit and turned instead to the "Professor Stopper"—a huge card shoe designed to hold over eight decks. The thinking was that having to count up to 400 cards would be too much for most card counters, but that wasn't the case. It just took a player longer to get to a winning position. The casinos kept losing.

Finally they decided to use Thorp's system against his own

Microbial life can survive on the cooling rods of a nuclear reactor.

disciples. Casino employees were taught the high-low system and, more importantly, how to spot card counters by their telltale behavior. Since card counting requires intense concentration, for example, card counters tend not to be very conversational or jovial when they play. Anyone suspected of card counting was shown the door and told not to come back. So was that the end of card counting? Hardly. In fact, the battle between counters and casinos had just begun.

## GAMING COMPUTERS

Keith Taft was an electronics engineer from California, and an aggressive card counter. He studied the books, learned the strategy, and spent hours at the tables trying to perfect his game. But the casinos loved him. Why? Because he was also a big loser. His problem was that he kept losing count. Then in 1969 he had a brainstorm: Why not invent a machine that would do his counting for him, a computer just for blackjack?

• **GEORGE.** Two years later Taft and his son, Marty, unveiled one of the first portable computers ever made, which they called "George." Wearing specially modified shoes, the player would use his toes to tap in the value of the card being played. The main computer, which was harnessed to the player's body, used the data to figure out the best way to play the next hand. That information was then flashed to the player through tiny lights embedded in the frame of a modified pair of glasses. George was a good prototype, but it was too bulky to use in a casino.

• **DAVID.** It took them another four years and the invention of the microchip to build the computer they wanted: about the size of a pocket calculator, with a keyboard no larger than a credit card. The device, called "David," was strapped to the player's thigh; he could work the keyboard through a strategically placed hole in his pocket. But David was more than a fine piece of miniaturization. It took Thorp's High-Low system to an exciting new level. What had made Thorp's system so attractive to blackjack players was that it relied on simple mental arithmetic, which made it accessible to almost any player. But that was also its weakness.

Thorp's system worked on approximations, not on the precise value of each card played. The player still had to make an educated guess on how to play a hand. But David could remember the values of every card played, analyze that information, and tell the player exactly how to play their cards. The player didn't have to guess at all. They just had to follow David's recommendations and rake in the dough.

## BET ON DAVID

The Tafts debuted David in April 1977 and racked up $40,000 in winnings the very first week. They quickly set up a production line and offered the new blackjack computer for sale at $10,000 apiece. But before they could cash in, Marty Taft was caught with David strapped to his leg. Casino security had never seen anything like it before. They were certain it was a cheating device, but they couldn't figure out how it worked (the Tafts' use of microchip technology was far ahead of its time) and had to let Marty go. He had made a narrow escape, and that was the end of the road for David. In 1985 the Nevada legislature passed the Nevada Devices Law, making it against the law to use a card-counting machine. The maximum sentence was 10 years. Once again, the house ruled.

Or did it?

*For part II of the story of the Las Vegas card counters, turn to page 431.*

\*     \*     \*

## WORLD'S FUNNIEST JOKE?

In 2002 the University of Hertfordshire set up a Web site where people could rate more than 40,000 jokes—the goal was to determine what joke was the world's funniest, across wide culture, age, gender, and nationality differences. The winner was from a 1951 routine by comedians Michael Bentine and Peter Sellers:

**Bentine:** Help! I just came in and found him lying on the carpet in there.
**Sellers:** Oh, is he dead?
**Bentine:** I think so.
**Sellers:** Hadn't you better make sure?
**Bentine:** Alright. Just a minute.
(He leaves. Sound of two gunshots.)
**Bentine:** He's dead.

---

Deep-sea fish can explode when brought rapidly to the ocean's surface.

# WHEN IN ROME...

*Uncle John is fascinated by the international rules of etiquette (especially anything bathroom-related). Over the years he's picked up quite a few tidbits of advice to help you get by in foreign countries.*

**Argentina:** People tend to stand very close. If you back away from someone, they'll assume you're shy and close the gap. Or they might just be offended by your rudeness.

**Austria:** Cut your food with a fork. To use a knife implies the food is tough and unappealing.

**Brazil:** Brazilian women can be romantically aggressive. It's not uncommon for a woman to send a note to a man in a restaurant asking for his phone number...even if he's with his wife or girlfriend.

**Bulgaria:** In this east-European country, shaking your head "no" actually means "yes." Nodding means "no."

**Czech Republic:** Raising your voice damages your credibility. You will be considered a buffoon.

**Denmark:** Never compliment other people's clothing. It's considered too intimate.

**Australia:** Don't say "g'day, mate" to an Australian. Avoid the temptation to talk about convicts (Australia was founded as a penal colony) or mention *Crocodile Dundee*. It's condescending.

**Egypt:** Don't add salt to a meal. It's insulting to the cook, implying that the food is unpalatable.

**France:** Bread will be waiting for you on the table in restaurants, but don't eat it until the main course arrives. It's not an appetizer—it's meant to accompany meals.

**Singapore:** Chewing gum, jaywalking, spitting, littering, and not flushing a public toilet are not only considered rude, they're also illegal...and you can be fined $500 per offense.

**South Korea:** If you want to get someone's attention, don't point and do the "come here" thing. Instead, extend your arm, palm down, and wiggle your fingers downward.

---

Hats off! Wearing a hat is considered disrespectful in Fiji.

**Japan:** It's considered rude to eat food on the street, especially if you're walking. Sit down to eat, even if it's a cup of coffee or an ice cream cone.

**Italy:** It's rude to get up to use the bathroom during a meal. Wait until the meal's over.

**The Netherlands:** Cafés and coffee shops aren't the same thing. Both sell food and both sell coffee, but "coffee shops" are also places where marijuana is sold and consumed.

**Hungary:** Never clink glasses. According to legend, 13 Hungarian generals were jailed by Austria in the 1848 revolution. Their Austrian captors clinked glasses at every meal, so Hungarians unofficially vowed to ban the practice for 150 years. Technically, the ban is now over, but it's still honored.

**Finland:** It's the home of Nokia, so cell phones are universal. But in public places, you must set your phone to "vibrate." If it rings in a theater, restaurant, library, or even at a sporting event, you will be asked to leave.

**Poland:** When dining at someone's home, thank them by saying *dziekuje* (jen-koo-yeh). But don't say it to a waiter in a restaurant unless you really mean it; in that context, it means "keep the change."

**Sweden:** If you touch something in a store or market, you're expected to buy it.

**Thailand:** Thailand is a Buddhist country, so all life is deemed precious there. Be careful not to step on spiders, and never swat at insects.

\*     \*     \*

## A RANDOM ORIGIN

On a 1976 Lynyrd Skynyrd live album, singer Ronnie Van Zant asks the audience, "What song is it you want to hear?" The audience demands "Free Bird!" and the band plays it. The tradition of shouting it at non-Skynyrd concerts started in Chicago in 1988. Disc jockey (and Lynyrd Skynyrd fan) Kevin Matthews instructed listeners to attend a Florence Henderson concert and shout out requests for "Free Bird" to torment the singer. Fans then started yelling the song at other unhip concerts, then at any concert at all.

Equal rights: By law, all tombstones in Norway must be the same height.

# HE SLUD INTO THIRD

*Verbal gems actually uttered on the air by sports announcers.*

"If only faces could talk."
—**Pat Summerall,
NFL announcer**

"Hector Torres, how can you communicate with Enzo Hernandez when he speaks Spanish and you speak Mexican?"
—**Jerry Coleman,
San Diego Padres announcer**

"A lot of good ballgames on tomorrow, but we're going to be right here with the Cubs and the Mets."
—**Thom Brennaman,
Chicago Cubs announcer**

"Lance Armstrong is about to join a list which includes only himself."
—**Mark Brown,
ESPN sports analyst**

"I don't think anywhere is there a symbiotic relationship between caddie and player like there is in golf."
—**Johnny Miller,
golf analyst**

"Referee Richie Powers called the loose bowel foul on Johnson."
—**Frank Herzog, Washington
Bullets basketball announcer**

"It's a great advantage to be able to hurdle with both legs."
—**David Coleman,
British sports announcer**

"The Minutemen are not tall in terms of height."
—**Dan Bonner,
college basketball analyst**

"Jose Canseco leads off the 3rd inning with a grand slam."
—**John Gordon,
Minnesota Twins announcer**

"The offensive linemen are the biggest guys on the field, they're bigger than everybody else, and that's what makes them the biggest guys on the field."
—**John Madden,
NFL announcer**

"Watch the expression on his mask."
—**Harry Neale,
hockey analyst**

"The game's in the refrigerator, folks. The door's closed, the light's out, the eggs are cooling, the butter's gettin' hard, and the Jell-O's a-jigglin'."
—**Chick Hearn,
L.A. Lakers announcer**

---

Lou Gehrig's only film role was as himself, in the movie *Rawhide*.

# ACTS OF SEDITION!

*Political arguments about one of America's most cherished freedoms, the right to free speech, have been going on since the United States was founded. And they continue to this day.*

**P**ARDON ME
In May 2006, Governor Brian Schweitzer of Montana officially pardoned 78 people who had been convicted of crimes in 1918, almost 90 years earlier. The crimes: sedition— "incitement of insurrection against lawful authority," or, in the case of these 78 Montanans, criticizing the government. Three of the people convicted had written something critical, and the rest had simply said something aloud in public and had been turned in by neighbors or townspeople. Forty-one of the 78 convicted—40 men and one woman—served prison sentences for their words. "I'm going to say what Governor Sam Stewart should have said," Schweitzer said, referring to the governor who signed the sedition law in 1918. "I'm sorry, forgive me, and God bless America, because we *can* criticize our government."

## THE ACTS

It wasn't the first time that people's words had landed them in prison in the United States.

In 1798, just nine years after the ratification of the U.S. Constitution, America's first two political parties—Alexander Hamilton's Federalists, and Thomas Jefferson's Republicans—were struggling for power. The Federalists controlled Congress and the White House with John Adams, and they used their power to pass the Alien and Sedition Acts. War with France was looming, they said, and these laws were necessary to thwart French immigrants within our own borders who might side with France. The Republicans saw the Acts as an attempt to crush the Republican Party. The Acts themselves, and how the Federalists prosecuted them, supported the Republicans' views. Four laws made up the Alien and Sedition Acts:

• The Naturalization Act extended the period an immigrant had to wait to become a resident from 5 to 14 years. (Most immigrants

---

The horse pictured on Wyoming's license plates has a name: "Old Steamboat."

at the time, particularly the French and the Irish, supported Jefferson and the Republicans, so the law made fewer of them eligible to vote.)

• The Alien Act and the Alien Enemies Act gave the president the power to imprison or deport any aliens he deemed dangerous to the United States. (This would allow the Federalists to silence any foreign-born critics, whether they were dangerous or not.)

• The Sedition Act, the most controversial of the statutes, made it illegal for anyone to criticize the government, the Congress, or the president, orally or through writing. (The only people who went to prison for violating the Sedition Act were Republicans.)

## WRONGING THE RIGHTS

The Republicans were outraged, calling the Alien and Sedition Acts an "unconstitutional reign of terror." And not just because the Sedition legislation didn't make it illegal to criticize the *vice* president, a position which was currently held by Thomas Jefferson. (Criticism of Jefferson continued to flow unabated.) The Republicans claimed that the Sedition Act was in direct violation of the First Amendment right to free speech.

Twenty-five people were arrested under the Sedition Act (the Federalists never charged anyone with violating the Alien Acts), most of them editors of Republican newspapers who had publicly lambasted the president. Some of them:

• Republican congressman (and Irish American) Matthew Lyon of Vermont. Lyon, known as "Spitting" Lyon for spitting in the face of another congressman on the floor of the House some years earlier, had published an article in a newspaper he owned criticizing President Adams and opposing going to war with France, which the Federalists supported. Lyon blasted the Adams administration for, among other things, its "unbounded thirst for ridiculous pomp, foolish adulation and selfish avarice." For that he was charged with sedition and found guilty—most historians say by a jury packed with Federalist supporters—receiving a fine of $1,060.96 and a sentence of four months in prison.

• James Callender, editor of the *Republican Richmond Examiner*, who said Adams was "mentally deranged" and a "hideous hermaphroditical character, which has neither the force of a man, nor the gentleness and sensibility of a woman." For that he was fined and sent to prison for nine months.

• Benjamin Franklin Bache, grandson of Benjamin Franklin and publisher of the *Philadelphia Democrat-Republican Aurora.* He had mercilessly and continually attacked the Federalists, at one point referring to the president as "old, querulous, bald, blind, crippled, toothless Adams." Bache died before going to trial.

Ultimately, the Alien and Sedition Acts backfired on the Federalists. Public opinion turned against the oppressive laws, and in 1799 the Jeffersonians were able to pass resolutions in Kentucky and Virginia that made the Acts unenforceable in those states. That same year "Spitting" Lyon ran for reelection—from his jail cell—and won. The Acts helped to unite Republicans across the country, and Thomas Jefferson was able to win the presidency in 1800. He immediately pardoned every person convicted of sedition and ordered the government to pay back their fines...with interest. The Alien and Sedition Acts expired in 1801, and Jefferson did not reinstate them. No American would be charged with sedition again...for more than a century.

*What events could lead American legislators to curtail one of the people's basic freedoms?* *Turn to page 469 to find out.*

\*      \*      \*

## REVENGE!

In a 1980s Far Side cartoon, two chimpanzees are grooming each other. One finds a human hair on the other and jealously says, "Doing a little more 'research' with that Jane Goodall tramp?" The Jane Goodall Institute cried foul and wrote a letter to Far Side cartoonist Gary Larson, calling the cartoon an "atrocity." But Goodall herself thought it was funny—she and Larson struck up a friendship, and all profits from sales of a T-shirt featuring the cartoon now go to the Goodall Institute. But was she *really* okay with it? Seems one of her chimp friends wasn't. In 1988 Larson visited Gombe National Park with Goodall and was attacked by a chimp named Frodo. Goodall apologized to Larson, who suffered cuts and bruises, telling him Frodo was "a bully." (Goodall had raised the 12-year-old chimp herself.)

# BATHROOM NEWS

*All the latest from the news stream.*

## LAWN BOWLING

When the zoning board of Anderson Township, Ohio, turned down Alan and Robin Sutton's request for permission to build a fence around their yard, the Suttons protested the decision by lining the perimeter of their yard with 15 flower-filled toilet bowls. And because their creation is technically not a "structure," the zoning board can't do anything about it.

## THE ELECTION IS GOING DOWN THE TOILET

Candidates seeking election in India may soon have to fulfill an unusual condition to prove their viability as a leader: toilet ownership. The proposal, the brainchild of rural development minister Raghuvansh Prasad Singh, is intended to force the poor to take sanitation seriously. "If you cannot build a toilet in your own house, what use can you be to voters?" says Singh.

## BATHROOM 101

The National Health Service of Scotland has distributed a pamphlet entitled "Good Defecation Dynamics" to thousands of people in the city of Dundee. Recent research by the department found that a third of Scotland's population suffers from bowel or bladder problems, and the booklet offers many useful tips and techniques, including recommended breathing habits and "proper posture for effective evacuation." (One tip: "Keep your mouth open as you bulge and widen.")

## PAY TOILET

A tax collector in Graz, Austria, took a black briefcase containing $28,000 in cash with him when he used the men's room at a local restaurant. Somehow, when he exited the bathroom he forgot to take his case with him. An hour later he remembered and went back to retrieve it…but it was gone. Despite a formal plea from the Graz police, neither the case nor the money have been recovered.

## BREAD BOWL

In April 2006, federal food safety investigators in Kuwait City shut down the Hawally Bakery because it was improperly storing its dough. Where? In a big clump in a toilet. The owner said the humidity and water in the toilet kept it fresh.

## LIGHTS...CAMERA...FLUSH!

Toilets ruined a day of filming on the Indian movie *Keep At It, Munnabhai*. In one scene filmed in a suburban Mumbai (formerly Bombay) mall, two characters have a secret meeting in a bathroom and then walk out. The only problem: Every time actors Sanjay Dutt and Arshad Warsi moved, the sensors on all the urinals in the bathroom were activated, making them all flush. The noise ruined every take, and the shoot had to be moved to another location.

## LIKE A VIRGIN

When musicians agree to do a concert, they provide promoters and the concert hall with a list of demands called a "rider," usually food and drink requests. Madonna has an unusual item on her rider: a brand-new toilet seat at every concert venue on every stop of her tour. (It must still be wrapped in plastic to prove it's new.) After the concert, the seat is to be removed and destroyed to stop anybody from trying to sell it on eBay.

## LOO WITH A VIEW

If you're looking for a bathroom in the Irish coastal town of Lahinch, it's going to cost you. A dilapidated shack containing a public toilet is on the market for the same price as the average home in Ireland—about 300,000 euros ($380,000). Three reasons: location, location, location. It overlooks a popular beach on Ireland's Atlantic coast. But if that's not in your price range, the Boston Red Sox offered the toilet from the clubhouse during their 2004 World Series winning season. Final price at auction: $624.47.

\*     \*     \*

"There is so little difference between husbands you might as well keep the first."

—Adela Rogers St. Johns

In 1981 an L.A. man was arrested for hiding under tables and painting women's toenails.

# DEATH CUSTOMS

*The treatment and disposal of a dead body is a sacred ritual in every culture, but each one does it a little bit differently.*

I N INDIA, custom calls for a body to be burned on a funeral pyre near a riverbank and a temple; the ashes are thrown into the river. Some adherents to Zoroastrianism place bodies atop towers; after the flesh is eaten by vultures, the bones are thrown into a pit at the center of the tower.

IN THE SOLOMON ISLANDS of the South Pacific, a body was traditionally placed on a reef where it would be eaten by sharks.

INUIT PEOPLE constructed small igloos around a corpse (like an "ice tomb"). The cold protected and preserved the body (unless a polar bear found its way in).

THE NAVAJO feared being haunted by the dead, so the body was burned and the deceased's house was destroyed. On the way back from the funeral, relatives took a long, circuitous route to confuse the spirit into not following them.

A VIKING FUNERAL: At sunset, the dead man was placed on a small boat. As it drifted out to sea, it was lit on fire. If the color of the sunset was the same as that of the fire, it meant the deceased was bound for Valhalla (Viking heaven).

MUSLIMS do not use caskets (unless required by law). The body is washed three times, wrapped in a white shroud, and placed directly in the ground with the head pointed toward Mecca.

THE IROQUOIS buried corpses in shallow graves, but exhumed them after a few months. Relatives then placed the bones in a community burial plot.

IN MODERN JAPAN, bodies are washed in a Buddhist temple, dressed (men in suits, women in kimonos), and put in a casket with a white kimono, sandals, and six coins, all for the spirit's crossing into the afterlife. After a funeral, the body is cremated. Relatives pick bones out of the ash, put them in an urn, and bury it.

# HONK IF ANYTHING FALLS OFF

*We keep thinking that we've seen every clever bumper sticker that exists, but every year readers send us new ones. Have you seen the one that says...*

If you lived in your car you'd be home by now.

OVER 50. BEEN THERE. DONE THAT. CAN'T REMEMBER.

Watch out! I'm late for Driver's Ed class.

I child-proofed my house but they still get in.

**This car is a status symbol. It symbolizes me being poor.**

Yes, this is my truck. No, I won't help you move.

The Earth is full. Go home.

I have the body of a god: Buddha.

EAT RIGHT, EXERCISE, DIE ANYWAY.

Honk if anything falls off.

He who hesitates not only is lost, but is miles from the next exit.

*End hunger: Eat a little snack.*

THINK THIS CAR'S TOO DIRTY? THEN YOU WASH IT.

**Am I living happily ever after yet?**

Don't believe everything you think.

*My child was inmate of the month at the county jail.*

4 out of 3 people have trouble with fractions.

**Blessed are the flexible. They never get bent out of shape.**

Don't make me release the flying monkeys!

Don't tailgate me or I'll flick a booger on your windshield.

**I have no idea where I'm going.**

---

**Carrot-toon character:** The variety of carrot that Bugs Bunny munches is a "Danvers."

# TAKING THE LOW ROAD

*What makes people do the sleazy things they do? Beats us.*
*Here's our non-salute to some really bad behavior.*

**N**AME: Matthew Shaner of Rostraver, Pennsylvania
BACKGROUND: Shaner, 21, was driving down Route 981 when he struck 15-year-old Sean Cossell, who was riding his bike along the road.

HOW LOW CAN YOU GO? According to witnesses, Shaner got out of the car and started yelling profanities at the kid he'd just hit—telling him to get off the hood of his car. When the injured Cossell rolled off the hood, Shaner jumped into his car and sped off. He was arrested a short time later. Cossell was treated for multiple (but not life-threatening) injuries at a local hospital and released.

NAME: Julie E. Hunt of North New Portland, Maine
BACKGROUND: Three middle-school girls brought some homemade cookies to their teacher.

HOW LOW CAN YOU GO? They were suspended from school because the cookies had Ex-Lax in them. The teacher didn't eat them—she gave the cookies to other students, four of whom became ill. Where does Julie E. Hunt fit in the picture? She's the mother of one of the girls who gave the "treats" to the teacher, and, according to her affidavit, actually taught the girls how to make them. She was arrested and charged with misdemeanor assault.

NAME: Gary C. Jones of Missouri
BACKGROUND: In October 2004, Jones, a Hazard Mitigation Counselor for the Federal Emergency Management Agency (FEMA), was sent to Brevard County, Florida, to assist with hurricane relief. While there, 72-year-old Diane Greco called Jones's office for help with her home in Melbourne Beach, which had a damaged roof as well as a mildew problem.

HOW LOW CAN YOU GO? Instead of helping Greco fix the problems, Jones bought the house—for $250,000 (its true value was estimated at nearly $1 million). In March 2005, Tony Pipitone, an investigative reporter from Orlando's Local 6 News, got a tip about the sale and questioned Jones at his home in Missouri, but Jones denied working for FEMA. When the station confirmed his employment, Jones said that Greco had set the price. When Pipitone contacted Greco, she confirmed setting the $250,000 price, based on a scant memory of an appraisal years earlier. "I thought it was fair," she told Local 6. "Now I guess I'm finding out otherwise." She filed a civil suit against Jones—who by then had moved into the house with his family—demanding he void the contract and return her house, which she and her husband had built in 1971. Her son, Marcus Greco, said Jones "100 percent took advantage" of his mother. The lawsuit is still pending.

**NAME:** Anthony Mesa, 22, of Deland, Florida

**BACKGROUND:** In 2006 Mesa was "playing practical jokes" with a co-worker in the Pix convenient store where he worked.

**HOW LOW CAN YOU GO?** One of the "jokes" Mesa played: he urinated in a bottle of Mountain Dew and put it back in the refrigerator. An unsuspecting customer…well, let's just say he later sued the store for an undisclosed amount of money. Mesa was arrested and sentenced to six months in prison.

**NAME:** Nicholas Buckalew, 18, of Morrisville, Vermont

**BACKGROUND:** In April 2005, Buckalew wanted to make himself a creative and unusual "bong" (large marijuana pipe).

**HOW LOW CAN YOU GO?** Buckalew went to a cemetery, broke into an above-ground tomb, and took the skull from an interred body, along with the eyeglasses and bow tie that were with it. Police said he told friends he was going to bleach the skull and make a pipe out of it. In 2006 Buckalew pleaded guilty to "intentionally removing a tombstone and intentionally carrying away the remains of a human body." He was sentenced to one to seven years in prison.

\*     \*     \*

**Celebrity Coincidence:** While filming an action scene for the movie *Troy* in 2004, actor Brad Pitt tore his Achilles tendon. The character he was playing: Achilles.

# WHY YOUR MOM SAYS, "WASH YOUR HANDS!"

*Here's a little science experiment to remind you that Mom was right—you really should wash your hands before you eat. One note before you start: If you're a kid, you'll need adult supervision and assistance. (And if you have a germ phobia, skip this story and read something else.)*

## WHAT YOU'LL NEED

1. Hands that haven't been washed for several hours.
2. A pair of rubber gloves.
3. Cotton balls and rubbing alcohol.
4. Masking tape or labels, and a pen.
5. A vegetable peeler and a paring knife that can be boiled.
6. Two apples and a dish to set them on. (If you don't have apples handy, you can substitute potatoes, pears, or any other fruit or vegetable that can be peeled.)
7. Two glass jars with screw-top lids, each large enough to hold cut pieces of apple.
8. A cutting board.

## WHAT TO DO

1. Wearing the rubber gloves, wash the jars, lids, dish, and cutting board in warm soapy water. Dry them off with a clean dish towel, then rub them inside and out with a cotton ball soaked in rubbing alcohol.

2. Boil the vegetable peeler and the paring knife in a pot of water, then drain and let them cool to room temperature before handling them.

4. Label the jars. Write "Jar 1—Unwashed Hands" on the label for the first jar, and "Jar 2—Washed Hands" on the second jar.

5. Now, still wearing the rubber gloves, wash both apples in warm, soapy water. Rinse them with clean water and set them on the dish.

6. Remove the gloves. Pick up one of the apples and peel it with

the apple peeler. When you finish, cut the apple into pieces small enough to fit inside one of the jars. Now rub your unwashed hands all over the pieces of apple. When finished, put them in the jar marked "Jar 1—Unwashed Hands" and screw the lid on tight.

**7.** Wash your hands thoroughly in soap and water for at least 30 seconds. Wash the potato peeler, paring knife, and cutting board, too, so that the second apple isn't contaminated by anything that touched the first apple.

**8.** Now that your hands are clean, peel the second apple and cut it into pieces just like you did with the first apple. Rub your clean hands all over the pieces of apple, then put them in the jar marked "Jar 2—Washed Hands" and screw the lid on tight.

**9.** Put the jars in a warm place and let them sit there for a week; then come back and see what they look like. Notice any difference in the two jars? *That's* why your mom wants you to wash your hands before you eat.

## EXPLANATION

If you did a good job cleaning your equipment and your hands were good and grubby when you peeled the first apple, you should see plenty of mold growing on the first apple and noticeably less on the second apple, even after a week has passed. The mold growing on the apples started out as invisible mold spores on the skin of your hands.

Mold is only the beginning—there's plenty of other stuff, including bacteria and possibly cold and flu viruses, on your unwashed hands, too. Washing your hands thoroughly removes the things you can see…and the things you can't.

## HANDS-ON SCIENCE

If you find the results of this experiment fascinating, try another. How does washing your hands for 5, 10, or 15 seconds compare to washing for 30? How does washing with regular soap compare to washing with antibacterial soap? What happens if you wash, but don't use any soap? How dirty are your hands one hour after washing them? After six hours? After 24 hours? Keep going. You'll learn a lot and—who knows?—if the sight of all those moldy apples kills your appetite, maybe you'll even lose a few pounds.

---

One isn't enough? Two rivers in Florida are named Withlacoochee.

# THE GOLDEN AGE OF RADIO, PART II

*What happened when a "ham" radio operator put a microphone in front of a record player? Modern radio was born. Here's Part II of our story (Part I is on page 77).*

**M**ORE THAN JUST MUSIC
Radio offered numerous advantages over phonographs in the 1920s: Listeners weren't limited to the records in their own collections, and they didn't have to get up every five minutes to flip the record over and wind the record player back up. (Long playing, or "LP," records, which had about 30 minutes of playing time on each side instead of four and a half minutes, weren't introduced until 1948.) Even better: radio broadcasts were *free*. Yet as early as 1926, opinion polls began showing that listeners were hungry for something to listen to besides music. The networks responded by developing a variety of shows for every member of the family.

### WHAT WAS ON
**Comedies:** Comedy shows were some of the earliest hits on radio—it was easy for vaudeville stars like Jack Benny, Eddie Cantor, and the husband/wife team of George Burns and Gracie Allen to move their acts to the new medium. At first these comedians did their usual standup routines, but over time they pioneered the "situation comedy" format that's still being used on TV today: A situation is set up at the beginning of the episode—Jack Benny has to go to the doctor, for example—and then it's milked for jokes for the rest of the show.

**Kiddie Shows:** These shows were on in the afternoon when kids got home from school, in the early evening, and on Saturday mornings. Established movie and comic-strip characters like Superman and Little Orphan Annie were quickly adapted for radio. In later years the trend reversed itself, as characters created for radio—like Captain Midnight, Sergeant Preston of the Yukon, and Jack Armstrong, the All-American Boy—moved on to comic books, movies, and eventually television.

**Soap Operas:** Soaps appealed primarily to housewives, and dominated the daytime. The soap-opera format came about only by chance in 1932, when NBC moved a show called *Clara, Lu 'n' Em* from its evening time slot to the middle of the day because that was the only place for it in the schedule. *Clara, Lu 'n' Em* was more of a satire than a soap, but it did so well that NBC began programming other shows for women during the day. Soaps proved to be the most popular shows; by 1940 the four networks offered more than 60 hours of soap operas a week.

**Dramas:** One of the nice things about radio is that you can transport the listener anywhere using only sound effects. You want to tell a story about space colonists on Mars? About cops in L.A.? Maintaining order in Dodge City, Kansas? You don't need fancy costumes or sets—you just need the right background sounds. Police and detective shows came early to radio. They were easy to produce because they were dialogue-heavy, filled with characters who spent a lot of time standing around trying to solve crimes. And they were popular with audiences.

Surprisingly, science fiction shows and Westerns targeted at adults appeared relatively late in radio and never really caught on. All four networks introduced science fiction series for adults in the 1950s, but only two of them, *2000 Plus* (Mutual, 1950–52) and *X Minus One* (NBC, 1955–58) lasted longer than two years.

*Gunsmoke*, the first adult-themed Western, didn't appear until 1952, but it fared much better than the science fiction shows. It became one of the most popular programs on the air and ran until the summer of 1961. (The TV version ran for 20 years, from 1955 to 1975, making it the longest-running drama in history.)

## SIGNING OFF

What ended the Golden Age of Radio? TV, of course. In retrospect it's amazing that radio lasted as long as it did—both NBC and CBS began making experimental television broadcasts from their New York stations in 1939, and both stations were issued commercial licenses in 1941. Were it not for World War II, TV might have swept the country over the next few years. But when the United States

---

Animal sounds: Apes gibber, deer bell, hippos bray.

entered the war, further development was halted as the stations cut their broadcasts back to almost nothing and TV manufacturers switched over to making electrical equipment for the war effort.

## AS SEEN ON TV

When World War II ended in 1945, fewer than 10,000 American households had a television, and most of the sets were in the New York City area. The industry got a big boost in 1947, when the World Series was broadcast on television for the first time. It's estimated that of the nearly 4 million people who watched the game, at least 3.5 million of them watched it on sets in their neighborhood taverns. Many of these patrons then went out and bought TVs for their own homes—and when curious neighbors came over to watch, they wanted TVs too. The TV craze was on.

By 1951 television broadcasts were available coast to coast and six million homes had TVs. People were buying them as fast as manufacturers could make them. By the end of the decade more than 60 million homes had TVs, and as Americans abandoned their radios in favor of television, so did the advertisers, and so did the stars. The most successful radio shows like *Gunsmoke* and *The Jack Benny Show* moved to TV (*Gunsmoke* stayed on the radio for a time as well); less successful shows just went off the air.

As the big advertising dollars left radio, big-budget shows became impossible to air. Many radio stations with hours of programming to fill and very little money to do it with went back to what radio had been in the very beginning: a single person, sitting alone in a booth, playing records for anyone who happened to be listening.

## THEY'RE BAAACK

Today the classic shows of the Golden Age of Radio are largely absent from AM and FM radio, but thanks to satellite radio and the Internet, they're more widely available now than they've been since they originally aired. Both XM Radio and Sirius offer channels that play classic radio shows 24 hours a day; and you can buy collections of old shows in bookstores or download them on iTunes. If you've never heard them, you're in for a treat.

*For a list of our favorite shows, check out
"Audio Treasures" on pages 298 and 451.*

If your cat snores, or rolls over on his back to expose his belly, it means he trusts you.

# STATE V. BIG HAIR

*Names of actual court cases tried in the good old U.S. of A.*

Friends of Kangaroo Rat v.
California Dept. of Corrections

U.S. v. Pipe on Head

United States of America v.
2,116 Boxes of Boned Beef,
Weighing Approximately
154,121 Pounds, and 541
Boxes of Offal, Weighing
Approximately 17,732 Pounds

Schmuck v. Dumm

Jones v.
God, Jesus, Others

Julius Goldman's Egg City v.
United States

Pam-To-Pee v.
United States

Klink v. Looney

United States ex rel.
Gerald Mayo v.
Satan and His Staff

Lexis-Nexis v. Beer

Muncher v.
Muncher

People v. Booger

Short v. Long

State of Indiana v.
Virtue

United States v.
$11,557.22 in U.S. Currency

Advance Whip & Novelty Co. v.
Benevolent Protective
Order of Elks

Fried v. Rice

United States v.
1,100 Machine Gun Receivers

Plough v. Fields

Frankenstein v.
Independent Roofing & Siding

Big v. Little

Ruff v. Ruff

State v. Big Hair

Hamburger v. Fry

I am the Beast Six Six Six of the
Lord of Hosts in Edmond Frank
MacGillevray, Jr., et. al. v.
Michigan State Police

---

**Louisiana is the only state that still refers to the Napoleonic Code in its state law.**

# IRONIC, ISN'T IT?

*There's nothing like a good dose of irony to put the
problems of day-to-day life into perspective.*

## ANIMAL IRONY

In 2005 Bob Schwartz, crime advisor to the governor of
New Mexico, authored a law that would allow felony
charges to be brought against any owner of a dangerous dog
involved in a vicious attack. A few months after the law passed,
Schwartz was in his backyard when his own dog attacked him, biting both of his arms and sending him to the hospital. (Schwartz
recovered but was not arrested.)

• John Fleming was riding his motorcycle on a road in Canberra,
Australia, when a kangaroo hopped onto the road and collided
with him. Fleming's job: making road signs that warn people about
kangaroo crossings.

• A building in Dundee, Scotland, was overrun by mice. "They've
been eating biscuits in our cupboard," says Johanna Girling, who
works in the building. "One of our staff even got an electric
shock because the mice had bitten through wires and left them
bare." But what the mice were feasting mostly upon was cat
food—the building is home to the Cat Protection League, and
houses dozens of stray cats. (The cats didn't take care of the
problem—there were too many mice—so an exterminator was
called in.)

## ENVIRONMENTAL IRONY

Greenpeace's flagship, *Rainbow Warrior II*, travels the world's
waterways trying to protect them. In October 2005, while studying
the effects of global warming on a fragile underwater coral reef in
the Philippines, the ship accidentally ran aground on the reef,
causing it significant damage. The environmental organization
was fined 384,000 pesos ($6,800).

## CELEBRITY IRONY

• Before becoming an actor, Margaret Hamilton was a kinder-

---

Q: What is the official state rock song of Ohio? A: "Hang On Sloopy."

garten teacher. In fact, she wanted to devote her life to children. But after she played the role of the Wicked Witch of the West in 1939's *The Wizard of Oz*, most kids were afraid of the mere sight of her. Even as an old woman, Hamilton was repeatedly asked by kids why she was "so mean to poor little Dorothy."

• One of comedian Redd Foxx's recurring jokes on the 1970s sitcom *Sanford and Son* was faking a heart attack any time things didn't go his way. "It's the big one!" he would yell. On October 11, 1991, Foxx was working on a new show called *The Royal Family*. During rehearsal, he suddenly clutched his chest and fell to the floor. The cast and crew started laughing at the star's brilliant performance…until they realized it wasn't a joke. Foxx died a short time later.

**Final Irony:** Before producers decided to call the show *The Royal Family*, its working title was *Chest Pains*.

## FLAMING IRONY

It was supposed to be a celebration marking the end of Fire Awareness Week in Shimohetsugi, a town in southern Japan. But festivities were cut short when the two-story fire station where the event was taking place caught fire. Everyone made it out, but the station was severely damaged. What caused the fire? A gas canister improperly connected to the barbecue grill the firefighters were using to cook dinner. "It's very embarrassing that this should happen to people whose job it is to go and put out fires," said one of the firefighters.

## HAPPY-ENDING IRONY

An elderly man was attending a banquet in Santa Barbara, California, in 2005 when he clutched his heart and collapsed. The event was the Heart Ball, and most of the 300 people in attendance were cardiologists. "Several doctors sprang into action and began performing cardiopulmonary resuscitation," newspapers reported. The man, who had no blood pressure or heartbeat, was revived and taken to the hospital. One of those who helped him, Dr. Richard Westerman, commented afterward: "If you have to go down, this was the place, I guess."

# WEIRD CANADA

*Canada: land of beautiful mountains, clear lakes, bustling cities…and some very weird news reports. Here are a few odd entries from the BRI news files.*

## YOUR (CANADIAN) TAX DOLLARS AT WORK

In June 2006, the federally funded Council for the Arts gave a $9,000 grant to a performance artist named Jess Dobkin. Her performance: She set up a bar called "Lactation Station" where patrons could sample human breast milk. Dobkin modeled the event after a wine tasting, providing milk from six different women. In similar news, the Ontario provincial government gave $150,000 to researchers at Laurentian University to study the sex drive of squirrels.

## AN "A+" FOR CREATIVE THINKING

In January 2006, history professor David Weale of the University of Prince Edward Island had a severely overcrowded class, with 95 students. His solution: He offered a work-free B-minus to any student who agreed not to show up for the rest of the semester. Twenty accepted. When administrators found out, Weale, who had come out of retirement to teach the class, was asked to re-retire.

## NAME GAME

James Clifford Hanna, a resident of the Yukon Territory, argued before a court that he didn't have to pay his taxes. Reason: "James Clifford Hanna" was a name given to him involuntarily. Since he never asked for nor accepted the name, he wasn't legally responsible for paying the taxes of anyone named James Clifford Hanna. Whatever his name is, he lost the case.

## A BIRD IN THE HEAD

Shawn Hacking, 13, of Winnipeg, suffered scraped knees, a sprained wrist, and a bruise on his face when a Canada goose landed on the boy's head and slapped a wing into his face at the same time. The force knocked Hacking off his skateboard. Hacking's friend Brent Bruchanski, who witnessed the event, said, "It was so funny…but I felt sorry for him at the same time."

Try it: It is physically impossible to tickle yourself.

## MORE! MORE! MORE!

After winning a $1.2 million lottery jackpot in 1989, Barbara Bailey of Montreal enjoyed her windfall modestly, buying a house for about $200,000 and loaning money to friends and relatives. Then she started blowing it on extravagances, and within two years she was broke and living on welfare. Desperate to recapture her millionaire lifestyle, Bailey got her niece, a bank teller, to divert $500,000 from other peoples' accounts into Bailey's. The bank quickly caught on. She was sentenced to a two-year jail term.

## THE REAL POOP

Bill Sewepagaham, a leader of the Cree tribe in northern Alberta, offered a good luck charm to the Edmonton Oilers during the 2006 National Hockey League playoffs: a necklace made of lacquered deer and moose feces. Sewepagaham claimed it was based on an ancient Cree tradition in which hunters who'd had a fruitless day would smear their weapons in animal droppings and the next day they'd have better luck. Unfortunately, the charm didn't work—the Oilers lost in the Stanley Cup finals.

## A SHOT IN THE...

Police were called to a home in Burnaby, British Columbia, when a local resident reported hearing a gunshot in the yard of the house next door. Police discovered a drunken 55-year-old man with a shotgun partially hidden behind his couch. The man admitted that he had fired the shot. Why? He was annoyed that his nephews were taking too long to finish their yard work, so he shot the gun into the air to motivate them. The kids ran away and the man went to jail.

## SPACE CADET

Former minister of defense Paul Hellyer recently announced that he believes in UFOs. Seriously. He said he once saw one, but then put the event out of his head...until he saw a TV show about UFOs in early 2005. That prompted him to read books about Roswell, New Mexico, which sealed his belief in aliens. At a political conference in Toronto in November 2005, Hellyer accused U.S. president George W. Bush of plotting an outer-space war, and the U.S. military of preparing weapons on a secret military base on the moon to use against aliens.

---

Big Red: The world's tallest tomato plant grew to a height of 65 feet.

# MMM...CANDY

*Who cares if it's bad for you?*

• Americans eat 25 pounds of candy per person each year. Worldwide leader: Denmark, at 36 pounds.

• Easter candy: 60 million chocolate bunnies are made each year; 74% of people eat the ears first.

• The melting point of cocoa butter is just below human body temperature, which is why it melts in your mouth.

• First candy: Ancient Arab, Egyptian, and Chinese cultures candied fruits and nuts in honey.

• Holidays in order of candy sales: Halloween, Easter, Christmas, Valentine's Day.

• In surveys, 90% of parents admit to stealing Halloween candy from their kids.

• Celebrate! January 3 is National Chocolate-Covered Cherry Day, April 12 is National Licorice Day, and May 23 is National Taffy Day.

• One chocolate chip provides enough food energy to walk 150 feet.

• Twizzlers contain no actual licorice.

• Hershey's Kisses weren't made during World War II: The foil for wrapping them was unavailable due to aluminum rationing, and chocolate-making equipment was being used to make candy bars for the military.

• Sales of KitKat bars surge in Japan around the time of college entrance exams. "KitKat" sounds like the Japanese phrase *kitto katsu*, which means "good luck." Parents buy the candy for their kids as a good luck charm.

• An average bag of M&Ms contains 10% blue ones, 10% green, 10% tan, 20% red, 20% yellow, and 30% brown.

• When Saddam Hussein was found in a hole in Iraq in 2003, he had Mars and Bounty candy bars with him.

• Some failed chocolate bars: Milk Nut Loaf, Fat Emmas, Big Dearos, Vegetable Sandwich, Kandy Kake, and Chicken Dinner.

# DUDE, YOUR PANTS ARE FALLING DOWN

*As a fad, baggy hip-hop jeans have lasted longer than bell-bottoms and parachute pants…combined.*

## DROOPY DRAWERS

Believe it or not, the modern fad of wearing oversized, low-riding pants originated in U.S. prisons. In the late 1980s, many prisons banned the wearing of belts. And because standard-issue prison pants were often too big for inmates, they sagged. Instead of being embarrassed by having to wear clothes that didn't fit, inmates turned it into a fashion statement. The fad spread to the outside world when gang members in Los Angeles started wearing their pants baggy and low in solidarity with their friends in prison. From there, it took off.

The style first found its way into pop culture through rap music. It started with M.C. Hammer's 1990 hit single "U Can't Touch This" and the video, which featured Hammer dancing in oversized "genie" pants. Within a year, the first beltless, boxers-revealing jeans showed up on rap artists such as Ice-T, Too Short, and Kriss Kross (who also ushered in a short-lived craze of wearing the baggy pants backwards).

The trend quickly caught on with teenagers—urban and suburban—and the fashion industry knew it had a winner. By the mid-1990s, brands such as Levi's, J. Crew, Tommy Hilfiger, Savanna, and Khakis had all released "anti-fit" jeans, and within a few years it was a multi-billion dollar industry.

## PULL THEM UP!

As with a lot of new clothing fads, many parents, school officials, and even lawmakers dislike baggy pants. Some say the pants are dangerous because they make it easier to conceal a weapon. A counter-argument: baggy pants make concealed weapons that much harder to *retrieve*. But the loudest objections to the style center on the fact that some people don't want to look at other people's underwear. A few examples:

---

Little known fact: The Chihuahua is the longest-lived breed of dog.

- Louisiana House Bill 1626, drafted by state lawmakers in 2004, tried to target any person who "intentionally exposes undergarments or intentionally exposes any portion of the pubic hair, or cleft of the buttocks." After a close vote, the bill was defeated.

- A year later, Virginia legislators tried to create the "Droopy Drawers Law," which would issue a $50 fine to any person whose pants were worn low enough to reveal their skivvies. "Underwear is called underwear for a reason," said one congressman. The bill was voted down.

- Many school systems have had better luck. In a move to ban baggy pants, Lynn, Massachusetts, public schools issued a dress code in 2006, requiring all male students to wear belts and have their shirts tucked in at all times.

Most kids, however, don't see what the big deal is. A 2005 *USA Today* poll asked 218,000 teenagers whether baggy pants should be banned. Results: Over 80% said "no." A Virginia high school student, Jessica Miller, when asked by the *Washington Post* about proposed anti-baggy pants laws, summed up the majority view: "They're using words like 'lewd' and 'indecent.' War is lewd. Homelessness is indecent. Boxers showing—that's tacky, but it's not worth spending taxpayers' money on."

## NO END IN SIGHT

After more than 15 years, the baggy-pants craze is still here. And between the hip-hop and skateboarding cultures, it looks like the trend won't be sagging anytime soon. In a June 2006 *TransWorld Business* fashion trends article, industry expert John Lacey reported that the "loose, baggy fit comprises more than 80% of the market, and we'll continue driving that." He goes on to say, however, that there is a growing market for tighter pants. Does that mean that when the baggy-pants craze finally ends, it will be replaced by the tight designer jeans John Travolta wore in the 1970s?

## WALK, DON'T RUN

Whether or not the style is offensive, baggy pants can be a crime deterrent, as these would-be crooks found out.

- A thief in Detroit stashed six stolen DVDs in his oversized pants, then tried to get away on a bike. Bad idea: the pants kept getting caught in the chain. So he ditched the bike and ran into an alley. That didn't work either—his pants fell down around his ankles, tripping him up. He got up, ran a few more feet, then fell down again, making it easy for cops to catch him.

• "That kid, he could run fast. But he got caught up by his pants, which were real big and baggy," said 55-year-old Vicki Chandler. She was walking to her car in Chattanooga, Tennessee, when the young man snatched her purse. Fortunately for Chandler, he had to throw the purse on the ground and use both hands to hold his pants up as he ran away.

• A would-be robber in North Carolina tried to hold up a Subway sandwich store…but his pants got caught on the counter when he tried to jump over it, sending him crashing to the floor. He fled without taking anything. Then, when he tried to make his get-away over a fence, his baggy pants got hung up on the links. Police found him hanging upside down and had to cut him down with a knife before arresting him.

• In 2004, a suspect in handcuffs tried to run away from Officer Denny Fuhrman. But he didn't get far—his jeans fell around his ankles while he tried to cross the street. "He was flopping around like a fish out of water," Fuhrman told reporters. The suspect got out of his trousers and continued running, wearing only a shirt and boxer shorts, prompting Fuhrman to make one of the strangest calls of his career: "White male, running, no pants, in handcuffs." The man was caught and arrested a few minutes later at the entrance of a J.C. Penney store after a 61-year-old grandmother grabbed him by his shirt collar and pulled him to the ground.

\*     \*     \*

## IRONY AT SEA

On a voyage in 2006, the luxury cruise ship *Crown Princess* suddenly—and unexpectedly—listed heavily to one side. More than 240 passengers were injured when the ship's four swimming pools emptied, flooding the decks. The accident, blamed on a faulty steering mechanism, occurred just before the start of the day's movie: *Titanic*.

# BEHIND THE HITS

*Popular songs are more than just background music—we mark the milestones in our lives by the songs we listened to. Here are the stories behind how some of our favorites were created.*

**ARTIST:** Marvin Gaye
**SONG:** "What's Going On" (1971)
**STORY:** By the end of the 1960s, Gaye had become unhappy with the way Motown was treating its artists, and with how it valued commercialism over content. Like a lot of other Americans, Gaye was also feeling disillusioned by the war in Vietnam, so in 1970, when Obie Benson of the Four Tops wrote "What's Going On" and asked Gaye to record it, Gaye jumped at it—he felt the song perfectly summed up his frustrations. But when they played the record for Motown chief Berry Gordy, Gordy refused to release it, claiming it "wasn't commercial enough." In protest, Gaye refused to record any more songs until "What's Going On" was released as a single. After a few tense weeks, Gordy relented. Good move: In January 1971, "What's Going On" hit the Top 5. Suddenly, of course, Gordy was all for Motown's music having a message, and Gaye recorded the rest of the songs for soul music's first concept album, written from the point of view of a Vietnam veteran (based on letters Gaye received from his brother, who was serving in the war). The album sold two million copies in 1971—Gaye's biggest success to date—and ushered in a decade of socially themed soul music.

**ARTISTS:** U2
**SONG:** "Where the Streets Have No Name" (1987)
**STORY:** This song took so long to record, and caused so much strife between the band and producer Brian Eno, that the track almost never saw the light of day. Eno was so frustrated with the band members' inability to agree on the melody lines and instrument sounds that one day he threatened to erase all the tapes—three weeks of work—on the theory that they would be better off starting over from scratch. The band had Eno physically restrained

and then asked engineer Steve Lillywhite to mix the tapes into the finished track. The song became the third big hit off their album *The Joshua Tree*, reaching #4 on the U.K. charts in 1987.

So exactly where are those no-named streets? The prevailing theory: Africa. Bono traveled to Ethiopia in 1985, and the impact the trip made on him found its way into many U2 songs. "The spirit of the people was very strong," he recalled. "There's no doubt that, even in poverty, they had something we didn't have. When I got back, I realized the extent to which the people in the West were like spoiled children." But when U2 performs the song onstage, Bono usually dedicates it to his love of God, leading many to believe that the place "where the streets have no name" is actually Heaven.

Bono has never stated specifically where the streets are, but he has said where they're not. "In Belfast (Ireland), you can almost tell what the people are earning by the name of the street they live on and what side of that street they live on. That said something to me, and so I started writing about a place where the streets have no name."

**ARTIST:** Nirvana
**SONG:** "Smells Like Teen Spirit" (1991)
**STORY:** Before Nirvana frontman Kurt Cobain fell for Courtney Love, he dated Tobi Vail, drummer of Bikini Kill, for a while in 1991. But she eventually lost interest in the troubled rocker and broke it off. One night, one of Vail's bandmates, Kathleen Hanna, was hanging out at Cobain's apartment, listening to him lament the break-up. At some point she grabbed a can of spray paint and scrawled the words, "Kurt smells like Teen Spirit" on Cobain's wall. (Teen Spirit was an underarm deodorant that Vail wore, and her scent was still lingering on Cobain.) The phrase immediately struck him and provided the inspiration for what he later called "the ultimate pop song." "Smells Like Teen Spirit" became the first big hit from Nirvana's seminal album, *Nevermind*. It reached #6 on the Billboard charts and has since been called the anthem of a generation. Ironically, Cobain later admitted that he didn't know that Teen Spirit was a deodorant until after the song was released—he would have never knowingly put the name of a mass-produced product for teenagers into the title of one of his songs.

# GEEZERS AND RODNEYS

*On a recent trip to the Emerald Isle, Uncle John picked up some Irish words and expressions, old and new. Here are some of his favorites.*

**Parish priest:** A pint of stout. It has a black body and white collar (the foamy head of the beer).

**Jingler:** A telephone.

**Donkey's grudge:** Day-old cake. If a cake didn't sell by the end of the day, the baker added layers of pastry on the top and bottom and sold it the following day. Add a layer of cream on top, and it's called a Donkey's Wedding Cake.

**Mooching shoes:** Today Ireland is one of Europe's wealthiest countries. But it used to be one of the poorest. Mooching shoes were dirty old shoes specially worn when asking merchants or banks for extra time to pay an overdue bill.

**Hogger:** Someone who mooches drinks off others. Originally referred to indigent alcoholics who drank the dregs out of empty Guinness barrels, or "hogsheads," left outside Dublin pubs for collection and refilling.

**In a rat:** In a bad mood.

**Rodney:** A twit.

**Petty:** Outhouse. From the French *petit*, or "little," referring to the little house out back behind the main house.

**How's your granny for slack?** A stock pickup line used by Dublin lads who were too shy to say anything else to girls they were interested in.

**Shuggly-shoe:** A seesaw.

**Swimmers and bricks:** Fish and chips.

**Tickle-the-bricks:** A sneaky person (they step very lightly).

**Black dog:** An unpaid bill; dates back to the days when pub tabs were written in chalk on slate blackboards.

**Chairwheeze:** A fart.

**Geezer:** A cat.

**Child:** In some parts of Ireland, the word *child* refers only to females. It's not uncommon to hear someone asking of an infant, "Is it a boy or a child?"

**Spadger:** Little boy; from the slang term for "sparrow."

**Mot:** A girlfriend.

**Shed a tear for Ireland:** To pee.

It is rumored that Napoleon owned a pair of spider-silk gloves.

# LIFE IMITATES ART

*Countless movies and TV shows are inspired by
real-life events. But when real-life events are inspired
by fiction, that's when Uncle John takes notice.*

**ON THE SCREEN:** In the TV sitcom *Seinfeld*, actor John O'Hurley portrayed J. Peterman, owner of the J. Peterman Catalog, for 21 episodes (1995–98).

**IN REAL LIFE:** In 1998 the real J. Peterman Catalog was in financial trouble and headed for bankruptcy. Desperate, the catalog company's owner (the *real* J. Peterman) called O'Hurley for help. The actor funneled money into it, and within a year, the company was again turning a profit. The J. Peterman Catalog now has two owners: the *real* J. Peterman and John O'Hurley, the *TV* J. Peterman.

**ON THE STAGE:** Tim Owens, lead singer for British Steel, a Judas Priest tribute band in Pennsylvania

**IN REAL LIFE:** Judas Priest had been without a lead singer for five years in 1996 when Christa Lentine, girlfriend of drummer Scott Travis, happened to see a British Steel show in a small nightclub in Erie, Pennsylvania. She videotaped the performance and showed it to the band, and they immediately flew Owens to London for an audition. After singing just one verse of one song, he got the job. Owens went on to record four albums with Judas Priest.

**ON THE SCREEN:** In a 1999 episode of *The Simpsons*, Homer invents "tomacco," a horrible-tasting, highly addictive hybrid of tobacco and tomatoes.

**IN REAL LIFE:** Inspired by the episode, Rob Baur of Lake Oswego, Oregon, did some research on tobacco and tomatoes, both members of the nightshade plant family. He then successfully grafted a tomato plant onto tobacco roots. Result: real-life tomacco. The plant even bore fruit that looked like regular tomatoes. But although tests on the fruit revealed no nicotine, Baur wouldn't eat them. One tomacco fruit was destroyed for testing, one was given to the *Simpsons* writers, and one was sold on eBay.

# DUSTBIN OF HISTORY: AL GROSS

*We recently came across the story of this unknown pioneer of modern communication. Who was he? Let's put it this way: if you can talk into it and it isn't plugged into a wall, thank Al Gross.*

## FDR'S REQUEST

Not long after the Japanese bombed Pearl Harbor in 1941, President Franklin Roosevelt summoned William Donovan, head of the Office of Strategic Services (forerunner of the CIA), to make a complaint. Winston Churchill always seemed to have more accurate, up-to-date information on the war than he did, Roosevelt explained. Churchill got his intelligence directly from spies behind enemy lines, but FDR had to wait for information to filter up through the chain of command. The president wanted Donovan to do something about it.

Donovan had recently read an article about a 23-year-old man named Al Gross who had invented a portable two-way radio with a range of several miles. Donovan thought Gross's "walkie-talkies" or something like them might help solve the president's problem. He arranged to meet Gross and get a demonstration.

Gross had been fascinated by radio since childhood and had built amateur, or "ham," radios out of parts he scrounged from junkyards. In those days ham radios were bulky—as big as today's microwave ovens—and too heavy to carry, and Gross didn't like being stuck inside the house every time he wanted to talk to other hams. It took two years of tinkering, but in 1938 he finally managed to build one small enough to hold in his hand.

Four years later, when Gross demonstrated the device to Donovan, the OSS chief came away so impressed that he hired Gross on the spot, gave him the rank of captain, and set him to work building radios that American spies could use behind enemy lines.

## JOAN AND ELEANOR

The first thing Gross did was take a trip in a high-altitude bomber over Nazi-occupied Europe. The bomber was loaded with radio scanning equipment, and as Gross studied the radio traffic he realized the Germans didn't have any equipment that worked on frequencies above 180 megahertz. So he came up with a system—codenamed "Joan-Eleanor"—that operated at 250 MHz and was composed of two kinds of radios: "Joan," a small walkie-talkie that spies could easily conceal, and "Eleanor," an enormous radio built into the belly of the high-altitude bombers that regularly flew over enemy territory.

The Joan and Eleanor radios had a range of more than 30 miles, which meant that spies operating behind enemy lines could talk to a bomber flying overhead for as long as 15 minutes. And because the Germans didn't have the technology to detect the radio traffic or listen in, the spies could use plain English instead of speaking in code. That meant that as soon as the bomber was back on the ground, the information could be sent on its way to President Roosevelt without having to be deciphered first. The radios even saved on training time, since people could be sent into the field without having to master secret codes.

## LIFESAVERS

Joan-Eleanor was a huge success: The Germans never intercepted any of the radio signals and didn't even know that such high-frequency radios existed. FDR got the intelligence he wanted, and the radios helped shorten the war, saving hundreds of thousands of lives in the process. The spy radios were a highly classified secret—so secret, in fact, that Vice President Harry Truman did not learn of their existence until he became president following FDR's death in 1945. Joan and Eleanor radios weren't declassified until 1976.

Gross also aided the war effort by inventing another kind of radio—a one-way device that received signals but could not transmit them. It was used to detonate bombs. Operatives would hide explosives under bridges, and then an aircraft flying overhead would transmit a radio signal to the receiver, causing it to detonate the bomb. As many as 600 bridges were destroyed using Gross's invention—another huge contribution to the war effort.

Both of Gross's wartime inventions later found peaceful uses. Just before the war ended, Ewell K. Jett, chairman of the Federal

Communications Commission, asked for a demonstration of the Joan-Eleanor radios. He was so impressed with the idea of portable radio communications that he created the Citizens Radio Service Frequency Band in 1946. After the war Al Gross founded a company that manufactured the first radios approved by the FCC for use on the "citizen's band"—the first CB radios. (He was the first person to receive a CB license.)

## THE OTHER RADIO

It took a little longer for the bomb-detonator radio to find a peacetime application. That idea came to Gross after he spent time in the hospital and got tired of hearing doctors and nurses being paged over a loud intercom. He reworked his radio so that when it received a radio signal, it would make a beeping sound, alerting the wearer that he was being paged—the world's first wireless pager.

Gross patented the pager in 1949 and the following year set up a paging system in New York City's Jewish Hospital, certain that the medical world would be quick to embrace it. He was wrong: Doctors worried that beeping pagers would frighten patients during working hours, and disrupt golf games and other leisure activities during their off-hours. And nurses balked at having to wear the bulky receivers on their uniforms. Gross eventually put the pager aside and moved on to other projects; in the meantime, an outside company licensed the technology and used it to make the first automatic garage door openers.

## AHEAD OF HIS TIME

Throughout the 1950s, Gross made repeated attempts to interest AT&T in his radios. The technology, he explained, would free telephones from having to be connected to the wall. People could make calls from anywhere in their homes or offices. But the phone company wasn't interested in cordless phones. He explained how CBs could be integrated into the telephone system, so that people would be able to make phone calls outdoors or even from their cars. The phone company wasn't interested in cellular phones either. Gross explained that his hospital pagers could be integrated into the system, too, so that people could reach someone even if they weren't near a phone, just by dialing a special number for the pager. Again the phone company said no.

What could he do? In those days AT&T had a monopoly on phone lines in America, so if they weren't interested, that was pretty much the end of the story. Gross couldn't get other companies to bite because they were afraid that AT&T would sue to stop them from using alien equipment on its phone system. Reluctantly, Gross gave up on the phone company and focused his attention on other things.

About the only person who showed an early interest in Gross's ideas was Chester Gould, the cartoonist who wrote the Dick Tracy comic strip. During a visit to Gross's workshop in 1947, Gould saw a demonstration of a wireless microphone that could be worn on the wrist; the following year Dick Tracy started wearing his famous two-way wrist TV.

## SIGNING OFF

If Al Gross had an unlucky number, it must have been 17, because his patents were only good for 17 years. After that, anyone could use his inventions without paying him a penny. His last radio patent expired in 1971—just in time for him to miss out on the communications revolution that his inventions made possible. The first successful consumer pager was introduced by Motorola in 1974; 20 years later, 61 million people around the world owned pagers. Their popularity only began to decline after the next invention based on Gross's patents, the cellular phone, became affordable enough for the general public. And cordless phones now outnumber corded phones. But he didn't make a penny off of that one, either.

After a lifetime of work, Gross had made more than enough money to retire, but he never did. He preferred to keep on tinkering, and spent his last years designing missile systems at an Arizona company called Orbital Sciences Corp. He kept on working until shortly before his death from cancer in 2000 at the age of 82, and somehow he managed not to be bitter about having missed out on the electronics boom. "I was born 35 years too soon," he liked to joke. Indeed, the sight of so many pagers, cordless phones, and cell phones in use thrilled him. "It makes me feel good," he said, "like I've had a part in the world."

Yet he never did get a cell phone of his own. "I go to the office and my wife calls me on the phone there," he told a reporter in 1998. "Why do I need one?"

Leonardo da Vinci invented an alarm clock that woke him by rubbing his feet.

# GOT YOUR EARS ON, COME ON?

*Some more of our favorite expressions
from the golden age of CB radio.*

**Tin can:** a CB radio.

**Kojak with a Kodak:** a State trooper with a radar gun. (Kojak was a 1970s TV detective.)

**Breaker, breaker:** What you say when you need to interrupt routine conversation to say something important, like when there's a Kojak with a Kodak up ahead.

**Come on:** I'm done talking and am waiting for your reply.

**Put the hammer down:** Step on the gas pedal; floor it.

**Hammer lane:** fast lane or passing lane.

**Sandwich lane:** middle lane.

**Granny lane:** slow lane.

**Dream weaver:** a sleepy driver who's weaving in and out of their lane of traffic.

**Roller skate:** a car.

**Pregnant roller skate:** a Volkswagen Beetle.

**Barbershop:** a low overpass.

**Draggin' wagon:** a tow truck.

**Pickle park:** a highway rest stop.

**Good buddy:** Used to mean "friend"; now it means "homosexual."

**Good neighbor:** What you call your good buddies now that "good buddy" means homosexual.

**Got your ears on?:** Are you listening?

**Seat cover:** a good-looking woman in a vehicle.

**Bumper sticker:** a car that's following *way* too close.

**Hole in the wall:** a tunnel.

**Bird dog:** radar detector.

**Bear bait:** a reckless trucker who's driving fast without a bird dog to spot the Kojaks with the Kodaks.

**We gone:** Bye-bye!

---

**Buzzards are legally classified as songbirds in Ohio.**

# CREATIVE CROOKING

*Kudos to the cops who caught these clever crooks.*

**B**AR CODES TO PRISON STRIPES
Twin brothers Justin and Nicholas Chitwood were arrested after a year-long investigation into their bar-code swapping scheme at Target stores all over Wisconsin. The two men would cover up the bar codes on items that cost about $150 with fake codes that put their cost at less than $10, buy them, and then sell them on eBay. They sold about $15,000 worth of items before they were caught. "The photocopying and sticking the new UPC sticker over the old ones is unique," said Detective Barry Waddell. "I've never seen this before." The two were charged with conspiracy, theft, and computer crime, and face 28 years in prison.

### FOOL PIGEONS

Police in the state of West Bengal, India, uncovered a bizarre robbery scheme when truck drivers reported being robbed of their cargo…after seeing ghosts. Drivers reported that they'd seen strange lights flying around their trucks while driving on remote highways. The sight disturbed them so much that they stopped their trucks and fled. On returning, they'd find the trucks empty. An investigation took the mystery out of the story: A gang of highway bandits was creating the "ghosts" with trained pigeons. They strapped battery-operated red lamps to the birds and released them before approaching trucks. "In the darkness of the night, all the drivers see are red lights flying all around," said a police official. "And being superstitious, most of them flee, leaving their consignments at the mercy of bandits." Undercover officers patrolling the highways caught several of the bandits (and their pigeons).

### FISH STORY

In April 2006, someone reported to Fish and Wildlife officers that they'd found something odd at Lake Barkley in Kentucky: a basket containing five live bass, tied to a dock just below the waterline. That aroused the suspicion of the officers, who knew that a fishing tournament was scheduled at the lake that weekend. So they marked the fishes' fins and watched the site. Sure enough, on Saturday morning a boat pulled up, retrieved the stashed fish, and left. The boat belonged to two Kentuckians—Dwayne Nesmith, 43, and Brian Thomas, 31—who were registered in the tournament. The officers posed as staff and were at the weigh-in when Nesmith and Thomas dropped off the marked fish. They didn't win anything (they were just ounces shy of earning prize money), so when the officers identified themselves the two could only be charged with misdemeanors. But an investigation revealed that Nesmith and Thomas had entered other tournaments as well— and had been uncannily lucky in them, netting thousands of dollars in prizes and even winning a $30,000 boat. The fishy fishing buddies were charged with 10 felony counts of theft and face several years in prison.

## YOU ARE FEELING VERRRRY GENEROUS

Police in the Eastern European nation of Moldova reported in 2005 that they were on the lookout for a robber who hypnotized bank clerks. The hypno-thief was identified as 49-year-old Vladimir Kozak, a trained hypnotist from Russia. Police said Kozak would start a conversation with a teller, make eye contact, and put the teller into a hypnotic trance. He would then have the teller hand over all the money in the till. Kozak's total haul: nearly $40,000 (one clerk in the city of Chisinau reportedly handed over more than $12,000). Police put wanted posters with Kozak's face around the nation…but warned bank clerks not to make eye contact with it.

\*　　\*　　\*

### SOME REALLY, REALLY, REALLY BAD PUNS

• A fisherman accidentally got some vinegar in his ear, and now suffers from pickled hearing.

• The king of an African country issued a royal decree: "No one may kill any wild animals." The decree was honored, but soon there were too many lions and tigers in the kingdom. The people revolted, and the king was removed from power. It was the first known instance of a reign being called on account of game.

# BEN KINGSLEY'S HAIR

*Critics agree: The 2005 sci-fi movie A Sound of Thunder was one of the year's worst. Why? In addition to the laughable dialogue and cheesy special effects, there was that poofy white wig worn by British actor Ben Kingsley.*

"The usually-bald actor has been given a thick thatch so white it almost glows in the dark. Now that's scary."
—**Movie Mom's Review**

"Ben Kingsley sports a white wig that looks like a lump of cotton candy perched on his head."
—**CNN**

"It's 2055. Ben Kingsley has grown a head of 'Man from Glad' hair and presides over Time Safari, Inc."
—*Toronto Star*

"They keep going back to the same spot and shooting the same poor dinosaur, allowing director Peter Hyams to use the same sequence over and over, thereby saving money to pay for Kingsley's snowy-white Chia Pet head."
—*The Arizona Republic*

"Kingsley is forced to wear an outrageous wig that makes it appear he has a massive White Persian cat perched atop his head."
—*Variety*

"Someone has also apparently gone back to the 20th century to retrieve a truckload of double-breasted chalk-stripe suits and—to judge from Mr. Kingsley's white pompadour—Jack Valenti's hair."
—*The New York Times*

"Ben Kingsley pits his hairdo against Edward Burns' space suit."
—**Roger Ebert**

"Perhaps the saddest thing is watching an actor of Ben Kingsley's caliber try and say his lines without being embarrassed. This is made even harder for Kingsley with the ridiculous wig he's forced to wear. Did these guys lose a bet or something?"
—**ThreeMovieBuffs.com**

"I'm talkin' pure white Cesar Romero Joker-style hair."
—**MovieJuice.com**

"Ben Kingsley has scary hair. It's tall and white and exceedingly strange, like Donald Trump's collided with Siegfried Fischbacher."
—**USA Today**

Surely you can't be serious: In the 19th century, Shirley was a popular name for boys.

# FLAG TRIVIA

*It turns out there's a lot more to flags than stars and stripes.*

A NATOMY OF A FLAG
There are more than 200 countries in the world, and all of them have flags. Most national flags are rectangular; two—the Vatican and Switzerland—are square. The flag of Nepal is the only one that doesn't have square corners: it has a "double pennant" shape that looks like one triangle on top of another.

• Modern flags are divided into four quarters, or *cantons*. These cantons are numbered clockwise from the top left, which is known as the first canton. On the American flag, the white stars against the blue background are in the first canton.

• It's so common for special symbols to be placed in the first canton that it alone is sometimes referred to as the canton, with the rest of the flag being called the *field* or *ground*.

• The first and the fourth cantons—the two closest to the flagpole —are known as the *hoist*. The second and third cantons—the ones that flap freely in the wind—are called the *fly*.

## AMERICAN FLAG FACTS
Here's a trick question: If the 50 stars on the American flag represent the 50 states in the union, which star represents *your* state? Answer: none of them. Collectively, the stars do represent the fifty states, but no star represents any particular state.

Another question: If a 51st state enters the union, can you still fly your old 50-star flag? Yes. If the United States ever does get a 51st state, the president will order a new American flag to be designed, one with 51 stars instead of 50. But the new flags will be phased in gradually; even on federal buildings, the 50-star flags will continue to fly until they're too worn for public display.

You may think that all American flags are exactly the same, but they're not. Flags that are meant to be displayed indoors often have extra decorative elements. For example:

• Gold cords, ending in gold tassels, may hang from the top of the *flagstaff* or flagpole.

- The flag may have a gold fringe running along its outer edges.

- The flagstaff may be topped with a *finial*, or ornament, shaped like a spearhead, an eagle, or some other three-dimensional figure.

## FLAG DESIGNER

In January 1959, an executive order from President Dwight Eisenhower resulted in a flag redesign. After Alaska became the 49th state, the stars had to be rearranged into seven rows of seven stars each. When Hawaii became the 50th state later that year, Eisenhower ordered the stars to be rearranged again—in nine rows staggered horizontally and 11 staggered vertically.

But who came up with the staggered design? A 17-year-old high school student from Ohio named Robert Heft. When statehood for Alaska and Hawaii were being discussed in 1958, Robert's teacher asked his students to redesign the flag. He got a B–; the teacher said his design lacked creativity. Robert thought he deserved better, so he sent his flag to his U.S. representative… and Congress approved it, making his school project the new, official American flag.

## MYTH UNDERSTOOD

The proper way to dispose of worn or tattered flags is by burning them in a dignified fashion. This tradition is often misunderstood to mean that if a national flag touches the ground for even a moment, it has been desecrated and must be disposed of by burning. This is untrue: A flag should not be dropped or allowed to touch the ground, but if it happens, it's not the end of the world (or the flag): Just pick it up, and if it's dirty, clean it. Tattered flags may be mended and restored to good condition.

## YOUR SCHWENKEL IS SHOWING

Picture an American flag. Now picture the topmost stripe, the red one, extending out beyond the rest of the flag to almost twice its length, as if a red streamer has been tied to it. That streamer, and the shape it gives to the flag, are known as *schwenkels*. (Seriously.)

Schwenkels aren't seen very often these days, but during the Middle Ages knights of low rank carried them as their personal flags. How could you tell when a knight had been promoted to the rank of *knight-banneret*? His flag had its schwenkel cut off (not as painful as it sounds), after which the flag was known as a *banner*.

# UNCLE JOHN'S PAGE OF LISTS

*Some random bits from the BRI's bottomless files.*

## Top 10 States for Deer/Car Accidents

1. Pennsylvania
2. Michigan
3. Illinois
4. Ohio
5. Georgia
6. Minnesota
7. Virginia
8. Indiana
9. Texas
10. Wisconsin

## 5 Requirements in Dick Cheney's Hotel Room

1. All lights on
2. Decaf coffee (brewed in advance)
3. Diet Sprite (4 cans)
4. Temperature set to 68°F
5. TV tuned to FOX News

## World's 5 Healthiest Foods (according to Health.com)

1. Olive oil
2. Soy
3. Yogurt
4. Lentils
5. Kimchee

## 6 Parts of the Circulatory System

1. Heart
2. Arteries
3. Arterioles (small arteries)
4. Capillaries
5. Veins
6. Venules (small veins)

## 3 Little Pigs

1. Fifer (straw house)
2. Fiddler (wood house)
3. Practical (brick house)

## The 4 Seasons

1. Frankie Valli
2. Tommy DeVito
3. Bob Gaudio
4. Nick Massi

## 7 Real Computer Programming Languages

1. Toadskin
2. Nietzsche
3. Beatnik
4. OWL
5. Bullfrog
6. Spaghetti
7. Argh!

## 5 Sports Nicknames Made Up by ESPN's Chris Berman

1. René "La Kook" Arocha
2. Rick "See Ya Later" Aguilera
3. Jim "Hey" Abbott
4. Chuck "New Kid On" Knoblauch
5. Mike "Enough" Aldretti

## 4 H's in the 4-H Club

1. Head
2. Heart
3. Hands
4. Health

## 5 Childless U.S. Presidents

1. George Washington
2. James Buchanan
3. Andrew Jackson
4. James Polk
5. James Madison

## 3 Events in an Ironman Triathlon

1. 2.4-mile swim
2. 112-mile bike race
3. 26.2-mile run

---

Nicole Kidman has *lepidopterophobia*...a morbid fear of butterflies.

# WORD ORIGINS

*Ever wonder where certain words come from? Here
are the interesting stories behind some of them.*

# HAGGARD

**Meaning:** Appearing tired or worn out

**Origin:** "When the Normans conquered England in 1066,
they brought with them their own style of falconry. The Old
French word *falcon* referred only to female hawks, while the male
was called a *tercel* (that's where Toyota got it). A wild bird trapped
for falconry was called a *haggard*. These haggards were often
uncontrollable and difficult to train, and soon haggard was being
used to describe unruly, intractable people, and, eventually, the
gaunt appearance of an exhausted person." (From *Once Upon a
Word*, by Rob Kyff)

## HUBRIS

**Meaning:** Arrogance

**Origin:** "In its original Greek sense (the Greek form is *hybris*) it
indicated insolence towards the gods, an unwise attitude that
would inevitably be followed by one's comeuppance (or *nemesis*).
If used to describe someone's current attitudes or behavior, the
speaker is looking forward to saying 'I told you so.'" (From *Faux
Pas?*, by Philip Gooden)

## PASTRAMI

**Meaning:** A cured or smoked, seasoned deli meat

**Origin:** "Pastrami has a Romanian-Roman history. In Bucharest
it's *pastrama*, from a verb meaning 'to preserve.' Pastrami is a kind
of prepared beef, most often taken from a shoulder cut, highly seasoned and smoked to preserve it." (From *A Pleasure in Words*, by
Eugene T. Maleska)

## PAPARAZZI

**Meaning:** Photographers who follow celebrities

**Origin:** "From a character in the 1960 Federico Fellini film, *La*

---

Aretha Franklin's voice has been designated a natural resource by the state of Michigan.

*Dolce Vita*, a photographer named Signor Paparazzo. When Fellini was growing up, one of his classmates was a boy who was always squirming and talking fast. A teacher gave him the nickname *Paparazzo*, an Italian dialect word for a mosquito-like insect that is always buzzing around in the air. When Fellini was writing *La Dolce Vita*, he gave his classmate's nickname to his fictitious photographer, a character who constantly flitted around the rich and famous. Before long the real-life photographers who follow celebrities everywhere began to be known as *paparazzi*, the plural of paparazzo." (From *Inventing English*, by Dale Corey)

## SCAVENGER

**Meaning:** A person or animal who collects junk or waste

**Origin:** "In the 14th century, many English towns levied a tax called a *scavage* on goods sold by nonresident merchants in order to give local merchants an advantage. The *scavegers* (the 'n' was added later) of London were officers charged with the collection of the scavage. The responsibility for keeping the streets clean later fell on their shoulders, as well. When the scavengers' original purpose was forgotten, they remained simple street cleaners. Now anyone who collects junk is a scavenger." (From *The Merriam-Webster Book of Word Histories*)

## SCHLEMIEL

**Meaning:** A fool

**Origin:** "The name comes from one Shelumiel (Numbers 2:12), leader of the tribe of Simeon. Of all the Hebrew captains of his day, he was the only one regularly unsuccessful in battle. The tradition was revived in 1814 by Adelbert von Chamisso, who wrote *Peter Schlemihl's Wonderful Story*, about a man who gives up his shadow to a stranger (the devil) in return for the never-empty purse of Fortunatus (a hero of European legend). The word became a synonym for a person who agreed to a silly bargain." (From *O Thou Improper, Thou Uncommon Noun*, by Willard Espy)

\*　　　\*　　　\*

"Desserts remain for a moment or two in your mouth, and for the rest of your life on your hips."

—**Peg Bracken**

It *is* unusual: Tom Jones was on Charles Manson's hit list.

# AUDIO TREASURES

*Uncle John loves old-time radio shows. Here are some of his favorites. (For a background on the Golden Age of Radio, turn to page 77.)*

(For a background on the Golden Age of Radio, turn to page 77.)

**D**RAGNET (NBC, 1949–57)

If you like to watch *CSI* or any other police "procedural" show, you have Jack Webb—*Dragnet's* Sergeant Joe Friday—to thank for it. Webb came up with the idea for *Dragnet* after playing a forensic scientist in the 1948 movie *He Walked by Night*. Other cops-and-robbers radio shows were mostly flights of fancy, but Webb, the creator and producer of the show as well as its star, was a stickler for authenticity. He rode along with police officers on patrol and sat in on classes at the police academy, soaking up details that he put to good use in his show. Even the ring of the telephones and the number of footsteps between offices were exactly as they were at LAPD headquarters.

**Things to Listen For:** Controversial subject matter. *Dragnet* was the first police show to tackle taboo topics, such as sex crimes, drug abuse, and the deaths of children. The grim storyline of the 1949 Christmas episode: An eight-year-old boy is shot and killed by the .22 rifle his friend got for Christmas. Gritty realism and attention to detail helped make *Dragnet* one of the most popular and long-lasting police dramas on radio. It has influenced nearly every police show—on radio and TV—since.

**Note:** Good writing is one of the things that makes *Dragnet* so much fun to listen to; *bad* writing is what gives another Jack Webb radio detective show, *Pat Novak for Hire* (ABC, 1946–47), its appeal. The endless stream of cheesy similes ("When Feldman hit me I went down like the price of winter wheat," and, "She was kind of pretty, except you could see somebody had used her badly, like a dictionary in a stupid family") pile up like cars on the freeway at rush hour.

## MY FAVORITE HUSBAND (CBS, 1948–51)

If you're a fan of *I Love Lucy*, give *My Favorite Husband* a listen. Lucille Ball stars as Liz Cooper, the screwy wife of George Cooper, played by Richard Denning. The show was so successful that CBS decided to move it to television in 1951. Lucy agreed on one condition: her real-life husband, Cuban bandleader Desi Arnaz, was to play her husband.

## YOURS TRULY, JOHNNY DOLLAR (CBS, 1949–62)

Detective series were commonplace during the golden age of radio. This one set itself apart from the pack by making Johnny Dollar a freelance investigator for insurance companies (instead of a typical gumshoe) and structuring the narration of the story as if Johnny was itemizing his expense account in a letter to his client. Each story began with "Expense account item one," followed by another item or two to get the story rolling. The show ended 30 minutes later with the last item on the account, followed by the signature—"Yours truly, Johnny Dollar." The gimmick worked: the show became one of the longest-running detective shows in radio.

## INNER SANCTUM (NBC/ABC/CBS, 1941–52)

Before *Inner Sanctum*, the hosts of horror shows were as deadly serious and spooky as the stories themselves. Then came Raymond Edward Johnson, a.k.a. "Your host, Raymond," who introduced each story with bad jokes and one morbid pun after another. He was the inspiration for all the smart-aleck horror hosts that followed, including *Tales from the Crypt*'s wisecracking Crypt-keeper.

**Things to Listen For:** The squeaking door that opened and closed each broadcast—probably the most famous sound effect in radio history. The sound was actually created by a squeaky office chair…except for the time that someone fixed the squeak without realizing its importance. That forced the sound man to make the squeak with his voice until the chair returned to "normal." Also, do you like tea with your nightmares? For a time Raymond was paired with Mary Bennett, the singleminded spokeswoman for Lipton Tea, who rarely approved of his jokes and always found a way to insert Lipton Tea and Lipton Soup into their conversations. Listening to how she does it is one of the best parts of the show.

## THE LONE RANGER (Mutual, 1933–54)

*The Lone Ranger* was one of the most popular radio shows of all time. It was targeted at children, but more than half of the listeners were adults. If you listen you'll understand why—crisp storytelling and vivid characters make the show a treat. Earle Graser, who played the Masked Man from 1933 until 1941, delivers a wonderfully over-the-top performance—sometimes he sounds like a crazy man who only *thinks* he's the Lone Ranger.

**Things to Listen For:** Tragedy struck the show in 1941, when Graser was killed in an automobile accident. For the next five shows, the Lone Ranger spoke only in a whisper until the producers found a replacement—Brace Beemer, the show's longtime announcer, who played the Ranger until the series ended in 1954.

## THE GREEN HORNET (Mutual/ABC, 1936–52)

*The Lone Ranger* was such a huge hit that the show's creators, Fran Striker and George Trendle, decided to create a second show by bringing the formula into the 20th century. Like the Lone Ranger, the Green Hornet wore a mask and had an ethnic sidekick (his valet, Kato, a Filipino of Japanese ancestry). The Lone Ranger had a horse named Silver; the Green Hornet drove a car called the Black Beauty. Trendle and Striker even made the Green Hornet the Lone Ranger's great nephew.

**Things to Listen For:** The show had several announcers over the years. One of them was Mike Wallace, who later became a correspondent for the CBS-TV show *60 Minutes*. One more thing: In the early episodes, the announcer claims that the Green Hornet goes after crooks "that even the G-men (FBI agents) couldn't reach." In later shows that line was dropped, after J. Edgar Hoover complained that *no* criminals were beyond the Bureau's reach.

## CHALLENGE OF THE YUKON (ABC/Mutual, 1938–55)

Why stop at *The Green Hornet*? In 1938 Trendle and Striker reworked the *Lone Ranger* format a third time, this time moving it to the Alaskan Gold Rush of the late 1890s, and combining the hero's sidekick and his animal companion into a single character, that of Yukon King, Sergeant Preston's lead sled dog.

**Things to Listen For:** Yukon King's astonishing insight into the human condition: He growls and barks at the bad guys before they are revealed to be bad guys, and whimpers in sympathy when murder victims are discovered. "That's right, King, he's dead!"

First television sitcom: *The Goldbergs* (1949).

# Q & A: ASK THE EXPERTS

*More questions and answers from the world's top trivia experts.*

## EATING RAINBOW

**Q:** *Why aren't there any blue-colored foods?*

**A:** "In the search for blue foods it is important to discount impostors like blueberries, blue cheese, and Blue Nun wine, which are usually gray or purple. There is, however, a variety of corn known as blue corn, commonly obtained in the form of blue tortilla chips. This is but one example of a large range of plant pigments of the *anthocyanin* family, which are pink when acid and blue when alkaline. Since most plant foods are mildly acidic when fresh, anthocyanin-colored foods are rarely seen in their blue form." (From *The Best Ever Notes & Queries*, edited by Joseph Harker)

## BARKING UP THE FAMILY TREE

**Q:** *Why do dogs bark so much, and what are they saying, anyway?*

**A:** "Breeding animals to make them more docile tends to make them more cublike. And that's what scientists believe happened naturally to the wolf-dogs, who for thousands of years hung out on the outskirts of human settlements, scavenging for food. As dogs evolved to be docile, they essentially became overgrown puppies. Even in the absence of danger, dogs may bark for no reason at all, just for the puppy-like thrill of it. So when a yapping dog is driving you crazy, think 'toddler.'" (From *How Come? Planet Earth*, by Kathy Wollard)

## NO $O_2$ FOR YOU

**Q:** *We need oxygen to breathe, and there is oxygen in water. So how come we can drown in water?*

**A:** "Sure, there's oxygen in the water, but we're not equipped to access it. Oxygen in the water is not in a free state as it is in the atmosphere. The one oxygen atom and two hydrogen atoms are so chemically bound together in the water molecule that they can only be separated by a complicated process called *electrolysis*, which involves running an electric current through the water to separate the hydrogen from the oxygen. Only then could you make use of the oxygen, now in a free state." (From *How a Fly Walks Upside Down*, by Martin Goldwyn)

## THE GRASS IS ALWAYS HOTTER

**Q:** *Why does a pile of grass clippings get hot in the middle?*
**A:** "What is happening is that the grass has already begun to rot and produce heat. It feels hotter in the middle because the heat is trapped. Chemical changes begin when organic materials begin to break down; it is these chemical changes that produce the heat." (From *Why?*, by Eric Laithwaite)

## FREE FALLIN'

**Q:** *How does a parachute work?*
**A:** "A parachute is deployed by a skydiver to increase the amount of air resistance and slow down the fall. Once it's deployed, the air resistant force is greater than the force of gravity, so the diver slows down dramatically. Terminal velocity with the open parachute is achieved within a second or so, allowing the person to land safely on the ground at a speed of about 9-16 mph." (From *The Handy Physics Answer Book*, by P. Erik Gundersen)

## LET'S JAM

**Q:** *What's the difference between jam, jelly, preserves, and marmalade?*
**A:** "The preparation of each involves adding sugar or other sweeteners to the fruit to insure flavor preservation, and the removal of water to increase the intensity of taste. Most also include citric acid (for tartness) and pectin (a jelling agent). The main difference is texture. Jellies are prepared from strained fruit juices and have a smooth consistency. Jams are made from crushed fruit. Preserves use whole fruit or pieces of whole fruit. Marmalades use citrus fruit only and include the peel." (From *When Did Wild Poodles Roam the Earth?*, by David Feldman)

# G.E. COLLEGE BOWL

*So you didn't suffer enough on page 61? Here's another bunch of questions to take your self-image down a couple of notches.*

## SCIENCE AND MATHEMATICS

**Tossup Question:** If a plane travels 300 yards in 10 seconds, how many feet does it travel in a fifth of a second?

**Bonus Questions:**

**1.** There's a rhyme that goes like this: "Poor James is dead. We see his face no more. For what he thought was $H_2O$ was $H_2SO_4$." What was the cause of death?

**2.** There are three states of matter: solid, liquid, and gas. Which state has a definite volume, but no definite shape?

**3.** Who discovered the radiation belts that surround the Earth? (*Hint:* They're named after him).

**4.** There are an infinite number of *prime* numbers (whole numbers that are divisible only by themselves and 1). How many of them are even numbers?

**5.** If you're suffering from a myocardial infarction, should you buy a larger pair of shoes, or call 911?

## U.S. HISTORY

**Tossup Question:** Only one crime is defined in the U.S. Constitution. Name it.

**Bonus Questions:**

**1.** Who was president when the United States bought Alaska from Russia? (Extra credit: Who was president when it became a state?)

**2.** Name the one U.S. vice president to preside over the Senate while under indictment for murder.

**3.** In 1858 a man named Duff Armstrong went on trial for murder. A witness for the prosecution claimed that he had been able to see the murder, which happened after dark, by moonlight from 150 feet away. Armstrong's lawyer won his freedom by producing an 1857 almanac, which showed that on the night in question the moon was too low in the sky for that to have been possible. Who was Duff Armstrong's lawyer?

**4.** The United States declared war on what three countries on June 5, 1942? (*Hint:* They're not the countries you're thinking of.)

**5.** When President Dwight D. Eisenhower called out the National Guard in Little Rock, Arkansas in 1957, he did it to enforce desegregation of the public schools. Why did George Washington call out the National Guard in 1794?

## GEOGRAPHY

**Tossup Question:** If you start from Pakistan and travel over the Khyber Pass, where will you end up?

**Bonus Questions:**

**1.** In 1917 the United States purchased some real estate from Denmark for $25 million. What territory did America buy?

**2.** The country of Liechtenstein is only about 5% the size of Rhode Island, and yet it still has room for a capital city. Name it.

**3.** New York City used to be known as New Amsterdam. What used to be known as New Holland?

**4.** What misleadingly named lake is the largest lake in the world?

**5.** The Fox Islands and Rat Islands are both part of what larger chain of islands?

## GENERAL KNOWLEDGE

**Tossup Question:** What four U.S. states refer to themselves as "commonwealths" instead of states?

**Bonus Questions:**

**1.** In the old days, this kind of produce (fruit or vegetable) was called a "love apple." What is it?

**2.** He fought in World War I, and other than George Washington, he's the only general to hold the rank "General of the Armies." What is his name?

**3.** The Sea of Tranquility is found on what kind of map?

**4.** John Chapman made a name for himself wandering around Ohio and Indiana at the turn of the 19th century. How'd he do it?

**5.** According to legend, what was the name of Robin Hood's wife?

*How'd you do? The answers are on page 514.*

---

# THAT'S AMORE?

*When the moon hits your eye like a big pizza pie, it hurts.*

In 2005 Ahmed Salhi, 24, was sentenced to nine months home arrest in Ferrara, Italy, for violating immigration laws. He begged the judge to change the sentence to nine months in *prison*...because he couldn't bear his wife's nagging. "I need some peace," he said.

• A couple in Aachen, Germany, had been sleeping in separate beds for months when the wife finally woke the husband up in the middle of the night and demanded he fulfill his "husbandly duties." He refused. She called the police and demanded they make him do it. "The officers did not feel able to resolve the dispute," a police spokesman said, "let alone issue any kind of official order."

• A woman in Newport, Arkansas, was arrested after she pulled a gun on Larry Estes, a preacher who had just started the service in his church. The woman was Tammy Estes, the preacher's wife. Witnesses later reported that Mrs. Estes was upset over text messages that she'd found from her husband to another woman. After holding Rev. Estes at bay for two hours, she surrendered to police.

• During the 1950s, a couple in Kuligaon, India, had an argument that resulted in the husband moving out of the house...and into a nearby treehouse. As of 2006, the 83-year-old was still living there. "We quarreled over a tiny issue," his wife told reporters. "I've tried to get him to come back, but he has refused all the time."

• In September 2005, Mark Bridgwood, 49, of Dartmouth, England, noticed a classified advertisement in his local paper for a yacht. It was *his* yacht. His estranged wife, Tracy, was secretly selling it for less than half its $180,000 value. "Any quick cash offer considered," the ad said. The fuming husband nixed any possible sale by taking an ax to seawater valves under the vessel's waterline. The 53-foot yacht went down immediately. "It was a beautiful boat," said Tracy, who works as a waitress. "And he sank it."

Coffee should be black as hell, strong as death, and as sweet as love. —Turkish proverb

# ZERO-SUM EXPANSION

*Every line of work has its own jargon, but corporate lingo—
"office speak"—has some of the best (and darkest)
euphemisms around. Here's a brief sampling.*

**Negative advancement:**
Demotion.

**Percussive maintenance:**
Kicking a machine to get it
to work.

**Sub-optimal results:** Failure.

**Temporarily displaced
inventory:** Stolen goods.

**Market correction:** The
stocks are plummeting.

**Opportunity:** Severe problem
with no clear solution.

**Realigned salaries:** Pay cuts.

**Mindsharing:** Brainstorming.

**De-layering:** Eliminating
middle management.

**Treeware:** Paper.

**Efficiency expert:** Outsider
brought in by a company to
decide who should be fired.

**Execution excellence:**
Success.

**Soft restructuring:** Quietly
selling off assets to raise cash,
while publicly denying that
any such action is going on.

**V2V:** "Voice to Voice," or
actually speaking with
someone.

**Enterprise environment:**
The office.

**Capital preservation:** When
a struggling company stops
spending money.

**Negative cash-flow experience:**
The company is losing
money.

**Structural constraints:**
Overhead.

**Zero-sum expansion:** An
attempt to sell more products
or hire more people with no
additional resources.

**We're right-sizing:** You're
fired.

**We're de-growing:** You're fired.

**We're putting you on
indefinite idle:** You're fired.

**We're considering you for
vocational relocation:**
You're fired.

**He left to pursue other
opportunities:** He was fired.

---

The Japanese word *koroski* means "death induced by overwork."

# BEAUTY SECRETS FROM THE GOOD OLD DAYS

*Here's a beauty tip from Uncle John: If your great-great-great-grandma is still living, don't ask her for beauty tips. If what we found in these old books is any guide, you'll probably get some pretty odd advice.*

**To lose weight:** "New York society women usually go upon the milk diet during Lent, as being the most convenient time, and for a week they take nothing into the system but milk. The dose for the milk diet is: Take a glass of milk upon rising, then follow it with a glass every hour all day. Add a pinch of salt if you prefer. The milk will wash all impurities out of the system, and milk taken thusly is not fattening."

—*The Household Physician* (1905)

**Another way to lose weight:** "Keep on bearing children as long and often as possible."

—*Creative and Sexual Science* (1876)

**For wrinkles:** "A wrinkle is like a crinkle in a piece of tissue paper. It is there, but is easily smoothed out. The plaster treatment has been tried with good results: The wrinkle is stretched flat, and slender strips of plaster are applied. When taken off, the wrinkle will be much lighter."

—*The Household Physician* (1905)

**Bathing:** "The vigorous and strong may bathe early in the morning on an empty stomach. The young and weak had better bathe three hours after a meal."

—*Cassell's Household Guide* (1880)

**"Bags under the eyes** destroy the beauty of the face. To get rid of these bags, massage persistently, and also reform the diet, for the eyes are particularly the sign of a bad liver. It is good to eat apples, cooked and raw; correct the liver and the eye sacs will disappear."

—*The Household Physician* (1905)

"Every intelligent dentist knows that the whiter the teeth are," the sooner and the more certainly they will decay. He also knows that those teeth last the longest and are the most useful, which have a yellowish tint."

—*Fun Better Than Physic* (1877)

"To enlarge the bust: An efficacious, yet safe method to enlarge the bust is a persistent massage with some bland oil, of which coconut or olive oil are good examples."

—*The Household Physician* (1905)

"To cure pimples: Take a fairly full breath and hold it momentarily while contracting the abdominal muscles and straining lightly. This brings a flush to the cheeks and fills the capillaries of the skin, insuring a better skin circulation. Standing on the head will have the same effect as the exercise given, and is worth a try."

—*Home Health Manual* (1930)

"Freckled hands in summer are caused by letting the sun touch the hands immediately after they have been washed. The freckles can be removed with lemon juice followed by cold cream."

—*The Household Physician* (1905)

"The very best way of making the hair grow is to rub paraffin into the roots but, of course, you must be very careful afterwards not to go near a fire or light of any kind."

—*The Girl's Own Annual* (1903)

"Fat faced women always have small eyes. As the fat increases, the cheeks puff up and the eyes dwindle. Eyes can be made larger if one massages the cheeks until the fat is less noticeable."

—*The Household Physician* (1905)

To freshen the breath: "A lump of charcoal held in the mouth two or three times in a week and slowly chewed, has a power to preserve the teeth and purify the breath. Those who are troubled with an offensive breath might chew it very often and swallow it but seldom."

—*Polite Manual for Young Ladies* (1847)

# THE NAKED TRUTH

*Writing is a profession that requires focus and concentration. Here are a few well-known authors who liked to strip away all distractions—literally—before they got down to work.*

**V ICTOR HUGO.** The French novelist who wrote *Les Misérables* and *The Hunchback of Notre Dame* hated the labor of writing and was a great procrastinator. So he came up with a unique way to force himself to work: He handed all of his clothes to his servant, with orders not to give them back until Hugo had completed a full day's writing.

**EDMOND ROSTAND.** The French author of *Cyrano de Bergerac* suffered so many interruptions from visitors that he resorted to working naked in his bathtub to get some privacy.

**ERNEST HEMINGWAY.** The American novelist (*For Whom the Bell Tolls*) wrote nude, standing up, with his typewriter at about waist level.

**ROBIN MOORE.** In a possible homage to Hemingway, Moore (*The Green Berets* and *The Hunt for Bin Laden*) says he also likes to type his novels while standing in the nude.

**JAMES WHITCOMB RILEY.** The American poet had a tendency to drink too much when he wrote. So he had himself locked inside a hotel room, naked, thus thwarting any temptation to stroll out to the bar for a cocktail.

**D. H. LAWRENCE.** This British novelist (*Lady Chatterley's Lover*) liked to climb mulberry trees in the buff and then write when he came back down.

**BENJAMIN FRANKLIN.** According to legend (which he probably helped spread), the statesman and author of *Poor Richard's Almanack* began each day by taking an "air bath"—sitting naked for hours in an extremely cold room—while he wrote.

---

Whole milk contains only 4% fat by weight—but 48% by calories.

# SCAM-O-RAMA

*The latest in scams, frauds, cons, and quacks brought to you by* Uncle John's Bathroom Reader, *the book that can spin straw into gold, cure the common cold, and prevent you from getting old.*

## THIS ISN'T HOT, IS IT?

A 42-year-old woman in South Bend, Indiana, called police after being sold a bogus flat-screen television. The woman had been approached by a man on the street about a great deal on the TV: just $500. When she said she couldn't afford that, the price got even better: $300. The woman bought the set, which was bubble-wrapped, had Wal-Mart stickers on it, and came with a remote control, and happily took it home. But when she opened it she discovered it wasn't a flat-screen television at all—it was an oven door. Police said the scam explained the recent theft of oven doors from several abandoned properties. (The suspect was arrested two months later...with an oven door in his truck.)

## FOWL PLAY

Transportation authorities in New Zealand uncovered an automobile-registration scam after a woman called a radio station to brag about it. She told the hosts that she had registered her car as a "noncommercial hearse" for carrying dead animals, which allowed her to pay only $36 instead of the normal $113. The dead animals she was transporting: chickens—frozen ones from the supermarket. A search quickly discovered 40 more people using the scheme, with possibly hundreds more to come. Land Transport spokesman Andy Knackstedt said, "The definition of a hearse is a vehicle used to convey coffins, not to convey groceries."

## MICROSPUD, INC.

In 2004 a man in the German city of Kaiserslautern angrily returned a computer to the store where he had just purchased it, claiming to have been taken in a scam. The computer's insides, he showed them, were full of potatoes, not computer parts. The store apologized and gave the man another computer. Turns out he was the scammer, not the scamee. He almost got away with it, too.

Store security called police when the man returned the second computer—again filled with potatoes—and said he didn't need the computer anymore, he wanted a cash refund. The man was arrested and charged with fraud.

## JUST A PHONE CALL AWAY

Hideto Tomabechi became famous in Japan as the man who "deprogrammed" brainwashed members of the AUM Shinrikyo cult in the 1990s. In 2004 he became famous again when he developed a cell phone ring tone...that increases breast size. Tomabechi claimed the song uses sounds that "make the brain and body move unconsciously" and called it "positive brainwashing." While that might seem so ludicrous that nobody would believe it, the tune, "Rockmelon," was purchased and downloaded 10,000 times in its first week alone. "We offer loads of *chakumero* [ringtones] at 300 yen [$2.60] a month," said a spokesman for Media Chic, the company selling the tune. "And the tune promising huge breasts would have to be in our top ten." Tomabechi was so pleased with the results that he's developing ringtones to cure baldness, improve memory, attract mates, and help people give up smoking.

## THEY RECEIVED STIFF PENALTIES

In 2003 a hospital employee in Harare, Zimbabwe, noticed a mortician entering the basement morgue carrying a coffin that had earlier been sent out for a funeral with a body in it. The employee notified authorities, and an investigation revealed that the mortician and an assistant had been renting corpses out to people...so they could cut in front of the long lines at gas stations. Gasoline is in short supply and extremely expensive in Harare, and most stations give priority to people with burial orders (which the duo also provided) and corpses. The cadaver dealers were arrested and charged with violating dead bodies.

\*     \*     \*

"If one morning I walked on top of the water across the Potomac River, the headline that afternoon would read: PRESIDENT CAN'T SWIM."

—Lyndon B. Johnson

Only four angels are mentioned by name in the Bible: Gabriel, Michael, Abaddon...and Lucifer.

# BUILDING THE WALL

*Today, the Vietnam Veterans Memorial is one of the most popular*
*memorials in the United States, but at the time it was conceived*
*it was so controversial that it's a wonder it got built at all.*

## MOVING PICTURE

One evening in March 1979, Jan Scruggs went to see *The Deer Hunter*, a movie about a group of friends who go off to fight in the Vietnam War. Scruggs had served in Vietnam, and the movie upset him so much that he sat up all night drinking whiskey to dull the pain. But something good came from the experience, too: Scruggs decided he wanted to try and get a memorial built for Vietnam veterans, to honor their sacrifices and aid in the healing process. In April he and an attorney friend, also a Vietnam vet, founded the Vietnam Veterans Memorial Fund to raise money to build the monument.

## LAYING THE FOUNDATION

After a slow start, the memorial fund began to make progress. More veterans joined the effort, the money started coming in, and legislation setting aside three acres on the Mall in Washington, D.C., for the memorial sailed through both houses of Congress. Jimmy Carter signed the bill into law on July 1, 1980.

As fundraising continued, the organization announced that the design for the memorial would be chosen in a national contest. Any U.S. citizen over the age of 18 was eligible to enter. The deadline for entry was March 31, 1981; the winning design would be chosen by a jury of eight architects, sculptors, and other professionals in May. For an entry to be considered it had to meet four criteria: 1) It had to be "reflective and contemplative" in nature; 2) It had to fit in with its surroundings on the Mall; 3) It had to contain the names of all U.S. personnel who died in the war or who were listed as missing in action; and 4) It could not make a political statement about the war.

In all, 1,421 people entered designs. The entries were identified only by number to prevent the judges from knowing who was responsible for each design. It took them four days to winnow the entries down to 232 and then to 39 and then finally to 1, entry number 1,026. That entry had been submitted by Maya Lin, a 21-year-old Yale architecture student who created it as a class assignment. (It got a B+). Her design won by unanimous vote.

## THE WALL

Lin's design was simple and stark: Two long black walls that meet at a 125° angle. The walls are just over 10 feet tall where they meet at the apex, and taper to just eight inches high at the far ends.

The names are listed in columns in chronological order of when they fell in battle or went missing. They start in the center of the memorial and move rightward down the length of the east wall, then pick up again at west wall, ending back at the center, so that the last person killed in the war is listed not far from the name of the first person killed.

The walls are made of black granite that was especially chosen for its reflective quality. A path running along the memorial allows visitors to touch the names; when they do, their faces are reflected in the granite. (Lin was at Yale when the names of the school's Vietnam War dead were being carved into the wall of one of the buildings; she found that she could not pass the building without stopping to touch the names, and she thought visitors to this memorial would want to touch the names, too.)

## SOMETHING NEW TO FIGHT OVER

Lin's design has since become one of the most popular war memorials in the country, if not the world. It's easy to forget how controversial it was when it was selected, not just because of what was included in the design, but because of what *wasn't*—there were no heroic statues, no patriotic verses carved in stone alongside the names, and no American flag. The name "Vietnam War" didn't appear anywhere on the wall, either. There was a wall. It had names carved in it—that was it.

People who were expecting something like the statue of the soldiers raising the flag on the Iwo Jima memorial were stunned. Members of the Memorial Fund were bitterly divided over the jury's decision; one member, a veteran named Thomas Carhart, called it an "open urinal" and vowed to stop it.

## THE DEVIL'S IN THE DETAILS

Opponents attacked every aspect of the design and saw conspiracies and hidden meanings behind many of the details:

The V shape? They thought it represented the two-fingered "peace" sign that had been popular with anti-war protesters. Actually, Lin chose an angle over a straight line so that the west wall would point toward the Lincoln Memorial, and the east wall would point toward the Washington Monument. That gave the memorial historical context while integrating it with its surroundings.

The black granite? Critics said it was intended to symbolize shame; they wanted white granite instead. Lin chose black granite so that people would see themselves reflected in the names of their loved ones, providing a link between the past and present. White granite wouldn't show reflections, and since the site faced south and into the sun, it would have been blinding to visitors.

Opponents objected to the idea of the wall being sunk into the earth and approached by walking down a grade. But this was integral to the design—Lin wanted the memorial to appear as "a rift in the earth," representing the upheaval of war. Making the memorial lower than the surrounding landscape also sheltered it from surrounding noise, making it a quiet spot for reflection.

## THE NAMES

The opponents of the design also wanted the names to be listed in alphabetical order, not in the order in which the men (and eight women) died or went missing. Many people also felt that the names should start at the far left of the memorial and end at the right. Lin explained that there were many duplicate names in the more than 58,000 people killed, including 600 people with the last name of Smith and 16 men named James Jones. When the family of one of the James Joneses came to honor his memory, how would they know which of the 16 names represented their loved one?

Having the name of the last person killed in the war meet at the apex with the name of the first person killed, instead of listing names from left to right, symbolized "a wound that is closed and healing." It also prevented the monument from becoming a "bar graph of slaughter," reflecting the increasing death toll as America got pulled deeper into the war, followed by a decline in deaths when the United States began to pull out of Vietnam.

Lin's explanation of the thinking behind the design didn't make the opponents any happier, and they had a powerful friend in Secretary of the Interior James Watt. Watt saw the memorial as "an act of treason." He was the Reagan Administration official in charge of the National Mall, and he refused to allow construction to begin unless the planners agreed to put a flagpole on top of the wall and a statue in front of it, right at the apex. Lin complained that it would have turned the wall into little more than a backdrop, and it would look like a putting green.

Lin was only a college student at the time, but she held her ground against Watt and other powerful opponents: She refused to compromise on her design. Watt wouldn't give in either, and the stalemate dragged on until Senator John Warner of Virginia, an early supporter of the monument, forced the two sides into a compromise. In the end it was the opponents who blinked—they got their flagpole and a statue titled *Three Soldiers*, but they were placed at the entrance to the memorial, about 300 feet away from the wall. Lin wasn't happy with the compromise; she equated it with a vandal scrawling a mustache on a portrait. But at least the wall itself was protected.

## OPEN FOR BUSINESS

The groundbreaking for the memorial took place on March 26, 1982; construction was completed in October, and the wall was dedicated on November 13. (President Reagan did not attend.) The wall will probably never be without controversy. Nevertheless, today it is one of the most popular memorials in the country, and more than three million people visit it each year. For those who cannot visit, a Vietnam veteran named John Devitt created The Moving Wall, a half-scale replica that he hauls around the country each year from April to November. That wall was so popular that he and other volunteers built a second wall and then a third that they take all over the country. These moving walls have been visited by tens of millions of Americans, about as many as have visited the genuine article in Washington, D.C.

## READING THE NAMES

• As of 2006, there are 58,253 names inscribed on the wall, including approximately 1,200 that are listed as missing in action. Since the wall was completed, 226 new names have been added—most of them when the geographic criteria were expanded to include people who died outside the war zone but while in combat or in support of direct combat missions. Fifteen of the names are those of servicemen who have since died from wounds they received in Vietnam.

• If you've visited the memorial, you probably noticed that each name on the wall has a symbol next to it. A diamond next to a name indicates that the person's death was confirmed. A cross means the person is missing and unaccounted for. (If a person's status changes from missing to confirmed dead, the cross is converted to a diamond.) If a person who is missing ever turns up alive, a circle will be drawn around their cross. As of July 2006, that has not happened once.

• Veterans who die from cancer related to exposure to the defoliant Agent Orange do not qualify to have their names inscribed on the wall, nor do veterans who commit suicide while suffering from post-traumatic stress disorder.

• Though the list of names was checked and rechecked several times before they were carved into the granite, the Vietnam Veterans Memorial Fund estimates that the names of as many as 38 living veterans may be on the wall as the result of clerical errors.

## PARTING GIFTS

It wasn't long after the wall opened that people started leaving objects for their loved ones whose names appear on the wall: dog tags, letters, photographs; even food, cigarettes, and beer. Originally it was thought that these items should simply be disposed of, but when maintenance workers could not bring themselves to toss them out, the National Park Service started saving personal, nonperishable items. Park rangers collect and catalog the items each evening and send them to a facility called the Museum Resource Center in Maryland. So far the National Park Service has collected well over 60,000 items. A representative sample is displayed at the Smithsonian's National Museum of American History.

\*     \*     \*

He who forgives ends the quarrel. —**African proverb**

Statue of Bedloe? Liberty Island was originally named Bedloe's Island.

# FORGOTTEN FIRSTS IN ROBOT HISTORY

*The first known robot was a mechanical wooden bird, powered by steam, built by Greek mathematician Archytas of Tarentum in 350 B.C. Here are some more robot firsts.*

**1927:** "Maria," a female robot, appears in Fritz Lang's science-fiction movie *Metropolis*. It's the first ever on-screen robot.

**1940:** Isaac Asimov publishes "Robbie" in *Super Science Stories*, the first piece of robot-themed fiction.

**1954:** George Devol receives the first patent for a robot. Five years later, his Unimate, a robotic arm, is installed at a General Motors plant in New Jersey. It moves pieces of hot metal from a die-casting machine.

**1966:** Shakey, developed by the Stanford Research Institute, becomes the first robot that can actually react to its surroundings. Using "reason," it can identify and move small objects.

**1968:** "Humanoid Boogie" by the British group Bonzo Dog Doo-Dah Band is released, making it the first pop song about robots.

**1969:** A remote-controlled robot washes the windows of the Tower of the Americas in San Antonio, Texas.

**1983:** Ropet-HR, built by Personal Robotics Corp., lobbies the House of Representatives for increased spending in robot technology. It is the first robot to address Congress.

**1983:** "Robot Redford" becomes the first robot to deliver a commencement address when it speaks to the graduating class at Anne Arundel Community College in Maryland.

**1984:** A robot named "Rebecca" runs for president of the United States as an independent. Her supporters say she's eligible because she was "born" in Maryland.

**2006:** A team at Carnegie Mellon University creates "McBlare," the first robot bagpipe player. (Was that really necessary?)

# PEMA CHÖDRÖN

*Born in New York City in 1936, Chödrön was an elementary-school
teacher until her husband left her in the 1970s. That's when she decided to
become a Buddhist nun. She is now an author and spiritual teacher, most
noted for her ability to apply Buddhist teachings to everyday life*

"Now is the only time. How we relate to it creates the future. If we're going to be more cheerful in the future, it's because of our aspiration to be cheerful in the present. The future is the result of what we do right now."

"If we learn to open our hearts, anyone, including the people who drive us crazy, can be our teacher."

"We think the point is to pass the test or to overcome the problem, but the truth is that things don't really get solved. They come together and they fall apart. The healing comes from letting there be room for it all to happen: room for grief, for relief, for misery, for joy."

"Only to the extent that we expose ourselves over and over again to annihilation can that which is indestructible be found in us."

"Without loving kindness for ourselves, it is impossible to genuinely feel it for others."

"Gloriousness and wretchedness need each other. One inspires us, the other softens us."

"We work on ourselves in order to help others, but also we help others in order to work on ourselves."

"The truth you cling to makes you unavailable to hear anything new."

"A sign of health is that we don't become undone by fear and trembling, but take it as a message that it's time to stop struggling and look directly at what threatens us."

"Rejoicing in ordinary things takes guts. Each time we drop our complaints and allow everyday good fortune to inspire us, we enter the warrior's world."

"This body that we have, that's sitting right here right now—with its aches and its pleasures—is exactly what we need to be fully human, fully awake, fully alive."

# EVERYBODY'S A CRITIC

*Even revered artists get bad reviews (and
some go out of their way to give them).*

"He is as unacquainted with art as a hog with mathematics."
**—The London Critic, on poet Walt Whitman**

"He might have been a great composer if his teacher had spanked
him enough on his backside."
**—Ludwig van Beethoven, on Rossini**

"I like his music better than any other. It is so loud that one can
talk the whole time without people hearing what one says. That is
a great advantage."
**—Oscar Wilde, on composer Richard Wagner**

"Never have I read such tosh. As for the first two chapters we will
let them pass, but the 3rd, 4th, 5th, 6th—merely the scratchings
of pimples on the body of the bootboy at Claridges."
**—Virginia Woolf, on James Joyce's *Ulysses***

"He sang like a hinge."
**—Ethel Merman, describing Cole Porter**

"Take from him his sophisms, futilities, and incomprehensibilities
and what remains? His foggy mind."
**—Thomas Jefferson, on Plato**

"*Howl* is meant to be a noun, but I can't help taking it as an
imperative."
**—Partisan Review, on Allen Ginsberg's poem *Howl***

"Composition indeed! Decomposition is the proper word for such
hateful fungi!"
**—Dramatic and Musical World, on the work of Franz Liszt**

"As a piece of good taste, it ranks with that statuette of the Milo
Venus with the clock in her stomach."
**—Dorothy Parker, on an essay by Upton Sinclair**

---

**Puppy love: 3% of pet owners give Valentine's Day gifts to their pets.**

# VOTE FOR ME!

*Do political campaigns bring out the best in people? Apparently not.*

## GRASSROOTS CAMPAIGN

In 2005 Edward Forchion, also known as "Weedman," ran for governor of New Jersey on the slogan "Take a Toke, Then Vote!" The self-proclaimed leader of the "Marijuana Party," Forchion had also run in 1998. About the 2005 campaign, he said, "It's a whole angrier thing." He was angry because he'd spent five months in jail in 2002 for filming a TV ad promoting the legalization of marijuana, which prosecutors said was a violation of his parole. (He was on parole after serving 16 months for distribution of marijuana.) When a federal judge freed Forchion, finding that the arrest violated his right to free speech, Forchion wanted revenge. "My whole reason for running for office is to specifically give the finger to the attorney general," he said. (Forchion got 8,271 votes, coming in 6th out of 10 candidates.)

## CANDIDATE FROM CELL BLOCK C

In November 2005, Randy Logan Hale won one of three available seats for the Romoland School District board in Riverside, California. People in the district were confused: They had never seen Hale at any board meetings, and he hadn't attended any of the candidate events, either. A call to his wife, Penny, cleared it up: He was in jail. The school board candidate had been incarcerated since September for parole violations stemming from a 1998 spousal-abuse conviction. Penny Hale said that her husband had run for a school board seat because "he cares about kids." When he won, she said, "He'll be glad." But you have to be a registered voter to run for office, and convicted felons aren't allowed to vote. In May 2006, Hale was charged with perjury, forgery, and voter fraud.

## HEART OF THE MATTER

When California farmer and businessman Tom Berryhill entered the Republican primary for assemblyman in 2006, he probably didn't expect his "heart" to be questioned quite the way it was. His opponent, former Modesto City Councilman Bill Conrad, sent out a mailer with the red-lettered headline, "Tom Berryhill

doesn't have the HEART for State Assembly." What was he referring to? The fact that Berryhill was a heart transplant recipient.
Conrad's letter continued with "Heart Transplant Facts":

- The Average Lifespan of a Heart Transplant recipient is seven
years. (Berryhill's heart transplant was six years ago.)
- Heart Transplant patients take anti-rejection medications for life,
which weaken the immune system making the recipient more susceptible to illness and death
- Severe stress SIGNIFICANTLY shortens the life expectancy of
Heart Transplant recipients.

The ad continued, "Can you imagine the costs to taxpayers for a
special election when poor health renders him unable to fulfill the
duties of office?" The letter was condemned, mocked, ridiculed, and
lambasted by the press (and voters in the district). "He's set a new
low," said Berryhill. "This is the type of thing that keeps good people from running for office." (Happy ending: Berryhill won.)

## MORALLY BANKRUPT

In early 2006, Arizona resident Mike Harris argued in court that
child-support payments to his ex-wife were putting him "near
bankruptcy." The judge cut the payments in half, from $2,000 a
month to $1,000. But just months after the case, Harris, a candi-
date for Arizona governor, somehow found his financial situation
improved—he donated $100,000 of his own money to his cam-
paign. Questioned by reporters, Harris said he was simply doing
better…but he wouldn't be increasing his payments to his ex-wife.

## OTHER STANDOUTS

- George W. Bush didn't win in 2004. Neither did John Kerry. It
was Green Party candidate David Cobb. A survey of dentists by
the California Dental Association said Cobb had the "most attractive" and "most trustworthy" smile.
- In June 2006, Republican Congresswoman Marilyn Musgrave
of Colorado received an unusual "gift" at her office. The package,
wrapped in one of the reelection campaign mailers that had been
sent to her constituents, was full of dog poop. Using the address on
the mailer, police tracked the package back to Kathleen Ensz, a
prominent local Democratic party official, who was cited for criminal use of a noxious substance (the dog poop).

Before the Rockies or the Alps were formed, the dinosaurs were already extinct.

# REVENGE!

*A dish best served cold. These people must have had theirs in the freezer.*

## PHOTO FINISH

In February 2006, a man who gave his address simply as "Wales" offered 200 photos of his sexily attired wife for sale on eBay. "She was playing away with my so-called best friend," he wrote, "and now it's payback time." He asked £4.99 ($8.75) each and sold them all in less than 24 hours. An eBay spokesman told reporters, "We saw no reason to take the listing off."

## HE WAS FRAMED

In the 1950s, Greek shipping magnate Stavros Niarchos commissioned Salvador Dali to paint his portrait. The price: $15,000. But Dali was incensed when Niarchos got up and left the sitting after just the face was done, telling Dali he could finish the painting without him. Dali did—he drew a very unflattering naked body to go along with the pompous man's head…and then sold it to Niarchos's rival, Aristotle Onassis, for $25,000. Years later, Onassis had Niarchos over for lunch one day, just so he could show him the embarrassing portrait hanging on his dining room wall. (Onassis finally agreed to let Niarchos buy it back…for $75,000.)

## NAUGHTY NEIGHBOR

In September 2005, Darren Wood began work on a new home for his family in Riverton, Utah. That started an ongoing feud with his neighbor-to-be, Stan Torgersen, who thought Wood was building too close to his existing home, endangering the foundation of his house and ruining his view. Torgersen tried to get the city to stop construction of the new home, which cost Wood time and money to plead his case. Wood got his revenge when, almost a year later, the house finally went up. It had a large, specially made window that directly faced his neighbor's house. Wood said it was a piece of art, made to look like a "beautiful cactus." Torgersen—and just about anybody else who saw the window—thought it looked a lot like a hand…with its middle finger raised.

# THE CULTURE CLUB

*Do you know what* pukana *is? How about a "walking marriage," or* bhoonda? *Neither did we, until we saw these news stories and decided to take a look.*

**C**ULTURE: Maori people of New Zealand

**IN THE NEWS:** In 2005 Michael Walker, one of New Zealand's leading jockeys, was ordered by racing officials to stop celebrating racing wins in his preferred way: by rolling his eyes and sticking out his tongue as he continues to ride around the track. They said he was being disrespectful of the other racers.

**BACKGROUND:** Walker is Maori, one of New Zealand's indigenous people, and he was performing the ancient ritual of *pukana*. "I am very proud of where I come from and my heritage. People probably thought I was doing it to be cheeky," Walker told the *New Zealand Herald.* "That is not the case."

"Pukana is an action derived from times of war, to make your face fierce and warlike," explained Pita Sharples of the nation's Maori Party. "Over time the fighting aspect had been modernized to now demonstrate solidarity with the Maori culture. It is now a sign of pride. He is saying, 'Hey, I am Maori and I have won.'"

Walker vowed to continue celebrating his wins with pukana. "I don't think it puts a bad image on racing," he said. "If anything, it has brought a bit of color."

**CULTURE:** Mosuo people of China

**IN THE NEWS:** In 2005 PBS's *Frontline* aired a TV program called "The Women's Kingdom." It told the story of the Mosuo people who live around Lugu Lake in the Himalayas of southern China, and are one of the world's few remaining matriarchal societies. Women are in charge in every aspect, including family finances, raising children…and the bedroom.

**BACKGROUND:** The Mosuo practice what is called "walking marriages." A woman gives a man a signal, either subtly or by simply telling him that he will be "walking to" her room that evening. In the morning the man goes home to his mother's house. The woman may choose the same man night after night

An Arctic woolly bear caterpillar can live 14 years before it turns into a moth.

for years, or she may choose another whenever she wants; it's up to her. Any children that result from a union are raised in the mother's house and are taken care of by her brothers. The father will have little to do with the child; his duties are at his own home, where he helps to raise the children of his sisters.

Some other peculiarities of the Mosuo: The religious script (*Tomba*) used by their priests is the world's only true ideographic (picture-based) language still in use today. Also, the Mosuo language contains no words for "murder," "rape," or "war," and they have no jails.

**CULTURE:** Hill towns of Himachal Pradesh, northern India

**IN THE NEWS:** In 2005 people in the town of Shimla in the Indian Himalayas strung a thick rope across a mountain gorge, one end higher than the other. A saddle was placed on the higher end of the rope. Thirty-five-year-old Kanwar Singh was then brought to the site. Sandbags were tied to his feet (to help him keep the balance he was going to need), he was placed on the saddle, a shroud was put over his head—and he was pushed down the 600-foot length of rope. His wife "readied herself for widowhood, already loose haired, wailing, breast-beating as death was certain," *India News* reported.

**BACKGROUND:** Singh was performing a ritual known as *bhoonda*. Experts say the ritual's origins are unclear, but it dates to at least medieval times. Traditionally, a man from the local community was chosen three months before the ceremony. While living in the village temple during this period, he wove a rope made of grass, approximately 500 *hath* long (a *hath* is the length between the elbow and the tip of the middle finger). On the appointed day, the man and his wives made a ceremonial march to the top of the hill in a "procession of the gods." There the rope was strung across the gorge and a woolen saddle laid on the rope. The man was then seated and at a signal from the priest, pushed downhill. His survival, according to historians, "depended purely on chance."

India outlawed *bhoonda* in 1962 because of its obvious dangers. But 10 years later it was made legal again after protests by people in the region. As for Singh, he had the gods on his side in 2005, and calmly stepped off the saddle after his hair-raising ride. "It was amazing. He was so calm when he slid down the rope," one spectator said. "He is truly a hero."

So *that's* why they're not allowed in church: Glow sticks contain an ingredient called *luciferin*.

# SUPERMAN, STARRING JAMES CAAN

*Some roles are so closely associated with a specific actor that it's hard to imagine that he or she wasn't the first choice for the part. Can you imagine, for example...*

**TOM HANKS AS JERRY MAGUIRE** (*Jerry Maguire*—1996) Cameron Crowe wrote the movie and created the role of a shallow sports agent specifically for Tom Hanks. But Hanks turned him down—he was too busy filming his directorial debut, *That Thing You Do*. Tom Cruise was reluctant to do the movie (he didn't want to be anybody's second choice), but did it and was nominated for an Oscar. Hanks's movie bombed.

**JOHN TRAVOLTA AS JIM MORRISON** (*The Doors*—1991) John Travolta was the front-runner for the Morrison role. He met with the surviving members of the Doors in 1986 and impressed them so much that they gave director Oliver Stone their approval to go ahead with Travolta. They even considered going on tour with him as lead singer. Ultimately, though, they decided Travolta was "too nice" to replace Morrison, both onscreen and off.

**JADA PINKETT-SMITH AS TRINITY** (*The Matrix*—1999) Readers of *Uncle John's Slightly Irregular Bathroom Reader* may recall that Will Smith turned down the role of Neo in *The Matrix*. But it could have been a family affair: Smith's wife, Jada Pinkett-Smith, went on multiple auditions for the female lead and thought she had nailed the part. Then little-known actress Carrie-Anne Moss auditioned once...and got it. But the film's directors, Larry and Andy Wachowski, did like Pinkett-Smith—so much that they cast her in both sequels, *The Matrix Reloaded* and *The Matrix Revolutions*.

**SYLVESTER STALLONE AS AXEL FOLEY** (*Beverly Hills Cop*—1984) The script was written in 1977 as an action movie for Stallone. But by the time production started in 1983, cop movies were stale. Producers wanted to make the film more of a comedy, but Stallone actually wanted *more* action and violence. Two weeks

---

Don't touch! The "warts" on a toad are actually toxin-filled glands.

before filming, Stallone quit. Producers decided to play up the comedy, ordered a rewrite, and hired Eddie Murphy.

### CHARLIZE THERON AS NOMI MALONE (*Showgirls*—1995)
Theron auditioned for the role of the criminal-turned-stripper, then took herself out of the running. The part went to Elizabeth Berkeley. The movie, one of the most notorious bombs of all time, flopped, and pretty much ended Berkeley's career. Theron later called her decision "a blessing."

### JAMES CAAN AS SUPERMAN (*Superman*—1978)
After starting off the 1970s with a starring role in *The Godfather*, by 1977 Caan was in a career slump. Director Richard Donner was working on the first *Superman* movie and offered Caan the lead. At the time, action-movie roles were mostly the territory of TV stars, and Caan, a serious actor, didn't want to be lumped in with those guys. He told Donner, "There's no way I'm getting into that silly suit." The part went to TV actor Christopher Reeve.

### JODIE FOSTER AS PRINCESS LEIA (*Star Wars*—1977)
Carrie Fisher got the part—she was director George Lucas's first choice. But Fisher was more interested in pursuing a career as a writer than as an actress, and Lucas feared she might drop out before filming began. So he had another actress ready to go: Jodie Foster, who was only 15 at the time. (Lucas had seen her act in the role of a child prostitute in *Taxi Driver* and was convinced she could do it.)

### HENRY WINKLER AS DANNY ZUKO (*Grease*—1978)
It's not too hard to imagine Winkler in this part. The role of a tough, leather-jacket-wearing 1950s greaser is pretty similar to Fonzie, the character Winkler played on *Happy Days*. And that's exactly why Winkler didn't do it: He didn't want to be typecast.

### GARY COOPER AS RHETT BUTLER (*Gone With the Wind*—1939)
Cooper was the producers' first choice, but he'd hated the book and thought a movie was a bad idea. "*Gone With the Wind* is going to be the biggest flop in Hollywood history," he said after Clark Gable had been cast, "and I'm just glad it'll be Clark Gable who's falling on his face and not Gary Cooper."

Yellow fever: The average American eats 28 pounds of bananas a year.

# NUDES & PRUDES

*News of the scantily clad and the folks they make mad.*

**NUDE:** In February 2005, an Auckland, New Zealand, man charged with indecent exposure arrived at the courthouse to answer the charges…naked. Simon Oosterman, 24, had been arrested a week earlier for taking part in the Auckland Naked Bike Ride, which was organized to protest dependence on automobiles. Now he was protesting the arrest. "There has to be a distinction," Oosterman said, "between people flashing young girls and simple public nudity."

**PRUDE:** In June 2004 Oleg Shlyk, the deputy governor of Kaliningrad, Russia, ordered female government employees to stop wearing short skirts and sexy makeup to work. His reason: The women were arousing the "animal instincts" of male government workers. But by trying to encourage public modesty, Shlyk ended the object of public ridicule. "If short skirts and makeup distract him and he cannot control himself to direct his energy correctly," said Yuri Matochkin, a deputy of the regional parliament, "he ought to change his job."

**NUDE:** Ontario, Canada, police arrested a 39-year-old man after he stripped off his clothes and jumped naked into a gas-station car wash when his taxi driver stopped at the station to fill up. The man, whose name was not released to the media, was still "bathing" when police came and took him away. He was later charged with being naked *and* intoxicated in a public place.

**PRUDE:** The city of San Antonio, Texas, has come up with a novel way to prevent strippers from stripping completely: They are now required to apply for business licenses, and must carry them on their person while performing. The licenses are about half the size of a credit card…so where are the dancers supposed to put them? "It can be on the wrist or ankle, or something like that," says Lt. Mike Gorhum, head of the city's vice squad.

# MORE BATHROOM NEWS

*Our continuing quest to keep commodes in the public eye.*

## PASTORAL PIT STOP

Rev. John Hawdon was filling in for the regular vicar at Longforgan Parish Church in Perthshire, Scotland, when, during a break in the service, he had to make a pit stop...forgetting that his wireless lapel mic was still attached to his robe. The stunned congregation listened to the sounds of the reverend "peeing, sighing with relief, flushing, and washing his hands." Said one parishioner, "It was mortifying. Every sound boomed and echoed around the church. We all sat there looking at each other, totally embarrassed. One or two folk managed a wee giggle."

## TAKE A SEAT

Rosemary Salce is a guidance counselor at Public School #18 in Manhattan. Because of overcrowding and budget cuts in New York City's public schools, Salce's counseling office had to be turned into a classroom, which left the school's only guidance counselor with no place to counsel. Her solution: She converted one of the school's restrooms into an office. It has room for only two chairs and a desk, but the small size isn't the biggest problem. "Every time a toilet flushes somewhere in the school, it stinks in here," Salce laments. But at least, she admits, the students have access to her services.

## DID A DEADHEAD STEAL THE DEAD'S HEAD?

One of Grateful Dead guitarist Jerry Garcia's most treasured possessions was his salmon-colored personal toilet, where he reportedly spent a lot of time thinking and writing songs. After his death in 1995, the toilet became the property of Henry Koltys, who had purchased Garcia's Sonoma, California, home. Koltys didn't want the toilet, though, and sold it to a casino for $2,550. The casino planned to add the potty to a traveling exhibit (they also purchased William Shatner's kidney stones for the show), but before they could claim the commode, someone stole it. Garcia's gardener, Jon Lipsin, thinks it was "liberated" by Deadheads. "It's a little gross," he said, "but I could see that toilet in a rock 'n' roll museum."

---

Prince Charles owns a collection of toilet seats.

# AMERICA'S MOST WANTED

*America's Most Wanted was the Fox network's first big hit. It was pretty controversial when it was launched in the late 1980s, but love it or hate it, it's hard to argue against a show that has led to the capture of nearly 1,000 wanted criminals.*

## MADE IN GERMANY

When Fox TV first went on the air on October 6, 1986, it had only one show—*The Late Show Starring Joan Rivers* —but it had ambitious plans to add others. One program that Fox wanted to copy was *Aktenzeichen XY...Ungelöst* (*File XY...Unsolved*), a German TV show that had been on the air since 1967. Each episode featured as many as five real-life unsolved crimes that were reenacted and presented to the viewing audience. The hope was that someone would call in with a tip that would help solve the crime.

*File XY* was the outgrowth of an earlier show called *Vorsicht, Falle!* (*Beware, Trap!*), which warned viewers about scam artists operating in Germany. Without being asked, so many viewers had sent in information about the con men depicted on the show that the producers decided to create *File XY* around the premise of asking viewers to send in tips. In 1984 the BBC began airing a similar show called *Crimewatch UK*; it too was successful. But would the concept work in the United States?

## PUTTING IT TOGETHER

Michael Linder, a former *Entertainment Tonight* producer, and Stephen Chao, a former *National Enquirer* reporter, were the Fox executives who fleshed out the show's details. They decided to focus the most attention on cases involving violent criminals who had committed crimes in the recent past and were likely to continue if they weren't caught right away. Escaped cons or repeat offenders were preferred; with these cases it was thought there would be less risk of violating the rights of someone who might later turn out to be innocent. Cases involving people who were only "wanted for questioning" were off-limits for the same reason.

One of the biggest challenges was getting law-enforcement agencies to cooperate with the show. Linder wanted to feature

---

Is this some kind of joke? In Quitman, Georgia, it is illegal for a chicken to cross the road.

someone on the FBI's Most Wanted list in the pilot episode, but the FBI wasn't sure it should get involved. Fox was a new network and *America's Most Wanted* was an unproven concept. The show would film reenactments of brutal real-life crimes—would they be done respectfully and in good taste? In the end the FBI did decide to cooperate...with the pilot. Future cooperation would depend on how the first show turned out.

FBI officials gave Linder information on each criminal on the Most Wanted list. After reading about them all, he decided to focus on the case of David James Roberts, an Indiana prison inmate who had escaped from custody in 1968 while serving six life terms for rape, arson, and murder, including the murder of two children. He'd been on the run for nearly 20 years.

The producers recruited actors to play Roberts and his victims, returned to the scenes of some of his crimes, and filmed reenactments. Stories on other wanted criminals were also filmed.

Now all the show needed was a host.

## FIRST CHOICE

Early on, Linder and Chao thought John Walsh, an outspoken advocate for missing and exploited children, would make a good host for the show. In 1981 Walsh's six-year-old son, Adam, had been kidnapped from a shopping mall in Hollywood, Florida. Weeks later, his partial remains were recovered in a drainage ditch 120 miles away; the rest of his body was never found. Since then, Walsh and his wife, Revé, had channeled their grief into lobbying to remove the legal and bureaucratic obstacles that made it difficult to recover missing children. The passage of the federal Missing Children Act of 1982 and the Missing Children's Assistance Act of 1984 were due in large part to their efforts.

Walsh understood from personal experience the impact that the media could play in solving crimes. His family's story was made into two TV movies: *Adam* (1983) and *Adam: His Song Continues* (1986). Each movie had ended with photos of and information on 55 missing kids, for a total of 110 for both shows. Dozens of the kids were then found or accounted for (by 1990, 71 of the cases would be solved).

Still, Walsh wasn't sure he wanted to host the show. Like the FBI, he didn't know what to make of it. He was worried that if it turned out to be cheesy and exploitative, it might hurt his ability to continue lobbying on behalf of missing children.

## HOST TO HOST

Walsh told Fox he wasn't interested, and the producers considered a number of other people to host the show, including a former commandant of the Marine Corps, former U.S. attorney Rudolph Giuliani, and several actors, including Treat Williams, Brian Dennehy, and Brian Keith. While some agreed to take the job, none of them had the credibility that Walsh did. Linder and Chao decided to wait.

Finally, after six months of saying no, Walsh changed his mind. He agreed to host the show provided that Fox would flash a phone number on the screen during the broadcast so viewers would know where to call. "What would be the point, otherwise?" he told *Newsday* in 1988. But the deciding factor for Walsh was David James Roberts, the escaped killer who was going to be featured on the pilot. Walsh decided that if there was anything he could do to put a murderer of children behind bars, he had to try.

## PREMIERE

The pilot of *America's Most Wanted* aired on Sunday, February 7, 1988. Nobody knew how it would do—nothing like it had been shown in the U.S. before. Would anyone watch? The FBI had questioned the show's merit; so had most of the other law-enforcement agencies who were asked to participate. So had John Walsh.

So had Fox—AMW was so unusual and so untested that instead of broadcasting the show to the nearly 100 stations in their fledgling network, Fox decided to air it only on the seven stations that it owned outright. They did very little to promote the show, and scheduled it to run following *21 Jump Street*, a program that didn't provide much of a lead-in audience. Those few people who did watch were asked to help find a man that police had been hunting nonstop for 19 years, and whose appearance must have changed considerably since 1968.

So how long did it take to catch Roberts after *America's Most Wanted* debuted on seven TV stations? Four days.

## GOTCHA!

Then, as now, *AMW* set up a phone bank to handle whatever

---

calls came in, even though "we didn't know if we'd get one call," Linder admitted in 1988. They did get calls, though—dozens of them, including 15 tips in the first 40 minutes that placed Roberts in New York City. One of the callers recognized him as the man running a homeless shelter on Staten Island. Police took Roberts into custody on February 11.

Other arrests followed: In the first two months alone, 15 other suspects profiled on the show were captured, eight of them caught solely on the basis of tips phoned in to the AMW hotline.

*America's Most Wanted* moved to the full network in early April and quickly became Fox's highest-rated show—and its first genuine hit. As torrents of viewer tips led to the arrest of one fugitive after another, the FBI and other law-enforcement agencies abandoned their skepticism. Soon they were fighting to get their most difficult unsolved cases on the air. By the end of the first year, more than 25 million viewers were tuning in each week; the tips they phoned in led to the arrests of 73 fugitives. By the end of 1989, *America's Most Wanted* was averaging one arrest every 16 days, a success rate of 44%.

## I WANT MY AMW

*America's Most Wanted* was a hit, but Fox may not have realized what a cultural force the show had become until 1996, when they announced they were pulling it from the upcoming fall season— even though its ratings were still on the upswing. Why kill a success? The up-to-the-minute nature of the show means that there isn't much of a market for reruns or DVD collections. Apparently Fox was hoping to replace AMW with something that had a greater potential for future profits.

Fox broke the news to John Walsh on a Monday, made the public announcement on Tuesday, and by Wednesday a campaign to save the show was well underway. FBI director Louis Freeh asked Fox to put the show back on; so did countless other law-enforcement agencies. So did the governors of 37 states. But it was the letters from fans, Walsh says—more than 200,000 of them— that got the show back on the air after an absence of just six weeks. "The public was the judge," he told reporters. "It was the shortest cancellation in the history of network television."

## ROGUE'S GALLERY

*America's Most Wanted* hasn't been perfect—Walsh admits that he cringes when he thinks back to how graphic the filmed reenactments were in the show's early days. And it's not uncommon for the actors who play the criminals to be mistakenly turned in to the police. One man in Louisiana was "apprehended" six times in one week in March 1990 just because he looked like someone who had been profiled on the show.

Even so, the number of criminals who have been captured over the years is astounding—as of August 2006, 900 fugitives had been captured and 42 missing children returned safely to their homes. Here's a look at some of the most notable captures:

• **Jack and Mona Volagres,** wanted for the murder of Mona's daughter Saleana. They were arrested only 29 minutes after the episode aired, the quickest arrest in the show's history.

• **James Charles Stark,** a repeat sex offender. The week before his segment was scheduled to air, *AMW* showed his picture for five seconds as part of a preview. That's all it took—six people phoned in tips that he worked at a car wash in Ann Arbor, Michigan. Police took him into custody the next day.

• **Stephen Randall Dye,** wanted for shooting a man and linked to the murder of a motorcyclist. After seeing himself profiled on the show, he went outside, flagged down the first police car that came along, and surrendered on the spot.

• **James Henderson,** wanted for kidnapping and assault in Arizona. Henderson wasn't on the show at all—Tucson police suspected that his wife was in contact with him, so they told her that an *America's Most Wanted* film crew was in town shooting reenactments of his crimes. Henderson's wife didn't know they were lying, and passed the information on to Henderson. He surrendered to police a short time later.

• **Steven Ray Stout,** wanted for the murder of his stepmother-in-law and stepsister-in-law. Arrested nine days after his story aired, Stout pled guilty to both murders and was sentenced to life in prison. One of the few subjects of the show who also admits to being a fan, Stout says he watches the program in prison every week. "There's no doubt that most of the people on the show need to be off the streets," he says.

# CAN YOU PASS THE U.S. CITIZENSHIP TEST?

*Bad news! The government lost the answers to the quiz you took on page 177. You need to take it again. Here are 21 "medium-hard" questions.*

**1.** What is it called when the president refuses to sign a bill into law and returns it to the Congress with his objections?

**2.** What do we celebrate on the 4th of July?

**3.** Name one of the five freedoms outlined in the first amendment of the U.S. Constitution.

**4.** How many justices are there in the U.S. Supreme Court?

**5.** Who is the commander in chief of the U.S. military?

**6.** Who alone has the power to declare war in the U.S.?

**7.** Who elects the Congress?

**8.** Who elects the president of the United States?

**9.** Name the three branches of the federal government.

**10.** Who is the head of the executive branch?

**11.** The Civil War was fought over what important issues?

**12.** What are the duties of the Supreme Court?

**13.** How many voting members are there in the House of Representatives?

**14.** How many senators are there in the U.S. Senate?

**15.** Why are there that many senators in the U.S. Senate?

**16.** What are the first 10 amendments to the U.S. Constitution called?

**17.** How long is the term of each U.S. senator?

**18.** How long is the term of each U.S. representative?

**19.** How many full terms can a president serve?

**20.** How many full terms can a U.S. senator or representative serve?

**21.** Who said, "Give me liberty, or give me death?"

*Whew! Check your answers on page 516, then try the "hard" test on page 473...if you dare.*

Old softie: President Andrew Johnson left crumbs out for the White House mice.

# DELICIOUSLY FAMILIAR PHRASES

*Hungry for some word play? You'll eat up
these juicy origins of popular phrases.*

## SPILL THE BEANS

**Meaning:** To give away a secret

**Origin:** "A tradition that began in ancient Greece for electing a new member to a private club was to give each existing member one white and one brown bean with which to cast their votes (white was 'yes'; brown was 'no'). The beans were then placed in a jar and then counted in secret by an official. The prospective member would never know how many people voted for or against him. Unless, that is, the jar was knocked over before the secret count and the beans spilled. Then the members' secret would be out." (*Red Herrings & White Elephants*, by Albert Jack)

## TO EGG ONE ON

**Meaning:** To persistently urge someone to do something

**Origin:** "Following the Norman Conquest, Anglo-Saxon peasants were treated brutally. Roped or chained together, they were often driven from place to place like cattle. Many prisoners were urged to move faster by a poke of their captor's spearpoint, or *ecg*. Later, children listened as their elders told of having been "ecged on" in this fashion. Tradition kept the stories alive long after Anglo-Saxon ceased to be spoken, with the result that later generations referred to their ancestors as having been *egged* on." (*I've Got Goose Pimples*, by Marvin Vanoni)

## EAT, DRINK, AND BE MERRY

**Meaning:** To feast and not worry about life's problems

**Origin:** "This phrase has its roots in the Bible, where, in Ecclesiastes 8:15, we read: 'A man hath no better thing under the sun, than to eat, and to drink, and to be merry.' There is a further reference in Isaiah 22:13, 'Let us eat and drink; for tomorrow we may die.'" (*Everyday Phrases—Their Origins and Meanings*, by Neil Ewart)

Until 2004, caffeine was on the International Olympic Committee list of prohibited substances.

## IN A PICKLE

**Meaning:** To be stuck in a difficult situation

**Origin:** "From *in de pikel zitten*, a Dutch phrase going back four centuries, literally meaning to sit in a salt solution used for preserving pickles, an uncomfortable or sorry plight." Dante used the idiom in his *Divine Comedy*; Shakespeare used it in *The Tempest* ("How camest thou in this pickle?"). It's now also used to describe the sorry plight of a baseball player caught in a rundown between two bases." (*Encyclopedia of Word and Phrase Origins*, by Robert Hendrickson)

## EASY AS PIE

**Meaning:** Simple to complete

**Origin:** This phrase came from Australia, by way of New Zealand, in the 1920s. When someone was good at something, they were considered "pie at it" or "pie on it." For example, a good climber was "pie at climbing." Although the modern phrase is associated with pie (the dessert), it is actually derived from the Maori word *pai*, which means "good."

## THE PROOF IS IN THE PUDDING

**Meaning:** Wait to pass judgement until a task is actually completed

**Origin:** "In its full wording this old English proverb runs, 'The proof of the pudding is in the eating'—with 'proof' meaning 'test' rather than its normal sense of 'verifying that something is true.' The expression has a long history in English, with recorded versions dating from the beginning of the 14th century. From that time until the present, it has remained unaltered." (*Bringing Home the Bacon & Cutting the Mustard*, Castle Books)

## OUT OF THE FRYING PAN AND INTO THE FIRE

**Meaning:** To escape one danger, only to land in another

**Origin:** "This expression is common to many languages; dating to the 2nd-century Greek equivalent, 'out of the smoke into the flame.' Its English usage is traceable to an ongoing religious argument in 1528 between William Tynedale, translator of the Bible into English, and Sir Thomas More, who wrote that his adversary 'featly conuayed himself out of the frying panne fayre into the fyre.'" (*Hog on Ice & Other Curious Expressions*, by Charles Earle Funk)

---

As a species, the platypus is 150 million years old. (Humans are about 200,000 years old.)

# ODD DOGS

*According to the American Kennel Club, the most popular dog breed is the Labrador Retriever. Here's a sampling from the opposite end of the spectrum—breeds that few people have ever heard of.*

## LÖWCHEN

First bred in France, this small but lively dog was the fashionable choice of Renaissance ladies throughout 16th-century Europe. It got its name, which means "little lion" in German, from the way owners groomed its long wavy coat into a mane. Traditionally a lap dog, the Löwchen is actually fearless and very assertive, often cowing larger dogs into submission. Its popularity peaked in the early 19th century, when Francisco Goya and other artists often pictured Löwchens in their paintings. By the end of WWII the breed had gone into decline. In 1960 the *Guinness Book of World Records* declared the Löwchen the rarest breed in the world, but it has since climbed back in popularity enough to be considered merely "rare."

## CATAHOULA CUR

The official canine of Louisiana, this tough working dog has an amazing story that begins in 1539. That's when Spanish conquistador Hernando de Soto crossed what is now the southern United States looking for gold. Dogs always traveled with the Spanish troops: Mastiffs for use in battle and Greyhounds to hunt game. When de Soto died in 1542, his army retreated back to Mexico, leaving their sick and wounded animals behind. The native tribes adopted the dogs, which then interbred with the local red wolf. Eventually a new cross emerged—tough, wily, quick, and known as the "wolf-dog." When French settlers arrived in the 1600s, they brought with them the Beauceron, a boar-hunting hound. This new dog was bred with the "wolf-dog" to create the Catahoula Cur, which looks like a dog designed by committee: Its motley short fur is multicolored in irregular spots, and its eyes are unusually glassy. But owners swear by the intelligence and uncanny abilities of these dogs as herders, guard dogs, and hunters. They've even been called "cat-dogs" because they like to climb trees.

There were over 300 banana-related accidents in Britain in 2001. (Most people slipped on peels.)

## SPANISH WATER DOG

This woolly-coated herding breed is thought to have come to Spain with the Moorish invasion of A.D. 711, although some experts claim they came from the north with the barbarian invasions of the Vandals and Visigoths. Either way, by 1100 they were popular all over the Iberian Peninsula, particularly in Andalucia in the southeast, where they were known as Turkish dogs. Great multitaskers, they not only herd goats and sheep but also are expert field dogs, adapted over the centuries to work the marshes retrieving birds and hares. Like their cousins, the Portuguese Water Dog (a more popular breed, to which Uncle John's dog, Porter, belongs), they often work with fishermen retrieving nets and lines. These days they are widely used by the Spanish government for bomb and drug sniffing.

## PERUVIAN INCA ORCHID

The origins of this breed, also known as the South American Hairless Sighthound, are lost in time. But by A.D. 750 they were common among the Moche, a Peruvian people whose empire predated the Incas. Primarily bred for swiftness, like the Greyhound, Peruvian Inca Orchids have hairless and coated pups in the same litter. The Incas kept the coated ones outside as hunters; the hairless ones were brought inside to be house pets and bed warmers, and were highly prized. Their name in the Quechua language of the Incas translates into "dogs without clothes." During the Spanish conquest, the conquistadors often found the dogs inside the orchid gardens of noble Incan homes, which is how they got their modern name.

## FOO

This ancient breed was long thought extinct. In appearance a combination of Spitz and Chow, today the Foo is best known as the traditional mascot of the mysterious Chinese tongs, the Chinese version of secret fraternal orders like the Masons, which dominated immigrant Chinese life in San Francisco and other American cities at the turn of the 20th century. Thought by its name to have originated in Foochow in southeast China, the Foo may be the missing link between the Chinese wolf and the modern Chow. This watchdog goes by many names: Sacred Dog of

Sinkiang, Chinese Choo Hunting Dog, Chinese Temple Forest Dog, Chinese Celestial Dog, or Chinese Dragon Dog.

## NORWEGIAN PUFFIN DOG

The Lundehund (its Norwegian name) is one of the rarest breeds in the world and the oldest purebred dog in Norway. Much like a miniature Spitz, the Lundehund is small, compact, and rarely weighs more than 15 pounds. The breed is known for several remarkable traits: six toes on each foot, and ears that shut tightly against its head to keep out dust and water. Its unusual neck joints enable the dog to bend its head so that its forehead touches its back, and its hyperflexible shoulders let it splay out its front legs at right angles, allowing it to lay flat on the ground like a rug. These traits are all useful when hunting puffins, small sea birds that nest in crevices and burrows along the rocky slopes of the Norwegian fjords. Breeders claim the Norwegian Puffin Dog is descended from *Canis forus*, a primeval dog that survived the last Ice Age. It's been around in its present form since 1432.

\* \* \*

## OFFICIAL STATE FOODS

- Florida's official pie is key lime.

- Grits is Georgia's "official prepared food."

- The official snack of Illinois: popcorn

- The official muffin of Massachusetts is the corn muffin. Minnesota's is blueberry; New York's is apple.

- The Oklahoma state meal consists of fried okra, squash, cornbread, barbecued pork, biscuits with sausage gravy, grits, corn, strawberries, chicken-fried steak, black-eyed peas, and pecan pie.

- The state cookie of New Mexico is the *bizcochito*, a Spanish shortbread.

- The official drink of Rhode Island is coffee milk (sort of like chocolate milk, but made with coffee syrup instead).

- South Dakota's official dessert is *kuchen*, a German-style cake.

- Official beverage of Ohio: canned tomato juice.

# THE REIVERS

*Think the American "Wild West" was wild? It was tame compared to the border between England and Scotland in the 14th century.*

## THRONE TROUBLES

In A.D. 1286, King Alexander III of Scotland died when his horse fell over a cliff (he was on it). The Scottish crown passed to his four-year old granddaughter, and when she died four years later, 13 different nobles stepped forward to claim the throne.

The Scots were unable to settle the issue themselves, so they appealed to King Edward I of England to select a king for them. Bad move. Although the Scots wanted to remain independent, the English wanted them to be weak. So, after more than a year of deliberations, in 1292 Edward selected a noble named John Balliol to be the next king of the Scots. Four years later, Edward invaded Scotland, defeated the Scots in battle, and forced John to abdicate.

England and Scotland fought almost continuously for the next 300 years. The people living on the border suffered terribly as armies from both kingdoms repeatedly sacked towns, burned crops, and slaughtered people by the thousands, collapsing the traditional rural economy and rendering the area a wasteland. Result: Many border families, or clans, on both sides resorted to raiding each other to steal what little food, livestock, and valuables were left. Raiding, or *reiving*, as it was known, began as a crime of necessity, but as generations passed it evolved into a way of life, one with no social stigma attached at all.

## MEET THE REIVERS

The reivers were the cattle rustlers of the Middle Ages. They worked as farmers, laborers, or tradesmen during the day—some were even members of the nobility—and raided at night. Their weapon of choice was the lance, a long wooden spear with a daggerlike metal blade. They were excellent horsemen, riding small, sturdy horses called hobblers. Their armor: steel helmets and leather vests with metal plates sewn on.

Nationality meant nothing—it was common for English reivers to raid the English side of the border, and the same was true of the

Scots. Reivers from both sides of the border even went on raids together.

About the only way to avoid being attacked was to pay a clan to protect you. But average citizens didn't appreciate having to pay thugs to protect them from other thugs, of course—the farmers who paid rent (or *mail*, as it was called) took to calling the payments *black mail*. (Blackmail isn't the only word that has entered the English language courtesy of the reivers: *Kidnap*, *debauchery*, and *bereaved* come from them, as well.)

Things didn't change until 1603, when Queen Elizabeth I died and her cousin, King James VI of Scotland, became King James I of England. Determined to bring reiving to an end, James offered amnesty to any reivers who ended their "foul and insolent outrages" and declared war on any who didn't. Most clans bowed to the inevitable and gave up reiving. Thanks to King James's diligence, by the 1640s only a few roving gangs of reivers remained, having been forced off their land and reduced to hiding in the hills.

## YOU REIVER, YOU

Are you of Scottish or English descent? If your last name is Henderson, Armstrong, Chamberlain, or any of the names listed below, you may be descended from one of the reiver clans.

| | | | |
|---|---|---|---|
| Archbold | Dodd | Laidlaw | Routledge |
| Beattie | Douglas | Little | Rutherford |
| Bell | Dunne | Lowther | Salkeld |
| Burns | Elliot | Maxwell | Scott |
| Carleton | Fenwick | Milburn | Selby |
| Carlisle | Forster | Musgrove | Shaftoe |
| Carnaby | Graham | Nixon | Storey |
| Carruthers | Gray | Noble | Simpson |
| Carrs | Hall | Ogle | Tait |
| Charlton | Hedley | Oliver | Taylor |
| Crisp | Heron | Potts | Trotter |
| Crozier | Hume | Pringle | Turnbull |
| Cuthbert | Irvine | Radcliffe | Wake |
| Dacre | Irving | Reade | Watson |
| Davison | Johnstone | Ridley | Wilson |
| Dixon | Kerr | Robson | Young |

Priciest painting by a female artist: *Calla Lilies with Red Anemone* (Georgia O'Keeffe, $6.1 million).

# STRANGE LAWSUITS

*Here are more real-life examples of unusual legal battles.*

**PLAINTIFF:** Curtis Gokey of Lodi, California
**DEFENDANT:** Curtis Gokey of Lodi, California
**LAWSUIT:** A city dump truck backed into Gokey's car, so he sued the city for damages. Gokey, a city employee, was driving the truck at the time.
**VERDICT:** Pending. The city denied the claim, saying it amounted to Gokey suing himself, so he filed suit again—under his wife's name. And she upped the amount of damages. "I'm not as nice as my husband is," she explained.

**PLAINTIFF:** John Melo of Massachusetts
**DEFENDANT:** Massachusetts Department of Correction
**LAWSUIT:** Melo was convicted of home invasion, assault and battery by means of a dangerous weapon, and armed assault in a dwelling house in 1997. He was sentenced to 10 years in prison. In August 2004, he sued the Department of Correction, saying that they had miscalculated his sentence—because they hadn't taken Leap Years into account. The suit claimed that his sentence of 10 years referred to 365-day years, and not the 366-day years that include a February 29. By the time of the suit he had already served in two Leap Years, 2000 and 2004.
**VERDICT:** The lawsuit was rejected by the court.

**PLAINTIFFS:** Nancy Alperin and Kendra Keller
**DEFENDANT:** The Gorilla Foundation
**LAWSUIT:** Alperin and Keller were animal handlers at the foundation in Woodside, California, home of the famous gorilla Koko. Koko uses sign language and knows more than 1,000 different signs. According to foundation president Francine Patterson, Koko also has a fascination with human nipples. In 2004 Alperin and Keller were fired, and they say it was because they refused to expose their breasts to the 300-pound gorilla. Their suit claimed sexual discrimination, as well as wrongful termination in retaliation

for reporting health and safety violations, and failure to pay overtime or provide rest breaks. They asked for more than $1 million in damages.

**VERDICT:** The foundation settled the lawsuit for an undisclosed amount.

**PLAINTIFFS:** Sue Storer of Bristol, England
**DEFENDANT:** The Bristol City Council
**LAWSUIT:** Story was deputy headteacher at Bedminster Down Secondary School in Bristol until she resigned in 2006. She then filed a lawsuit, saying that she had been harassed at the school—especially by being forced to sit in a chair that made "farting noises." She claimed that all her requests for a replacement chair were ignored. "It was a regular joke that my chair would make these sounds," she said, "and I regularly had to apologize that it wasn't me—it was my chair." The lawsuit asked for $1.9 million in damages.

**VERDICT:** Storer lost. The court ruled that there was no evidence of harassment, and that as headteacher, she could have replaced the farting chair herself.

\* \* \*

## AN ILLUMINATING ORIGIN

It was so dark and rainy on the first day of the Woodstock festival in August 1969 that concert promoters passed out candles to the crowd. Folk singer Melanie took the stage in near darkness and a total downpour and the concert's announcer told the audience to "light a candle to keep away the rain." The rain didn't stop, but as Melanie sang, little bits of light started to appear across the huge crowd. The next day, Melanie wrote the song "Lay Down (Candles in the Rain)" about the experience, and lighting candles during performances of the song became a tradition at her concerts. Within a few years, cigarette lighters replaced candles, and it became commonplace to hold up a lit lighter during a ballad by nearly any rock band. Lighters aren't allowed in most concert halls anymore (they're a fire hazard), so today people use flashlights or hold up their cell phones.

# BEULAH LAND, PART II

*In Part I (page 94), freed slaves moved west after the Civil War in search of land, dignity, and opportunity. But for those who established all-black towns in Oklahoma, their battles weren't over. Here's Part II of the story.*

## THE GREENWOOD RIOTS

In 1921 the town of Greenwood, Oklahoma—dubbed "The Black Wall Street"—was one of the most prosperous black communities in America. More than 190 businesses were licensed to operate in the community of 11,000 residents. (Tulsa at the time had a population of 70,000.) There were fifteen doctors, three lawyers, two dentists, and a chiropractor, as well as two schools, two theaters, several hotels, a library, and a hospital. Greenwood was a model of black enterprise and self-sufficiency.

It all changed on May 31, 1921. There are varying accounts of how it began, but like so many acts of race-related violence in the United States, it involved a white woman and a black man. Something happened in a building in downtown Tulsa between a 17-year-old elevator operator named Sarah Page and 19-year-old Dick Rowland. The most commonly accepted version of the story is that Rowland stepped on the girl's foot. When she started to fall, he tried to catch her. She screamed, and he ran away. Word quickly spread through the white community that Rowland had "assaulted" the girl. When a local paper ran an inflammatory headline encouraging local whites to "nab the negro," events spiraled out of control.

## CHAOS AND DISASTER

Whites gathered outside the courthouse where Rowland was being held, demanding that he be turned over to the mob. Meanwhile, worried blacks came together in Greenwood, determined to stop the lynching. The crowd at the courthouse swelled to 2,000. About 75 blacks went to the courthouse, and in the confrontation that followed, a shot was fired. Within seconds the street erupted in a gunfight. The outnumbered blacks retreated to Greenwood, pursued by a rampaging mob that looted and burned stores and homes along the way.

Violence raged for the next 16 hours. Bands of whites drove through the streets of Greenwood, shooting any black person they saw. One black man tried to escape by running into a theater; the mob caught and murdered him on the stage. Many blacks fled the city. Those who stayed behind were rounded up and placed in internment camps. When the National Guard finally restored order, Greenwood was in ruins. At least 150 people were dead and 1,200 homes and businesses had burned to the ground. Aside from the loss of life, property damage was estimated at $1.5 million. The black community never recovered from the disaster. No arrests were ever made, and some months later the case against Dick Rowland was dismissed when Sarah Page chose not to press charges.

## SURVIVORS

The financial crash of 1929, followed by the hard times of the Great Depression and agricultural losses of the Dust Bowl, brought an end to those early glory days of black self-sufficiency in the Midwest. Many black township residents fled west to California or north to Chicago, looking for work or a better way of life.

Today only 13 of the 29 predominantly black towns in Oklahoma still exist: Boley, Brooksville, Clearview, Grayson, Langston, Lima, Redbird, Rentiesville, Summit, Taft, Tatums, Tullahassee, and Vernon. They remain a living testimonial to the courage and grit of the former slaves who founded them, and the American Dream they hoped to find out West.

\*       \*       \*

## MORE SPICY FACTS

• Cinnamon and cassia were essential ingredients in the embalming methods of the ancient Egyptians, as were anise, marjoram, and cumin.

• The famous legal code of King Hammurabi contains numerous regulations controlling the use of spices in Babylonian medicine.

• When the Visigoths besieged Rome in A.D. 408, they demanded (and received) a ransom of pepper, along with gold and silver, to call off their attack.

# MODERN MYSTERIES

*Even in a world of science, some things still can't be explained.*

## POISONOUS PRIEST

According to the *United News of India*, Hindu priest Biswanath Kanwar of Jharkhand was bitten by a king cobra in 2005…and the *cobra* died. The priest was feeding milk to the 3½-foot-long snake, something he did regularly at the Nagdevata temple, when it suddenly bit him on the hand. The cobra immediately became very still, started vomiting, and then died. Kanwar was taken to a local hospital, where doctors said he was fine.

## DON'T GO IN THE GARAGE

In November 2005, remote garage door openers in a section of Ottawa, Ontario, suddenly stopped working. Hundreds of them. "It affects a 25-mile radius," said J.P. Cleroux of Ram Overhead Door Systems. "That's huge." According to Cleroux, there was a powerful radio signal—at 390-megahertz, the same as the signal used by the remote door openers—interfering with the devices. Where did it come from? A rumor quickly circulated that it emanated from the American Embassy, but the embassy denied transmitting the signal, and two weeks after it began…it went away. And, just as mysteriously, the doors started working again.

## A LIGHT MEAL

Hira Ratan Manek of Kerala, India, claims he hasn't eaten since 1995. Manek says he started studying "sun-gazing" after retiring in 1992 at the age of 55—and now gets all his nourishment from it. "Every evening, I gaze at the sun for an hour without batting an eyelid. This is my main food." From 2000 to 2001, an international team of doctors and scientists observed Manek as he went for 411 days without food; NASA scientists observed him at Thomas Jefferson University in Pennsylvania as he fasted for 130 days. They verified that Manek went the entire time—more than four months—with only water and his sun-gazing technique. They now identify the mysterious technique with Manek's initials, calling it the "HRM" phenomenon.

---

Venice gondola rule of thumb: If it isn't painted black, it belongs to a high official.

# READING TOMBSTONES

*If you've ever walked through a cemetery, you've probably noticed that many tombstones, especially older ones, are decorated with flowers, animals, and other symbols. Here's a look at what some of them represent.*

**B**utterflies: The three stages of the butterfly's life—caterpillar, cocoon, and butterfly—represent life, death, and rebirth.

**Daisies:** Innocence. Daisies are frequently found on the graves of children.

**Sheaf of wheat:** A long and productive life. Frequently found on the graves of people who lived past the age of 70.

**A woman holding a candle, lamp, or cross:** Faith.

**Pomegranates:** Holiness, unity, love, and hope of immortality and resurrection.

**Two hands clasping each other:** A married couple. Look closely at the hands— one hand will be masculine, the other feminine.

**Curtains, doors, or gates:** Transition to the next world.

**Elephants:** Strength and happiness. Sometimes it just means the deceased liked to travel to exotic places.

**Pine cones:** Immortality.

**A crane standing on one leg:** Vigilance; these birds are often found perched atop mausoleums and other monuments. (Legend has it the birds sleep standing on one leg while holding a small stone in the claw of the other leg. If they sleep too deeply, they drop the stone onto the other leg, which wakes them up.)

**A human foot:** Humility (it's the part of the body that touches the ground).

**An empty chair, often with a small pair of shoes nearby:** The death of a child.

**A broken Roman column:** A life cut short.

**Acorns:** Prosperity.

**An angel, a lion, an ox, and an eagle:** The authors of the four gospels: Matthew, Mark, Luke, and John, in that order.

**Coins:** Charity.

**Chrysanthemums:** Longevity, immortality. (The plants are hardy and their flowers last well into winter.)

**A closed book:** A completed life.

**A candelabra:** It's lighting the way to the next world.

**A woman holding a bottle:** The bottle is a tear bottle and represents the sadness of those who mourn the deceased.

**Oxen:** Patience, humility, and hard work.

**Snails:** Often used purely for decoration; sometimes they represent self-sufficiency. (Snails carry their houses with them wherever they go.)

**A woman nursing an infant:** Charity. She can also be depicted carrying food or clothing for the needy.

**Hummingbirds:** Purely decorative, they mean absolutely nothing, except perhaps that the deceased liked hummingbirds.

**A crescent hanging from a scimitar:** The deceased was a Shriner.

**An elk:** The deceased was a member of the Elks Club.

**An ear of corn:** Fertility and rebirth.

**Pelican:** Self-sacrifice. People used to believe that a mother pelican fed her young her own blood, taken from a gash she tore into her own breast.

**A pair of dice:** The deceased was a Christian. After Jesus was crucified, the Roman soldiers cast dice to see who got to keep his undergarment. (Either that, or the deceased liked to gamble.)

**A "Buddhist" or backwards swastika:** Sometimes seen on Japanese gravemarkers. Christianity was banned in Japan in the 17th century, so Christians who wanted a cross on their tombstone often disguised it by making it into a swastika.

**A coffin and some shovels:** A *sexton*, whose duties included digging graves in this very cemetery, is buried here.

**A nude figure:** Innocence. You're born naked and you don't get to take anything with you when you die, either.

\*　　\*　　\*

"Is life not a hundred times too short for us to stifle ourselves?"

—**Friedrich Nietzsche**

The letter combination "ough" can be pronounced in eight different ways.

# MATT'S MUSINGS

*Matt Groening (rhymes with raining) majored in philosophy in college...and then went on to create the world's most popular cartoon,* The Simpsons.

"I grew up completely over-whelmed by TV, and part of the reason I went into televi-sion is as a way to justify to myself all those wasted hours of watching TV as a kid. I can now look back and say, 'Oh, that was research.'"

"Of all the Simpsons, I like Homer the best because he is basically free of guilt. He loves what he loves, hates what he hates with every fiber of his being, but his addiction to heavily salted snacks and unre-pentant laziness is something that I certainly relate to."

"Animation is like being God, creating these living beings out of pen and ink and making them do your bidding and punishing them for their folly."

"I think it's a mistake for car-toonists to demand cartoons be treated as art. Cartoons are cartoons. I don't care if you call them art, literature—they're cartoons! They're the most fun things out there! So what if you don't get respect?"

"*The Simpsons*' message over and over again is that your moral authorities don't always have your best interests in mind. Teachers, principals, clergymen, politicians—on *The Simpsons*, they're all goof-balls, and I think that's a great message for kids."

"Love is a perky elf dancing a merry little jig and then sud-denly he turns on you with a miniature machine gun."

"It's always fun to tell a joke that makes all the kids laugh but which confuses and annoys the teacher. And that's what I try to do as a grown-up: entertain part of the audi-ence and annoy another part."

"The history of TV has tradi-tionally been not to do any-thing that would scandalize grandma or upset junior. Our solution on *The Simpsons* is to do jokes that people who have an education can get. And the ones who don't, it doesn't matter, because we have Homer banging his head and saying, 'D'oh!'"

---

Hugo's *Les Miserables* contains one of the longest sentences in French literature—823 words.

# LEGALLY SPEAKING

*So you're watching* Law and Order *on TV, or maybe you find yourself in court (we won't ask why), and you suddenly realize you have no idea what the judge and lawyers are talking about. Ta-da! Here's a handy legal-phrase guide.*

**Litigant.** A participant in the trial or hearing.

**Plaintiff.** The side that filed the lawsuit.

**Defendant.** The person on trial (or being sued).

**Prosecutor.** The lawyer who represents the state (or city) in a criminal case.

**Defense attorney.** The lawyer who represents the defendant.

**Brief.** A document written by each side that outlines and supports their arguments.

**Deposition.** Testimony of a witness taken outside the courtroom, usually in a lawyer's office.

**Arraignment.** The first court appearance of a person accused of a crime, usually when a plea is entered.

**Writ.** A legal paper filed to start various types of civil suits.

**Affidavit.** A written statement made under oath.

**Bail.** Also called "bond." Money accepted by the court for the temporary release of a defendant, given as a guarantee they will show up for trial.

**Statute of limitations.** The window of time during which someone can be charged with a crime.

**Bench warrant.** If a defendant out on bail doesn't show up for trial, the judge issues this to order that person's immediate arrest.

**Cross-examination.** Questioning by the other side's attorney.

**Contempt of court.** Being disrespectful in court or disobeying a judge's order. It often comes with a punishment of a night in jail.

**Felony.** A criminal offense carrying a sentence of more than one year in prison.

**Misdemeanor.** A minor crime with a maximum penalty of a year in jail or a fine of no more than $2,000.

---

**Subpoena.** An order to appear in court to testify.

**Infraction.** A minor offense, like a speeding ticket. It doesn't require a court case.

**Criminal case.** A lawsuit in which the government charges a person with a crime.

**Civil action.** When one party sues another, not involving the government, such as a divorce or child-support suit.

**Testimony.** A witness's oral account, presented as evidence.

**Jury trial.** A group of citizens hear testimony and evidence presented by both sides, and decide the winner of a lawsuit, or whether a criminal act was committed.

**Bench trial.** Trial by a judge, not by a jury.

**Grievance.** A complaint filed by litigants against an attorney or judge.

**Habeas corpus.** A court order used to bring a person physically to court.

**Voir dire.** The process of questioning prospective jurors or witnesses. It's Latin for "to speak the truth."

**Continuance.** The postponement of a case to a date in the near future.

**Tort.** A civil injury or wrong to a person or their property.

**No contest.** A plea in a criminal case that allows the defendant to be convicted without an admission of guilt.

**Plea bargain.** An agreement the defendant makes to avoid a trial, usually involving pleading guilty to lesser charges in exchange for a lighter sentence.

**Hung jury.** When a jury cannot agree and reaches no verdict.

**Capital crime.** A crime punishable by death.

**Damages.** Monetary compensation paid for a legal wrong.

**Injunction.** A court order to do (or not do) something, like pay child support or attend drug counseling.

**Appeal.** Asking a higher court to review a previous court's decision (or sentence).

**Trial de novo.** A new trial or retrial.

# DESTINATION: CANADA

*Why visit the CN Tower and Edmonton Mall when*
*you can see Joe's Scarecrows and Happy Rock?*

Attraction: Happy Rock
Location: Gladstone, Manitoba
Story: High atop a building the size of a storage shed sits the Happy Rock (nicknamed "the Canadian Ambassador of Smiles")—a 15-foot-tall fake rock wearing a tuxedo, top hat, and white gloves. Why a "happy rock"? Because it's the city of "Gladstone" (get it?). The rock was designed by a 10-year-old boy in 1993 and built specifically to draw visitors to this tiny town of 900 people. According to the Chamber of Commerce, if you get your picture taken under the Happy Rock, it will bring you good luck.

Attraction: Joe's Scarecrows
Location: Cheticamp, Nova Scotia
Story: In 1946 someone told Joe Delaney not to bother putting a garden in his yard—the area was too close to salt water for anything to grow—so Delaney decided to raise scarecrows instead. At first he just put in a few and dressed them up to look like actors and politicians. Tourists started stopping to look at them, so Delaney started adding more. Today more than 100 scarecrows occupy his yard.

Attractions: The World Famous Gopher Hole Museum
Locations: Torrington, Alberta
Story: The Gopher Hole Museum showcases real gophers (dead, stuffed, and dressed like people) in dioramas depicting life in Canada, past and present. Scenes include gophers hunting, playing hockey, eating dinner, going to church, and perhaps strangest of all, attending the Gopher Hole Museum. But wait! Canada is a big country—big enough for *two* tourist attractions featuring stuffed gophers. The other one, sadly closed now, was Gopherville in Langenburg, Saskatchewan—a miniature Wild West town where the gophers were dressed like cowboys, sheriffs, and frontier prostitutes, posed in Wild West situations like saloons and gunfights.

---

First Canadian in space: Marc Garneau (1984).

**Attraction:** Criminals Hall of Fame Wax Museum

**Location:** Niagara Falls, Ontario

**Story:** Many museums around the world display wax statues of famous, familiar people. This is the only one that exclusively features criminals (most of them American). Outside, a police car parked in front sets the mood. Inside are notorious murderers rendered in wax, including old-school criminals such as Al Capone and Bugsy Siegel, and modern creeps like cannibal Jeffrey Dahmer (getting a "snack" from a refrigerator) and Oklahoma City bomber Timothy McVeigh in an orange prison jumpsuit. At the end of the tour, visitors can have their picture taken in an electric chair that buzzes when you sit in it.

**Attraction:** World's Largest Hockey Stick (and Puck)

**Location:** Duncan, British Columbia

**Story:** For the 1986 Vancouver World Fair, the Canadian government commissioned this, the ultimate symbol of Canada. The world's largest hockey stick—made of Douglas fir and steel—measures 205 feet (five feet longer than an NHL rink) and weighs 61,000 pounds. The giant puck which, like the stick, is 40 times life size, sits atop a pole next to the stick. After the Fair, both stick and puck were moved from Vancouver to Duncan, where they currently sit in front of the Cowichan Community Centre.

**Attraction:** Funomena Mobile Museum of the Weird and Strange

**Location:** Regina, Saskatchewan

**Story:** Calling itself the "world's smallest museum," it features 13 exhibits, a souvenir shop, and a tour guide, all inside a 10-foot-long camper trailer. Exhibits include a set of silverware that supposedly belonged to Satan, a weeping statue, artifacts of Bigfoot, a half-human half-fish creature, a "miracle healing chair," and a portrait of Elvis Presley made with Presley's own hair.

\*     \*     \*

### MARK TWAIN ON BOOKS

"I like a thin book because it will steady a table, a leather volume because it will strop a razor, and a heavy book because it can be thrown at the cat."

For more than 600 years, the official language of England was...French.

# MAKING
## *THE GODFATHER*, PT. II

*Is this part two of our story of the making of* The Godfather: Part I...
*or is it part one of our story of the making of* The Godfather: Part II?
*Leave the gun. Take the cannoli. Read on and see for*
*yourself. (Part I is one page 91.)*

# THE SALESMAN

If *The Godfather* had a shot at becoming a good movie, it was a very long shot indeed. Robert Evans, Paramount's vice president in charge of production, wasn't sure he wanted Francis Ford Coppola for the director's job, and Coppola was willing to do it only if he got a big enough budget to direct the film that *he* wanted to direct: a period piece, shot on location in the United States and Sicily, and faithful to the novel.

If you could boil Coppola's entire career down to the single moment that put him on the path to his future successes, it must have been the meeting he had with Evans and Stanley Jaffe, the president of Paramount, to win final approval to direct *The Godfather*. When producer Albert Ruddy picked Coppola up at the airport to take him to the meeting, he peppered the young director with all the arguments the studio heads were going to need to hear: He could finish the picture on time, he could keep within the budget, etc.

Coppola considered all this and then decided to go his own way.

## REVERSAL OF FORTUNE

Rather than talk about schedules and finances, as soon as the meeting began, Coppola launched into a vivid and passionate description of the characters and the story as he thought they should be portrayed. "Ten minutes into the meeting he was up on the f*#$%ing table, giving one of the great sales jobs of all time for the film as *he* saw it," Ruddy told Harlan Lebo in *The Godfather Legacy*. "That was the first time I had ever seen the Francis the world got to know—a bigger-than-life character. They couldn't believe what they were hearing—it was phenomenal."

Evans and Jaffe were floored. "Francis made Billy Graham look like Don Knotts," Evans remembered. On the strength of that one meeting with Coppola, Evans and Jaffe abandoned the idea of a "quickie mobster flick," increased *The Godfather*'s budget to $6 million (it would later grow to $6.5 million), and announced that it would be Paramount's "big picture of 1971."

## CASTING CALL

Getting Paramount to take *The Godfather* seriously would come at a price—now that the studio had so much money tied up in the film, it was determined to oversee every big decision. Take casting: Even when he was writing the novel, Mario Puzo had pictured Marlon Brando playing the Godfather, Don Corleone, and Coppola agreed that he was perfect for the part. Though he was widely considered one of the world's best actors, Brando had been in a rut for more than a decade; he had appeared in one money-losing film after another and had a reputation for being the most difficult actor in Hollywood. When he made his directorial debut in the 1961 film *One-Eyed Jacks*, his antics caused so many delays that production costs doubled and the film lost a bundle of money.

Paramount had produced *One Eyed Jacks*, and it wasn't about to make the same mistake again. "As long as I'm president of the studio," Jaffe told Coppola, "Marlon Brando will not be in this picture, and I will no longer allow you to discuss it." The studio wanted someone like Anthony Quinn to play the part; Ernest Borgnine was the Mafia's top pick for the job (according to FBI wiretaps). Rudy Vallee wanted the job; so did Danny Thomas. Mario Puzo remembered reading in the newspaper that Thomas wanted the part so badly that he was willing to buy Paramount to get it. The thought of that happening put Puzo into such a panic that he wrote Brando a letter begging him to take the part.

## I'LL MAKE HIM AN OFFER HE CAN'T ACCEPT

Coppola was as determined to get Brando as Puzo was. He pushed Jaffe so hard, in fact, that Jaffe finally put him off by agreeing to "consider" Brando, but only if the World's Greatest Actor agreed to three conditions that Jaffe was certain he would never accept: Brando had to agree to work for much less money than usual, he had to pay for any production delays he caused out of his own pocket, and he had to submit to a screen test, something he *knew* Brando would see as a slap in the face.

## MAKING THE MAN

Coppola gave in—what choice did he have? While all this was going on, Brando read both the book and the script and became interested in playing the part. Coppola didn't tell him about Jaffe's conditions; Coppola just asked if he could come over and film a "makeup test." Brando agreed.

At their meeting, Brando told Coppola he thought the Godfather should look "like a bulldog." He stuffed his cheeks with tissues, slouched a little, and feigned a tired expression on his face. Then he started mumbling dialog. That may not sound like much, but with these and other subtle techniques, the 47-year-old actor turned himself into an old Mafia don. The change was so complete that when Coppola brought Brando's test back to Paramount, Ruddy and the other studio executives didn't even realize it was him. The "makeup test" closed the deal—Brando not only *could* play Don Corleone, the executives decided, he *had* to play him.

## GET SHORTY

Coppola also had someone in mind to play the character of the Don's youngest son, Michael Corleone. He'd recently seen a play called *Does the Tiger Wear a Necktie?*, a story about a psychotic killer, and he was convinced that the star of the play, 31-year-old Al Pacino, was just the guy for the part. Pacino was beginning to make a name for himself on Broadway, but he was still largely unknown to movie audiences.

Paramount wouldn't hear of it. Pacino was a nobody, the studio complained. The part of Michael Corleone was as big a part as Brando's, and studio wanted someone with star power to fill it. Pacino was too short, they argued. (He's about 5'6" tall). The son of Sicilian immigrants, Pacino looked "too Italian" to play the son of a Sicilian mobster, the executives argued. Dustin Hoffman was interested, and names like Jack Nicholson, Warren Beatty, Ryan O'Neal, and even Robert Redford were also being tossed around. O'Neal and Redford didn't look anything like Italians, but they were big stars. Paramount figured they could pass as "northern Italians."

*So how did Pacino land the role? Part III is on page 508.*

*So how did Pacino land the role? Part III is on page 508.*

Q: What is a *paleoscatologist*? A: An archeologist who studies ancient poop.

# BATHROOMIO READERUS

*Most people know that the Latin name* Homo sapiens *refers to human beings. But few know how names like that came to be. Here's the* Storius completicus.

# M AKING SENSE OF LIFE

For centuries, scientists struggled with the task of classifying and naming the more than two million species of plants and animals on Earth. Beginning with the ancient Greeks, many attempts were made, but each naming system was too complicated for the average person to use.

But in 1735, a Swedish botanist named Carl Linnaeus finally accomplished it. In his pamphlet *Systema Naturae*, he introduced the basics of *taxonomy*—a system that grouped and identified organisms according to their physical similarities and differences. His work has required alterations through the centuries to keep up with new discoveries, but it still forms the framework of the system used worldwide today.

## DIVIDE AND ORGANIZE

Taxonomy divides all life on Earth into seven categories, called *taxa*, meaning "divisions," beginning with the most general *kingdoms*. From there it divides all living things into smaller and smaller groups, right down to the most specific—*species*. The seven taxa: *kingdom, phylum, class, order, family, genus,* and *species*. (An easy mnemonic device to remember them: King Phillip Came Over For Good Soup.)

**Kingdoms:** There are six kingdoms of life: *Bacteria, Archaea, Protista, Fungi, Plantae,* and *Animalia*. The first four are all single-celled, microscopic organisms; the last two comprise all plants and animals.

Every member of a kingdom shares only very basic physical characteristics. In the *Animalia* kingdom, every member is, among other things, made up of more than one cell, and reproduces sexually (requiring two individuals to make offspring). That's a very wide and diverse group, including such animals as lizards, humans...and sponges. All members of the *Bacteria* kingdom,

---

Tool trivia: The side of a hammer is called a "cheek."

on the other hand, are single-celled and reproduce asexually (each individual can reproduce by itself).

**Phylum:** Each kingdom is made up of several *phyla*. All organisms in one phylum share a basic physical design. For example, the phylum *Chordata*, which is in the kingdom *Animalia*, consists only of animals that, among other characteristics, have a *notochord*—a backbone—at some point in their development. This includes lizards and humans…but not sponges, which have no backbone. (Sponges are so unique that they have their own phylum, *Porifera*.)

**Class:** Each phylum is divided into different *classes*, with members having more noticeable similarities. All members of the class *Aves* (birds), for instance, have feathers. And all members of the class *Mammalia* have hair.

**Order:** Classes break down into *orders*. This is where animals such as primates and rodents are separated.

**Family:** Families are yet again more alike. Dogs and cats are in the same order, *Carnivora* (the carnivores), but they are in different families, *Canidae* and *Felidae*.

**Genus:** *Genera* consist of organisms that are now very much alike. Example: Cats are all part of the same family, but lions, tigers, and housecats are in different genera.

**Species:** The last stop in the taxa line is *species*, and it has very detailed criteria. Members of the same species of animal, for example, must be able to breed *and* produce offspring that can breed. (Horses and donkeys can breed, but their offspring—mules—cannot. So horses and donkeys are different species.)

## THE NAME GAME

Linnaeus furthered his contribution to taxonomy with the publication of his *Species Plantarum* in 1753. A guide to all the known plants in the world, it introduced "binomial nomenclature," a Latin-based two-name system.

Botanists were already using Latin names for plants, but they were often ridiculously long: *Solanum caule inermi herbaceo, foliis pinnatis incisis*, for instance, meant the "solanum with the smooth stem which is herbaceous and has incised pinnate leaves." In other words: the tomato. Linnaeus knew his scientific naming method would have to be simpler than that to be universally accepted, so he shortened it to a two-name system for each species. (Today the tomato is known as *Lycopersicon esculentum*.) Linnaeus continued to use Latin because it was already the language of science, and because it was a "dead" language (no longer used by any culture), there was less chance it would be changed over time. His system was quickly adopted by the scientific community.

## THE RULES OF THE NAME
The rules for naming new species can be complex, but there are a few basic guidelines:

• The first word in a scientific name, such as *Homo*, is the name of the genus and is always capitalized. The second, such as *sapiens*, is the name of the species and is always lowercase.

• Once a name has been recognized officially, it cannot be used for any other species.

• Many species names are followed by an "L," such as *Rosa canina L* (the briar rose, or "dog rose" in Latin). The "L" stands for "Linnaeus," since he named so many species while devising the system of taxonomy. Though other scientists have species named after them, his is the only name designated by a single initial.

## CHANGING TAXONOMY
Linnaeus's system has been revised several times through the years:

• Linnaeus originally designated only two kingdoms: *Plantae* and *Animalia*—plants and animals. What set them apart? Animals ate and could move; plants didn't eat and couldn't move. That worked for the visible world—but what about the microscopic world? Microscopes were still primitive in the mid-1700s. As they improved and more and more microorganisms were discovered, it became apparent that many didn't fit into either category. Some moved but didn't eat; some ate but didn't move. And although this was known as early as the 1800s, the system didn't officially change until 1969, when five kingdoms were accepted. (The sixth, *Archaea*, was added in the late '70s.)

• Linnaeus believed that all species were fixed, and created his system accordingly. But the discovery of evolution and later, breakthroughs in DNA studies, have revealed much more about the relationships of organisms—and created new problems for scientists. For example, the lungfish and the salmon have always been in the same class—*Pisces*—and the cow has always been in the class *Mammalia*. But the lungfish and the cow, it was recently learned, are more closely related genetically than the lungfish and the salmon. So how do you classify them? (Scientists are still working it out.)

• According to Linnaeus's rules, every name had to be in Latin and, in some way, describe the species it refers to. (*Canis latrans*, for example, is the coyote, meaning "barking dog" in Latin.) But this rule no longer holds. Any language can now be used, as long as the name is put into a Latin-like form. Greek words, proper names, and even sly jokes have found their way into taxonomy. For instance, *Arthurdactylus conandoylensis*, an extinct reptile of South America, was named after Arthur Conan Doyle in honor of his novel *The Lost World*. Some modern examples: a wasp named *Preseucoila imallshookupis* (for Elvis), three species of wasp called *Polemistus chewbacca*, *Polemistus vaderi*, and *Polemistus yoda*, and a trilobyte with an hourglass-shaped head named *Norasaphus monroeae* (for Marilyn Monroe).

## DECLASSIFIED

• Linnaeus is known by four different names: Carl Linnaeus, Carolus Linnaeus, Carl von Linné, and Carl Linné. The confusion stems from the Swedish custom of taking a Latin name when registering at a university. Carl's father, Nils Ingemarsson, made up the name "Linnaeus" when he was a student, and Carl used it as well. Carl later changed it to "von Linné" when he was knighted in 1761.

• Linnaeus originally named humans *Homo diurnis*, or "man of the day." He later changed it to *Homo sapiens*, or "wise man."

• *System Naturae* introduced a controversial method of plant classification: the "sexual system," which organized the plant world according to the number a plant's *stamens* (male parts) and *pistils* (female parts). This caused an outcry, with one rival, Johann Siegesbeck, calling the work "loathsome harlotry." (Linnaeus would later name a small European weed *Siegesbeckia*.)

*Spongebob Squarepants* creator Steve Hillenburg studied marine biology in college.

# RANDOM ORIGINS

*You know what these are...but do you know where they came from?*

## WALLPAPER

It wasn't long after the Chinese invented paper more than 2,000 years ago that they began gluing pieces of it to the walls of their homes. Wallpaper was also popular in medieval Europe, where it was a cheap alternative to tapestries and murals. But these early examples were only imitations of the items they replaced, depicting scenes similar to those woven into tapestries and painted in murals. It wasn't until about 1688 that wallpaper as *we* know it came into being: that was when Jean Papillon, a French engraver, invented the first paper with repeating patterns that matched on every side when the sheets were pasted next to each other.

## TUXEDO RENTALS

Charles Pond made his living entertaining at London parties in the 1890s. He couldn't afford a formal suit of his own, so he borrowed them from his friend Alfred Moss, who ran a clothing store. Eventually Moss got tired of Pond's mooching and started charging him a small fee to rent a suit overnight. Today, Moss Bros. is the largest formalwear rental chain in the U.K.

## ORGAN TRANSPLANTS

On June 17, 1950, an Illinois surgeon named Dr. Richard Lawler removed a kidney from a donor who'd been declared brain dead moments earlier and transplanted it into a 44-year-old woman named Ruth Tucker. Kidney dialysis had only recently been invented and was not yet widely available; for most people, failing kidneys were still a death sentence. A transplant wasn't very promising either—doctors still hadn't figured out how to stop the human body from rejecting transplanted organs. Lawler went ahead with the surgery anyway. The transplanted kidney did fail three months after the surgery, but not before taking strain off of Tucker's remaining kidney, which began functioning normally again. Tucker lived another five years before dying of *heart* disease;

---

Lights on, nobody home: Only 55% of Americans know that the sun is a star.

Dr. Lawler never performed another transplant. "I just wanted to get it started," he explained years later. (The first successful organ transplant, between two identical twins for whom rejection was not an issue, followed in 1954.)

## GPS (GLOBAL POSITIONING SYSTEM)

Not long after the Soviet Union launched Sputnik in 1957, a team of American scientists monitoring the satellite's radio transmissions noticed that the frequency of its signal increased as it approached and decreased as it travelled away from them—a classic example of the "Doppler" effect. They realized they could use this information to pinpoint Sputnik's precise location in space; conversely, if they knew the satellite's location, they could use it to determine their own location on Earth. This principle served as the basis for the U.S. military's NAVSTAR GPS system, which became operational in 1993. The U.S. intended to restrict the system to military use, but when the Soviets shot down a Korean Airlines flight in 1983 after it wandered into Soviet airspace, President Ronald Reagan announced that the system would be made available for public use.

## DETECTIVE STORIES

In 1841 Edgar Allan Poe wrote a short story titled "The Murders in the Rue Morgue," the first of three tales featuring the exploits of a French detective named Auguste Dupin. Why a Frenchman? Because detective work as a profession was barely 30 years old, and France, where it was invented, was still the only country that had detectives. "Each of [Poe's stories] is a root from which a whole literature has developed," *Sherlock Holmes* author Sir Arthur Conan Doyle later acknowledged. "Where was the detective story until Poe breathed the breath of life into it?"

\*     \*     \*

## YUM...OR YUCK?

Ever feel like having dessert for dinner? Try something from the *Twinkies Cookbook*. Among the 50 "creative" uses for the cream-filled Hostess sponge cake are Twinkie Sushi, a Twinkie Burrito, Pigs in a Twinkie, Chicken-Raspberry Twinkie Salad, Twinkie Lasagna, and a red, white, and blue Patriotic Twinkie Pie.

# MAKE YOUR OWN (ORIGAMI) TOILET

*Okay, technically, this isn't origami. But when paper engineer Gary Martin came to us with his "garygami" toilet, we just couldn't resist. In addition to paper, you'll need glue and scissors. Happy folding!*

First, photocopy the patterns below and on page 364 onto white paper (glossy, if you can get it). Enlarging the patterns 200% will fit them onto two 8½ x 11" sheets. Now cut around the patterns along the solid lines. (Dashed lines are folds, solid lines are cut.) Now follow the steps on pages 365 and 366.

**THE TANK: Steps 1–2:** Fold along the dashed lines as shown. **Step 3:** Fold sides so the tabs meet in the back. **Steps 4–6:** Twist slightly to interlock the two slots (tabs should join on the *inside*). Slide them together so they align at the top. **Steps 7–8:** Fold down the larger flap first and tuck it inside, then do the same with the smaller flap.

**THE BOWL: Step 9:** Fold along the dashed lines. **Steps 10–11:** Overlap and lock toilet lid tab into slot as shown, keeping the toilet "seat" on the inside. **Step 12:** Now lock toilet seat tab in place with tab facing the outside. **Step 13:** Push bottom oval into toilet base. **Step 14:** Glue the tank to the toilet where marked so the bottom of tank aligns with the bottom of the outside tab on the toilet. *Voilà!* You're done! Your origami toilet can stand up on its own, or you can put a string through the hole in the "lid" to hang it as an ornament.

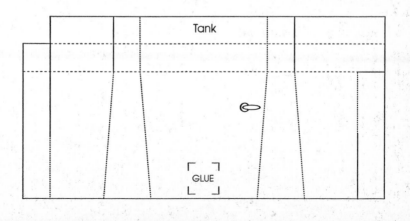

The King Ranch in Texas is bigger than the entire state of Rhode Island. (Size: 825,000 acres.)

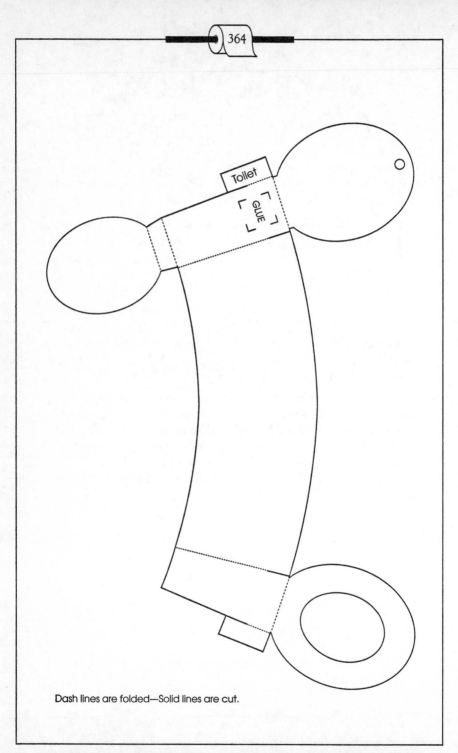

Toilet

GLUE

Dash lines are folded—Solid lines are cut.

George Harrison owned a musical toilet. It played "Lucy in the Sky With Diamonds."

**The Tank:**

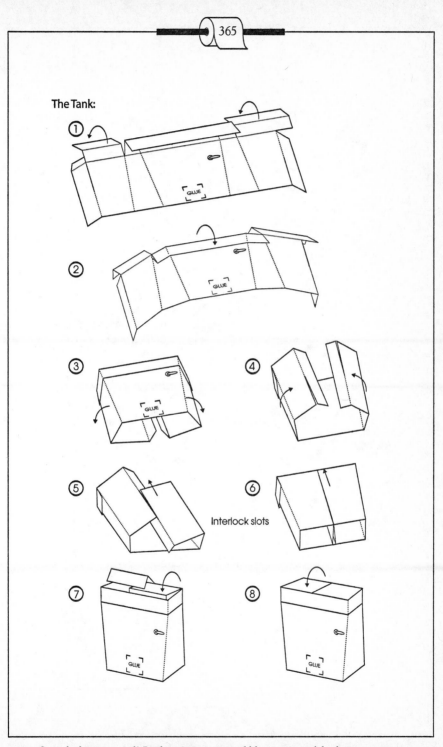

Scared of going to jail? In the 1800s, you could be imprisoned for being nervous.

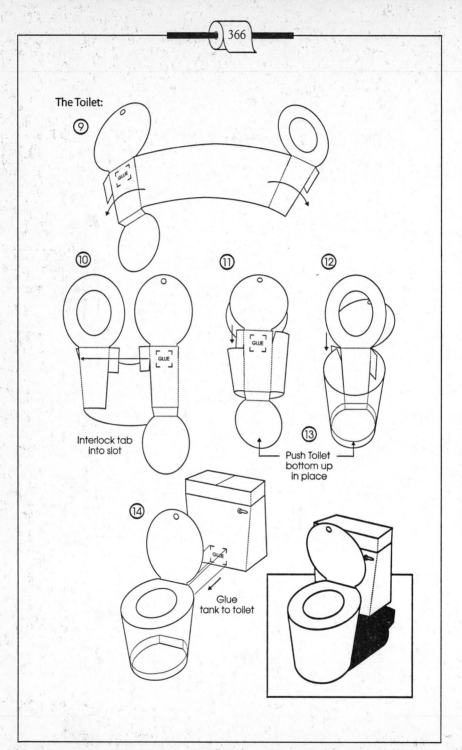

**The Toilet:**

⑨

⑩ Interlock tab into slot

⑪

⑫

⑬ Push Toilet bottom up in place

⑭ Glue tank to toilet

# MORE DUMB JOCKS

*More goofy gaffes by players, coaches, and announcers.*

"Sure. I'm proud to be an American."
—**Steve Foster, Cincinnati Reds player, asked by Canadian customs if he had anything to declare**

"We kind of looked at each other and said, 'That was fun.' It was a couple guys beating on each other. Good times."
—**Scott Parker, San Jose Sharks hockey player, after fighting Columbus's Jody Shelley**

"It's permanent, for now."
—**Roberto Kelly, San Diego Padres player, announcing he was changing his name to Bobby**

"It is beyond my apprehension."
—**Danny Ozark, Philadelphia Phillies manager, on his team's losing streak**

**Louise Goodman:** "Jonny, it's started to rain. How will that affect the track?"
**Jonny Herbert:** "Well, it makes it wet, usually."
—**British auto racing announcers**

"I'll be sad to go, and I won't be sad to go. It wouldn't upset me to leave St. Louis, but it would upset me to leave St. Louis. It's hard to explain. You'll find out one of these days, but maybe you never will."
—**Brett Hull, St. Louis Blues player, on a possible trade**

"Well, that kind of puts the damper on even a Yankee win."
—**Phil Rizzuto, after hearing Pope Paul VI died**

"Not only is he ambidextrous, but he can throw with either hand."
—**Duffy Daugherty, Michigan State football coach**

"The advantage of the rain is that if you have a quick bike, there's no advantage."
—**Barry Sheen, British motorcycle racing analyst**

"If Rose's streak was still intact, with that single to left, the fans would be throwing babies out of the upper deck."
—**Jerry Coleman, San Diego Padres announcer**

Hey, sports fans—if one team forfeits a baseball game, what's the score? (It's recorded as 9–0.)

# HEY, HO, LET'S GO!

*Rock critic Nick Tosches coined the term "punk" in 1970 to
describe a wave of raucous bands that had just come on the
music scene. Here's the story of punk rock. Riot!*

## ROCK IS DEAD

In the mid-1970s, the most popular musical acts in America
were middle-of-the-road, mellow-rock artists like the
Eagles, John Denver, Olivia Newton-John, ABBA, and Barry
Manilow. But while that was what was happening on Top 40
radio, an emerging scene of musicians in New York City was doing
something different. "We were all pretty disgusted with what was
going on in rock and roll," said Joey Ramone. "There was no
excitement in music—everything was totally superficial and pre-
fabricated." Rock music lacked the danger and energy that it had
had in the 1950s and '60s. They also thought rock 'n' roll was
supposed to be simple: Pick up a guitar, learn a few chords, and
write some songs.

In 1973 a failed country musician named Hilly Kristal opened
a bar in New York's Bowery neighborhood called CBGB and
OMFUG (short for Country, Bluegrass, Blues, and Other Music
for Uplifting Gormandizers). Kristal planned to feature country
and bluegrass music...until Tom Verlaine and Richard Hell convinced him to let their band, Television, play a weekly gig at the
bar in 1974. Over the next few years, CBGB became *the* home of
punk and alternative music, featuring bands like Blondie, the Patti
Smith Group, the Clash, Mink DeVille, the Talking Heads, Elvis
Costello, the Damned, Richard Hell and the Voidoids, the Police,
the Dictators, Tuff Darts, the Shirts, the Heartbreakers, and the
Fleshtones.

## ONE, TWO, THREE, FOUR

Probably the most famous—and most important—band to get
their start at CBGB was the Ramones. They pared rock music
down to its essentials: catchy melodies, simple lyrics, four chords,
songs no more than three minutes long. Their sound was loud,
fast, raw, and hard-driving, with lots of smart-aleck humor (they

had songs titled "Now I Wanna Sniff Some Glue" and "I Wanna Be Sedated"). The band members—Joey, Johnny, Dee Dee, and Tommy—all took the last name Ramone (from "Paul Ramone," an alias of Paul McCartney) and dressed identically in jeans, sneakers, leather jackets, and long hair that covered their eyes. All songs started with Johnny counting off "one, two, three, four!"

But the Ramones weren't the first band to combine musical simplicity, noise, and a bad attitude.

• In the late 1960s in New York, the Velvet Underground (fronted by Lou Reed) played slow, minimalist, creepy songs about depression and drugs.

• A Detroit band, the Stooges, would do things like play the same riff over and over, faster and faster, working frontman James Osterberg (who later took the stage name "Iggy Pop") into a frenzy. He'd cut himself with broken glass and dive into the audience.

• The New York Dolls screeched on guitars and dressed in makeup, high heels, and gold lamé. Their music, like their look, was loud, abrasive, and confrontational.

But the Ramones, Velvet Underground, Stooges, and New York Dolls all looked back to another band for inspiration: the MC5. This Detroit band released their first album, *Kick Out the Jams*, in 1968. The music was noisy and the lyrics were political, reflecting band members' involvement with countercultural groups like the Black Panthers (the first line of the title song contained profanity, shocking for 1968). Controversial in their day, they're now regarded as one of the greatest bands of all time—and they set the whole "punk" movement into action.

## ANARCHY IN THE U.K.

In 1974 former New York Dolls manager Malcolm McLaren saw Television perform at CBGB. McLaren was taken with the look of singer Richard Hell, who wore a torn shirt, studded dog collar, and a leather jacket. McLaren thought Hell looked the way punk sounded, and he concluded that punk was destined to be a hit among young people. He publicly stated that he wanted to form a punk rock band and "make a million pounds." So McLaren returned to his hometown of London and opened a punk-themed clothing store he called SEX. He then assembled some amateur

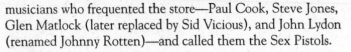

musicians who frequented the store—Paul Cook, Steve Jones, Glen Matlock (later replaced by Sid Vicious), and John Lydon (renamed Johnny Rotten)—and called them the Sex Pistols.

The Pistols toured England in 1976, and their sneering attitude and distinct lack of musical ability (none could play more than four chords on a guitar) caused a sensation. Their songs called for revolution, insulted the queen, and were brash, sexual, and violent. Young English kids loved it; the Sex Pistols' first single, "Anarchy in the U.K.," even achieved minor hit status.

But all that changed in December 1976, when the Sex Pistols appeared on the British show *Talk of the Town*. Guitarist Steve Jones got into a verbal spat with host Bill Grundy and swore profusely on the air. The controversy immediately made the Sex Pistols widely known and the band's first album, *Never Mind the Bollocks*, shot to #1 in England, spawning three Top 10 hits.

## CODA

For most fans, the intensity of punk rock and its lifestyle were too difficult to maintain long term. As musical tastes in the early 1980s shifted to more melodic "New Wave" rock and electronic-based pop music, punk went back underground. But it never died. A revival of '70s-style punk rock came about in 1994 when the Berkeley, California punk band Green Day sold 10 million copies of their album *Dookie*. This inspired a new wave of punk bands such as the Offspring, Rancid, and Blink-182, who all sold millions of albums. What was once an underground movement is now mainstream. In 2005, Green Day's *American Idiot* even won the Grammy Award for Album of the Year.

\*       \*       \*

Punk rock's other innovation: rude and funny band names, such as:

The Buzzcocks, 100 Demons, Agent Orange, I Killed the Prom Queen, Armed and Hammered, the Flesh Eaters, the Battered Wives, Bad Brains, Bastard, Gorilla Biscuits, I Hate You, the Stranglers, Suicidal Tendencies, Choking Victim, Deep Wound, Kinetic Destruction, Butthole Surfers, Dead Kennedys, A Chorus of Disapproval, Jerry's Kids, the Casualties, the Damaged, the Germs, Ed Banger and the Nosebleeds, the F.U.'s, the Vandals, Murder Disco X, Vitamin X, the Urinals, D.O.A., the Exploited, Shark Attack, the Misfits, the Vomit Pigs

Who was Edward Despard? He was the last criminal to be drawn & quartered in England (1803).

# THE RANKIN FILE

*This political pioneer was first and foremost a woman of conscience, whatever the consequence. You may not agree with her, but you've got to admire her spirit.*

## FIRST LADY

In November 1916, a short, feisty suffragette from Missoula, Montana, named Jeanette Rankin beat seven male rivals to become the first woman ever elected to Congress. And that made her the first woman ever elected to a national legislature in any Western democracy. "I knew the women would stand behind me," she said, "and I am deeply conscious of the responsibility. I will not only represent the women of Montana, but also the women of the country, and I have plenty of work cut out for me."

Rankin was not afraid of work. Born in 1880, the University of Montana graduate had worked as a teacher, seamstress, and social worker until, at age 30, she joined the fight for women's right to vote in Montana. "Men and women are like right and left hands," she declared. "It doesn't make sense not to use both." And when Montana women got the vote in 1914, Rankin decided to run for Congress. With her brother Wellington as her campaign manager, she was triumphant and took her seat in the House of Representatives on April 2, 1917.

## STANDING ALONE

Rankin was not welcomed with open arms. The congressional wives were unfriendly, afraid she'd have designs on their husbands. The U.S. Capitol at that time had no bathrooms for women—there'd never been a need. To make matters worse, four days after she took her seat in Congress, Rankin made the extremely unpopular decision to vote *against* America's entry into World War I (the vote was 373–50). It is customary to vote without comment, but Rankin broke with tradition, announcing dramatically, "I want to stand behind my country, but I cannot vote for war."

Rankin championed many causes during her two years in Congress: women's rights, birth control, equal pay, and child welfare.

In 1919 she proudly introduced the Susan B. Anthony Amendment, which gave women the right to vote, on the floor of the House; it passed and was ratified by the country as the 19th amendment to the Constitution. "If I am remembered for no other act," she later said. "I want to be remembered as the only woman who ever voted to give women the right to vote."

## WAR NO MORE

The ratification of the 19th Amendment was a triumph for Rankin and the suffrage movement. But her earlier anti-war vote had sealed her political fate. When she ran for the Senate in the next election, she was soundly defeated. Yet that loss only fueled her fire. For the next two decades, Rankin worked for peace through the Women's International League for Peace and Freedom and the National Conference for the Prevention of War. She saw war as a terrible waste and was fond of saying, "You can no more win a war than win an earthquake."

In 1940, when she was nearly 60, Rankin made another successful run for Congress on the slogan, "Prepare to the limit for defense; keep our men out of Europe." Then, in 1941, the Japanese bombed Pearl Harbor. The next day President Franklin Delano Roosevelt asked Congress to declare war on Japan. Despite pressure from the president, Congress, and her family, Rankin cast the lone dissenting vote, saying, "As a woman I can't go to war and I refuse to send someone else." Her vote caused a near-riot in the House chamber. She was showered with boos from the angry crowd in the gallery and had to hide in a phone booth until the Capitol police escorted her out. Jeanette Rankin was the only member of Congress to vote against both world wars.

## STICKING TO HER BELIEFS

Though she never ran for public office again, she continued to work for peace. In 1968 at the age of 88, when the United States was sending soldiers to fight in Vietnam, she led the Jeannette Rankin Brigade—5,000 women in black—in a silent protest march on Washington.

Before Rankin passed away at 92, she said, "If I had my life to live over, I'd do it all the same—but this time I'd be nastier."

# IT'S A WEIRD, WEIRD WORLD

*More proof that truth is stranger than fiction.*

**C**LOSED DUE TO AWESOME WEATHER
"Instead of enduring a day of inattention and spring fever, Bellingham (Washington) Christian School declared a 'sun day' in April 2006 and gave everyone the day off. School administrators had told the students there would be no school on the first sunny day that hit at least 63 degrees. After the forecast called for a high of 65, school was closed. Students were told to return the next day, when the forecast called for rain."

—*Arizona Republic*

**GOOD OMEN**

"A horror film fan who prayed that her baby would be born on 6/6/06 (he was) named her new boy Damien. The boy—weighing 6 pounds, 6 ounces—was born six days after his mother's labor was first induced. Suzanne Cooper chose the name because *The Omen* is her favorite film. 'He's a perfect baby—nothing at all like Damien (the son of the devil) in *The Omen*.'"

—*The Sun* **(U.K.)**

**PHONIES**

"In an inversion of the Third World call center set-up, a British man was fined for advertising that his 'sex chat' phone line offered 'Filipino girls,' when the women in question were in fact working from central England. He was unmasked when clients found the alleged 'Filipinas' had strangely familiar accents."

—*The Standard*

**HOPPING MAD**

"Bryan Johnson, who portrayed the Easter Bunny at the Bay City (Michigan) Mall in 2005, was pummeled in an unprovoked attack

---

What do you call a part-time bandleader? A semi-conductor.

on the job. Police say the attacker was a 12-year-old boy who sat on Johnson's lap the day before the incident. Johnson, 18, suffered a bloody nose. He kept his cool during the attack, deeming it inappropriate for the Easter Bunny to fight back."

—*Detroit News*

## FINGER FOOD

"Brandon Seinna ordered a meal in a T.G.I. Friday's in Bloomington, Indiana, in 2005. When the food arrived, he spied what looked like human flesh on the plate. It was, and T.G.I Friday's had to scurry to do damage control. 'A manager cut his finger while working in the kitchen,' the company said in a statement. 'In the rush of attending to his medical needs, the team members were unaware that a small piece of skin from the individual's finger top had fallen onto a plate, and that plate was subsequently served to a guest.' The statement went on to say that safety procedures were reviewed and another such incident would not occur."

—*Pittsburgh Tribune-Review*

## TRUE ROMANCE

"A 104-year-old Malaysian woman has gotten married for the 21st time—to a man of 33. It's his first trip to the altar. The bride, Wook Kundor, caught Muhammad Noor Che Musa's eye because she was childless, old, and alone. And no, she hasn't got money. Before this, Muhammad reportedly said, he never stayed anywhere long enough for a relationship."

—*Parade*

## JUST VISITING

"In Denmark, a 43-year-old man was arrested in jail after passing himself off as a bona fide prisoner and spending a night voluntarily behind bars. Per Thorbjoern Lonka said he carried out the prank to prove that rich people could easily pay someone else to serve their prison terms. He was right—the prison guards who locked him up failed to ask for his identity papers. But it didn't matter—the judge sentenced Lonka to two months in prison."

—*Daily Times* (Pakistan)

# UNCLE JOHN'S STALL OF FAME

*One woman's quest to do what the cops would not.*

**H**onoree: Katja Base, mother of six, from Norco, California
**Notable Achievement:** Solving "the Great Paper Caper"
**True Story:** One February morning in 2006, Base awoke
to find her house had been "TP'd"—wrapped with dozens of rolls
of toilet paper. But the vandals didn't stop there: They damaged
landscaping, broke light fixtures, ruined the finishes on the family's cars, and left the front yard covered with dry dog food, cheese,
flour, and hundreds of plastic forks. Base called the police, who
said they'd file a report but were too busy to chase down "teenage
pranksters." Unwilling to give up so easily, Base went into action.

• First, she went to the local supermarket and asked the manager
if there had recently been any large sales of toilet paper. Sure
enough, two days earlier, someone wiped out their entire supply—
144 rolls, to be exact. Also included in the sale: "cheese, dog food,
flour, and plastic forks." But because it was a cash transaction,
there was no way to trace the buyer.

• Base convinced the manager into letting her review the security
tapes from that afternoon, which showed four teenage boys in line
purchasing said items. One of them wore a letter jacket from the
local high school with his name printed on the back.

• A parking-lot camera captured the teens climbing into a pickup
truck, and Base was able to get the make and model.

• That night, Base looked through the school yearbook and
found the culprits. Then she entered the teens' names into an
online database and found their addresses. Base neatly packaged
up all of the evidence and brought it to the police.

Result: The cops brought the culprits in, showed them the
evidence, and got a confession. The boys were arraigned on felony
vandalism charges. Base told reporters, "Mainly, I pursued this as
a lesson for my daughters. I don't want them to ever come to me
and ask why I didn't do anything about this."

---

Yum! Eww! Yum! Eww! An earthworm eats and excretes its own weight every day.

# WEIRD PITCHES

*Lots of celebrities have endorsed products. Sometimes it helps sales.*
*The George Foreman Grill, for example, has sold millions.*
*Sometimes, on the other hand, it's just a weird idea.*

• In the 1880s, **Pope Leo XIII** endorsed a "medicine" called Vin Mariani in newspaper ads. (It was really wine laced with cocaine.)

• Former Chicago Bears linebacker **Dick Butkus** made TV ads for the Kwik-Cook, a portable grill that burned newspapers for fuel. More football news: Bassett Furniture carries a line of furniture designed by former Denver Broncos quarterback **John Elway**.

• Teen star **Hilary Duff** endorsed a line of ottomans.

• In 1994 Hong Kong TV station ATV used images of **Adolph Hitler** in print ads, claiming that Hitler would have been more "successful" had he advertised on ATV.

• Today, **Fred Flintstone** and **Barney Rubble** appear in ads for Flintstones vitamins, but they once starred in TV ads selling Winston cigarettes.

• **Cybill Shepherd** was hired by the Beef Industry Council in 1987 for the "real food for real people" campaign, despite Shepherd's public admission that she was a vegetarian.

• **Joe Namath** plugged Beautymist Panty Hose, which he claimed to have worn under his football uniform.

• In 1959 former First Lady **Eleanor Roosevelt** became the television spokesperson for Good Luck margarine.

• **Ricardo Montalban,** who once helped sell the Chrysler Cordoba (upholstered in "soft Corinthian leather"), also appeared in an infomercial for the Nativity Cross—a gold cross set with a stone said to be from a cave near Jesus's birthplace.

• Wrestler **Hulk Hogan** lent his image to a line of cameras for kids. His face was painted on the lens, inserting Hulk into the corner of every photograph.

---

Early Mountain Dew bottles featured a cartoon character called "Willy the Hillbilly."

# I'VE GOT A
# CUNNING PLAN…

*Un-genious schemes from un-genious people.*

## WHAT A PHONEHEAD

In January 2004, Jack Painter of Plainville, Connecticut, called 911 and reported a robbery in process at a Dairy Mart store. He then proceeded to rob a Dairy Mart on the *other* side of town. Only problem: He accidentally gave the dispatcher the address of the Dairy Mart he was robbing, not of the decoy one, as he'd planned. Police showed up and arrested him in the middle of the robbery.

## NOT TOO SWIFT

In 2005 Stewart and Cathryn Bromley of Manchester, England, got two camera-detected speeding tickets totaling about $200. Not wanting to pay the tickets, they told authorities that a friend named Konstantin Koscov had been visiting from Bulgaria and he was driving the car at the time of the tickets. Police were suspicious and started investigating…so Cathryn flew 1,400 miles to Bulgaria and mailed a postcard from the "friend," thanking them for the use of their car. When police contacted Interpol to locate "Koscov," the couple finally admitted that they'd made the whole thing up. Instead of the original $200, they ended up paying more then $20,000 in fines and court costs (plus a flight to Bulgaria).

## BY THE BOOK

In June 2006, Asante Kahari was charged with several counts of fraud for bilking a Michigan woman out of $38,000. He'd met her in 2001 on an Internet dating chat room, befriended her, and got her to deposit several (forged) checks into her bank account. Then he got her to withdraw the money in cash, took it, and disappeared. When police caught up with him, he pleaded innocent to the charges, but prosecutors were able to convince jurors of his guilt by reading excerpts of a novel they found on Kahari's Web site. The book, titled *The Birth of a Criminal* and billed as "the new autobiography from Asante Kahari," describes meeting a woman from Michigan on an Internet dating chat room, mailing her counterfeit checks worth about $38,000, going to meet her, getting her to withdraw the money in cash, taking it, and disappearing. He was convicted on six counts of fraud.

## NO EXIT

When 30-year-old Larry Bynum of Ft. Worth, Texas, decided to break into a liquor store in June 2006, he failed to take a couple of things into account. The first was how to get safely into the store. Bynum broke in through a ceiling ventilation hatch. A surveillance camera showed him crashing through the ceiling tiles of the store and falling the almost 20 feet to the floor. He remained on the floor, barely moving, for almost five minutes. He finally got up and emptied the cash register. The second thing he hadn't thought of was how to get *out* of the store. He tried to climb a display shelf back to the ceiling, but fell and broke the shelf. Then he tried bashing through the front door with a beer keg, but that didn't work, either—it was made of Plexiglas. Finally, after Bynum had spent more than an hour trying to escape from the store, a cop happened to drive by and see him. The surveillance video shows Bynum calmly sitting down on the beer keg and lighting a cigarette, waiting to be arrested.

\*　　\*　　\*

## CHILDHOOD NICKNAMES

- **Lucille Ball:** "Bird Legs" (*she had skinny legs*)
- **Frank Sinatra:** "Slacksey" (*he was a dapper dresser*)
- **Jerry Lewis:** "Id" (*short for "Idiot"*)
- **Cameron Diaz:** "Skeletor" (*super-skinny teenager*)
- **Dustin Hoffman:** "Tootsie" (*it was he who suggested his cross-dressing film be called* Tootsie, *in honor of his childhood nickname*)
- **John Lennon:** "Stinker" (*he was a notorious practical joker*)
- **Jenna Elfman:** "Bucky Beaver" (*she had quite the overbite*)
- **Samuel L. Jackson:** "Machine Gun" (*he stuttered*)
- **Jay Leno:** "Chinzo" (*no explanation necessary*)

# BOODLE AND BINGO

*Yo! It may be difficult to imagine your great-great-grandparents as teenagers, using slang back in the 19th century. But it turns out their language was as colorful as ours. For example:*

**Acknowledge the corn:** To admit a mistake.

**Wake snakes:** To make a noisy racket.

**Guttersnipe:** A homeless child who lives in the streets.

**Codfish aristocracy:** People who have become wealthy—*heavens!*—by earning money in business.

**Puke:** A person from Missouri.

**Bingo:** Liquor.

**Border ruffians:** People living in the untamed American West.

**I snore:** "I swear" was considered rude conversation in polite company, so people said "I snore" instead.

**Boodle:** Counterfeit money.

**Set your cap for (someone):** When a woman sets out to win over a particular man.

**Spark it:** To cuddle, kiss, or become affectionate on a date.

**Give (someone) the mitten:** When a young lady rejected the advances of a young man, she "gave him the mitten."

**Barking iron:** A gun.

**Row (someone) up Salt River:** To beat someone up.

**Sockdologer:** A powerful punch—the kind that would row someone up Salt River.

**Whip your weight in wildcats:** Defeat a powerful opponent.

**Bloke buzzer:** A pickpocket who specializes in stealing from men. (A moll buzzer steals from women.)

**It's a sin to Moses:** It's shameful.

**Long nine:** A cheap cigar that's nine inches long.

**Spider:** A frying pan with three legs, used for cooking over an open fire.

**Bang-up:** An overcoat.

**Bit:** A coin worth 12.5 cents—an eighth of a dollar ("two bits" is 25 cents).

**Short bit:** A dime.

**Talk like a book:** To speak eloquently.

**Bucket shop:** A distillery.

**Arkansas toothpick:** A big knife.

**Shinplasters:** Cheap paper currency, valued in denominations as little as a nickel and issued when banks were out of coins.

**Nerve tonic:** Whiskey.

**Anti-fogmatic:** Nerve tonic.

**Have a brick in your hat:** To be drunk.

**Virginia fence:** Drunks who staggered back and forth were said to be "making a Virginia fence."

**Savagerous:** Savage.

**Slantindicular:** Slanted.

**Cut up didoes:** To get into trouble.

**Poor as Job's turkey:** *Very* poor.

**Bummers:** What bums were called before the name was shortened.

**It's not your funeral:** It's none of your business.

**Have a pocket full of rocks:** To have lots of money.

**Inexpressibles:** What people called trousers when they were thought to be too vulgar to mention in polite company. (Also known as unwhisperables and sit-down-upons.)

**Make a fist:** To succeed.

**Hang up your fiddle:** Give up.

\*　　\*　　\*

## OOPS!

• On September 16, 2005, police in Bel Aire, Kansas, raided the home of the former mayor and his wife. They searched every closet, cabinet, and drawer looking for drugs and drug paraphernalia. Nothing was found. A marijuana plant had been seen, and photographed, in the former mayor's back yard. It turned out that it was a sunflower plant. The sunflower is the state flower of Kansas.

• NBC's broadcast of the 2006 Emmy Awards began with a film montage of host Conan O'Brien making mock appearances in the year's most popular TV shows, including *Lost*, a show about plane-crash survivors. Tragic coincidence: In some parts of the country the *Lost* skit immediately followed round-the-clock news coverage of a fatal plane crash in Lexington, Kentucky. NBC later apologized.

• In 1994 Salton Inc. contacted wrestler Hulk Hogan to attach his name to an indoor grill. He missed the call, so Salton signed another athlete instead. Too bad for Hogan: George Foreman has earned $150 million from the George Foreman Grill.

# LET'S DO A STUDY!

*If you're worried that the really important things in life aren't being researched by scientists...keep worrying.*

I n 2005 the publicly funded Mental Health Foundation of Britain did a year-long study on the psychological reasons behind alcohol use. Conclusion: People drink because it makes them feel better.

• Edward Cussler of the University of Minnesota led an experiment in which 16 people swam in a pool filled with water, and then in a pool filled with 700 pounds of guar gum—a dense syrup commonly used to thicken ice cream. Why? Cussler wanted to see if humans swim slower in syrup than they do in water. (Surprisingly, they don't.)

• After studying overweight children playing with weighted and unweighted blocks, researchers at Indiana State University concluded that lifting weights burns more calories than *not* lifting weights. (They had to do a study to figure that out?) The scientists plan to use the findings to help fight obesity by manufacturing teddy bears with three-pound weights inside.

• In 2005 John Mainstone and Thomas Parnell of the University of Queensland (Australia) determined that congealed tar flows through a funnel at a rate of about one drop per nine years. How did they know? They'd been monitoring the tar for 78 years. (Parnell actually died before the results were announced, and to date, nobody has actually been in the room when a tar drop dripped.)

• In 2003 two scientists went to Antarctica to find the exact velocity by which penguins expel waste. Their report: "Pressures Produced When Penguins Pooh: Calculations on Avian Defecation."

• In 1999, Harvard University conducted a study called "Gorillas in our Midst." Test subjects were instructed to watch people pass a basketball back and forth. Meanwhile, the subjects failed to notice a person in a gorilla suit walking around the room. Researchers' conclusion: When we're paying too close attention to one thing, we tend to overlook what's going on right around us. (Even a person in a gorilla costume.)

# THE TWO GRAVES OF MAD ANTHONY WAYNE

*Historians tell many stories about heroes who are so
beloved that everyone wants a piece of them. In
the case of this man, they mean it literally.*

## WHAT'S IN A NAME

Great generals frequently earn descriptive nicknames: "Blood and Guts" Patton, "Black Jack" Pershing, and "Stonewall" Jackson, to name a few. Revolutionary War hero "Mad Anthony" Wayne got his nickname for his bravery in battle—he was bold, he took big risks…and he won. His forces smashed the British in a surprise attack on Stony Point, New York; he led the American victory at Monmouth, New Jersey; and he prevented a disastrous rout at Brandywine in Pennsylvania. Washington's reports repeatedly praised Major General Wayne for his leadership and valor, and the Continental Congress awarded him a special gold medal celebrating the victory at Stony Point.

Wayne was born near Philadelphia on New Year's Day, 1745. He grew up to be a surveyor, then took over as manager of the family tannery until the Revolutionary War began. When the war ended, Wayne returned to civilian life, but his fighting days weren't over yet. In 1792 President Washington called him out of retirement for one last combat mission.

## BACK IN ACTION

The British were arming and sponsoring a coalition of the Miami, Shawnee, Delaware, and Wyandot Indian tribes in Ohio, hoping to protect the British-held Northwest Territory by blocking further westward expansion by the United States. Wayne was given command of the Legion of the United States, with the mission of driving the British out and destroying the coalition.

General Wayne spent almost two years recruiting and training his command, then went into action. On August 20, 1794, the U.S. Legion destroyed the tribal army at the Battle of Fallen Timbers, near present-day Toledo. The Treaty of Greenville was signed

August 3, 1795, opening the Northwest Territory to American settlement.

His mission accomplished, Wayne headed home...but never made it. He fell ill en route and died of complications from gout on December 15, 1796, at the age of 51. His body was buried in a plain oak coffin near Erie, Pennsylvania, almost 300 miles west of his family home in Radnor, near Philadelphia. There he rested for 13 years, until his family decided they wanted to bring their hero's body home for a proper funeral. His son, Isaac, was given the task of bringing the general's remains back to the family.

## CARRY ME BACK

Isaac Wayne made the long journey to Erie in a one-horse sulky— a two-wheeled cart more suitable for carrying light loads in urban areas than for carrying a heavy casket all the way back to Radnor. When his father's body was exhumed, it was remarkably well preserved, but there was no way it could bear bouncing along rutted dirt roads for 300 miles. It was a dilemma for the son. He couldn't return empty-handed—he had to find another solution. So he asked Dr. Wallace, who had cared for his father during his final illness, to dismember the body. (He refused to watch the operation, saying he wanted to remember his father as he looked in life.)

Next, the body parts were boiled in a large iron pot. Wallace and four assistants then carefully scraped the flesh from the bones, which were reverently placed in a wooden box and presented to the old soldier's son. The flesh was returned to the original oak casket and reburied in the original grave.

## THE OTHER FINAL RESTING PLACE

Isaac returned home with his precious cargo, and, after the long-delayed funeral, the bones of "Mad Anthony" Wayne were finally interred in St. David's Episcopal Church Cemetery in Radnor, giving the Revolutionary War hero two graves.

But that's not the end of the story. Today, Radnor is connected to Erie by paved freeways instead of rutted dirt roads. There is a legend that some of the bones were lost on the grueling trip home ...and the ghost of "Mad Anthony" haunts the freeways, searching for his lost leg.

## WAYNE'S WORLD

• **Have you every been to...**Wayne City, Illinois; Waynesville, North Carolina; Fort Wayne, Indiana; Wayne, Michigan; Waynesboro, Virginia; Wayne, Waynesburg, or Waynesboro, Pennsylvania; Waynesfield or Waynesville, Ohio; or Wayne Township, New Jersey?

• **Did you attend...**Wayne State University in Detroit, Michigan; Wayne High School in Huber Heights, Ohio; Wayne Middle School in Erie, Pennsylvania; Wayne High School in Fort Wayne, Indiana; Anthony Wayne Middle School in Wayne, New Jersey; or General Wayne Elementary School in Paoli, Pennsylvania?

• **Did anyone in your family...**perform military service at Fort Wayne in Detroit, Michigan?

• **Did you ever...**picnic in Anthony Wayne Recreation Area in Harriman State Park, New York, or drive across the Anthony Wayne Suspension Bridge near downtown Toledo, Ohio?

• **Have you ever driven on...**Anthony Wayne Drive in Detroit, Michigan; Wayne Avenue in Ticonderoga, New York; or Anthony Wayne Avenue in Cincinnati, Ohio?

• **Did you ever...**see a film at the Anthony Wayne Movie Theater in Wayne, Pennsylvania; get your hair cut at the Anthony Wayne Barber Shop in Maumee, Ohio; or fish on the Mad River in Dayton, Ohio?

They're all named after Mad Anthony Wayne.

## MORE MAD-NESS

• In 1930 actor Marion "Duke" Morrison was about to get his first starring role, in director Raoul Walsh's Western, *The Big Trail*. But Fox Studios didn't like the name "Duke Morrison"—it wasn't American-sounding enough. So Walsh suggested changing it to "Anthony Wayne," after the general. The film's producer thought that Anthony Wayne sounded "too Italian," and that Tony Wayne "sounded like a girl." So they changed his name to John Wayne.

• According to many pop-culture historians, the comic book character Bruce Wayne—better known as Batman—was named after Scottish patriot Robert the Bruce...and Mad Anthony Wayne.

The world's smallest park—452 sq. inches—is in Portland, OR. (It was designed for snail racing.)

# TOILET TECH

*Better living through bathroom technology.*

**P**roduct: Fresh-Air Breathing Device (a.k.a. Toilet Snorkel)
**How It Works:** The biggest cause of fire-related injury and death isn't the flames—it's the smoke. In 1982 William Holmes received a patent for a device designed to access a source of fresh air during fires in high-rise buildings, where help may be slow to arrive. Snake this slender breathing tube down through any toilet and into the water trap, and access fresh air from the sewer line's vent pipe. At the user end, the breathing tube is connected to a strap-on mask. Good news: The Toilet Snorkel comes with an odor-eating charcoal filter.

**Product:** No-Flush Urinal
**How It Works:** In recent years, some states, such as Arizona and California, have required all new toilets to be low-flow, water-conserving models. Waterless Co. of Vista, California, went one step further: They invented a urinal that uses no water at all. The No-Flush uses a glazed, ultrasmooth drain so slick and so narrow that urine is whisked away via gravity. Waterless claims that one of their devices can save 45,000 gallons of water a year.

**Product:** Intelligence Toilet
**How It Works:** The Japanese manufacturer Toto has a commode with a computer chip and a built-in urine analyzer. But that's not all you'll find in Toto's integrated bathroom: There's also a blood-pressure cuff housed in the sink countertop, a scale in front of the counter to weigh the user, and a device above the sink that measures body fat when briefly gripped after washing your hands. All results are recorded automatically on the toilet's hard drive and sent via the Internet to a home computer, which then dispenses dietary and health recommendations. Cost: $5,230.

**Product:** Compost Toilet
**How It Works:** It's essentially a litter box for people. According to the World Toilet Organization, a trade group based in Singa-

pore, this Chinese toilet is a steel box filled with sawdust. It has a microcomputer that senses when the box has solid waste in it, and a mechanical arm that rotates the sawdust, burying the waste (which the company says can later be used as organic fertilizer). The device stays at a constant temperature of about 120°F, hot enough to make liquid waste evaporate, and has specially formulated low-odor sawdust that needs to be changed only once a year.

**Product:** Indipod

**How It Works:** First there were car phones, then car DVD players. Now there's a car toilet. Indipod is a small chemical toilet within an inflatable opaque "bubble," designed to work inside most SUVs. A fan, powered by the car's cigarette lighter, inflates the tentlike bubble, creating a private bathroom in the back of the car. Chemicals in the toilet break down waste into a "sweet-smelling" liquid housed in a detachable, disposable container. Bonus: The fan noise masks any...um...sounds made inside the bubble. The company's motto: "Freedom to go wherever you want to go."

**Product:** New Plunge

**How It Works:** This product aims to replace the traditional toilet plunger. New Plunge is a straight rod of flexible plastic that you stick down the drain and twist around until the obstruction is cleared. But wait—there's more. New Plunge can also be used to *prevent* toilet clogs: One end of the plastic rod is a dull blade that can be used to "slice and dice" waste into smaller, more easily flushable chunks. What's more, says the manufacturer, it cleans up easily with toilet paper ("simply run the tissue down the length of New Plunge") and leaves no toilet residue on the floor.

**Product:** iCarta

**How It Works:** Now you can really "go anywhere" with your iPod. The iCarta resembles an ordinary wall-mounted toilet paper dispenser. But while TP comes out the roll on the bottom, the top has an iPod "docking station." Music comes out two moisture-resistant speakers.

# THE ICE AGE

*This article isn't about what you think. It's about the other*
*ice age—the 19th century, when ice was big business*
*and the iceman delivered right to your door.*

## COLD COMFORT

Humans have used freezing as a way to preserve food since the days they lived in caves. The practice was probably discovered around 12,000 years ago during the last ice age. By 4,000 years ago, the earliest civilizations in Mesopotamia were commonly using ice pits to store food and chill drinks. The Chinese got into it around 1100 B.C. The Egyptian pharaohs had ice shipped from Lebanon. Alexander the Great ordered ditches to be dug at the cave city of Petra and filled with snow so his troops could have chilled wine during the blistering Jordanian summer. In each case, the ice had to be imported from the mountains, and most of it melted along the way, making ice as valuable a commodity as gold. In Persia, Greece, and later Rome, it was a sign of affluence to be able to enjoy icy treats in summer. By the Renaissance, European nobility competed to display the most lavish ice sculptures at their banquets, accompanied by indulgent sherbets and *gelati* (soft ice cream).

## PUT IT ON ICE

The technology of storing ice was simple—dig a pit, line it with some insulating material such as sawdust or straw, cart the snow or ice down from the nearest snowcapped mountain, cover it with more straw, and enjoy it while it lasted. With very few modifications, this is how ice was stored for centuries.

Eventually, people realized that ice lasted longer if it was kept aboveground in an icehouse, usually just a simple roofed pen built of boards and insulated with sand, wood chips, and branches—the first coolers. By the 19th century, sawdust had become the insulator of choice. It would be spread two or three feet deep across the floor of the icehouse. Once the ice blocks were loaded in, more sawdust was spread over and around them. If the icehouse was built in the shade, this well-insulated winter ice could easily last into August. Ice harvesting was an equally simple process: Find a frozen lake, get a saw, cut the ice into chunks, load it on a cart, and race like crazy to the nearest icehouse.

## THE ICEMAN COMETH

Early Americans seemed to have had a particular fixation with ice. One of the first things the colonists at Jamestown did was build pits for the ice they cut from winter ponds. In parts of North America, like Maine, the ice-harvesting season could last until March, which led enterprising New Englanders to try exporting it. Ice harvesting was expensive—every block had to be sawn by hand—but it was also lucrative. A ton of ice was worth hundreds of dollars at a time when most commodities were valued in pennies. The first recorded American ice shipment went from New York to Charleston, South Carolina, in 1799. By 1805, ice harvesting was one of New England's biggest businesses—and one man dominated that business like a colossus.

Around 1800, Frederic Tudor passed up a chance to go to Harvard in favor of a visit to the Bahamas. While sweating in the islands, it occurred to him that shipping ice from Boston to the Caribbean could be very profitable. At the time, New England produced very little that could be exported. Ships that brought goods into Boston left with empty holds, meaning ship owners made money only in one direction. Even worse, they often had to fill their holds with rocks for ballast on the outward voyage. Ice made a perfect substitute: It was plentiful and it was heavy. Ship owners remained skeptical; people had tried transporting ice over long distances before, and it was a risky proposition.

## THE ICE KING

Tudor persisted, and in 1805 he shipped his first load of ice to Martinique. But that and subsequent attempts failed so badly that he wound up in debtor's prison for a time. Still, he kept at it, experimenting with ways of better insulating his cargo. He introduced the use of cavity walls in his icehouses and ships, which kept the sawdust from getting wet and protected the ice from being soiled by sawdust. His innovations worked: By 1816 the Tudor Ice Company dominated the ice trade to Cuba and the Caribbean.

But ice exports were necessarily limited by the handmade

nature of the product. In 1825 Tudor's employee, Nathaniel Wyeth, harnessed a cutting blade to a team of horses. The "ice plow" tripled Tudor's ice production. Needing new markets for his now plentiful ice, Tudor began looking west to what would become the greatest ice market of all…India.

## OH, CALCUTTA!

At first, the idea of shipping ice to India was absurd. Calcutta, the Indian port closest to Boston, was 16,000 miles away, and a four-month journey by ship. When Tudor announced his intention to send a shipment to India, people thought he was either joking or out of his mind. He wasn't. On May 12, 1833, Tudor watched from the pier as his crew loaded 180 tons of winter ice on board the brig *Tuscany* and set sail for the Orient. Boston wags started taking bets on how big a loss Tudor would sustain this time.

The *Tuscany* sailed into the Ganges estuary in September. When the ship docked in Calcutta, there were still 100 tons of marketable ice in the hold. For the next 20 years, Calcutta was the most profitable destination for Tudor's ice ships. By 1840, the Tudor Ice Company had icehouses in Madras, Bombay, and Singapore, and the profits rolled in. Tudor died in 1864, when the ice-cutting business was at its peak.

## CLEAR BLUE

By the end of the Civil War, having ice in the United States was no longer a luxury but a fact of everyday middle-class life. The first icebox for home use was sold in 1861; by 1865 two out three homes in Boston had ice delivered to them every day. The expansion of the railroads made the distribution of ice faster and less expensive. Ice companies (and ice wagons) became a fixture in communities across America.

Prices were determined by the purity of the frozen water used. River ice was the least valued because it was often milky. Still-pond ice was best. Blocks of "clear blue" were always in highest demand. Clear-blue ice from Wenham Lake near Boston became world-famous for its exceptional clarity. It was especially popular in London, where at one time no dinner party was considered a success if it didn't have Wenham Lake ice.

## FREEZE-OUT

"Ice famines," caused by unseasonably warm winter weather, put a cramp in the ice trade in 1889 and 1890, but it remained a lucrative business into the 20th century. Even the invention of artificial refrigeration couldn't slow it down. Primitive refrigerators had been invented as early as 1748, but they were too slow and too expensive to compete with natural ice. What brought an end to the ice-cutting industry? Pollution. As the Northeast and other centers of North American ice making became more industrialized, the rivers and ponds the ice cutters used became fouled with factory waste. Deliveries were constantly disrupted by the collection of contaminated water. In the meantime, electric refrigerators became cheap enough to deliver the final blow. By the 1920s ice houses had started to disappear from most cities. They hung on in rural areas through the 1930s, but with the end of World War II in 1945, the American Ice Age was history.

\*　　　\*　　　\*

## FIRST 20 VIDEOS PLAYED ON MTV

**1.** "Video Killed the Radio Star," the Buggles

**2.** "You Better Run," Pat Benatar

**3.** "She Won't Dance," Rod Stewart

**4.** "You Better You Bet," the Who

**5.** "Little Susie's on the Up," PhD

**6.** "We Don't Talk Anymore," Cliff Richard

**7.** "Brass in Pocket," the Pretenders

**8.** "Time Heals," Todd Rundgren

**9.** "Take It on the Run," REO Speedwagon

**10.** "Rockin' the Paradise," Styx

**11.** "When Things Go Wrong," Robin Lane and the Chartbusters

**12.** "History Never Repeats," Split Enz

**13.** "Hold on Loosely," .38 Special

**14.** "Just Between You and Me," April Wine

**15.** "Sailing," Rod Stewart

**16.** "Iron Maiden," Iron Maiden

**17.** "Keep On Loving You," REO Speedwagon

**18.** "Message of Love," the Pretenders

**19.** "Mr. Briefcase," Lee Ritenour

**20.** "Double Life," the Cars

# WORD ORIGINS

*Here are some more of our favorite stories
behind words we use every day.*

## CUE

**Meaning:** A signal for an actor to speak or do something

**Origin:** "A cue, in its theatrical use, was used in Shakespeare's *A Midsummer Night's Dream*: 'Pyramus, you begin: when you have spoken your speech, enter into that brake; and so every one according to his cue.' Many etymologists believe that it was a phonetic spelling of the letter 'q,' a marking used by actors in their scripts as an abbreviation of the Italian *quando* ('when')." (From *The Story Behind the Word*, by Morton S. Freeman)

## MARGARITA

**Meaning:** A popular tequila-based cocktail

**Origin:** "The margarita was first concocted in 1948 by Dallas socialite Margarita Sames at a Christmas party. Margarita liked to play a poolside game with her guests: She would get behind the bar and concoct several drinks for them to rate. When she mixed together three parts tequila with one part triple sec and one part lime, everyone loved it. Named in her honor, the margarita travelled to Hollywood and then to the rest of the country." (From *Why Do Donuts Have Holes?*, by Don Voorhees)

## HURRICANE

**Meaning:** An intense tropical storm with very high winds

**Origin:** "The *Popol Vuh* (an ancient Maya holy text) relates how the world began as a watery waste, over which the god *Hurakán* passed in the form of a mighty wind. As the god of thunder and lightning, Hurakán was greatly feared. The now-extinct aborigines of the West Indies, the Taínos, called the evil spirit that brought tropical storms a *hurrican*. To the Carib Indians the word *hyorocan* meant 'devil.' The Spanish borrowed these names to create the word *huracán*, which they used to describe the storms they encountered in the New World." (From *From Achilles' Heel to Zeus's Shield*, by Dale Dibbley)

---

**All U.S. telephones were turned off to honor Alexander Graham Bell during his funeral in 1922.**

# DUMB CROOKS

*More proof that crime doesn't pay.*

## KEEP THE CHANGE

"A judge gave Vickey Siles of New Haven, Indiana, just a suspended sentence and probation, ostensibly out of pity for the lousy job she did altering a check from Globe Life and Accident Co. Siles had tried to obliterate the '$1.00' amount of the check by typing '$4,000,000.00' over it, and then attempted to cash it at a neighborhood check-cashing store."

—*Washington Post*

## MISTAKEN IDENTITY

"Police conducting a roadblock operation in Texas stopped a man for not wearing his seatbelt. During the stop, the police observed three silver pipe-like packages on the floor. The police began to question the man as to whether or not the objects were pipe bombs. That's when the man blurted out, 'Man, that ain't no pipe bomb. That's cocaine.'"

—lwcbooks.com

## IS THIS SEAT TAKEN?

"A thief in Munich, Germany, who stole a woman's World Cup ticket from her purse in 2006 was caught after he sat down to watch the game...next to the victim's husband. The unidentified 34-year-old numbskull mugged 42-year-old Eva Standmann while she was en route to the Munich stadium for the game between Brazil and Australia and came across the ticket in her bag. As he sat in what was supposed to be the woman's seat, he was met by her hubby, 43-year-old Berndt Standmann, who promptly notified stadium security and had the crook arrested."

—Dumbcrooks.com

## LIFE IN THE SLOW LANE

"The timing was off for a bank robber in Cheshire, Massachusetts. He pulled off his heist at 4:30 p.m. and tried to make his getaway through downtown North Adams. Stuck in rush-hour traffic, he was apprehended by an officer on foot."

—*The Stupid Crook Book*

## STRONG ARMED

"The man on the witness stand in New Orleans was in obvious pain. Moving his right arm ever so slightly caused him to wince. He had injured his arm six months earlier in a job-related accident and was suing his former company for permanent disability. After a series of questions his client answered perfectly, his attorney asked the clincher, 'How high can you raise your arm right now?' Straining, the man slowly lifted his outstretched arm to shoulder level. 'And how far could you lift it before the accident?'

Without hesitation, the man proudly shot the same arm straight above his head, exclaiming, 'This high!' He was still holding his arm up when the judge slammed down his gavel and announced, 'Case dismissed!'"

—*Crimes and Misdumbmeanors*

\*      \*      \*

## "THE \*@%#SONS!"

*In 2006 Matt Groening, creator of* The Simpsons, *released these memos from network censors about the show's content.*

• "To discourage imitation by young and foolish viewers, when Homer begins to pour the hot wax in his mouth, please have him scream in pain so kids will understand that doing this would actually burn their mouths."

• "Although it is only a dream, please do not show Homer holding a sign that reads 'Kill My Boy.'"

• "When Marge worries that Bart may become jealous of newborn Lisa, Homer's previously unscripted line, 'Bart can kiss my hairy yellow butt!' is not acceptable; we believe this crude phrase plays as especially coarse since it is directed at a two-year-old child."

• "It will not be acceptable for Itchy to stab Scratchy in the guts and yank his intestine out and use it as a bungee cord."

At the end of the Beatles' "A Day in the Life," there's an ultrasonic whistle, audible only to dogs.

# LOL (LOVE ON-LINE)

*Single? Odds are that you've at least* thought *about trying an Internet dating site.*
*Some of these may seem weird…or you might find one that suits you perfectly.*

| | | |
|---|---|---|
| **Farmers**<br>(*FarmersOnly.com*) | **Deaf people**<br>(*DeafPeopleMeet.com*) | **Smokers**<br>(*DatingForSmokers.com*) |
| **People with herpes**<br>(*H-date.com*) | **Wheelchair-bound**<br>(*FriendsLikeMe.org*) | **Geeks**<br>(*Nerdlicious.com*) |
| **Boston Red Sox fans**<br>(*MatchingSox.com*) | **Golfers**<br>(*DateAGolfer.com*) | **Lawyers**<br>(*LawyersInLove.com*) |
| **"Beautiful" people**<br>(*BeautifulPeople.net*) | **Atheists**<br>(*SecularSingles.com*) | **Ivy Leaguers**<br>(*GoodGenes.com*) |
| **Millionaires**<br>(*MillionaireMatch.com*) | **Rockabilly fans**<br>(*RockabillyDate.com*) | **Wine aficionados**<br>(*GrapeDates.com*) |
| **Doctors**<br>(*Date-a-doc.com*) | **Scientists**<br>(*SciConnect.com*) | **Redheads**<br>(*PlanetRedhead.com*) |
| **Ayn Rand fans**<br>(*TheAtlasphere.com*) | **Biracial couples**<br>(*MixedRace.com*) | **Introverts**<br>(*ShyPassions.com*) |
| **Pet lovers**<br>(*DateMyPet.com*) | **The overweight**<br>(*LargeAndLovely.com*) | **Diabetics**<br>(*Prescription4Love.com*) |
| **Bicyclists**<br>(*CyclingSingles.com*) | **Single parents**<br>(*SingleParentsMingle.com*) | **Buddhists**<br>(*DharmaDate.net*) |
| **Scuba divers**<br>(*DiverDating.com*) | **Runners**<br>(*RunningSingles.com*) | **Patriots**<br>(*SinglesOfAmerica.com*) |
| **Bikers**<br>(*BikerKiss.com*) | **Tennis players**<br>(*1stServe.com*) | **Non-smokers**<br>(*SmokeFreeSingles.com*) |
| **Republicans**<br>(*conservativematch.com*) | **Vampires**<br>(*VampireRave.com*) | **Vegetarians**<br>(*VeggieDate.org*) |
| **Democrats**<br>(*LiberalHearts.com*) | **Witches**<br>(*PaganFriendSearch.com*) | **Vegans**<br>(*VeganPassions.com*) |
| **Equestrians**<br>(*EquestrianCupid.com*) | ***Star Trek* fans**<br>(*TrekPassions.com*) | **Goths**<br>(*GothicLoveOnline.com*) |

---

**Good news for teenagers: There is no evidence that eating chocolate makes acne worse.**

# TOM SWIFTIES

*This classic style of pun was originally invented in the 1920s. They're atrocious and corny, so of course we had to include them.*

"I've had my left and right ventricles removed," Tom said half-heartedly.

"We've taken over the government," Tom cooed.

"Dawn came too soon," Tom mourned.

"My hair's been cut off," Tom said distressfully.

"Company should be here in about an hour," Tom guessed.

"Where did you get this meat?" Tom asked hoarsely.

"You dropped a stitch," Tom needled.

"Blow on the fire so it doesn't go out," Tom bellowed.

"I suppose there's room for one more," Tom admitted.

"That's no purebred," Tom muttered.

"I couldn't believe we lost the election by two votes," Tom recounted.

"I'm losing my hair," Tom bawled.

"Measure twice before you cut," Tom remarked.

"Thanks for shredding the cheese," Tom said gratefully.

"Please put some folds in these trousers," Tom pleaded.

"I've located the dog star," Tom said seriously.

"You look like a goat," Tom kidded.

"I used to own that gold mine," Tom exclaimed.

"Another plate of steamers all around!" Tom clamored.

"I memorized the whole thing," Tom wrote.

"That's the last time I'll pet a lion," Tom said offhandedly.

"No thanks to that Frenchman," said Tom mercilessly.

"You're not a real magician at all," Tom said, disillusioned.

"I've never had a car accident," said Tom recklessly.

"It's made the grass wet," said Tom after due consideration.

# THE PILGRIMS, PT. III: SAILING TO AMERICA

*Historical fact: The Pilgrims never called themselves "Pilgrims."*
*In fact, they weren't known by that name until the 1840s.*
*Here's Part III of our story: the journey to freedom in*
*the New World. (Part II starts on page 215.)*

CRAMPED CONDITIONS

The Pilgrims finally set off from Plymouth, England, on September 6, 1620, more than a month behind schedule. Historians can only guess as to the *Mayflower*'s exact size and shape (no pictures of her were ever painted), although most agree that she had two decks and three masts. "Considering the proportions of a number of known merchant vessels of the era," writes William Baker in *Colonial Vessels*, "the *Mayflower* might have had a keel length ranging from 52 to 73 feet, a breadth of 24 to 27 feet and a depth of 10 to 13 feet." Other historians say she may have been as long as 90 feet. Even so, that's roughly the size of a two-story, three-bedroom house. And that's what 102 passengers, 25 crew members, two dogs, many cats, and even more rats squeezed into for 66 days on rough and often stormy seas.

The *Mayflower* was designed to carry cargo, not people, so there were few cots or hammocks to sleep on. Some of the wealthier families paid the ship's carpenter to build cots, but most of the passengers slept on hard wooden floors on a constantly rocking boat. Seasickness was common. Because these people were heading to a new life in an unknown land, they brought along as many of their possessions and rations as they could pack in…which made the living quarters below decks extremely cramped. A few of the passengers even slept in the shallop, a surveying boat that was stowed on the gun deck.

SMOOTH START

The first few weeks of the voyage saw relatively calm weather, and the mood among the Pilgrims was good. It is commonly believed that the Pilgrims were a bunch of staid old men who wore black clothes and black hats with buckles. That's a myth. In reality, there was only one man over 60; the average age was 32; and there were 30 children on board. The Pilgrims even wore colorful clothes; William Bradford, for example, owned a "green gown, violet cloak, lead colored suit with silver buttons, and a red waistcoat." And unlike the stricter Puritans, the Pilgrims liked to sing and play games.

## ROUGH SEAS AND ROUGHER SAILORS

But after those first couple of weeks, the fun came to a stormy end. The sky grew dark and the ocean swelled. Then the rain began pouring and the wind blew—and hardly let up for the rest of the journey. The foul weather forced the Pilgrims to huddle in the crowded holds. The rain leaked in through the creaky deck boards, making their lives cold and damp. The children suffered the most—from both sickness and boredom. On the few nice days, kids were permitted to climb up on deck and run around. But Master Jones and the *Mayflower's* crew of roughnecks weren't interested in cavorting with or entertaining their devoutly religious passengers. One of the sailors especially despised the Pilgrims, telling them that his only wish was "to throw your dead bodies into the sea and claim your treasures for myself." Luckily for the Pilgrims, he never got the chance. Bradford wrote:

> It pleased God before they came half seas over, to smite this young man with a grievous disease, of which he died in a desperate manner, and so was himself the first that was thrown overboard.

Bradford and Master Jones also had more than a few heated discussions, arguing about the route, the crew's attitude, and whether the creaky old ship was seaworthy. Jones made it very clear that even though Bradford was the leader of the Pilgrims, *he* was in charge of the *Mayflower*. Besides, in addition to the Pilgrims and the ship's crew, there were other paying passengers on board, about 30 regular folks booking passage to America. (Little is known about who these people were or where they ended up.)

## MORE TRIALS AND TRIBULATIONS

For the most part, the Pilgrims kept to themselves and stuck together, spending their days and nights below decks praying, reading the Bible, singing songs, and sleeping. In the mornings and evenings, the 20 women prepared the meals, which consisted of salted meats, peas, beans, hard cheese, water, and beer.

During a particularly rough storm, one of the *Mayflower's* main support beams cracked and splintered. This beam had been holding the ship together, and for a brief time it looked and felt like the old wooden ship might break apart. Luckily, one of the passengers had brought a "great iron screw," which was used to repair the beam and bind it back together.

During yet another storm, a 25-year-old Pilgrim named John Howland went up on deck to try to assist the crew, but when the *Mayflower* listed heavily, he fell overboard and was nearly lost in the North Atlantic. Howland was able to grab a rope hanging down from one of the masts…right before the current pulled him under. If Howland had been a little slower, or if the crew had not been on hand to haul him in, America might be different today, because two of Howland's descendants would become president of his future homeland: George H. W. Bush and George W. Bush. (Other presidents whose ancestors came over on the *Mayflower*: John Adams, John Quincy Adams, Zachary Taylor, Theodore Roosevelt, and Franklin D. Roosevelt.)

## LIFE AND DEATH

Two of the Pilgrim women had especially rough voyages. Elizabeth Hopkins and Susanna White were each seven months pregnant when the *Mayflower* left England. The constant rain and the ship's incessant tossing and heaving during six straight weeks of storms made their pregnancies that much more difficult. And the Pilgrims all wondered which would happen first: landfall or childbirth? Hopkins gave birth to a baby boy while at sea. He was called Oceanus. White didn't give birth until shortly after they landed, when she delivered a boy named Peregrine.

Oceanus's birth did little to liven the mood—the Pilgrims were cold and weary, and many were sick. A 12-year-old boy named William Butten fell ill early in the voyage and, despite the best efforts of the Pilgrims, died only two days before the *Mayflower* reached land.

*The Pilgrims would find life in their new home even harder than it was at sea. For the final installment of the story, turn to page 489.*

Widespread use of wooden coffins began about 200 years ago.

# BILLY MITCHELL'S BATTLE, PART II

*Here's Part II of our story on one of the first Americans
to realize the crucial role airplanes would play in the
future of warfare (Part I is on page 185).*

## FROM THE SUGGESTION BOX...

After World War I, Brigadier General Mitchell fired off one proposal after another to his superiors in Washington, describing the innovative ways the military could organize and develop its air power. Among other things, he believed that the Army and Navy air services should be combined to form one independent air force, just as the British had done to create the Royal Air Force in 1918. He also told the military that it should develop aircraft carriers, long-range bombers, and heavily armored "flying tanks" that could fly over battlefields and attack ground troops. And he proposed developing transport planes that could carry troops across oceans without fear of enemy submarines.

But what would prove to be Mitchell's most controversial proposal was that planes carrying bombs and aerial torpedoes could sink enemy battleships—behemoths that were thought to be unsinkable, except when fired upon by another battleship.

## ...TO THE CIRCULAR FILE

Airplanes sinking *battleships?* The top brass laughed off Mitchell's recommendations and tossed them onto what became known as the "Flying Trash Pile." Besides, even if they had believed in his ideas, there was no money to fund them. Now that the war was over, the military budget had been cut to the bone, and the Army had its hands full just fighting with the Navy over what little money was left. They weren't about to create an independent Air Force and then have to fight *it* for money, too.

Mitchell had tried to work through the chain of command, but when he realized that his ideas were being ignored, he decided to go public. He began writing articles, making speeches, and giving interviews to newspaper and magazine reporters. He figured that if

---

So you *can* take it with you! Neanderthals sometimes buried their dead with tools and food.

he could generate enough pressure from the public and Congress, the military might finally begin to act.

## I DARE YA

Mitchell's public relations campaign worked. In January 1921, he was called before a hearing of the House Naval Affairs Committee and testified that the age of the battleship was over. Since airplanes could easily sink them, he explained, they weren't going to be of much use in the next war. He even offered to prove his point—all he needed was a surplus battleship to sink.

It just so happened that one was available: The Germans had surrendered their battleship *Ostfriesland* to the United States after the war, and the Navy was planning to sink it as part of a test of battleship heavy guns. The Navy refused to budge from this plan, until Senator William Borah of Idaho threatened to cut off funding for new ships until it was determined whether they were as vulnerable as Mitchell claimed.

If ever a ship deserved to be called unsinkable, the *Ostfriesland* was it. Nearly two football fields long and boasting numerous watertight compartments, it had a four-layer steel hull that was nearly a foot thick in places. Airplanes, by contrast, were flimsy little things made of wood, wire, and canvas. How could an airplane sink a battleship? The Navy was so certain that Mitchell would fail, it decided to have him fail on as grand a scale as possible, to put the issue to rest once and for all.

Why stop at a single battleship? The Navy offered to let Mitchell try his luck against four ships—a submarine, a destroyer, a light cruiser, and the *Ostfriesland*—in a series of tests off the Virginia coast. It even made a troop ship, the USS *Henderson*, available for any politicians, journalists, foreign diplomats, and military officials who wanted to be there when Mitchell fell on his face. Nearly the entire Atlantic fleet would be floating nearby, too.

## GETTING READY

The tests were scheduled to begin in June, which gave Mitchell and his pilots barely six months to teach themselves how to bomb warships from the air. They didn't have any real ships to practice on, so they traced the outline of a 600-foot battleship in a marsh and attacked it with dummy bombs made of concrete. Mitchell believed that the best way to sink a ship was to drop a bomb in the water next to it, causing a "water hammer" effect that would damage the hull below the waterline and make the ship more likely to sink than if the bomb landed on the deck. When Mitchell's men got good at that, they moved to the Chesapeake Bay and practiced bombing runs on wrecked ships that were visible on the bottom.

Meanwhile, bomb makers at the Frankford Arsenal in Philadelphia began welding tail fins and steel nose cones onto converted torpedo tubes and filling them with TNT. When finished, the bombs weighed 2,000 and 4,000 pounds apiece, making them the heaviest ever built. By the time June rolled around, Mitchell was so sure of success that he arranged for 18 planes filled with photographers to film the tests. "I want newsreels of those sinking ships in every theater in the country," he said. The military was so certain he would fail that they let him do it.

## MOMENTS OF TRUTH

The first test, on the German submarine *U-117*, took place on June 21, 1921. The tests were structured to assess the effectiveness of different sizes of bombs, so the first attack was made with Navy seaplanes carrying 165-pound bombs. As VIPs on the troopship *Henderson* observed from a safe distance, bombers hit the sub three times and sank it in 16 minutes. The officers onboard the *Henderson* shrugged off the sinking as meaningless—submarines have thin skins, they explained to observers.

The second test took place on July 13. This time the target was the German destroyer *G-102*. In a wave of attacks, Mitchell's pilots hit the ship with machine gun fire, then with 25-pound, 100-pound, and finally, 600-pound bombs. The 600-pounders did the trick—the *G-102* broke in half and sank in 19 minutes. Once again, military observers dismissed the results. And they did the same thing five days later, when Mitchell's pilots sank the German cruiser *Frankfurt*, again with 600-pound bombs. Destroyers and cruisers weren't battleships, the officers explained to anyone who would listen. Just wait until Mitchell's pilots came up against the *Ostfriesland*—then he'd meet his match.

## FINAL TEST

The attack on the *Ostfriesland* began on July 19. Mitchell's planes attacked the "unsinkable" battleship with 250- and 600-pound bombs, which did some damage, until an approaching storm forced the test to be postponed.

When the attacks resumed the next day, Mitchell's pilots hit the *Ostfriesland* with three 1,100-pound bombs. Then the attack was called off so that Navy observers could examine the damage. Then, at the last minute, the Navy tried to change the rules, and told Mitchell that he could drop only three 2,000-pound bombs on the *Ostfriesland*—instead of as many as it took to score two direct hits, as had originally been agreed. Mitchell ignored the change and ordered seven bombers, each loaded with a 2,000-pound bomb, to attack the *Ostfriesland*.

## THAT SINKING FEELING

The first bomb hit 100 feet off the starboard (right) side of the ship, close enough to do plenty of visible damage. The second bomb hit the water in front of the ship, and the third hit so close to the starboard side that it blasted a giant hole in the hull. The fourth hit near the port (left) side and so did the fifth, exploding just 25 feet away and striking the ship with so much force that it lifted the bow out of the water. By now the battleship had received so much damage that it was clearly going to sink, but Mitchell's pilots kept bombing.

The sixth bomb was the coup de grâce: It hit near the stern, the bow lifted farther, and the ship rolled over and sank. Mitchell never did get a chance to drop the 4,000-pound bombs.

The officers and other observers onboard the *Henderson* were stunned into silence. "No one spoke," Douglas Waller writes in his biography of Mitchell, *A Question of Loyalty*. "Politicians, many of whom had staked their careers on funding the battleships, looked as if they had just witnessed a murder. Some admirals sobbed like babies."

*Billy Mitchell's success made him a hero, right? To find out, turn to Part III of the story, on page 485.*

---

Scarier than a ghost: There are an estimated 5,435 calories in the average trick-or-treater's bag.

# THE DOCTOR IS OUT (OF HIS MIND)

*Some news that might make you sick…and might make you never want to get sick again.*

## BEDSIDE HAMMER

A doctor in Japan was reprimanded after performing an operation during which the elderly female patient started wiggling and yelled, "Please stop the operation!" The improper administration of anesthesia wasn't why the doctor was reprimanded, though—it was his reaction to the distressed woman's cries: He smacked her on the forehead and told her to shut up. Hospital reports say that the doctor was punished, and that the patient's operation was completed three weeks later…by another doctor.

## FIRST, DO NO HARM

Dr. Brian Boughton of Devon, England, does not like seagulls. So much so that he founded DAGAS, the Dartmouth Action Group Against Seagulls. And on a May afternoon in 2006, he showed everyone just how much he didn't like them when he shot one in his backyard and hung its corpse from an apple tree. "The purpose," he said, "is to scare off other seagulls and avoid me having to shoot any more." He went on to explain that while his family was dining in their yard, that particular gull had deposited some droppings in his wife's salad. "I believe the risk to my family was extreme," Dr. Boughton said. He was convicted of violating the Wildlife and Countryside Act and fined £400.

## WEED IT AND WEEP

Dr. Totada Shanthaveerappa, 70, of Atlanta, was arrested in 2005, accused of treating patients with unauthorized drugs and filing false insurance claims. The drugs: several not yet approved by the FDA, including dinitrophenol—a commercial weedkiller and insecticide—which Shanthaveerappa was injecting into patients. The strangest part, though, was that prosecutors couldn't claim that anybody was actually harmed by the treatments. Several people came forward and said that the doctor—who faces 87 counts in federal court—had actually saved their lives.

## STING OPERATION
Health officials on the island of Crete in Greece ordered an immediate investigation after the inspection of an operating room found a live scorpion. It came just a few weeks after a rat tail was found in a bowl of soup in another hospital, and renewed a national debate about the quality of healthcare. Greek newspapers reported that a similar incident had occurred in 2002 in the city of Salonika, when a cat was found in an operating room.

## DR. NO
In 2006 Dr. John Veltman, 52, of Martinsburg, West Virginia, was charged with driving under the influence, battery on an officer, obstructing an officer, and refusing to be fingerprinted. The doctor had been driving a backhoe in his yard while intoxicated, and drove it through a fence protecting a gas main, then backed up and hit a building, then went forward again and ran into a neighbor's garage door, then drove through another neighbor's yard and into a tree. When police tried to give him a sobriety test, Veltman became abusive and struck an officer. When they tried to fingerprint him, he said "I am a [expletive surgically removed] doctor and you are below me!" He faces 18 months in prison.

*  *  *

## WORDPLAY WITH YOGI BERRA
**Interviewer:** Alright Yogi, we are going to play Word Association.
**Yogi:** What's that?
**Interviewer:** I'm going to say a word and you give me the first word that comes to your mind when I say it. Okay?
**Yogi:** Sure.
**Interviewer:** Are you ready?
**Yogi:** Okay.
**Interviewer:** Mickey Mantle.
**Yogi:** What about him?

In 5 of 6 Gallup polls, nurses were chosen as the "most honest and ethical workers" in the U.S.

# ROLLER DERBY

*What sport was popular in the 1930s and the 1970s, helped make TV popular, and helped set the rules for televised sports? No, it's not badminton. Here's the story of a strange sport that will not go away.*

R ACE ACROSS AMERICA
Along with other bizarre fads, such as flagpole sitting and goldfish swallowing, "marathon" entertainments were popular in the 1920s. Depression-era audiences seemed to enjoy watching other people suffer as they danced for 20 hours, bicycled for six days, or walked around a track until they dropped. But by 1935 the fad was pretty much over, and a dance-marathon promoter from Portland, Oregon, named Leo Seltzer had to find another way to make a living. He'd read in a magazine that 97% of Americans had roller skated at some point in their lives, and that gave him the idea to switch from dance marathons to roller-skating marathons.

He held the first one on August 13, 1935, in the Chicago Coliseum. A large, flat oval track was constructed in the center of the arena; 18 laps equaled a mile. The rules were simple: Teams of one man and one woman raced to skate 57,000 laps—about 4,000 miles. They would skate 11 hours a day every day for a month. The skaters earned $25 a week, good money at a time when jobs, if they could be found, paid about $12 a week.

## THE RACE IS ON
The event drew 20,000 people. It was so successful that Seltzer decided to select the best 20 skaters and take the show on the road, calling it the "Transcontinental Roller Derby Association." He added a few flourishes, such as a giant map of the 4,000-mile New York–to–Los Angeles trip with lights along Route 66 indicating the skaters' "progress." He also created "sprints," special periods in which skaters could earn bonus points for lapping other skaters. Fast-paced and competitive, sprints were a crowd favorite. But despite the urge to push other skaters out of the way, physical contact and fighting were strictly forbidden.

Seltzer continued to tweak the contest format, ultimately turn-

---

Acid rock, country rock, and hard rock were all geological terms before they were music genres.

ing the marathon into a game. In the middle of the national tour, he changed the troupe of 20 skaters from 10 pairs of players to two 10-person teams of five men and five women each. That change increased the instances of what the audience loved most: lapping. The Route 66 map was eliminated in favor of a pass-for-points system. They got a point every time they lapped an opponent.

## RACING TO VIOLENCE

Two events would permanently alter the tone of the game.

• At a race in Louisville, Kentucky, in 1936, skater Joe Laurey passed two opponents and purposely smashed into them. As they lost their balance, he threw them over the railing. Laurey was immediately kicked out of the game, and as he stormed out of the arena and threw his skates on the track, the crowd went wild.

• In Miami in 1937, some of the faster—and skinnier—skaters tried to break through a pack of slower, more muscular opponents and steal laps. The larger skaters pushed back, elbowing and shoving. But when the referees moved in to break up the tussle, the audience booed. They loved the violence.

Seltzer decided to lift the ban on physical contact. Not only did he make it part of the game, it soon became a vital part of the scoring process. Sprints became "jams" (the crush of skaters resembled a traffic jam), and that became the final element of the roller derby: A skater could earn one point for his or her team by passing another skater, even if it involved beating them up to do it.

## GOING IN CIRCLES

Roller derby grew steadily in popularity as it toured from town to town around the United States. By 1940, the league had expanded from two squads to eight traveling teams, the same year roller derby events attracted four million people. It looked like the sport would continue to grow, but when America entered World War II in 1941, most of the male skaters were drafted into military service, reducing the league back to two teams. The squads kept playing the circuit, cheering up wartime crowds the way early skating marathons had entertained Depression-era audiences. But with only two teams touring, there were fewer derby events, and by the

---

Air brakes: From a 100 mph dive, an African eagle can come to a complete halt in 18 feet

late 1940s, the sport's popularity dwindled. With more pressing world issues going on, the sport seemed silly and old fashioned.

But Leo Seltzer wasn't about to give up. He had invested his life—and his life savings—in roller derby. And, fortunately, there was a new tool at his disposal: television. Seltzer theorized that if the derby could be beamed all over the country, it would draw paying customers to the live events. CBS agreed to run derby matches once a week for 13 weeks in 1947. (The same two teams, the New York Chiefs and Brooklyn Red Devils, played each other every time.) The idea paid off: After five weeks of TV exposure, the derby was a top 10 show and the 69th Regiment Armory in New York City sold out all 5,300 of its seats for the event.

The broadcasts were so successful that after the initial 13-week run a bidding war ensued. Seltzer ultimately signed with ABC. ABC was a brand-new network and needed to fill a lot of airtime cheaply, so it aired roller derby three nights a week and on Saturday afternoons. To meet the demand, Seltzer expanded for the first time in nearly a decade, creating a six-team organization he called the National Roller Derby League, consisting of the two New York teams plus the Jersey Jolters, the Chicago Westerners, the Philadelphia Panthers, and the Washington Jets. It was ABC's most profitable broadcast. But Seltzer was unhappy: He envisioned the roller derby as a legitimate sport. He wanted to air derby matches for 40 weeks a year with an end-of-season championship game. ABC didn't see it that way. To them it wasn't a sport, it was a TV show, and they wanted to air it 52 weeks a year…and ABC got their way.

## BE CAREFUL WHAT YOU WISH FOR

Although 82,000 people packed New York's Madison Square Garden for the 1951 championship game, in 1952 the league didn't have enough money to pay its skaters. Why? ABC's 52-week schedule had overexposed the roller derby. The ratings dropped, and by 1952 it was off TV and could barely scrape by without the broadcast and advertising revenue. And like movies and other live entertainment, roller derby saw its attendance diminish as TV became more popular in the early 1950s. Seltzer realized that for the derby to survive, it would have to get back on TV, so he moved the league headquarters from New York to Los Angeles to court the TV industry. But none of the networks were interested.

Something to shout about: 50 gallons of fake blood were used during the filming of *Scream.*

By 1958, Leo Seltzer was tired of struggling to keep the derby going and turned over management duties to his son, Jerry Seltzer, who promptly moved league headquarters to San Francisco. Smart move: The city was in the midst of a professional sports boom. The New York Giants baseball team had just moved to San Francisco, and the 49ers football team had enjoyed their first winning season in 1957. The roller-derby team based in the area, the Bay Bombers, became a local hit. Once again, the derby was about to be pulled out of a financial hole…by television.

## REEL CHANGE

But this time games wouldn't be broadcast live. They were recorded on a new format: videotape. The harsh, fast-moving look of videotape made the games appear, ironically, *more live*. What's more, there was very little videotaped product in 1959, so this set the derby apart. Local TV stations around the country were looking for inexpensive content to plug the holes in their schedules and by 1963, 120 stations were airing Bay Bombers games. The games were taped according to Jerry Seltzer's careful specifications. He told cameramen to *not* film all the fights and punches. The crowd would go wild, but the TV audience would hear it, not see it, which Seltzer thought would draw crowds to the live matches. He even made the crowd louder on the broadcasts to increase the air of excitement. Seltzer's ideas worked. The Bombers went on a national tour in 1962 and sold out everywhere they appeared.

Roller derby was the most popular sport in northern California, too. The Bombers outdrew professional basketball, professional wrestling, professional soccer, hockey (and the Oakland A's) in the Bay Area from 1962 to 1972. It did well elsewhere, too:

• In 1970, two million tickets were sold for derby races in 100 cities. Eight million people watched weekly on television.

• Fifty thousand people attended a 1972 event in Chicago's White Sox Park.

• The sports pages of several major newspapers began printing roller derby results in 1972.

• Raquel Welch starred in *Kansas City Bomber*, based on the life of star skater Joan Weston.

---

• Until the WNBA started in 1997, the roller derby was the only national, professional, team sport that featured female players.

## ROLLING AWAY

For a number of reasons, the derby was in financial trouble again in 1972. The sport's popularity was waning and attendance was inconsistent. Skaters wanted more money (stars made $50,000 a year, but rookies made $5,000) and went on strike in 1972. The expense of setting up the large skating track, for both home games and road tours, ate into profits. The 1973 oil crisis made travel more expensive. The higher costs forced Seltzer to cancel entire tours. He thought that a massive four-team championship series in May 1973 at New York's Shea Stadium might put the derby back in the black. Instead, it was a disaster: Because of a computer glitch, only a fraction of the tickets were sold.

In December 1973, Jerry Seltzer announced to his players that the roller derby was folding. The last game was played on December 8, 1973, in Long Island. The game ended not with players punching, shoving, and throwing each other over the railings, but with them joining hands and crying.

## RACING BACK?

Since then, several attempts have been made to revive roller derby.

• From 1989 to 1991, a syndicated TV series called *RollerGames* aired. It was more violent than previous derby incarnations and even featured an alligator pit in the middle of the track.

• In 1999 the Nashville Network played down the violence and campiness with a more athletic roller derby called *RollerJam*. But the show's creators had failed to see that the violence and campiness were what made the roller derby attractive to fans, and *RollerJam* also bombed.

• What set the derby apart from other sports in its heyday was that women competed. Today, more than 80 small women-only leagues are reviving roller derby. One is the Texas Rollergirls Rock N' Roller Derby, a Texas-based league that's heavy on the theatrics and violence. It began play in 2003, with teams that include the Honky Tonk Heartbreakers, Hotrod Honeys, and the Hell Marys.

# THE GREAT DIAMOND HOAX OF 1872, PART II

*Here's the second installment of our tale of what may have been the biggest con job of the 19th century. (Part I is on page 178.)*

**E**MPIRE BUILDER

As Arnold and Slack made their getaway, William Ralston was hard at work putting together a $10 million corporation called the San Francisco and New York Mining and Commercial Company. He'd already lined up 25 initial investors who contributed $80,000 apiece, and now he was preparing to raise another $8 million. New York newspaper publisher Horace Greeley had already bought into the company; so had British financier Baron Ferdinand Rothschild.

A *Rothschild* investing in the diamond field? The house of Rothschild was a world-renowned banking firm and experienced at spotting good investments. With Tiffany and Rothschild involved, the excitement surrounding the diamond field grew to a fever pitch. No one but Arnold and Slack knew where the mine was, but so what? When rumors began spreading that it was somewhere in the Arizona Territory, fortune seekers by the hundreds began making their way there in the hope of finding strikes of their own.

## LOCATION, LOCATION, LOCATION

The stage was now set for the swindle to grow much bigger, which meant that a lot more people would have lost a lot more money. That it didn't happen was due purely to chance: When Arnold and Slack picked the location of their "diamond field," they unknowingly chose an area where a team of government geologists had been conducting surveys for five years.

The leader of the geological team was a man named Clarence King. When he learned of the diamond strike, he couldn't believe what he was hearing. He'd been all over the territory and had already filed a report stating that there were no deposits of precious gems of any kind anywhere in the area. If the story were true, he and his team of experts had missed a significant diamond field that two untrained miners had been able to find on their own. His professional reputation was on the line: If there really was a diamond field and word of it got back to Washington, D.C., he would be exposed as incompetent and funds for the survey would be cut off.

## TOO GOOD TO BE TRUE?
King arranged to meet the engineer Henry Janin over dinner to get a firsthand account of the diamond field story. As he listened to Janin describe his trip to the site, he started to smell a rat. Janin reported finding diamonds, rubies, and sapphires next to each other, and as a geologist, King knew that was impossible. The natural processes by which diamonds are created are so different from those that create rubies and sapphires that they are never found in the same deposits.

Because Janin had been blindfolded on the trip to the site, he couldn't tell King where it was. But King was so familiar with the area that after quizzing Janin, he was able to figure out exactly which mesa he was talking about. The next day he and some other members of his team set out to visit the site themselves.

## ON THE SPOT
They arrived at the site a few days later. It was fairly late in the day, so they set up camp and then started exploring the area. As had been Janin's experience, it didn't take long for them to find raw diamonds, rubies, and other gems. By the time King was ready to turn in for the night, he'd found so many precious stones that even *he* had a touch of diamond fever. He went to bed wondering if the field really was genuine, and maybe even hoping a little that it was. That hope vanished early the next morning.

• Shortly after sunrise, another member of the party found a diamond that was partially cut and polished. Nature is capable of many things, but it takes a jeweller to cut and polish a diamond—the stone had been planted there by human hands.

• King noticed that wherever he found diamonds, he found other precious stones in the same place, and always in roughly the same quantities, something that does not happen in nature.

• Upon close examination, the team also noticed that the

crevices in which the gems were found had fresh scratch marks, as if the gems had been shoved into place with tools.

• When precious stones were found in the earth, it was always in places that had been disturbed by foot traffic. When they went to areas that were undisturbed, they never found anything.

## DIGGING DEEP

King knew that if the field was real, diamonds would also be found deep in the ground as well as on the surface. As a final test, he and his men went to an undisturbed area where they thought diamonds might occur naturally and dug a trench 10 feet deep. Then they carefully sifted through all of the dirt that had been removed from the trench, and found not a single precious stone in any of it. There was no question about it: the find was a hoax. Arnold and Slack had planted the gems.

As soon as King got to a telegraph station, he sent word to Ralston in San Francisco that he'd been conned. Ralston was shocked and angry. He closed the company and returned the unspent capital to the original 25 investors. Then, because his reputation was on the line, he refunded the rest of their investment out of his own pocket, which cost him about $250,000. It turns out that Ralston's bad judgment wasn't limited to diamonds: He poured millions into the building of San Francisco's Palace Hotel and other money-losing schemes, which contributed to the Bank of California's collapse in 1875. His body was found floating in the San Francisco Bay the following day, though the cause of death remains a mystery.

## THE HOAX EXPOSED

The Great Diamond Hoax of 1872, as it came to be known, received widespread newspaper coverage not just in America but also in Europe. As reporters in the United States and abroad researched the story, details of how the hoax had been perpetrated began to emerge:

• Arnold had once been a bookkeeper for the Diamond Drill Company of San Francisco, which used industrial-grade diamonds in the manufacture of drill bits. He apparently stole his first batch of not-so-precious gems from work, then bought cheap, uncut rubies and sapphires from other sources and added them to the mix. None of the people he duped had been able to tell industrial-grade diamonds and second-rate gems from the real thing.

• When Ralston and the other early investors paid Slack the first installment of $50,000 for his share of the mine, he and Arnold made the first of two trips to London, where they bought $28,000 worth of additional uncut stones from diamond dealers there. Most of the gems were used to salt the claim in Colorado; the few that were left over were the ones that Tiffany and his assistant had foolishly valued at $150,000.

## AFTERMATH

Philip Arnold and John Slack made off with $650,000, which in 1872 should have set them up for life. Neither of them fared very well, though: Arnold moved to Kentucky and bought a 500-acre farm. When the law eventually tracked him down, he paid a reported $150,000 to settle the claims against him, then used the remaining money to start his own bank. Six years after the diamond hoax, he was injured in a shootout with another banker; he died from pneumonia six months later at the age of 49.

Less is known about Slack. He apparently blew through his share of the loot and had to go back to work, first as a coffin maker in Missouri and then as a funeral director in New Mexico. When he died there in 1896 at the age of 76, he left an estate valued at only $1,600.

Uncovering and exposing the fraud gave Clarence King's career a huge boost; in 1879 he became the first director of the U.S. Geological Survey. But he was a better geologist than he was a businessman, as he learned to his dismay in 1881 when he quit working for the government and took up ranching. He failed at that, then went on to fail at mining and banking. He died penniless in 1901 at the age of 59.

## FOOL'S GOLD

So did anyone come out ahead from the experience? Apparently only Henry Janin, the mining engineer who had vouched for the authenticity of the diamond field. He suffered a blow to his reputation when the hoax was exposed, but by then he'd already sold his $10,000 worth of shares to another investor for $40,000. Janin was never implicated in the scam; as far as anyone knows, his good fortune was just a case of dumb luck.

# GENTLEMAN GEORGE

*Every American school kid knows (or should know) that George
Washington is called the "Father of Our Country," because he led
the American victory over the British in the Revolutionary War
and became the first president of the United States. Here's a
story about Washington that might surprise you.*

## CLASS WARFARE

When American colonists revolted against England in
1775, they knew that the British army would try to quash
the rebellion by force. They had to raise an army of their own
quickly and prepare to fight back. To lead the new militia, they
selected a plantation owner and former military commander from
Virginia named George Washington. The class-conscious English
didn't take the American commander seriously. To them, only
noblemen were capable of commanding an army, and Washington
was a commoner.

His opponent, General William Howe, the fifth Viscount
Howe, was a true gentleman, raised in the royal court, and was also
a decorated war hero and one of England's best soldiers. But Howe
learned to respect his American adversary. "He conducted himself
like a gentleman," he would often say. He based his evaluation on
several incidents, especially two events concerning Washington's
scrupulous following of an honored rule of war: a soldier could be
taken prisoner, but his personal property must be returned to him.

## MAN OF (UNREAD) LETTERS

When American troops occupied a British encampment early in
1776, they found a packet of letters left by a high-ranking British
officer in Howe's command. Washington read them, searching for
information of intelligence value. But there was none—just an
indication of some personal indiscretions by the officer. Under a
flag of truce, Washington sent the letters to Howe. He added a
personal note, asking his adversary to pass the letters along to the
officer without reading them. Shortly thereafter, Washington
received a personal note from Howe, thanking him for his courtesy and assuring him the letters had been passed along unread.

## THE DOG

A second exchange took place after the Battle of Germantown, on October 4, 1777. After initial success, the American attack failed. Somehow, a small white dog ended up with the retreating soldiers. When they halted, they checked his collar. They had lost the battle…but they had captured Lord Howe's pet fox terrier.

Washington's staff wanted him to keep the dog as a mascot. But Washington refused: The dog was Howe's personal property and would be returned. While the terrier was being combed and fed, Washington dictated a note to his aide-de-camp, Alexander Hamilton. "General Washington's compliments to General Howe, does himself the pleasure to return to him a Dog, which accidentally fell into his hands, and by the inscription on the collar, appears to belong to General Howe."

## AN HONORABLE ACT

Washington then ordered one of his men to backtrack 25 miles, carrying the dog in one hand and a white flag in the other. The missing pup was safely returned to his master, who discovered a second—hidden—note. One of Howe's staff officers described the reunion:

> The General seemed most pleased at the return of the dog. He took him upon his lap, seemingly uncaring that the mud from the dog's feet soiled his tunic. Whilst he stroked the dog, he discovered a tightly folded message that had been secreted under the dog's wide collar. The General read the message, which seemed to have a good effect upon him. Although I know not what it said, it is likely to have been penned by the commander of the rebellion.

So what did the second note say? No one knows—neither Washington nor Howe ever disclosed its contents. However, we know Howe appreciated the gesture. He referred to the exchange many times as "an honorable act of a gentleman."

\*       \*       \*

## FAMOUS FOLKS AND WHAT THEY FEAR THE MOST

| | |
|---|---|
| **Michael Jordan:** Swimming | **Andre Agassi:** Spiders |
| **Alfred Hitchcock:** Eggs | **Barbra Streisand:** Performing |
| **Queen Elizabeth I:** Roses | **Augustus Caesar:** The dark |
| **Sid Caesar:** Getting a haircut | |

# SHOCKERS!

*They didn't see it coming.*

## HOW SEW?

**Setup:** In 1993 Gennady Varlamov of Ekaterinburg, Russia, went to the doctor because he had a bad headache. The doctor could find nothing besides minor flu symptoms, so he took an X-ray of Varlamov's head.

**Surprise!** Varlamov had three sewing needles in his brain. "My hair stood on end when I saw the X-ray," Varlamov said. "This is incredible that I have had them all my life!" They were from 1½ to 3 inches long, at the top of his brain just beneath the skull. The headache went away—the doctor said the needles probably weren't the cause and recommended *not* removing them surgically, since they posed no danger to Varlamov. He kept the story to himself until 2006, when his local news station offered a chance to win a television for an unusual story. Varlamov won. Neither he nor the doctor has any idea how the needles got there. (Uncle John's theory: aliens.)

## HAVING A BALL

**Setup:** A group of 10 boys, aged 7 to 14, were playing street hockey in Fairhaven, Connecticut, in January, 2006. They were using a tennis ball they had found in a parking lot.

**Surprise!** One of the boys took a slapshot at the ball and it exploded. It was described by a witness as a loud "Bang!" followed by sparks. Police examined the ball and found that it had been stuffed full of gunpowder, firecrackers, and match heads. None of the boys were hurt.

## HE AIN'T HEAVY

**Setup:** Thirty-five-year-old Russian Igor Namyatov went to a doctor for back pain when he was a teenager. Doctors told him he had a "fatty growth" in his back, but that it was harmless. The pain eventually subsided and Namyatov forgot about it...until it came back 20 years later. Doctors then said it wasn't a fatty growth, it was a tumor, and they scheduled an operation to remove it.

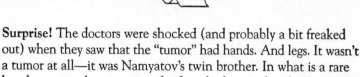

**Surprise!** The doctors were shocked (and probably a bit freaked out) when they saw that the "tumor" had hands. And legs. It wasn't a tumor at all—it was Namyatov's twin brother. In what is a rare but documented occurrence, the fetus had merged with Namyatov's while they were still in the womb and had never developed. Some of Namyatov's neighbors, newspapers reported, were disappointed that doctors had removed it. "They should have waited to see what would become of it later on," one said.

## HOME REMODEL

**Setup:** In January 2006, a real estate agent in Sandpoint, Idaho, took a couple and their son to look at a rental house near town.

**Surprise!** The agent entered the house, turned on a light...and the house exploded. All four of them were blown off the porch and into the snow. There had been a propane leak in the house, and the tiny arc of electricity caused by turning on the light had ignited it. They all had to be flown to Seattle to be treated for burns, but eventually everyone was okay. The house survived, but many of the walls were damaged and all the windows were blown out.

## GOOD NEIGHBORS

**Setup:** The couple in the story above, Cody and Jodi Greve-Likkel, and their six-year-old son, Mason, returned home to Idaho a few days later. An ironic twist to their tale was that they were looking at the rental home because their own house had burned down just two months earlier. And they had no insurance.

**Surprise!** When they got back home to Sandpoint, they found that people in their community—many of whom didn't know them at all—had held a fundraiser for them. Besides receiving a generous amount of cash, they were met at the airport by Chud Wendle, owner of Wendle Motors, the local Ford dealership. He presented them with the keys to a new car.

\*      \*      \*

"After twenty years in Washington, I often long for the realism and sincerity of Hollywood."

—**actor and former U.S. Senator Fred Thompson**

# PIG OUT

*According to statistics, Super Bowl Sunday is more than just a sporting event—it trails only Thanksgiving as America's biggest food feast. So what's wrong with a little overindulgence? Read on.*

## PUTTING ON THE FEED BAG

Every year on a Sunday in February, almost half the population of the United States gathers in groups around their TV sets to watch the Super Bowl—130 million people did it in 2005. As they watch, they eat. And eat. According to the Snack Food Association of America, during the Super Bowl Americans will snarf down roughly 30 million pounds of snack food—double the nation's average daily consumption—including 11.2 million pounds of potato chips, 8.2 million pounds of tortilla chips, 4.3 million pounds of pretzels, 3.8 million pounds of popcorn, 2.5 million pounds of nuts, and 13.2 million pounds of avocados (for guacamole). Here are some more fascinating Super Bowl food facts:

• Americans spend $50 million on Super Bowl snacks, but that pales next to the $237 million spent on soft drinks.

• What's the most popular item sold in food stores on Super Bowl Sunday—beer? Wrong. It's pizza. In fact, Pizza Hut claims that it sells more pizzas on Super Bowl Sunday than on any other day of the year.

• During the Super Bowl an average fan might easily pig out on more than 3,000 calories of snack food and beer. (And that's not taking into account calories consumed with pregame snacks and a postgame dinner and dessert.) A plate of nachos contains around 1,400 calories. A dozen chicken wings with blue-cheese dip adds another 1,000. A 180-pound man would have to jog 18 miles in three hours to burn off all those calories.

• Want to hedge your bet on who will win next year's Super Bowl? Each year before the game, the California Avocado Commission whips up guacamole recipes reflecting the competing teams (for instance, the entry for the Seattle Seahawks had shrimp as an ingredient) and holds a "taste-off" to see which is best. The winner of the "C.A.C. AvoBowl" has always won the Super Bowl.

# OSCAR'S BLOOPERS

*Even films that won the Academy Award for
Best Picture can't escape the scrutinizing
eyes of our movie-blooper hunters.*

**M**ovie: *The English Patient* (1996)
**Scene:** During a flashback, Almásy (Ralph Fiennes) writes a note that ends with "December 22, 1938."
**Blooper:** When Hana (Juliette Binoche) reads the note in the present, it ends with "December 22." What happened to the year?

**Movie:** *Rain Man* (1988)
**Scene:** Raymond (Dustin Hoffman) is spouting off air-travel statistics, stating that QANTAS is the only major airline to have never had a fatal crash.
**Blooper:** Between 1927 and 1951, QANTAS had eight fatal crashes. (QANTAS, by the way, was the only major airline that didn't delete this scene for its in-flight movie.)

**Movie:** *The Godfather, Part II* (1974)
**Scene:** Toward the end of the movie, the characters are talking about Pearl Harbor and how it happened on "Pop's birthday."
**Blooper:** The Japanese attacked Pearl Harbor on December 7. According to the tombstone from the end of *The Godfather*, Pop's birthday is April 29.

**Movie:** *Gladiator* (2000)
**Scene:** During the Battle of Carthage in the Colosseum, one of the chariots flips over.
**Blooper:** Look closely when the dust settles and you can see that this ancient Roman chariot was equipped with a gas tank.

**Movie:** *The Lord of the Rings: The Return of the King* (2003)
**Scene:** After defeating the big spider, Sam (Sean Astin) rushes over to Frodo (Elijah Wood), who has been paralyzed.

Hey movie buffs—can you name the Warner Brothers? (Harry, Albert, Sam, and Jack.)

**Blooper:** When Frodo is lying on the ground unconscious, his eyes are open. When Sam picks him up, Frodo's eyes are closed. When he's on Sam's lap, his eyes are open again.

**Movie:** *Amadeus* (1984)
**Scene:** Mozart (Tom Hulce) is watching a parody of his operas.
**Blooper:** When the last little person pops through the paper backdrop with a toy horse, a member of the film crew—wearing blue jeans—can be seen walking backstage.

**Movie:** *Ben-Hur* (1959)
**Scene:** The famous chariot race.
**Blooper:** Do the math: Nine chariots start the race, six of them crash, but somehow four finish.

**Movie:** *Schindler's List* (1993)
**Scene:** Oskar (Liam Neeson) is in a car with Jewish investors.
**Blooper:** Look at the passenger window and you can see the reflection of a movie camera and its operator. (Though it's not entirely clear, the reflection may belong to director Steven Spielberg, wearing his famous "Class of '61" hat.)

**Movie:** *Rocky* (1976)
**Scene:** While Rocky (Sylvester Stallone) is training, he does several one-arm push-ups.
**Blooper:** A careful look reveals that Stallone did only one push-up —the shot was then looped to make it look like he did a lot.

**Movie:** *Casablanca* (1942)
**Scene:** Rick (Humphrey Bogart) is driving through France.
**Blooper:** He's driving on the left; the French drive on the right.

**Movie:** *Million Dollar Baby* (2004)
**Scene:** Maggie (Hilary Swank) is driving to the new home she just bought for her mother.
**Blooper:** The house is supposed to be in Missouri, so why are there palm trees on the side of the road?

---

# EXIT, STAGE RIGHT

*There's nothing funny about dying onstage, but for these unfortunate performers, it was somewhat ironic.*

• **CARL BARNETT.** This 59-year-old music teacher died in 1974 while conducting a Bach piece at a Tulsa, Oklahoma, high school. The name of the piece: "Come, Sweet Death."

• **EDITH WEBSTER.** In 1986 the veteran stage actress sang "Please Don't Talk About Me When I'm Gone" during her big death scene in the play *The Drunkard*. Then she had a heart attack—a real one—and died instantly.

• **MOLIÈRE.** The 17th-century French playwright and actor (real name: Jean-Baptiste Poquelin) collapsed during the performance of one of his plays. He had a coughing fit, was carried home, and promptly died. The name of the play: *Le Malade imaginaire*, or *The Hypochondriac*.

• **LORD ULLI.** The Lords were a German band who had a string of minor hits in the 1960s, including "Over in the Gloryland," which included the lyric "When I die, I'd like to drop dead from the stage." That's exactly what happened in 1999 at the band's 40th anniversary concert. Lead singer Lord Ulli fell off the stage, hit his head, and died shortly afterward.

• **RICHARD VERSALLE.** The tenor was performing in the opera *The Makropulos Case* in 1996. He climbed a ladder and belted out the line, "Too bad you can only live so long." He then had a heart attack and fell to the ground, dying instantly. *The Makropulos Case* is about the discovery of the secret to eternal life.

• **DICK SHAWN.** In April 1987, the veteran comedian was performing a satirical monologue in which he made fun of politicians. After reciting a string of campaign slogans—ending with "I will not lay down on the job!"—Shawn fell to the floor and lay face down. At first the audience thought it was part of the act, but Shawn didn't get up. A theater employee finally checked him for a pulse: He was dead.

The role of *Dirty Harry* was originally intended for Frank Sinatra. (They wouldn't do it his way.)

# SNEAKY CORPORATIONS

*Powerful corporations often set up fake "institutes"*
*and programs that sound like independent foundations*
*promoting the public good—when in fact they're just*
*the opposite. Here are four examples.*

## VERY INCONVENIENT

The documentary film *An Inconvenient Truth* received a lot of attention and attracted huge audiences when it was released in May 2006. The film argues that global warming caused by industrial pollution is slowly altering the Earth's climate and melting the polar ice caps, and will eventually flood major cities and leave the planet uninhabitable.

But shortly after the movie came out, "public service" commercials began appearing on TV, calling global warming a myth and claiming that carbon dioxide—a byproduct of industrial pollution and automobile emissions (and the "villain" of the movie)—is actually not a pollutant at all, because "plants breathe it." They went on to say that industrial waste is not only harmless, it's essential to life.

So who made the "public service" ads? A think tank called the Competitive Enterprise Institute, whose members are almost exclusively oil and automobile companies, including Exxon, Arco, Ford, Texaco, and General Motors.

## CHEMICALS ARE COOL!

In 1997 students in hundreds of high schools across America got a few hours off from class to attend "Chem TV." Supposedly designed to get kids excited about chemistry and science, it was a traveling multimedia extravaganza featuring loud music, videos, lasers, games, skits, dancers, free T-shirts, a huge set with giant TV screens, and a cast of enthusiastic performers.

Educational? Sort of. Chem TV (meant to sound like "MTV") said it was about *chemistry*, but it was really about the *chemical industry*. It was part of a million-dollar public relations campaign by Dow Chemical—one of the world's biggest polluters—to help change their image. Dow had a controversial history: It supplied

---

Cereal trivia: The marshmallows in Lucky Charms cereal are technically known as "marbits."

napalm and Agent Orange to the government during the Vietnam War, and lawsuits over faulty breast implants nearly bankrupted the company in 1995.

Critics charged that the Chem TV presentations were misleading (in one example, an actor took off his clothes to demonstrate that "your entire body is made of chemicals"). Chem TV didn't differentiate between a *chemical* (a man-made, often toxic combination of ingredients) and an *organic compound* (molecules that fuse together naturally—like water). Despite the criticism, the program toured schools for three years and won numerous awards. (And it was tax exempt because it was "educational.")

## INDEPENDENT THOUGHT

In May 1998, the federal government filed a lawsuit against Microsoft, accusing the software giant of monopolistic behavior. In June 1999, the Independent Institute, a California-based legal think tank, ran full-page ads in the *New York Times* and *Washington Post* that staunchly defended Microsoft. In the form of an open letter (signed by 240 "economists"), it stated that prosecuting Microsoft would hurt consumers and weaken the economy. What exactly is the "Independent Institute"? It's not independent at all. Though its mission statement says it is "dedicated to the highest standards of independent scholarly inquiry," in 1998 it had exactly one source of funding: Microsoft.

## JUNK FOOD = FITNESS

The American Council for Fitness and Nutrition was formed in 2003 to combat the United States' growing obesity problem. At least that's what they said. Shortly after its formation, the Council held a press conference to announce its latest findings: Contrary to numerous government and medical studies, they reported, too much fast food and vending machines filled with junk food did *not* make children fat.

Turns out the ACFN's interest in childhood obesity is purely business related. The ACFN is actually a lobbying group…for snack-food makers and fast-food restaurants. Its members include Pizza Hut, Taco Bell, Sara Lee, Pepsi, Nestle, McDonald's, Hershey, Coca-Cola, and the Sugar Association.

# THE GREAT BOSTON FIRE

*For many cities—Chicago and San Francisco, especially—
it took a disaster to finally improve building codes and
safety regulations. Boston was no exception.*

## CALM BEFORE THE STORM

November 9, 1872, was a quiet Saturday night in Boston's downtown business district. Everything was closed, and only a handful of people were on the street. Then, at about 7 p.m., a fire broke out in the Klous Building, at the corner of Summer and Kingston streets. The three businesses housed in the three-story building sold dry goods, neckties, and hoopskirts, with boxes full of back stock stuffed into every empty room. In effect, the Klous Building was a giant pile of kindling, just waiting for a spark to set it on fire.

And that's what happened. The fire started in the basement, when a spark from the coal-burning steam boiler that powered the elevator ignited a box of hoopskirts. The elevator shaft sucked the flames up, fueled by the shaft's wood lining, and they spread quickly to other floors. Five minutes later, the entire building was a raging inferno.

## LAZY PEOPLE AND SICK HORSES

The fire could be seen from blocks away, and a crowd gathered to watch the blaze. After standing around for about 15 minutes, many wondered aloud why they couldn't hear a fire alarm. Surely *someone* had alerted the fire department. No, nobody had—they all assumed somebody else had done it. The fire department was finally summoned at 7:25 p.m. by a policeman half a block away who saw smoke in the air.

By that time, smoke was already visible five miles away across Boston Harbor in East Boston. Without waiting for an alarm, a pumper engine from the East Boston Fire Department boarded a ferry and was at the fire within minutes. But once the firefighters got there, tragically they couldn't do anything: Their fire hoses weren't compatible with Boston's fire hydrants. All they could do was watch the building burn and the fire spread. The Klous Building was gone by 7:30. Metal shutters had slid down the building in molten streams; shingles and roof tiles had fallen to the ground and struck onlookers.

Though firefighters all over Boston had heard the alarm, they couldn't get to the spreading fire because the horses that pulled their water-pumper engines had been stricken by an epidemic of horse flu. Some engines tried to get to the fire anyway, only to have their sick horses die along the way. The city had had the foresight to keep 500 men on call to carry the engines by hand, but by 7:45 p.m., only 75 of them had shown up.

Shortly after 8:00, Fire Chief John Damrell knew he'd need more help. He sent telegrams requesting fire engines and firemen to every town within 50 miles. The word spread, and 1,700 fire-fighters from 27 towns headed for Boston... but most didn't get there until well after 10 p.m.

## GRANITE, HYDRANTS, AND COAL

The fire had started to spread to adjacent buildings as early as 7:20, before any firefighters even arrived. Most of the buildings in the district were made of granite, which normally isn't flammable. But anything—including stone—will burn if it comes into contact with the proper oxidizing agent. The burning materials inside the Klous caused a chemical reaction that created the necessary agents, making the granite burn.

Granite burns hotter and creates a wider perimeter of heat than burning wood. A building across the street from the Klous caught fire without even being touched by flames; the heat from the fire was enough to ignite it. Now buildings on both sides of the narrow street were ablaze. This created a "wind of heat"—a 16-mph backdraft that blew embers and cinders in every direction, igniting even more buildings.

By 8:30 p.m., entire blocks were burning. There were 50 engine crews on the ground, but not enough fire hydrants in the business district to beat back the spread of flames. In some cases the nearest hydrant was 700 feet away. By the time the water came out of the hose, there wasn't enough water pressure to fight the fire. Other crews hooked up multiple hoses to a single hydrant. That also killed water pressure. The hot winds were so strong that what little water did come out was reduced to a mist.

The pumpers ran on coal, and fire engines usually carried 500 pounds of it—enough for an hour of firefighting. Ordinarily that would be sufficient, but on this night the engines ran through their coal and then, because the coal carts couldn't replenish the supply fast enough, resorted to using stray boxes, garbage, broken-off fenceboards—even shutters and blinds from nearby buildings—for fuel. Ironically, there was a large coal yard nearby, but it, too, caught on fire, making its thousands of tons of coal unusable.

## FIGHTING FIRE...WITH GUNPOWDER

At 10 p.m., the firemen were still concentrating on dousing the burning buildings, instead of trying to contain the fire. Fire Chief Damrell finally agreed to Mayor William Gaston's demand to use explosives to blow up houses and buildings in the fire's path. That was how the Great Chicago Fire had finally been extinguished— if there is nothing in a fire's way to burn, it will eventually stop. Would it work in Boston? They decided to find out: The police department donated kegs of gunpowder, and volunteers and business owners ignited them. The explosions eliminated the buildings...but it also ignited gas lines connected to street lamps. For a time, the fire raged hotter than ever, but because there were no buildings left, it could finally be controlled. It was largely extinguished by noon the next day.

## TAKING ADVANTAGE

The crowds didn't disperse as the fire spread. They actually grew, and not just to watch: They came to loot. By midnight, police had arrested 750 people, some of whom were business owners trying to salvage stock from their own burning stores. By 2 a.m., even some of the out-of-town firemen, convinced they had no hope of fighting the blaze, had joined in the looting. And to top it all off, many of the firefighters were drunk. As early as 8:00, police had passed out whiskey in a misguided attempt to keep firefighters awake and alert. One news report told of a drunken firefighter who claimed he saw fireballs falling from the sky, signifying the apocalypse. (It turned out to be the flames reflected on the white feathers of some passing geese.)

## TOLL OF DESTRUCTION

In the 17 hours the fire raged:

• Thirty people died, including 12 firefighters.

• Property totaling $75 million was destroyed (worth about $3.5 *billion* today).

• A total of 776 buildings, tenanted by 960 companies, burned to the ground.

• More than 300 warehouses full of wool, leather, shoes, paper, and hardware were lost.

• Thousands of people were left jobless and homeless.

• The blocks bordered by Washington, Summer, Broad, and State streets were completely destroyed—an area of 65 acres.

## AFTERMATH

Perhaps the greatest tragedy of all: The Boston Fire had been predicted. During the Chicago fire just a year earlier in 1871, more than 300 people had lost their lives and over 300,000 acres of the city had burned down. In the wake of that fire, insurance companies surveyed other large cities to assess their potential future losses. Their conclusion: Boston would be the next to go because it had no enforced building code or fire regulations. Many business owners ignored the report, mistakenly believing that granite was fireproof; some didn't even bother to insure their property. Other businesses understood the message and insured their buildings for up to six times their worth to collect when their businesses were inevitably destroyed. Result: The Boston fire bankrupted 35 insurance companies.

The district was completely rebuilt in less than two years—financed mostly by money from insurance claims. And the fire brought needed changes to the city: Streets were widened to prevent flames from jumping them, a citywide board of fire commissioners was formed, and a uniform building code was passed. As a result, this was the last major fire in Boston—but it wasn't the last in North America. In the next 40 years, Atlanta, Seattle, Baltimore, and Toronto would all suffer similar fires. But, except for the Chicago fire and the citywide inferno after the San Francisco earthquake of 1906, Boston's fire was the deadliest and most costly.

# WHY YOU GET MOTION SICKNESS

*If you're reading this book in a car on a windy road, you'll know why you feel queasy.*

**B**ALANCING ACT

Your ears do more than just hear—they are also home to your *vestibular system*, the set of tiny organs that your brain uses to maintain your balance. Even when you're sitting still, your body is moving ever so slightly. Your vestibular system is so sensitive that it is able to detect these slight movements and send signals to your brain, which responds by instructing various muscles to counteract the movement. This continuous process of movement and response is how your body maintains its balance when you're sitting, standing, walking, running, or moving in any other way. The bad news is that the organs of balance are *so* sensitive that when they're overstimulated by too much motion, they can cause motion sickness. Here's a look at how the organs of balance work…and how they can make you sick as a dog.

## ON THE LEVEL

The anatomy of your vestibular system is pretty complicated—so complicated, in fact, that scientists still haven't unlocked all its secrets. But the general principle is simple. Have you ever used a carpenter's level to straighten a picture on the wall? The level contains a small round cylinder filled with liquid, and the liquid has an air bubble floating in it. You put the level on the picture, then adjust the picture until the bubble moves to the center of the cylinder. When the bubble is centered, the picture is level.

The vestibular system works kind of like a carpenter's level: It consists of several chambers in your inner ear, each of which is filled with liquid. But instead of containing bubbles of air, each chamber contains tiny hairs that sprout from the bottom of the chamber like blades of grass. When your body begins to move or accelerate, the fluid in the chambers begins to slosh around, which causes the hairs to move, too.

---

Q. What's the all-night diner's term for 2:30 a.m., when the bars close? A. "Drunk Thirty."

Each time the hairs move, nerve cells at their bases send signals to the brain. Your brain then interprets the signals coming from the different chambers to determine how your body is moving through space.

It takes only one carpenter's level to straighten a bookshelf, but it takes several fluid-filled chambers to detect and measure all the different kinds of motion your body is experiencing. Some are sensitive to *linear* acceleration—whether you are moving in a straight line, up or down, forward or backward, left or right. The chambers that sense linear acceleration also sense the Earth's gravitational pull. Are you lying on your side? Hanging upside down? Other specialized chambers detect *angular* acceleration—they can tell when you're spinning in a circle, turning left or right, or tumbling head over heels. Your brain processes the signals coming from these chambers to figure it out.

## WHY YOU GET SICK

This complicated system has its limits—if the motion your body is experiencing becomes too extreme, the vestibular organs send more signals to your brain than it can handle.

The situation is made even worse when your eyes send contradictory information to your brain. For example, if you're riding in a car that is travelling on a winding road, your organs of balance are sensing the car's movement and reporting all of it to your brain. But if you're staring at the seatback in front of you, your eyes see a more stable scene—you and the seatback are moving more or less in sync—and they report much less movement to your brain. So are you moving a lot, or a little? Your brain can't tell, and the confusion caused by the mixed signals makes you more likely to get motion sickness.

## FALSE ALARM

So how do mixed signals end up as nausea? Scientists who study the vestibular system have uncovered evidence that it has a second purpose: helping your body detect when it has ingested poison. When certain poisons are detected in your bloodstream, your vestibular system bombards your brain with more signals than it can process…just as it does when you're rocking back and forth on a boat.

Astronauts get "spacesick" so often that the space shuttle toilet has a special setting for vomit.

Scientists theorize that when your brain becomes overloaded with signals reporting lots of motion, it may be misinterpreting the signals to mean that you have eaten poison. Your brain then tries to limit the damage by causing you to expel whatever poisons may still be in your stomach before they can enter your bloodstream and poison you further. It does this by making you vomit.

Why are some people more susceptible to motion sickness than others? It could be some people are better at telling the difference between poison and rapid motion than other people are. Another possibility: Some people are sensitive to even the tiniest traces of poison in their system, and the price they pay for this powerful survival trait is getting sick in the car a lot.

## HOW TO AVOID MOTION SICKNESS

• If you take Dramamine or another motion-sickness medicine, take it at least an hour before you leave on your trip. Eating food containing ginger may also help.

• Don't overeat, and don't drink a lot, either. If your stomach isn't full, you're less likely to get motion sickness.

• If you're travelling by plane, try to get a seat over the wings. The plane moves the least there. Taking a cruise? Ask for a cabin near the center of the ship.

• Don't read in moving vehicles. Look out the window and off into the distance. That allows your eyes to report more of the motion that your vestibular system is also sending to your brain, which minimizes the contradictory signals that make motion sickness worse. If you can't look out a window, try closing your eyes.

• Put your head against the headrest. That minimizes movement by keeping your head in sync with the rest of your body. Recline your seat or lie down, if you can. Another thing to try: Open a window (air blowing on your face seems to help).

\*     \*     \*

### IS THIS WARNING LABEL NECESSARY?

**On a smoke detector:** "This product will not extinguish a fire."
**On a bottle of drain cleaner:** "If you cannot read these directions and warnings, do not use this product."

The Russian Imperial Necklace has appeared as a prop in 1,215 Hollywood films.

# CARD SHARKS, PART II

*Part II of our story about card counting and how some kids from MIT won millions at gambling casinos with a system that was unbeatable...almost. (Part I is on page 251.)*

## THE HOUSE RULES

The casinos in Nevada had developed ways to uncover and thwart card counting...but they had no idea that the greatest threat to their control of blackjack gaming was being quietly developed 2,500 miles away.

The Massachusetts Institute of Technology has some of the smartest minds in the world among its student body. What's less known is that MIT students are notorious for their maverick attitude: They love to crack seemingly unsolvable problems just for the fun of it. Sometimes the problems can involve quantum mechanics and string theory. In this case, the question was: "How do we beat the casinos?" The answer was elegantly simple—and, for the casinos, very expensive.

## DREAM TEAM

In 1992 a group of MIT students formed an underground club innocently named "Strategic Investments." Their real intent was to apply Thorp's card-counting system in a radical new way. Previous card counters were all lone wolves. They worked solo, using a technique called *bet spreading*—betting low when the deck is against you, betting high the minute it turns in your favor. And that made them easy targets for casino security.

The MIT card counters played as a team. One person was the "spotter." His job wasn't to play but to observe the game and count cards, watching for the crucial moment when a deck went positive. Next was the "controller," a decoy who bet small while verifying the spotter's count and, most importantly, calculating when to make the big bet. The controller wouldn't make the bet, though. That was the role of the aptly named "big player." He'd wait for the controller's signal, then sweep up to a table and wipe it out with one massive bet. To all appearances—and to casino security—he was just another high roller who happened to get lucky one time.

The MIT team trained for months before trying out their system. Then they went to Las Vegas…and proceeded to win millions. At their peak they had 125 people working the tables. For months the casinos couldn't figure out what was going on, but they knew that, whatever it was, they had to stop it quickly or they'd be out of business. It was that serious.

## RAISING THE ANTE

To make matters worse for the casinos, in 1993 three of the best MIT players split from Strategic Investments to form their own group. Semyon Dukach (big player), Katie Lilienkamp (controller), and Andy Bloch (spotter) were one of the most successful SI teams in the field. But they were tired of sharing their winnings. Why was this a bad development for the casinos? Because the new team (they called themselves the Amphibians) was convinced they could come up with a system that was even better.

Counting cards is difficult for most blackjack players, but it had never been an issue for the nimble brains of these young math wizards. The Amphibians decided that if they were going to raise their game they had to focus on the betting side of the equation. They started by writing a complex computer program that could run simulations of every type of hand they had encountered. Their analysis brought them to a level of hand recognition that was simply awesome, and the new combination—perfect card counting and flawless betting strategy—was devastatingly effective. The Amphibians went on a winning rampage. But the casinos were about to respond with a powerful counterpunch—a woman named Beverly Griffin.

## A FACE IN THE CROWD

Griffin ran a private-investigation company specializing in casino operations. In the summer of 1993, she was hired by a consortium of desperate casino owners. Their instructions: Find a way to stop the card counters for good. She started by creating a database of suspected card counters based on information supplied by the casinos. Then she started looking for connections. Names weren't very helpful, as many gamblers (including the Amphibians) routinely used aliases when they played. Addresses—required by the casinos before they can pay out—were another matter, and that's where Griffin made her breakthrough.

She noticed an unusual concentration of winners from the Boston area. More telling was that most of them appeared to play only on weekends and were in their early 20s—college age. Acting on a hunch, Griffin got hold of some MIT yearbooks. She opened one up and, as she said later, "Lo and behold, there they were. Looking all scholarly and serious, and not at all like card counters."

Working with the casinos and using the MIT yearbooks to build a new database, Griffin and her team helped develop some of the first facial-recognition software. Using images taken from the hundreds of security cameras on the casino floor, a suspected card counter's face could be compared against the computer database and picked up before he or she reached the blackjack tables. Once the Amphibians learned of the casinos' "secret weapon," they knew their card-counting days in America were over. So they decided to take their show on the road. They went to Europe.

## THE LAST STAND

For three weeks the Amphibians—Dukach, Lilienkamp, and Bloch—played and won in London, Paris, and other major gambling locales. Finally they arrived at the mecca of gambling—the Grand Casino in Monte Carlo. The evening started well. All three played the same table, and they were winning. Then Katie Lilienkamp decided to take a potty break. On her way back to the table she was stopped by four security guards and ushered into a side room.

Semyon Dukach and Andy Bloch were already there. A picture of the three of them was scanned and uploaded to the Griffin Investigations office in Las Vegas. The Internet had made the Las Vegas database a global one, so when the identification came back positive (since they were all known Las Vegas card counters), they were unceremoniously shown the door. As Bloch recalled, "The guy said if we ever set foot in the country again we were going to be really hurt."

Wisely, the Amphibians chose that moment to disband their club and retire.

## ENDGAME

The war between the casinos and the best card counters in the world was over. As for the Amphibians, they went on with their

---

lives. Although they had won lots of money, the whole operation had been mostly a lark, an intriguing hobby that paid out as much in adrenaline as it did cash. (None of the MIT groups will say how much cash they won.) "I love playing," Semyon Dukach said later. "I love beating the casinos, knowing that my team was ahead of them, and tricking this huge $50 billion industry." Remember, what they did was not illegal (only Taft's personal computer fell into that category). Katie Lilienkamp went back to MIT and became an engineer. Andy Bloch became a professional poker player. Dukach teaches blackjack for a living.

And what about Edward Thorp, the genius who started it all? He took his mastery of probability theory to the biggest gambling table of all: Wall Street. He founded hedge funds and made untold fortunes managing them using techniques based on his understanding of the odds—and his willingness to place well-calculated bets.

\*　　\*　　\*

## GAMBLING TRIVIA

• The expression "rolling the bones" means to roll dice. And it used to be literal. Dice were made from animal bones—the Romans used sheep's knuckles—for thousands of years.

• The oldest known dice with regular sides were found in northern Iraq. They're made of baked clay and date to about 3000 B.C.

• President Richard Nixon won $6,000 playing poker in his first two months in the U.S. Navy during World War II. He used it to help fund his first campaign for Congress. (He won that, too.)

• More than 50 million decks of cards are sold in the U.S. every year.

• Do you know the book *According to Hoyle*? It's considered the seminal book on the rules of poker (and many other games of chance). It refers to Edmond Hoyle, who wrote the book *A Short Treatise on the Game of Whist* in 1742 (whist was a popular card game at the time). Hoyle died 150 years before poker was invented.

# RALLY 'ROUND THE FLAG

*Every country has one of its own; so do the queen of England and the president of the United States. Here's a look at the history and traditions associated with flags.*

## POLE POSITION

If you had to guess what came first, the flagpole or the flag, what would your answer be? If you guessed the flag, you guessed wrong: The pole predates the flag by thousands of years. It dates back to prehistoric times, when rulers of civilizations as diverse as the Aztecs, the Mongols, the Persians, and the Egyptians carried decorated ceremonial staffs or spears as symbols of their authority. These staffs were often topped with ornaments carved in the shape of animals, gods, or other religious symbols. Some were also decorated with feathers, horse tails, strips of cloth, or dried grasses, which gave the staff a broomlike appearance. Soldiers marched with these staffs in ceremonial processions and even carried them into battle.

It wasn't until after the Chinese discovered the secret of making silk in about 2,700 B.C. that they became the first civilization to attach banners to ceremonial staffs. Silk was well suited for the purpose—it was lightweight and strong, which allowed flags to flow freely, even in the lightest breeze. In the centuries that followed, flags spread to Mongolia, India, and Persia, and then to Rome and on to the rest of Europe.

## QUITE A SIGHT

These early banners had important ceremonial and symbolic value, just as national flags do today. They also served a practical purpose. They could be seen from great distances in battle, which meant generals could follow the course of the fighting by watching the flags, and even use them to signal subordinates. Flapping flags also indicated how strongly and in which direction the wind was blowing, which enabled archers to adjust and improve their aim.

Wardrobe malfunction: Jayne Mansfield "popped out of her dress" during the 1957 Oscars.

"Defending the flag" was more than just an expression—soldiers literally fought to defend their colors, and if the person carrying the flag was killed or wounded, the other soldiers "rallied around the flag" to prevent it from being captured by the enemy. If the flag was lost, the battle was more likely to end in defeat.

## FLAG ETIQUETTE

There is no single international set of guidelines detailing how national flags should be handled and displayed. Nevertheless, many countries have adopted similar rules. For example:

### Respecting the Flag

• National flags should be displayed during daylight hours and taken down at sunset. They should only be left up all night if they are well illuminated, and they should not be allowed to fly if the weather is so severe that the flag could be damaged.

• Flags should be treated with respect—never made into clothing or used as curtains, tablecloths, and so on. Indoors, they should not touch the floor; outside, they should not touch the ground or water. Flags should not be printed on napkins, shopping bags, or anything intended to be disposable.

• The national flag has precedence over regional, local, and other flags. In ceremonies in which more than one flag is being raised, the national flag should be raised first, followed by state, county, and city flags, in that order; and it should be lowered last.

### Flying Many Flags

• In centuries past, it was common in wartime for a conquering army to communicate its victory over the enemy by hoisting its battle flag over the enemy's on a single flagpole. Because of this, when the flags of more than one nation are displayed together, each flag must be flown on its own flagpole, and every flag must be flown at the same height.

• At gatherings hosted by an international organization, such as the United Nations or the Olympic Games, national flags are displayed in alphabetical order, according to the official language of the host country. For example, in England, the Spanish flag is alphabetized by the letter S, for "Spain." In Mexico, where Spanish is spoken, it would be alphabetized under E, for "España."

## The Host Country's Flag

At gatherings hosted by a particular country, it is common for the flag of the host country to be displayed in a special position of honor. That position depends on how many flags are being flown and in what configuration. If two flags are flown, the host country's flag should be flown to the left of the other flag, as seen by observers. If three flags are flown, it should be flown from the middle pole. If four or more flags are flown, it should be on the left again, or two host country flags may be flown, one at each end.

If the flags are flying from flagpoles organized in a circle, the host flag should fly from the place of greatest prominence, as seen by viewers as they approach or enter the circle.

\* \* \*

## POLI-TALKS

*Sen. Ted Stevens (R-Alaska) describes the Internet*

"There's one company now that you can sign up with and you can get a movie delivered to your house daily by delivery service. Okay. And currently it comes to your house, it gets put in the mailbox when you get home and you change your order but you pay for that, right. But this service isn't going to go through the Internet and what you do is you just go to a place on the Internet and you order your movie and guess what, you can order 10 of them delivered to you and the delivery charge is free. Ten of them streaming across that Internet and what happens to your own personal Internet?

"I just the other day—an Internet was sent to me by my staff at 10 o'clock in the morning on Friday and I just got it yesterday. Why? Because it got tangled up with all these things going on the Internet commercially...

"No, I'm not finished! I want people to understand my position, I'm not going to take a lot of time. They want to deliver vast amounts of information over the Internet. And again, the internet is not something you just dump something on. It's not a truck. It's a series of tubes. And if you don't understand those tubes can be filled and if they are filled, when you put your message in, it gets in line and it's going to be delayed by anyone that puts into that tube enormous amounts of material, enormous amounts of material."

# LINCOLN'S DUEL

*Politics can be a dirty, nasty business. And this forgotten bit of Americana reminds us that some people take it very seriously.*

## THEM'S FIGHTIN' WORDS

In 1842 a scandalous letter to the editor appeared in the *Sangamo Journal* in Springfield, Illinois. The newspaper was loyal to the Whig party (forerunner of the Republican party), and, not surprisingly, the target of the letter was a member of the opposition Democrats—Illinois state auditor James J. Shields.

The letter was biting. Signed by "Aunt Becca" from "The Lost Townships," it mocked Shields in every possible way: as an auditor, as an American, even as a man. Among many other insults, "Aunt Becca" described Shields as "a ballroom dandy, floatin' about on the earth without heft or substance, just like a lot of cat-fur where cats had been fightin'." The attack became the talk of Illinois, and Shields, known as a vain and pompous man, was enraged. He threatened to find out who wrote the letter and to "meet them on the field of honor."

## AUNTIE ABE

Illinois was in terrible financial shape in 1842, as was most of the United States. The Panic of 1837, one of the worst economic depressions in the country's history, had left the state in enormous debt. Shields, as state auditor, took the brunt of the blame, even though it was no fault of his: he had been appointed to the office in 1839. The state's mounting debt culminated in the closing of the State Bank of Illinois in 1842, and Shields ordered that notes from that bank would no longer be accepted for tax payments. People were enraged—and the Whigs saw an opportunity to score some political points. One of them was a young congressman named Abraham Lincoln. Known already for his caustic wit and sarcasm, he had penned the letter from "Aunt Becca."

Soon after news of the letter and Shields's response spread, another letter appeared from "Aunt Becca," this one written by two of Lincoln's friends, Julia Jayne and Mary Todd (the future

Mrs. Lincoln). Their letter was even more inflammatory than Lincoln's: "I will give him a choice, however, in one thing," it said in response to Shields's fighting words, "and that is whether, when we fight, I shall wear breeches or he petticoats, for I presume this change is sufficient to place us on an equality."

Shields went to the editor of the newspaper and demanded to know who had written the letters. The editor, as instructed, told him it was Lincoln (who didn't want to get his friends in trouble). Shields wrote an angry letter to Lincoln and demanded an immediate retraction. Lincoln replied that if the request were made a bit more gentlemanly, he might honor it. That only made Shields angrier—and he publicly challenged Lincoln to a duel.

## IT'S ON

By this point, Lincoln realized that the situation was getting out of hand—but he had to accept the challenge. He was a politician, and duels were still respected shows of a man's courage. (It may also have had something to do with Lincoln's desire to impress Mary Todd.) In any case, he accepted Shields's challenge, and the upcoming match between the two politicians was the biggest news story in Illinois.

Because Lincoln was the one who had been challenged, the choice of location and weapons was his. Dueling was illegal in Illinois, so he chose an island in the Mississippi River between Illinois and Missouri, the island being part of Missouri. For weapons, he chose cavalry broadswords.

The fight was to take place in a circle 10 feet across and 12 feet deep, with a plank across the middle that neither man could cross. This, historians say, was Lincoln's way of saying how ridiculous he thought the whole thing was—but it also gave him a distinct advantage if they were actually going to fight. He was 6'4" and long-armed; Shields was much shorter. Judge William H. Herndon, Lincoln's friend and law partner, wrote, "There is little doubt that the man who had swung a beetle [a heavy wooden hammer] and driven iron wedges into gnarled hickory logs could have cleft the skull of his antagonist, but he had no such intention." Lincoln hoped Shields would see his disadvantage and call the fight off, but Shields wasn't about to back down.

## A SHOW OF FORCE

On the morning of September 22, 1842, the two men and their respective parties showed up on the island. The "seconds," friends of the fighters charged with securing the location and weapons and so forth, immediately began negotiating to try to bring about a peaceful solution. When Shields refused, Lincoln started hacking branches off a nearby willow tree with his sword—high above his head. The sight apparently took some of the stubbornness out of Shields. The two sides soon came to an agreement, with Lincoln agreeing to admit in writing that he had written the letters, and saying he "had no intention of injuring your personal or private character or standing as a man or gentleman." The ordeal was over.

## AFTERMATH

Lincoln and Shields never became friends, but their near-duel didn't ruin their relationship as politicians—or soldiers. When the American Civil War began 19 years later, Lincoln was president and commander-in-chief. Shields, a onetime Army officer, joined the Union Army, and Lincoln made him a brigadier general. And after Shields was wounded in 1862 while his troops gave Confederate General "Stonewall" Jackson his only defeat of the entire war, Lincoln approved his promotion to major general (it was blocked by Congress). Shields served with distinction and went on to serve in Congress after the war, becoming the only man in history to be elected U.S. Senator in three different states (Illinois, Minnesota, and Missouri). He died, still in office, on June 1, 1879.

Historians say that Lincoln was terribly embarrassed about the duel and the events leading up to it, and refused to speak about it afterward. In an 1865 letter, Mary Todd Lincoln wrote that an army officer once visited the White House and asked President Lincoln, "Is it true…that you once went out to fight a duel and all for the sake of the lady by your side?" Lincoln answered, "I do not deny it, but if you desire my friendship, you will never mention it again."

\*　　\*　　\*

"The illegal we do immediately. The unconstitutional takes a little longer."

—Henry Kissinger

America's first public park: Boston Common, established in 1634.

# THE BRISTOL SESSIONS

*Or, how one man with a microphone changed
the face of American music.*

# MAKING MUSIC HISTORY

For two weeks in the summer of 1927, a vacant store in the Appalachian town of Bristol, Tennessee, became the scene of one of the pivotal moments in music history. Johnny Cash later called it, "the single most important event in the history of country music." Scores of "hillbilly" musicians came out of the mountains and hollows, and performed their songs in an improvised recording studio run by a 35-year-old producer named Ralph Peer. With each acetate master Peer made, American roots music left its rural isolation farther behind and began down the path to worldwide acclaim. Two of the artists Peer recorded—Jimmie Rodgers and the Carter Family—became so influential that they defined the style of country for generations to come.

## THE HITMAKER

In the early days of the recording industry, most records were made for urban markets. Peer noticed that many new record players were being sold in rural areas, but relatively few records were being sold in those same regions. He figured that there was probably an untapped market of rural people hungry for their own kind of music. When Peer became recording director for Okeh Records in 1920, he seized his chance to go out and find that music.

Ralph Peer knew a good thing when he heard it. His first success was getting Mamie Smith's "Crazy Blues" on wax—the first blues recording targeted specifically for a black audience. He also gets the credit for making what experts agree is the first country music record: a medley of fiddle tunes called "Little Old Log Cabin in the Lane/That Old Hen Cackled" by Fiddlin' John Carson. Peer wanted to make more country records, but he was limited by the small number of artists he could convince to come from their Appalachian homes to his New York recording studio. His solution: Take the studio to the mountains.

Oh, be-have! State dance of South Carolina: the Shag.

## SETTING UP SHOP

By 1925 Peer had left the Okeh label and moved to the Victor Talking Machine Company, because, as he said later, they "wanted to get into the hillbilly business and I knew how to do it." After a long talent search through the South, Peer decided to set up shop in Bristol, Tennessee. The town of 32,000 was the largest in the area, and, more important, it lay right where the borders of Tennessee, North Carolina, Kentucky, and Virginia come close together. Peer was convinced that true "mountaineer melodies" still survived in these states. He rented the second floor of the Taylor-Christian Hat Company at 410 State Street, put an ad in the local paper announcing that the Victor Recording Company would be recording local talent, and went back to New York to alert his bosses.

On June 23, 1927, Peer drove back to Bristol with his wife, two engineers, and a carload of recording equipment. After hauling their gear up the stairs into the vacant office, the team hung blankets on the walls to deaden the sound and prepared to receive an onslaught of hopeful musicians and singers. The only problem: Almost no one showed up.

## ALERT THE MEDIA

A desperate Peer ran down to the local paper and talked the editor into running a front-page feature about his makeshift studio. The article appeared the next day, touting the great opportunity available to the locals. One paragraph mentioned that session musicians often made as much as $100 a day in New York, and that Peer was prepared to do the same for the musicians he recorded. By noon the makeshift studio on State Street was full of hungry musicians looking to make some easy money.

Peer was ecstatic. The recording sessions ran day and night to accommodate the rush. By August 5, Peer had 76 masters by 19 different acts to take back to New York. Some of the groups he recorded: the West Virginia Coonhunters, Dad Blackard and the Shelors, Red Snodgrass, Ernest Phillips and His Holiness Quartet, Blind Alfred Reed, the Alcoa Quartet, and the Bluff City Church Choir. Nearly all of these singers and musicians went on to have solid careers in the infant country music industry. But two of the acts that walked in the door at 410 State Street ended up doing much more than that.

## BRISTOL BOYS

Down in North Carolina, word of the sessions in Bristol reached a local band that was working the Asheville music scene. Three of the band members—brothers Claude and Jack Grant, and Jack Pierce—were from Bristol, so they talked their lead singer, a skinny railroad worker from Mississippi named Jimmie Rodgers, to come along with them. The night before their session, they got into a disagreement over how to bill themselves. The argument grew heated until finally the singer said in disgust, "All right, I'll just sing one by myself."

The next day Rodgers recorded two songs: a World War I tune, "The Soldier's Sweetheart," and a lullaby called "Sleep, Baby, Sleep" that featured his distinctive yodel. The session lasted just over two hours, and Peer paid Rodgers $100. When the record was released in October 1927, it proved enough of a success to convince Peer to record more of Rodgers's songs. This time Rodgers went to the Victor studios in Camden, New Jersey, and one of the tunes he recorded there, "T for Texas (Blue Yodel)" sold half a million copies. Rodgers became the first superstar of country music until his career was cut short by tuberculosis in 1933.

## FAMILY BUSINESS

At the time of the Bristol sessions, Alvin Pleasant Carter, known as A. P., was managing a general store in nearby Maces Springs, West Virginia. He and his wife, Sara, sang together and were popular with the locals. After he heard about the sessions, A. P. packed Sara into their jalopy and headed for Bristol. At the last minute he asked Sara's sister, Maybelle, to come along to play guitar and add a little harmony.

When he first met the Carters at the studio, Peer was unimpressed. As they climbed out of their broken-down car in their overalls and homemade dresses, Peer suspected that they were "too hillbilly" to be any good. A. P. had such a thick mountain accent that he was almost unintelligible. Then they set up and began to play. For Peer it was like striking gold. Although she was only 18, Maybelle was already a virtuoso guitar player, picking in a unique style that Peer had never heard before (it came to be known as the "Carter scratch"). But it was Sara's voice that sold the deal for him: a clear, thin alto, it seemed the essence of pure mountain singing.

---

Monkey business: Mother orangutans breastfeed their young for as long as 7 years.

On August 1 and 2, the Carter Family, as they decided to call themselves, recorded six tunes, including "Bury Me Under the Weeping Willow" and "The Poor Orphan Child." Within months, they were nationally known recording stars and went on to be the bestselling country artists of the 1920s and 1930s.

## THE UNBROKEN CIRCLE

It's hard to overstate the influence that the Carter Family and Jimmie Rodgers had on the development of country music as a result of the Bristol sessions. The recordings Ralph Peer made, not only of the Carters and Rodgers but also of the other mountain artists, were the first to be widely heard in rural America. For many Americans, this was their first exposure to records at all, and they took to the music and new technology with gusto. By the 1940s, an entire generation had grown up listening to Rodgers's "blue yodel" and the tight harmonies of the Carter Family.

Country music continued to evolve, from the bluegrass innovations of Bill Monroe and Earl Scruggs to the honky-tonk of Hank Williams to the intricate harmonies of the Louvin and Everly Brothers. And out of that grew the crossover blend of country and R&B that, in the hands of Elvis Presley and other early rockabilly artists, morphed into rock 'n' roll—another direct descendant of those crude acetate masters recorded in a makeshift studio in Bristol, Tennessee.

\*   \*   \*

## WORLD CUP MADNESS

"A Beijing soccer fan refused to let the small matter of his house burning down disturb his enjoyment of the 2006 World Cup match between France and Spain. A fire broke out in a *hutong* in the center of the Chinese capital at kick-off time and gutted the traditional courtyard dwelling, the *Beijing Daily Messenger* reported. 'When the neighbors shouted "fire!" I took my little baby and ran out in my nightclothes,' the man's wife said. 'My husband paid no attention to the danger, just grabbed the television and put it under his arm. After getting out of the house, he then set about finding an electric socket to plug in and continue watching his game.'"

—**Reuters**

The word *calzone* literally translates to "pant leg" in Italian.

# THE *GLOMAR EXPLORER*

*Shh! This story details one of the most incredible examples
of nutty spy technology. Ever. (But don't tell anyone.)*

L OST AT SEA
On March 8, 1968, the submarine USS *Barb* was on a mission, secretly monitoring shipping activity near Vladivostok,
home of the Soviet Union's largest naval base on the Pacific
Ocean. Suddenly five Soviet submarines came racing out of the
port at full speed. Subs are supposed to be stealthy and silent—
these were anything but. They were noisily "pinging" the ocean
floor with active sonar, and repeatedly diving and surfacing. It was
clear they were looking for something, and a dozen surface warships soon joined in the hunt. Radio communication between
the ships was frantic and unencrypted, another indication of the
urgency of the search. What were they looking for?

## CHECKING THE RECORDS

The U.S. Navy's Office of Undersea Warfare, responsible for inter-
cepting the radio traffic of enemy submarines, quickly started poring
over the logs of recent radio traffic, looking for clues to what was
going on. Sure enough, *K-129*, a diesel submarine carrying
nuclear torpedoes and ballistic missiles with four-megaton nuclear
warheads, had failed to report in, as scheduled, the day before.
More than 24 hours had passed since then and there was still no
word from the sub. It was missing and now presumed sunk. And
judging from the haphazard nature of the search, the Soviets didn't
have a clue where it had gone down.

Did the Americans? The Navy operates a large network of
"hydrophones"—underwater microphones—in strategic locations all over the Pacific. This Sound Surveillance System
(SOSUS) can distinguish between sounds made by military
ships and submarines, and those given off by ordinary maritime
traffic. It also records background noise. Analysts went over the
recordings, looking for any sound that might have been *K-129*
exploding or being crushed by tremendous pressure as it sank to
the ocean floor.

---

60% of Americans can name the Three Stooges. 17% can name three Supreme Court justices.

## TAKING PICTURES

They found what they were looking for: a single unexplained loud popping sound that they traced to the same area of the Pacific where they believed the *K-129* was likely to have gone down. The USS *Halibut*, a submarine capable of dropping a camera to the ocean floor at the end of a long cable, was dispatched to the area to search for the missing sub.

Analysts narrowed the search to a five-square-mile section of ocean floor about 1,700 miles northwest of the Hawaiian Islands. That's still a lot of ocean—it took two trips to the site and more than 13 weeks of methodically inching across the ocean floor before *Halibut* finally found the wreck of the *K-129*, three miles below the surface.

The camera showed that a 10-foot-wide hole had been blown in the sub's hull right behind the conning tower. That led the analysts to speculate that the sub had suffered a catastrophic explosion while charging its batteries. The batteries give off explosive hydrogen gas while they're charging, and a spark from the engines could have ignited the gas.

The Navy had found the Soviet sub. Now what?

## SUNKEN TREASURE

Apparently, telling the Soviets where to find their submarine was never given serious consideration—after all, this was during the Cold War. And the Soviets never did figure out where *K-129* was, so eventually they called off their search. There the submarine lay, at the bottom of the ocean, a potential treasure trove of intelligence information:

• Recovering a nuclear warhead would enable the United States to gauge the sophistication of Soviet weapons.

• Recovering a torpedo would make it possible to build counter-measures against them.

• Recovering cryptographic machines and materials would help the U.S. decipher encoded communications.

• Examining sections of the hull might reveal how deep Soviet subs were capable of operating.

The problem was that the sub was more than 17,000 feet under water. American submarines operate at a depth of only about 1,300 feet; if they go any deeper, they can be crushed by the tremendous pressure of the ocean. The Navy proposed sending unmanned mini subs to recover the nuclear warheads and the cryptographic equipment. But the CIA, which by now had joined the project, proposed a much more ambitious scheme: why not pull the entire submarine up to the surface?

## STARTING FROM SCRATCH

Picking up something as massive as a submarine from the ocean floor had never been done before. When CIA director Richard Helms first heard the idea, he replied, "You must be crazy." But the United States already had a secret program to recover Soviet missiles that had been test fired over the Pacific, and recovering a submarine was the same thing, only on a larger scale. Besides, if the U.S. developed the capability to recover Soviet subs, they could use it to recover any American subs that might sink, preventing their secrets from falling into Soviet hands. The program was approved; the CIA set to work designing a ship that could do the job.

## THE NUTTY BILLIONAIRE

Raising a sub from the ocean floor was a tricky enough problem in its own right. Doing it without the Soviets realizing you were doing it was another thing entirely. How was the CIA going to keep it a secret?

They decided to work through the eccentric industrialist (and billionaire) Howard Hughes. Hughes had a lot to offer: His companies had done classified work for the government, and he was obsessed with secrecy. His Glomar Marine Corporation was interested in undersea mining—a field that involves pulling tons of material up from the ocean floor—which made it a good cover. And Hughes had a reputation as being a bit of a nut, so when he announced that he was building the world's first deep-sea mining ship—the *Glomar Explorer*—to harvest "manganese nodules" from the ocean floor, no one suspected that he was really acting as a front for the CIA. The cover story was so effective, in fact, that after his announcement, other companies began looking into mining for the "potato-sized" manganese nodules too.

## SPY SHIP

Another Hughes subsidiary, the Hughes Tool Company, designed the 50,000-ton ship, which was 618 feet in length—twice as long as the *K-129*. It would serve as the mother ship to a giant submersible barge called the *Hughes Mining Barge-1*, which would do the actual lifting of the *K-129*.

The barge was about as big as a football field and contained eight sets of giant claws, similar to salad tongs, suspended from a large platform. The system worked like this: the *Glomar Explorer* would lower the *Hughes Mining Barge* all the way down to the wreck of the *K-129*, then the giant claws would close around the sub. Once the claws were secure, the barge and the submarine would be slowly and carefully floated back to the surface. Once there, it could either be hidden inside the *Glomar Explorer*, which had a 200-foot-long trapdoor beneath the waterline, or it could be left on the *Hughes Mining Barge* under a giant curved roof, similar to a Quonset hut, to prevent the sub from being observed by Soviet spy planes or satellites.

## PROJECT JENNIFER

It took more than two years to build and test the system, and it wasn't until the summer of 1974 that the *Glomar Explorer* was ready for action. The ship left port with a 170-man crew of CIA agents, only 40 of whom knew what the real mission was.

What happened next depends on who you believe. The details of the recovery mission, code-named "Project Jennifer," are still classified, and the various sketchy accounts of the mission that have been published contradict each other on many points. They don't even agree on whether the *K-129* lay intact or broken into pieces. At the very least, it was in very fragile condition, having been damaged first by the initial explosion that crippled it and caused it to sink, then by the tremendous ocean pressure that crushed it like a soda can as it sank three miles to the bottom. The *K-129* slammed into the ocean floor at an estimated 200 mph, which caused still more damage.

The *Glomar Explorer* arrived at the site, found the sub, and was able to lower the barge down to the wreck without incident. But getting its giant hooks around the damaged sub was another story: Because it was partially buried, the claws had to dig through the sea bed to get a proper grip. They apparently dug a little too deep—some of the hooks were so badly damaged that they couldn't grasp the submarine. The decision was made to try and raise the sub anyway. Lifting at a rate of six feet a minute, the *Glomar Explorer* managed to lift the submarine 5,000 feet off the ocean floor… only to have it break apart, with some of the most valuable parts—including the nuclear missiles—falling back to the ocean floor.

## UNANSWERED QUESTIONS

That's *one* version of the story, anyway. Another is that the entire submarine—nukes, torpedoes, cryptographic machines, everything —was successfully recovered, and that the tale about the sub falling back into the ocean was created as a cover story to conceal one of the greatest intelligence coups of the 20th century.

Still another version of the story says that after blowing more than $300 million on the project, the CIA watched everything but a tiny, worthless scrap of the sub slip from its grasp, leaving it with nothing to show for all the money that had been spent. The CIA then made up the story of salvaging part of the sub to cover up their blunder.

Which story is true? Your guess is as good as ours.

## THE SECRET GETS OUT

One thing that is certain is that the secret of the *Glomar Explorer* had already begun to leak out even before it set out to sea in the summer of 1974. The *Los Angeles Times* broke the story on its front page on February 7, 1975, reportedly while the *Glomar Explorer* was at the site of the *K-129*, making a second attempt to recover more of the wreckage. Because the mission was still underway and lives were at risk, William Colby, the new director of the CIA, managed to get the story pushed back to page 18 in the later editions of the *L.A. Times*, and accomplished the same with a similar story in *The New York Times* the following month. The story finally blew wide open on March 18, when columnist Jack Anderson reported it on national television.

## 15 MINUTES OF FAME

The exposure of the *Glomar Explorer* in newspapers all over the world, complete with photographs, ruined its effectiveness as a spy ship. Now that the Soviets and everyone else knew what it really was, it could no longer be sent on clandestine missions without causing an international incident.

## OUT OF ACTION

For the next five years it went back to what it claimed to have been doing the whole time—working as a deep-sea mining ship. Then in 1980 Hughes Global Marine returned the ship to the U.S. Navy, which added it to the "mothball fleet" of inactive naval ships anchored in Suisun Bay outside of San Francisco. Anyone crossing the Benicia Bridge could see it clearly.

The *Glomar Explorer* sat at anchor for the next 16 years, until Global Marine leased it back from the government in 1996 and spent a reported $150 million refitting it to drill for oil on the ocean floor. The retrofit removed much of the equipment used to raise the *K-129*, so the *Explorer* will likely spend the remaining time on its 30-year-lease exploring for oil just like Global Marine says it will.

…Or maybe that's just what the CIA *wants* us to think.

\*　　\*　　\*

## FROM THE BAD JOKE FILE

A man who wanted to achieve enlightenment made a pilgrimage to a Buddhist monastery high in the mountains. There he found the wisest monk and told him his goal. The monk replied, "To reach enlightenment, you must take a vow of silence for 10 years."

After 10 years of silent meditation, the monk said to the man, "You may now speak."

"My bed is too hard," said the man.

"You have not yet reached enlightenment," replied the monk. "You must not speak again for 10 years."

So the man remained silent for 10 more years, and then the monk came to him and said, "You may now speak."

"The food here is too cold," he said.

"You still have not yet reached enlightenment," said the monk.

So the man took another vow of silence. Ten years later—after 30 years of meditation—he was again allowed to speak.

"I quit," he said.

"Good," replied the monk. "All you do is complain, anyway."

# AUDIO TREASURES

*More of Uncle John's favorite old-time radio shows.*

## GUNSMOKE (CBS, 1952–61)

*Gunsmoke,* radio's first Western series for adults, is considered by many fans to be the best radio drama ever produced. The show's creators placed great emphasis on realism; episodes dealt with mature themes like scalpings, massacres, and the relationship between Marshall Dillon and Miss Kitty, the "saloon girl." (Although it was never stated explicitly, it was much clearer on the radio series than on the TV show that Kitty was a prostitute.) On *Gunsmoke* there was no guarantee of a happy ending, either—the good guys sometimes got killed, and it wasn't unusual for criminals to skip town before they were punished for their crimes.

**Things to Listen For:** The show's incredible attention to detail. If a character fired a Winchester rifle, the sound crew recorded a real Winchester rifle shot to use on the show. Saloon scenes were taped with a piano player in a roomful of extras who were milling around just as if they were in a real saloon. And does Marshall Matt Dillon's voice sound familiar? That's William Conrad, who worked on numerous other radio shows, did voiceovers on dozens of TV and radio commercials, and narrated the *Rocky & Bullwinkle* show. Why didn't he play Marshall Dillon on television? Conrad's radio portrayal was terrific, but TV producers thought he was too overweight to be believable as a U.S. marshall. Conrad finally did make it to TV—first in 1971, starring in the detective series *Cannon,* and again in 1987, starring in the appropriately titled *Jake and the Fatman* (hint: he didn't play Jake).

## JOURNEY INTO SPACE (BBC, 1953–58)

Unlike most science fiction programs which were complete flights of fancy, this British show was grounded in the real physics of space flight. In one episode a group of reporters is given a tour of a launch pad on the moon; the description of the spacecraft is so true to life that the modern listener may forget that the show predated the Apollo moon landing by 15 years. The realism helped make it one of most listened-to radio series in the history of the BBC, and the last one to attract a larger audience than the television shows that were on at the same time.

**Things to Listen For:** Lemmy, the clueless Cockney member of the crew. He has presumably spent years training for the first mission to the moon in episode 1, yet after the ship blasts off he is surprised to find out that he is weightless in space. Why? In the early 1950s, most listeners had no understanding of space flight; having someone explain it to Lemmy was the show's way of telling the audience what a trip to the moon would really be like.

## GANGBUSTERS (CBS/NBC/Mutual, 1935–1957)

*Gangbusters* wasn't the first show about gangsters vs. lawmen, but it was the first one based on the case files of real-life criminals. Creator Phillips H. Lord won the cooperation of FBI director J. Edgar Hoover by promising that he would only present stories based on closed cases—the ones in which the crooks had already been apprehended by the FBI.

**Things to Listen For:** Ever watch *America's Most Wanted*? (See page 329.) *Gangbusters* was the first show to broadcast the descriptions of real, at-large criminals who were wanted by police and the FBI.

## THE CHARLIE McCARTHY SHOW (NBC/CBS, 1937–56)

Edgar Bergen was a ventriloquist who got his big break in radio when he was discovered at a Hollywood party and invited to appear on the *Rudy Vallee Show*. He and his dummy, named Charlie McCarthy, were such a hit that they got their own radio show the following year. (Bergen's young daughter, Candice, also appeared on the show and later became a well-known actress.)

**Things to Listen For:** A ventriloquist act on the *radio*? One thing that made this improbable show a success was Charlie McCarthy's sharp wit. As a wooden dummy, he got away with insults, double entendres, and racy dialogue (for the time) that network censors would never have allowed to be spoken by "real" people. Mae West's risqué 1937 appearance—a "blasphemous" Adam and Eve sketch—sounds innocent today, but it got her banned from NBC. She didn't appear again on radio until 1968.

---

**Like fingerprints and snowflakes, no two Holstein cows have exactly the same pattern of spots.**

## THE GOON SHOW (BBC, 1951–1960)

The most influential comedy show ever broadcast by the BBC, *The Goon Show* was written by Spike Milligan and starred Milligan, Peter Sellers, and Harry Secombe. The show's bizarre, satirical sketches and clever sound effects revolutionized British comedy. The creators of *Monty Python's Flying Circus* and even the Beatles have cited the Goons as a major influence on their work.

**Things to Listen For:** Indian characters spouting genuine Hindi obscenities that were snuck past BBC censors. Also: laughs in odd places. The show was recorded before a live audience, and Harry Secombe was fond of yanking Sellers's suspenders off in mid-show, causing his pants to fall down. Does their speech sound slurred at times? Liquor was banned at the BBC, so the Goons drank milk during their broadcasts. (The milk was spiked with brandy.)

## OTHER FAVORITES

• *Calling All Detectives* (Syndicated/Mutual, 1945–50). A combination quiz show and detective drama starring actor Paul Barnes, who does the voices for every character. Once all the clues were in place, the show paused for a five-minute commercial break while the station called listeners chosen at random and asked them to solve the mystery on the air. When the five minutes were up, the drama resumed and the real solution was revealed.

• *Mary Noble, Backstage Wife* (Mutual/NBC, 1935–59). An unintentionally funny soap opera about a small-town girl from Iowa who marries Larry Noble, "a matinee idol of a million other women." Mary spent the next 24 years defending her marriage from the tramps and scam artists who continually try to pry her and her husband apart.

• *Richard Diamond, Private Detective* (NBC/ABC, 1949–53). This show about an NYPD cop turned private detective was written by Blake Edwards, who went on to direct the Pink Panther movies, as well as *Breakfast at Tiffany's*, *Days of Wine and Roses*, and *10*.

• *Queen for a Day* (Mutual, 1945–57). A game show in which contestants compete for fabulous prizes by sharing their real-life hard-luck stories with the studio audience. The audience then votes, and the woman with the most miserable life gets crowned "Queen for a Day"…and then goes back to her miserable life.

---

Belleville is the Unidentified Flying Object Capital of Wisconsin.

# IT'S A WEIRD, WEIRD WORLD

*News from the outer reaches of normal.*

## HITTING THE HIGH NOTES

"Mystery surrounds Ben Nevis, Britain's highest mountain. Why? A piano was discovered near its 4,418-foot summit. The instrument was found by volunteers from the John Muir Trust, a conservation charity. 'They couldn't believe their eyes,' said trust director Nigel Hawkins. 'The only thing that that was missing was the keyboard—and that's another mystery.' He added that a cookie wrapper with an expiration date of December 1986 was found under the piano, giving a clue as to when it was taken there, but not why."

—*The Guardian*

## LAST FISH STORY

"A Hungarian fisherman drowned while trying to catch a 150-lb. catfish. Gabor Komlosy was dragged into a river when he refused to let go of the line. The 53-year-old's body was later pulled from the Szamos river still clinging to his rod. The 4-foot monster catfish was still hooked on the end. Police in Hungary believe he had been yanked down the river bank by the fish. It then pulled him through the water until he hit his head on a rock and drowned."

—Sky News

## HANDY

"A man has been jailed on assault charges after a police officer, prosecutor, and courtroom bailiff became seriously ill after shaking hands with him. During a court appearance on a traffic charge, John Ridgeway pulled out a vial of an unknown liquid, rubbed his hands with the contents and insisted on shaking hands with the three people. All of them got sick within an hour, suffering from nausea, headaches, and numbness that lasted about a day. The FBI was running tests on the substance to identify it. Ridgeway, 41, told officials the vial contained olive oil."

—Associated Press

The last Bonaparte, Jerome Napoleon Bonaparte, died in 1945 after tripping over his dog's leash.

# ETHICALLY DISABLED

*There are few things more pathetic than people pretending to be disabled—and few things more satisfying than catching them.*

## FUTBOL FAKERS

Their dream was to watch their country's soccer team play in a World Cup game in Germany in 2006, but the admission price was more than the three Argentinians wanted to pay. Determined to see the match, they found a loophole: Discounted seats were being offered to disabled people. So they somehow got themselves three wheelchairs and rolled into the match against Holland, claiming a handicapped viewing spot near the field.

The ruse probably would have worked, too, if one of them hadn't gotten so excited after a play that he jumped out of his chair with his arms raised in the air. "A person near us thought there was a miracle happening," one of the fakers told reporters outside the stadium—which is where the three fans spent the second half of the game after security escorted them out (on foot).

## PARALYMPIC FAKERS

The 2000 International Paralympics were a resounding success for Spain: The country won 107 medals overall, highlighted by the gold medal awarded to its developmentally disabled basketball team. A few months later, one of the players, Carlos Ribagorda, made the shocking admission that "of the 200 Spanish Paralympic athletes, at least 15 had no physical or mental handicap." Ribagorda, a journalist for the Spanish magazine *Capital*, had joined the intellectually disabled basketball team to expose the corruption. In the two years Ribagorda played for the team, no one ever tested his I.Q. Not only that, says Ribagorda, the team was told to slow down their game so they wouldn't attract suspicion.

A subsequent international investigation concluded that only two members of the basketball team were intellectually disabled. In addition, as Ribagorda had discovered, some members of Spain's Paralympic track, tennis, and swimming teams were found to be only...*morally* handicapped.

## LAWSUIT FAKER

In 2006 Las Vegas authorities suspected that wheelchair-bound Laura Lee Medley was taking them for a ride. After four separate lawsuits against four California cities over faulty handicapped access to public buildings, investigators smelled fraud. They tracked Medley to Las Vegas, where they arrested the 35-year-old woman—who was sitting in her wheelchair. Medley immediately began complaining of pain and begged for medical attention. Skeptical—but not wanting to doubt her if she really was in pain—police officers drove her to a nearby hospital. But moments after she was wheeled through the entrance, the "paralyzed" woman got up and started sprinting through the hospital corridors. She was quickly apprehended and cuffed. Medley was charged with four counts of fraud and resisting arrest.

## BEAUTY PAGEANT FAKER

Dee Henderson was crowned Mrs. Minnesota International in a 1999 beauty pageant, thanks in part to the aerobic exercises she performed for the talent competition. Henderson owned and operated two businesses selling beauty pageant supplies, *and* was the director of three Midwest beauty pageants. Those are amazing accomplishments, especially considering the fact that at the same time, she was getting disability payments from the government. Henderson claimed she couldn't work, couldn't sit for more than 20 minutes at a time or lift anything heavier than her mail. She also had difficulty with "walking, kneeling, squatting, climbing, bending, reaching, and personal grooming." The injuries, she said, stemmed from a 1995 car accident. From 1996 to 2003, Henderson received Social Security benefits totaling $190,000.

But her case unraveled when a video taken by a private investigator showed her doing activities such as snorkeling and carrying heavy luggage (not to mention the aerobics). More damning evidence: an email in which Henderson claimed she would "keep going and going and going and going" like the Energizer Bunny. She did keep going...to prison for 46 months.

\*     \*     \*

If I die, I forgive you. If I recover, we shall see.
—**Spanish proverb**

---

The average child eats over 15 pounds of cereal in a year.

# TALK TO THE SWORD

*Dutch Schultz was a notorious New York mobster who made his name in bootlegging and numbers rackets. But Schultz had another claim to fame: the grisly story of his death and bizarre last words.*

## BACKGROUND

On October 23, 1935, 33-year-old Dutch Schultz (real name: Arthur Flegenheimer) was dining at the Palace Chophouse, a restaurant in Newark, New Jersey, that also served as a mob hideout. Schultz was in the bathroom when three Murder, Inc. hit men working for a rival gang burst in—"Charlie the Bug" Workman, Emanuel Weiss, and a third man known only as "Piggy." They went into the back room and shot Schultz's associates Otto Berman, Abe Landau, and Lulu Rosenkrantz. Schultz heard the shots but couldn't stop urinating fast enough to flee.

While he was still peeing, the hit men came into the bathroom. Schultz turned around and they shot him in the stomach. The bullet pierced his liver, colon, and gall bladder, and exited out his back.

Not wanting to be found dead with his pants unzipped in a men's room, Schultz stumbled into the restaurant; Rosenkrantz, still alive, called an ambulance from a phone booth and then collapsed. The police arrived first and loaded Schultz up on brandy to numb the pain. It didn't work. When they finally got to the hospital, Newark police sergeant Luke Conlon interrogated Schultz. In a state of physical agony, high fever, drunkenness, and morphine-induced euphoria, Schultz babbled on for nearly two hours. What follows is an actual transcript of Schultz's talkfest.

## LAST WORDS

**Schultz:** George, don't make no bull moves. What have you done with him? Oh, mama, mama, mama. Oh stop it, stop it; eh, oh, oh. Sure, sure, mama? Has it been in any other newspapers? Now listen, Phil, fun is fun. Aha...please! Papa! What happened to the sixteen? Oh, oh, he done it? Please...please...John, please. Oh, did you buy the hotel? You promised a million sure. Get out. I wish I knew. Please make it quick, fast, and furious. Please. Fast and furious. Please help me get out; I'm getting my wind back, thank God. Please, please, oh please. You will have to please tell him, you got no case? You get ahead with the dot dash system. Didn't I

---

Dark-roasted coffee is "weaker" than medium roast. Roasting burns off caffeine.

speak that time last night. Whose number is that in your pocketbook, Phil? 13780. Who was it? Oh, please, please. Reserve decision. Police, police, Henny and Frankie. Oh, oh, dog biscuit and when he is happy he doesn't get snappy please, please do this. Henny, Henny, Frankie! You didn't meet him; you didn't even meet me. The glove will fit what I say oh, kayiyi, kayiyi. Sure, who cares? When are you through! How do you know this? How do you know this? Well, then, oh, Cocoa; no…thinks he is a grandpa again and he is jumping around. No Hoboe and Poboe I think mean the same thing.

**Conlon:** Who shot you?

**Schultz:** The boss himself.

**Conlon:** He did?

**Schultz:** Yes, I don't know.

**Conlon:** What did he shoot you for?

**Schultz:** I showed him, boss; did you hear him meet me? An appointment. Appeal stuck. All right, mother.

**Conlon:** Was it the boss shot you?

**Schultz:** Who shot me? No one.

**Conlon:** We will help you.

**Schultz:** Will you help me up? Okay, I won't be such a big creep. Oh, mama. I can't go through with it, please. Oh, and then he clips me; come on. Cut that out, we don't owe a nickel; fold it; instead, fold it against him; I am a pretty good pretzeler. Winifred—Department of Justice. I even got it from the department. Sir, please stop it. Say listen, the last night.

**Conlon:** What did they shoot you for?

**Schultz:** I don't know, sir. Honestly I don't. I don't even know who was with me, honestly. I went to the toilet and when I reached the…the the boy came at me.

**Conlon:** The big fellow gave it to you?

**Schultz:** Yes, he gave it to me.

**Conlon:** Do you know who the big fellow was?

**Schultz:** No. See, George, if we wanted to break the ring. No, please I get a month. They did it. Come on. *(Unintelligible)* cut me off and says you are not to be the beneficiary of this will. I will be checked and double-checked and please pull for me. Will you pull? How many good ones and how many bad ones? Please! I had nothing with him. He was a cowboy in one of the seven days a week fight. No business; no hangout; no friends; nothing; just what you pick up and what you need. I don't know who shot me. Don't put anyone near this check—you might have—oh, please, please do it for me. Let me get up, sir, heh? In the olden days they waited and they waited.

---

**In 1908 New York City passed a law forbidding women to smoke in public.**

Please give me a shot. It is from the factory. Sure, that is a bad. Well, oh good ahead that happens for crying. I don't want harmony. I want harmony. Oh, mama, mama! Who give it to him? Who give it to him? Let me in the district-fire-factory that he was nowhere near. It smoldered. No, no. There are only ten of us and there are ten million fighting somewhere in front of you, so get your onions up and we will throw up the truce flag. Oh, please let me up. Please shift me. Police are here. Communistic...strike... baloney. Please, honestly this is a habit I get; sometimes I give it and sometimes I don't. Oh, I am all in. That settles it. Are you sure? Please let me get in and eat. Let him harass himself to you and then bother you. Please don't ask me to go there. I don't want to. I still don't want him in the path. It is no need to stage a riot. The sidewalk was in trouble and the bears were in trouble and I broke it up. Please put me in that room. Please keep him in control. My gilt-edged stuff and those dirty rats have tuned in. Please mother, don't tear, don't rip; that is something that shouldn't be spoken about. Please get me up, my friends. Please, look out. The shooting is a bit wild, and that kind of shooting saved a man's life. No payrolls. No walls. No coupons. That would be entirely out. Pardon me, I forgot I am a plaintiff and not defendant. Look out. Look out for him. Please. He owes me money; he owes everyone money. Why can't he just pull out and give me control? Please, mother, you pick me up now. Please, you know me. No. Don't you scare me. My friends think I do a better job. Police are looking for you all over. Be instrumental in letting us know. They are Englishmen and they are a type I don't know who is best, they or us. Oh, sir, get the doll a roofing. You can play jacks and girls do that with a softball and do tricks with it. I may take all events into consideration. No. No. And it is no. It is confused and its says no. A boy has never wept nor dashed a thousand kin. Did you hear me?

**Conlon:** Who shot you?

**Schultz:** I don't know.

**Conlon:** How many shots were fired?

**Schultz:** I don't know. None.

**Conlon:** How many?

**Schultz:** Two thousand. Come on, get some money in that treasury. We need it. Come on, please get it. I can't tell you to. That is not what you have in the book. Oh, please warden. What am I going to do for money? Please put me up on my feet at once. You are a hard-boiled man. Did you hear me? I would hear it, the Circuit Court would hear it, and the Supreme Court might hear it. If that ain't the payoff. Please crack down on the Chinaman's friends and Hitler's commander. I am sore and I am going to give you honey if I can. Mother is the best bet and don't let Satan draw you too fast.

---

Turkish turkeys don't gobble—they say *gloo-gloo*.

**Conlon:** What did the big fellow shoot you for?

**Schultz:** Him? John? Over a million, five million dollars.

**Conlon:** John shot you, we will take care of John.

**Schultz:** That is what caused the trouble. Look out. Please get me up. If you do this, you can go on and jump right here in the lake. I know who they are. They are French people. All right. Look out, look out. Oh, my memory is gone. A work relief police. Who gets it? I don't know and I don't want to know, but look out. It can be traced. He changed for the worse. Please look out; my fortunes have changed and come back and went back since that. It was desperate. I am wobbly. You ain't got nothing on him but we got it on his helper.

**Conlon:** Control yourself.

**Schultz:** But I am dying.

**Conlon:** No, you are not.

**Schultz:** Move on, Mick and mama. All right, dear, you have got to get it.

*(Schultz's wife, Francis, arrives.)*

**Mrs. Schultz:** This is Francis.

**Schultz:** Then pull me out. I am half crazy. They won't let me get up. They dyed my shoes. Open those shoes. Give me something. I am so sick. Give me some water, the only thing that I want. Open this up and break it so I can touch you. Dennie, please get me in the car.

**Conlon:** Who shot you?

**Schultz:** I don't know. I didn't even get a look. I don't know who can have done it. Anybody. Kindly take my shoes off. *(They're already off.)* No. There is a handcuff on them. The Baron does these things. I know what I am doing here with my collection of papers. It isn't worth a nickel to two guys like you or me but to a collector it is worth a fortune. It is priceless. I am going to turn it over to—turn you back to me, please Henry. I am so sick now. The police are getting many complaints. Look out. I want that G-note. Look out for Jimmy Valentine for he is an old pal of mine. Come on, Jim, come on. Okay, okay, I am all through. Can't do another thing. Look out mama, look out for her. You can't beat him. Police, mama, Helen, mother, please take me out. I will settle the indictment. Come on, open the soap duckets. The chimney sweeps. Talk to the sword. Shut up, you got a big mouth! Please come help me up, Henry. Max, come over here. French-Canadian bean soup. I want to pay. Let them leave me alone.

Schultz died two hours later, without saying another word.

---

# "THE GREATEST CANADIAN"

*Today, Canada has free universal health care. The man who made it happen:*
*former Saskatchewan premier Tommy Douglas. Here's his story.*

L IFE AND DEATH
In 1910, when Tommy Douglas was six years old, he injured
his leg and it never healed properly. Four years later he
developed a life-threatening bone infection, and because his family couldn't afford a specialist to treat it, the doctors wanted to
amputate the leg to stop the infection from spreading. Tommy's
leg was saved only by chance—a teaching surgeon took an interest
in the case and offered to operate on Tommy for free, provided
that his students could watch the procedure and learn from it.

Tommy never forgot the experience. A medical crisis could
affect anyone—what would happen to the people who weren't as
lucky as he had been? His situation wasn't at all unusual in the
early 20th century. In most industrialized nations, there were few
options if you were poor and happened to get sick. Hospitals
would occasionally admit "charity cases," but only rarely. For the
most part, if you needed life-saving surgery and couldn't pay for it,
you died.

## HUMAN RIGHTS

After spending his teens at a variety of jobs (printer, whiskey dis-
tiller, actor, boxer), Douglas became a Baptist minister and in 1930
took a job as a preacher at Calvary Baptist Church in Weyburn,
Saskatchewan. The rural, blue-collar town was devastated by both
a drought and the Great Depression. Even if families had money
for food, there was none left over for medicine. It reminded Douglas of his own near-tragedy from childhood. "I buried two young
men in their 30s with young families who died because there was
no doctor readily available and they hadn't the money to get proper care," he wrote. Douglas came to believe that medical care was a
basic human right and should be available to everyone.

In 1934 Douglas realized that he could do more for the poor in
politics than he could at a small-town church, and joined the Cooperative Commonwealth Federation. Like Douglas, they advocated

The year on a bottle of wine refers to when the grapes were picked, not when the wine was bottled.

health care access. (The party also agitated for social reforms to end the Depression, including workers' compensation and unemployment insurance.) Douglas ran on the CCF ticket for the Saskatchewan legislature in 1934...and lost. But in 1935, he won a seat in the national legislature, the House of Commons.

## WINS AND LOSSES

Douglas served in the House for nine years but never got the support he needed to institute health care on the national level. The CCF wasn't well regarded in mainstream Canadian politics; their idea of tax-supported, government-run medicine was too reminiscent of the complete state control of the Soviet Union. But Douglas was no communist, and had no interest in totalitarian government. He just wanted universal health care.

Frustrated with the lack of progress at the national level, Douglas resigned from the House in 1944, returned to Saskatchewan, and tried to get his health care plan going on the provincial level. The voters were with him: In the 1944 election, the CCF won 47 of the 52 seats in the Saskatchewan legislature. And since Douglas was the head of the Saskatchewan CCF, the election landslide made him the premier (governor) at age 39. Now he'd have a chance to prove to the rest of Canada that his social welfare programs, especially universal health care, could succeed.

## PRESCRIPTION FOR SUCCESS

Douglas's entire plan for governing was built around the idea of universal health care, or "medicare." Seventy percent of the 1944 budget was allocated to health, welfare, and education. That year, Douglas's government passed 72 social and economic reform laws, most of them directly or indirectly related to health care:

• Douglas ordered the University of Saskatchewan to expand to include a medical school to create and train more doctors.

• Utilities, lumber, fisheries, and other corporations became state-run, generating substantial revenue to pay for health care.

• Douglas and his cabinet took a 28% pay cut.

• Retirees were immediately given free medical, hospital, and dental coverage. Treatment of cancer, tuberculosis, mental illness, and venereal disease were made free to everyone in Saskatchewan.

By 1947, Saskatchewan had one of the strongest economies in

Canada. After just three years as premier, Douglas made the province financially stable enough to introduce universal hospitalization for all residents of Saskatchewan for an annual fee of $5.

Free hospitalization and surgery were in place, but drugs and doctors visits were not. There just wasn't enough money. Still, the rest of Canada was beginning to see how well Douglas's program was working and warmed to the idea. When new prime minister John Diefenbaker—a conservative—was elected in 1958, he offered matching federal funds to any province that started a free hospitalization program. The following year, Saskatchewan had a budget surplus, and in 1959, after 15 years of work, Douglas was finally able to introduce complete universal health care to the province.

## JUST THE BEGINNING

Seeing how well Saskatchewan did with health care, legislation began in 1961 to expand it to all of Canada, and by 1966 it was in place, paid for by the provincial and federal governments, each contributing 50%. His goal reached, Douglas returned to national politics in the early 1960s. He led the New Democratic Party, a new version of the CCF, and held seats in the House of Commons off and on before retiring from politics in 1979. In 1988 he was elected to the Canadian Medical Hall of Fame. He's one of the few non-doctors honored, but without Douglas's efforts, the Canadian medical—and social—landscape would be far different today.

**Some other Tommy Douglas facts:**

• In a 2004 poll conducted by the Canadian Broadcasting Corporation, Canadians were asked to name "the greatest Canadian." Tommy Douglas was voted #1.

• Douglas's daughter, Shirley Douglas, was arrested in 1969 for ties to the Black Panthers—they had helped Douglas organize a free breakfast program for African-American children living in poor sections of Los Angeles. Following her arrest, Tommy Douglas said "I'm proud that my daughter believes that hungry children should be fed, whether they are Black Panthers or white Republicans."

• Actor Kiefer Sutherland is the grandson of Tommy Douglas. (His mother is Shirley Douglas.) As a boy, Sutherland asked his grandfather what defined a Canadian. Douglas's response: the harsh winters and Medicare.

# THE NIAGARA FALLS MUMMY

*Canada has never had a king or queen of its own...but did it have a pharaoh? Here's the story of a famous missing mummy.*

WHO'S THAT GIRL?
Have you ever heard of Nefertiti? After Cleopatra, she's probably the most famous queen of ancient Egypt. Nefertiti was the wife of Akhenaton, who ruled from 1353 to 1336 B.C. A famous limestone bust of her is on display at the Egyptian Museum in Berlin, and because of this she is a popular historical figure in Germany.

Queen Nefertiti's mummy has been missing for more than 3,000 years...or has it? In 1966 a German tourist named Meinhard Hoffmann paid a visit to the Niagara Falls Museum, a cheesy tourist museum and freak show on the Canadian side of the falls. He looked at their famous Egyptian mummy exhibit, which had been displayed alongside two-headed calves, five-legged pigs, and other fascinating oddities for nearly 150 years. One mummy in particular caught his attention: It was unwrapped—removing a mummy's linen bandages had been common practice in the 19th century—and the body was partially covered by a shroud. Hoffmann wondered if the mummy might actually be Nefertiti, but how could he prove it? He couldn't—there was no way to verify his suspicion. Still, he took plenty of pictures of it before returning to Germany.

## CROSS MY HEART

A decade passed. Then one day in 1976 Hoffmann read in an article that Egyptian queens of Nefertiti's era were mummified with their left arm, but not their right arm, folded high across the chest. He remembered that one arm had been folded across the naked mummy's chest, and when he dug out his photographs, he saw that it was indeed the left arm. *Could it be Nefertiti?* He couldn't tell whether the right arm was also folded across the chest, because it was obscured by the shroud.

Hey, sports fans—how big is home plate? (It's five-sided: 17" x 8½" x 12" x 12" x 8½".)

Hoffmann got a photograph of the Nefertiti bust in the Egyptian Museum and compared it to his photographs of the mummy. Sure, the mummy's face was shriveled and wrinkly, while the face on the bust was pristine and beautiful. Even so, Hoffman thought they were astonishingly similar.

## ON SECOND THOUGHT...

Having convinced himself that the mummy was Nefertiti, Hoffmann set out to convince others as well. Over the next several years he gradually developed his case, and in 1985 he managed to persuade a TV producer at Germany's Channel Two that he'd found the lost mummy. The producer made plans to do a TV special on the subject and flew Hoffmann and a camera crew to the Niagara Falls Museum. There an Egyptologist would remove the shroud and examine the mummy to confirm that it was the mummy of a queen, and most likely that of Nefertiti.

The examination got no further than the removal of the shroud—as soon as the Egyptologist removed it, it was clear that *both* arms were folded across the chest, not just one, which pretty much ruled out the possibility of the mummy being a queen. It was also clear that the naked mummy was anatomically a male, which ruled out the queen theory for sure.

## LOOK ON THE BRIGHT SIDE

That was a pretty big letdown after such a huge buildup, but it was here that Hoffmann demonstrated a remarkable capacity for optimism. Not a queen? Not a problem—"It must be a pharaoh!" he exclaimed.

Hoffmann actually had a point: Kings of the period *were* mummified with both arms folded high across the chest. That (and their male anatomy) was what distinguished them from the mummies of queens. But kings weren't the only people in Egypt who were embalmed with their arms folded that way: About 1,300 years after Queen Nefertiti passed from the scene, Egypt was annexed by the Roman Empire and it then became fashionable for commoners to be embalmed with their hands folded high across their chest. This made it difficult to tell an ancient king from a newer commoner. The two had been confused many times in the past, especially by amateurs and wishful thinkers like Hoffmann.

## BACK TO SQUARE ONE

The suspicion that the mummy was a Roman-era commoner seemed to be confirmed when the mummy was X-rayed and dark masses were seen inside the chest cavity. Mummies from Nefertiti's era had their organs removed and their chest cavities stuffed with linen to retain their natural shape. During the Roman Era, on the other hand, the organs were wrapped in linen and placed back in the chest cavity. The dark masses in the X-rays appeared to be organ packets, which led the group to conclude that the mummy was that of a commoner of the Roman Era.

Who wants to watch a TV show about a mummified commoner? Channel Two cancelled the special—it never aired.

## DEJA VIEW

That's where things stayed until the late 1980s, when an Egyptology student named Gayle Gibson began visiting the museum in Niagara Falls to study four well-preserved coffins that were part of the Egyptian collection. She noticed the folded arms on the mummy and wondered about it, too, but the idea of a royal mummy lying undiscovered in such tacky surroundings for so many years seemed too farfetched to be true.

Then, in 1991, Gibson brought a mummy expert named Aidan Dodson, who was visiting from the U.K., to look at the collection. As soon as Dodson laid eyes on the mummy and saw its exquisite condition, the obvious skill of the embalmers, and of course the position of the arms, he, too, began to seriously suspect that the mummy might be a pharaoh. The next step was to try to get a scientific estimate of the mummy's age using carbon dating. In 1994 the museum agreed to allow the mummy to be tested, and scientists gave it a date of somewhere between 800 and 1500 B.C.—far too old to have been embalmed during the Roman Era. This mummy was no commoner.

## HEADING SOUTH

So who was it? Given the mummy's age, the chances that it was indeed that of a king increased considerably. But events still moved slowly; it wasn't until after the Niagara Falls Museum closed in 1998 and the entire Egyptian collection was sold to Emory University in Atlanta (for $2 million) that further testing was done. Researchers at the university submitted the mummy to a battery of sophisticated tests that had not been available previously, including CT scans and computer imaging. This enabled them to get a much better look at the dark masses in the chest, which turned out not to be organ packets after all. They were tightly wound rolls of linen, which have been found in other royal mummies of the period.

The piece of evidence that had been thought to rule out a royal connection now seemed to confirm it, as did a CT scan of the skull. It showed that the skull cavity contained a large amount of tree resin, a precious and very rare material in ancient Egypt—further evidence that the mummy was indeed that of a king.

## THE CANDIDATE

But *which* king? As researchers unlocked the mummy's secrets, mounting circumstantial evidence pointed increasingly away from other missing pharaohs and toward a single candidate: Ramses I, founder of the 19th Dynasty, which ruled Egypt from 1291 to 1183 B.C. On the throne for less than two years, he was the grandfather of Ramses II, or Ramses the Great, whose 66-year reign was the second longest in Egyptian history.

Ramses I's body was believed to have been removed from a tomb containing several royal mummies in the mid-19th century, at about the same time that a collector representing the Niagara Falls Museum was touring Egypt acquiring the mummies that ended up in the collection. He bought it for £7, or about $34.

## LIKE FATHER, LIKE SON

Ramses I's mummy had been missing from Egypt for more than 140 years, but those of his son, Seti I, and his grandson Ramses the Great are both in the Egyptian Museum in Cairo. Their faces bear a striking resemblance to the mummy from the Niagara Falls Museum, and that similarity was backed up when X-rays of the mummy's skull was compared to X-rays of all of the Egyptian Museum's royal mummies, taken in the 1960s. The shape of a human skull is hereditary, so if the mummy was related to Seti I and Ramses II, measurements of his skull were likely to be similar to theirs. Sure enough, the measurements of the Niagara Falls mummy matched those of Seti I and Ramses II more closely than those of any other royal mummy in the Egyptian Museum.

The case for the mummy being Ramses I is based entirely on circumstantial evidence, but there's so much of it that there is now very little room for doubt: The Niagara Falls mummy is almost certainly that of a king, and most likely that of Ramses I.

## A BARGAIN AT TWICE THE PRICE

Scooping up the Niagara Falls Museum's entire Egyptian collection for $2 million seemed to be a pretty good bargain—the mummy of Ramses I is a priceless treasure. But rather than keep it, as soon as the mummy's identity was established to everyone's satisfaction, Emory University announced that they were giving the mummy to Egypt. In October 2003, Ramses was flown back to his home after an absence of 150 years.

"There was never any question about whether the mummy would be returned to Egypt if it proved to be a royal," the university museum's curator, Peter Lacovara, told *National Geographic*. "It was simply the right thing to do."

## DELAYED GRATIFICATION

So who gets credit for finding Ramses I in his hiding place at Niagara Falls? Meinhard Hoffmann thinks it should go to him. Even when "experts" assured him that the mummy was a commoner, he was so convinced it was a pharaoh that he documented his claim in writing and hired a lawyer to notarize it. In the document, Hoffmann even suggested three possible identities for the mummy: Aye, Horemheb…and Ramses I.

"Here's the real reason I did that," says Hoffmann. "Because if all of a sudden you come out and say, 'Oh, I knew all that 20 years ago,' people will doubt you and say you're nothing but an opportunist."

\*     \*     \*

## FLUSH LIKE AN EGYPTIAN

The birthplace of the toilet seat (and the human litter box) was the ancient Egyptian city of Akhetaten. There is archaeological evidence that around 1350 B.C., "seats" made of wood, stone, and pottery were commonly placed over large bowls of sand.

# MORE ACTS
# OF SEDITION!

*What can you say about freedom of speech? Anything you want. But at a few points during America's history, that right was called into question. (For a background on sedition, turn to page 258.)*

(For a background on sedition, turn to page 258.)

## THE GREAT WAR

T HE GREAT WAR
President Woodrow Wilson won reelection in 1916 largely because "he kept us out of the war," which became the unofficial slogan of his campaign. That war was World War I (or "The Great War," as it was known then), which had been raging in Europe since 1914. The United States' position of "noninvolvement" was widely supported by the American people. A big reason was that a large segment of the American people—fully one-third of the entire population—were immigrants. Most of them were from Europe, and there were many different sentiments regarding the many nations involved in the war.

But by 1917 the mood in America had shifted. German submarines had been attacking civilian ships for two years by then, including the British passenger ship, the *Lusitania*, in an assault that killed 1,200 people, 129 of them Americans. Then, in March, the "Zimmerman telegram" was released—a secret message sent from Germany to Mexico, intercepted and decoded by the British, that proposed an alliance between the two nations against the United States. The ensuing outrage led to a dramatic change in public opinion, and on April 6, 1917, Wilson declared war on Germany.

## THE WAR ON HYPHENS

Wilson had a delicate game to play with the public. Between 1900 and 1915, more than 15 million people emigrated to the United States, most of them from Germany. Wilson feared that these new Americans might feel more loyalty to their homeland (on whom he had just declared war) than to their adopted country, and that their conflicting attachments might hurt conscription efforts or, worse, induce them to spy for Germany.

The next largest group of immigrants were the Irish, and the

Easter Rising, an outbreak of violence against the English by the Irish that would lead to the formation of the Irish Republican Army, had taken place in April of 1916. England was now an ally in the war, and Wilson feared Irish-Americans would not support a war on the side of their age-old oppressor. "Any man who carries a hyphen around with him," Wilson said, referring to German- and Irish-American immigrants, "carries a dagger that he is ready to plunge into the vitals of the republic." Feelings such as these led to the passing of the Espionage Act in 1917, which made it a crime to aid an enemy during wartime. In 1918 it was amended with the Sedition Act.

## WATCH WHAT YOU SAY

The Sedition Act made it a crime to "utter, print, write, or publish any disloyal, profane, scurrilous, or abusive language about the form of government of the United States, or the military or naval forces of the United States, or the flag." One of the more controversial sections of the law was that it allowed the postmaster general to refuse to deliver any publications he deemed unfriendly to the war—any magazine or newspaper that criticized the president or the war. In essence, the Acts made it illegal to criticize in almost any way—through speech or through the press—the American government or its involvement in the war.

Opponents of the law saw it as a way to silence political dissent. Eugene Debs, a union leader and head of the Socialist party who had run for president against Wilson in 1912 (he got nearly a million of the 15 million total votes), was arrested for giving a speech against the war. He was sentenced to 20 years in prison. Rosa Pastor Stokes, another prominent Socialist and a feminist, was arrested for writing a Letter to the Editor of the *Kansas City Star*, saying "no government which is for the profiteers can also be for the people. I am for the people while the government is for the profiteers." She was sentenced to 10 years in prison.

The laws also fueled the already widespread problem of prejudice against immigrants. And that was especially true in Montana.

## MONTANA

When the federal government amended the Espionage Act in 1918, it did so by copying, almost word for word, the Sedition Act that the Montana legislature had passed earlier that year. Some historians say the law was largely a result of efforts by the Anaconda Copper Mining Company, the largest industrial employer in the state, to quash growing activity by labor organizers.

More than half of the 78 people convicted there were immigrants, most of them poor blue-collar workers: miners, farmers, butchers, and bartenders. All but three of them had simply said something in public and were turned in to police. A few of them had said things that most people would consider inflammatory, such as the woman who said that "she wished the people would revolt and that she would shoulder a gun and get the president the first one." (She served two years in prison.)

But most of the so-called seditious statements were benign criticisms. A liquor salesman in a bar was reported to have said that wartime food regulations were a "joke." He got a 7-to-20-year prison sentence for that. A furniture salesman standing in a lobby of a motel said, "This is a rich man's war and we have no business in it." He, too, was sentenced to 7 to 20 years. One man served 10 months because somebody claimed he had said something critical ...even though they couldn't remember exactly what it was.

More than 1,500 people nationwide were arrested before the Sedition Act was repealed in 1921 (the Espionage Act remains in place). No new laws regarding sedition have been enacted since.

## THE PARDONS

In October 2005, University of Montana, Missoula, journalism professor Clem Work published the book *Darkest Before Dawn: Sedition and Free Speech in the American West*. The book sparked law professor Jeff Renz to ask seven of his students to see if they could find legal grounds for posthumous pardons of the "seditionists." They contacted living relatives of the convicted, and in March 2006 wrote to Governor Brian Schweitzer to urge him to formally pardon them. Schweitzer, a descendant of German immigrants himself, was happy to do it.

On May 3, 2006, Work, Renz and his students, and 40 family members of the long-dead "criminals" gathered for a ceremony in the capitol rotunda in Helena, where they watched Schweitzer sign the proclamation of pardon. Drew Briner, the grandson of Herman Bausch, a German immigrant who served 28 months in prison, read from his grandfather's memoirs, written long after his imprisonment: "No, I do not regret what I have done or rather what I refused to do," Briner read. "I have lost much, but I am more than ever in possession of my soul, my self-respect, and the love and affection of my beautiful wife. I end with a prayer for the early establishment of world peace, for a greater humanity, a greater love among men."

"Neighbor informing on neighbor—this isn't the American way, it isn't the Montana way, it isn't the cowboy way," Governor Schweitzer concluded. "We weren't the only state to have this kind of hysteria, but we will be the first state to say, 'We had it wrong.'" His pardons were the first in Montana's history.

*     *     *

## HOW TO PLAY WITH "TOUNGE OF FROG"
*The misspelled, mistranslated English
instructions for a toy made in Taiwan.*

• Frog. If it is thrown with full of your strenght, it will spit out the tounge, which is like the genuine one from the frog.

• A product has the stickness and is just like a soft rubber band with high contractility. It can be played to stick the remote objects.

• Inspite of it is sticky, it is never like the chewing guns which is glued tightly and cannot be separated.

• If the stickness is not good enough, it can be washed by soap. After it is dried, it can be used continously many times.

• The packing paper has printed the bug picture, which can be cut as per the black frame and placed on the table; then you can stick the picture with your tounge of frog.

Cautions:

• Never throw out the other person's head.

• Inspite of it is non-toxic, it cannot be eaten.

• Never pull out tounge of frog hard, as it might be separated.

• Never put on surface of any object, shall keep in polybag.

• Its content has the oil, so if it touches on cloth, precious object or wall, the stains will remain if you don't care about it.

8 flavors of NECCO wafers: lemon, orange, lime, clove, cinnamon, wintergreen, licorice, chocolate.

# CAN YOU PASS THE U.S. CITIZENSHIP TEST?

*Bad news! You were supposed to use a #2 pencil on your citizenship test on page 334, and you used a ballpoint pen. Let's try it again. This time there are 17 "hard" questions. (The answers are on page 517.)*

**1.** What is the most important right granted to United States citizens?

**2.** Who was the principal author of the Declaration of Independence?

**3.** How many amendments are there to the U.S. Constitution?

**4.** If both the president and the vice president die, who becomes president?

**5.** Name the original 13 colonies.

**6.** What three qualifications does the U.S. Constitution require of candidates for president?

**7.** In what year was the U.S. Constitution written?

**8.** Name your U.S. representative and your two senators.

**9.** Name the four amendments that guarantee or address voting rights.

**10.** What officials and departments make up the executive branch of the federal government?

**11.** What is the introduction to the U.S. Constitution called?

**12.** Whose rights are guaranteed by the U.S. Constitution and the Bill of Rights?

**13.** Who was president during the Civil War?

**14.** Name the major river running north to south that divides the United States.

**15.** What type of democratic government does the U.S. have?

**16.** What is the basic belief of the Declaration of Independence?

**17.** Where is the White House located? (Include the street address.)

---

**Thanks, Mom: Clark Gable was listed on his birth certificate as a girl.**

# RARE CONDITIONS

*If you're like Uncle John, when you get an ailment—say, a cold—you ask yourself, "Why is it called a 'cold?'" If you get one of these odd diseases, you probably won't have to ask how it got its name.*

• **MAPLE SYRUP URINE DISEASE.** An inherited metabolic disease that makes the urine and sweat smell like maple syrup.

• **KABUKI MAKEUP SYNDROME.** This birth defect causes facial features to distort, resembling the overpronounced and elongated made-up faces of Japanese Kabuki actors.

• **PRUNE-BELLY SYNDROME.** An absence of abdominal muscles gives the stomach a wrinkled, puckered look and a severe pot belly that stretches out grotesquely.

• **JUMPING FRENCHMAN.** An acquired condition first discovered in the 19th century among Canadian lumberjacks. Patients have extreme reactions to sudden noises or surprises: they flail their arms, jump in the air, cry, scream, and hit people.

• **HAIRY TONGUE.** Due to tobacco use or poor oral hygiene, the tiny hairs on the tongue grow to be several inches long and the tongue itself turns black.

• **FOREIGN ACCENT SYNDROME.** After a severe brain injury or stroke, a person begins speaking their native language with a foreign accent. English-speaking Americans might suddenly sound Russian, for example.

• **WANDERING SPLEEN.** The muscles that hold the spleen in position are missing or undeveloped, causing the spleen to "wander" around the lower abdomen and pelvic region.

• **ALICE-IN-WONDERLAND SYNDROME.** Vision is distorted, making objects appear much smaller than they actually are. For example, a house may appear to be the size of a shoebox or a cat may look no bigger than a mouse.

---

North Dakota is the only state in the U.S. never to have had an earthquake.

# BINGHAM'S LIST

*You've probably heard of Oskar Schindler, but how about Hiram Bingham? Here's the recently uncovered story of a U.S. State Department employee who secretly helped thousands of Jews escape Europe during World War II.*

## CHARMED LIFE

Hiram Bingham IV was born into a prominent New England family. His ancestors settled in Connecticut in 1650, his great-grandfather was a missionary in the South Pacific, and his father was a globe-trekking archaeologist and senator. Hiram attended the best schools, and the world was wide open to him when he graduated from Yale University in 1925. Like his relatives, he immediately went overseas—he worked in Japan and traveled through India—then, at his father's behest, returned home to attend law school.

But young Bingham had other ideas: He yearned to be far, far away again. So after less than a year of law school, he dropped out and took the Foreign Service exam, then landed a job with the State Department. After some paper-pushing assignments in China, Poland, and England, in 1939 Bingham was given a post as vice consul at the U.S. consulate in Marseille, France.

## ESCAPE CLAUSES

Within a year, World War II was underway in Europe. Germany invaded France in June 1940; France surrendered and agreed to a Nazi-controlled puppet government in the southern part of the country, called the Vichy regime. Meanwhile, thousands of Jewish refugees from Austria, Germany, and Poland were passing through southern France, trying to get out of Europe as quickly as possible to escape the Nazis. Their favored destination: the United States, which hadn't yet entered the war.

But the American government didn't want the refugees. It didn't want to antagonize Germany, or get involved in the escalating European conflict. Plus, thousands of political refugees would put added strain on the country's financial resources, and there was always the possibility that they could be spies. Congress imposed immigration limits, decreasing the number of visas allowed to central Europeans from 27,000 in 1939 to 5,000 in 1940—not nearly enough to go around. To further hinder the visa process in southern France, the consulate was moved from downtown Marseille to the less-accessible suburb of Montredon.

## BOLD MANEUVERS

Bingham didn't care about the restrictions; he knew they weren't fair. Every day outside his office window, he saw thousands of Jewish people waiting in a line that stretched for miles. By leaving them in Europe, he knew, the United States was ultimately sending them to their deaths. Bingham decided to use his position as vice consul and subvert the system: At work, he granted as many visas as he legally could. Outside of work, he came up with some creative ways to get the refugees out of the country.

• German novelist Lion Feuchtwanger was jailed for writing anti-Nazi articles. He fled to France, where he was caught and sent to a prison camp. Bingham met Feuchtwanger in a remote section of the camp, snuck him out, and dressed him in a woman's coat, dark glasses, and head shawl. He told police at checkpoints that the novelist was his elderly mother-in-law. Feuchtwanger made it to the United States.

• Until he could get them to the United States, Bingham hid refugees in his villa, including the family of German writer Thomas Mann and artist Alma Mahler.

• He forged papers allowing refugees to cross from France into Spain, and then to Portugal. Just in case, he'd stuff their pockets with cigarettes to bribe German guards.

• Bingham would lie to prison camp guards, demanding the release of certain Jewish prisoners by producing fake documentation that proved the prisoner was American and could not be held. He got the French painter Marc Chagall out this way. Other artists Bingham helped escape: Max Ernst, Jacques Lipchitz, and Marcel Duchamp.

• Bingham personally funded many escapes. His consulate salary didn't even cover his rent, but he had a large family inheritance to work with: his mother was the heiress to the Tiffany jewelry fortune. That money paid for bribes, travel expenses, and forged visas.

## THE JIG IS UP

German prison officials eventually complained to the Vichy government about Bingham's "subversive activity." They in turn complained to the U.S. government. In September 1940, Secretary of State Cordell Hull warned Bingham, in a letter to the French consulate, not to smuggle out refugees, because "they are carrying on acts evading the laws of countries with which the United States maintains friendly relations."

Bingham ignored the letter and kept on forging documents, hiding refugees, and granting visas. In April 1941, the U.S. State Department had finally had enough. They transferred him to Buenos Aires, Argentina, far from the war. Bingham's superiors thought this would get him out of their hair. It didn't. After the war's end in 1945, he started reporting on Nazi activities in Argentina, including evidence of the transfer of Nazi assets to South American banks and sightings of fugitive war criminals. But Bingham's reports were ignored. Frustrated, he quit his job in 1946 and returned to his family's Connecticut estate.

Bingham never worked again. He lived off his inheritance and focused on his hobbies: tennis, painting, and playing the cello. He rarely spoke of his wartime activities—he actually felt guilty. "I remember him saying there were so many more he could have saved and didn't," his daughter Tiffany said.

## RECOGNITION

It was only after Bingham's death in 1988 that his children discovered the full extent of what their father had done during World War II. When William Bingham was cleaning out his father's house, he found a hidden pantry behind the fireplace containing a box with his father's wartime journal as well as letters, photos, and other materials...documenting nearly every person he'd helped escape, more than 2,500 people in all.

The Bingham family lobbied the government for recognition of their father's heroics. It finally came in 2004. At a lavish ceremony, Secretary of State Colin Powell presented an award for "constructive dissent" to Hiram Bingham's family. In 2006 he was honored on a postage stamp. Hiram Bingham was no longer an insubordinate—he was a hero.

# IN THE BLOOD

Other famous Binghams:

• Bingham's great-grandfather, the first Hiram Bingham (1789–1869), led the first missionary group to the Hawaiian Islands in 1819, and adapted the Hawaiian language to a written form, enabling Hawaiians to read and write for the first time. He also translated the Bible into Hawaiian. His group established schools, introduced Western medicine, and took the first census of Hawaii.

• Hiram Bingham, Jr. was an ordained minister and a linguist. He led missions to the Marquesas Islands and Micronesia. He translated the Bible into Gilbertese (a major language of Micronesia) and wrote dictionaries, books, and hymnals in that language. From 1877 to 1880, he was the U.S. government's advisor on Hawaiian affairs.

• Rather than follow the family into religious work (and poverty), Hiram Bingham III, Bingham's father, joined the academic world and married into money. Later he went into politics, serving as a Connecticut delegate at the 1920 Republican National Convention, and as the state's lieutenant governor in 1922. In 1925 he was elected to the Senate, where he served for eight years. But it was as a professor of Latin American studies at Yale that he made his mark. He led several expeditions into South America, and in 1911 stumbled upon the lost Incan city of Machu Picchu. Does the college professor–archaeologist–jungle adventurer image sound familiar? It should: Hiram Bingham III was widely reported to be the inspiration for the movie character Indiana Jones.

\*　　\*　　\*

# IRONIC, ISN'T IT?

"Police in Daytona Beach are investigating the burglary of the police chief's home over the weekend that took place while he was giving a lecture on crime prevention. Police Chief Michael Chitwood was speaking to Neighborhood Watch members Friday about working with the police department to prevent burglaries when his home was targeted. Chitwood returned home to find the place ransacked and his TV, stereo, laptop, watch, and other items missing."

—WKMG-TV (Orlando, Florida)

W.C. Fields was the first choice for the wizard in *The Wizard of Oz*. (He was too busy to do it.)

# THE ÜBER TUBER

*Oh, the poor potato—a symbol of laziness (couch potato) and
unhealthy eating (cheese fries). But it deserves much better. Here's
how the lowly potato altered the course of human history.*

## SPUDS OF THE INCAS

For at least 4,000 years, potatoes have been cultivated in
the Peruvian Andes. The Incas called them *papas*, and
although the flowers are toxic (they're members of the deadly
nightshade family), the part that grows underground—the tuber—
is one of the healthiest foods humans have ever cultivated. Consider this: The average potato has only 100 calories, but provides
45% of the U.S. Recommended Daily Allowance of vitamin C;
15% of vitamin B6; 15% of iodine; and 10% of niacin, iron, and
copper. Potatoes are also high in potassium and fiber, with no fat
and almost no sodium.

But the papas that the Incas cultivated looked more like purple
golf balls than today's potatoes. More than 5,000 different varieties grew in the Andes, and there were more than 1,000 Incan
words to describe them. The potato was so integral to Incan culture
that they buried their dead with potatoes (for food in the afterlife)
and measured time based on how long it took a potato to cook.

## THE EDIBLE STONE

When the Spanish conquistadors invaded the New World in the
1500s, they resisted this strange new food at first, not wanting to
lower themselves to eating anything so "primitive." But when
their own food stores ran low, the Spaniards were forced to eat
potatoes. They liked them so much that they brought some tubers
back to Europe in 1565.

Europeans balked at what they called the "edible stone." It was
dirty, had poisonous leaves, and tasted horrible when eaten raw
(which led to indigestion). The Catholic Church condemned
potatoes as "unholy" because there was no mention of them in the
Bible. Farmers started growing them, but only to feed livestock.
It's amazing that potatoes ever caught on, but thanks to a few key
events, that's exactly what happened.

## KING'S EDICT: JUST EAT IT

The potato's first big boost in Europe came from Frederick the Great, ruler of Prussia. In the 1740s, Prussia was mired in a war against Austria. Faced with the prospect of his nation's crops (and food supply) being trampled by invading armies, Frederick urged his farmers to grow potatoes. Why? Because potatoes grow underground. A potato field could be marched over or even burned, and survive, where wheat and barley fields would be devastated.

But the Prussian people didn't understand why the king wanted them to eat animal fodder, and most refused. So Frederick sent his personal chefs out to travel the countryside and distribute potato recipes to his subjects. When that didn't work, he issued an edict that anyone who refused to eat potatoes would have their ears cut off. Potatoes caught on relatively quickly in Prussia after that.

## PRISON FOOD

But they didn't in France. Along with most other French people, King Louis XVI reviled the potato. "It has a pasty taste," wrote an 18th-century French historian. "The natural insipidity, the unhealthy quality of this food, which is flatulent and indigestible, has caused it to be rejected from refined households."

During the Seven Years War (1756–1763), a French pharmacist named Antoine Parmentier was imprisoned in Germany, where he was fed the same food as the pigs: potatoes. But when he was released, he felt stronger and healthier than before his imprisonment. He credited his health to the potato and became its biggest advocate. Granted an audience with the king, Parmentier told his prison story and urged him to fund a series of potato farms to feed the hungry. Louis was intrigued, but not enough to carry out Parmentier's grand scheme. Instead, he donated a few acres of the worst possible land near Paris. Historically, nothing would grow there— nothing, that is, until Parmentier grew potatoes. They thrived.

But how would Parmentier convince his fellow citizens to eat them? Knowing that people usually want what they can't have, Parmentier devised a plan. First, he positioned soldiers around his field in order to "protect" the valuable crop from theft. Second, he instructed the soldiers to take bribes and allow peasants to sneak in at night to steal the spuds. The plan worked, and within a few decades, potato farms became as common as wineries in France.

In 1767 Benjamin Franklin traveled to Paris, where he attended a banquet hosted by Parmentier consisting of nothing but potato dishes. Franklin was instantly won over by their taste and versatility and took some seedlings home to the Colonies, where he gave them to his friend, Thomas Jefferson. Jefferson, too, was enthusiastic about the vegetable and urged every farmer he knew to grow it. Yet even with the statesman's endorsement, the potato didn't catch on quickly in the Colonies. The Old World cultural and religious stigmas against it were still too strong.

## THE BLIGHT

It was a different story in Ireland. The potato, first brought there around 1590, quickly became one of the country's main crops. The Irish climate and soil—in many areas too poor to grow grain—were perfect for growing potatoes. In addition, potatoes could go straight from the earth to the kitchen without having to be refined at a mill, which made the crop very appealing to the poor. The potato is actually credited with saving Ireland from famine…but no one knew how devastating Ireland's reliance on it would become.

For all of its attributes, the potato has one major drawback: it is susceptible to potato blight. Caused by a funguslike organism called *Phytophthora infestans*, which travels in airborne spores, an outbreak can destroy every potato plant for hundreds of miles. Even today, scientists have not found a cure.

In 1845 Ireland was hit hard with blight, and the country's entire potato crop failed. As food stores dwindled, Ireland begged neighboring England, which ruled them at the time, for help. But the British did nothing. When the blight hit again the following year, the British sent soldiers and farmers to help out, but by then there was little anyone could do—tens of thousands of acres of potato fields were dead or dying. When the crops failed yet again in 1847, families that relied on their potato crops to pay rent were evicted from their land, causing a mass exodus from Ireland. Result: About a million people died, and millions more fled to Europe and the Americas (including the families of John F. Kennedy and Henry Ford).

Before the Potato Famine, Ireland was on its way to becoming a major political force in the West: High-yielding potato crops were boosting the country's economy, and its eight million citizens were close to gaining independence from England. Within three years, however, the population was cut almost in half and the land was scarred from repeated attacks of blight. Many Irish held their English rulers responsible, claiming that they waited too long before helping. The Irish Potato Famine only intensified the bad blood between the two nations that continues to this day.

## THE BIRTH OF THE MODERN POTATO

The potato blight hit North America as well, but because the United States also grew corn, oats, wheat, and barley, Americans were able to compensate for it. Besides, even with Franklin's and Jefferson's endorsements 50 years earlier, the potato was still primarily used as livestock feed.

The potato did have its advocates in America, though—none more important than horticulturist Luther Burbank. Burbank spent 55 years developing more than 800 new varieties of fruits, vegetables, nuts, and grains. His goal was, simply, to feed the world. Burbank's greatest achievement came in 1871 when he developed a hybrid potato—the Burbank—that produced twice as many tubers per crop and was much larger than any potatoes that had existed before. Most importantly, this new potato showed more resistance to blight than previous varieties. Burbank sent some tubers to Ireland to help rebuild the potato crop, which, even 20 years later, was still suffering the effects of the famine.

Thanks to Burbank's advances, the potato started to catch on in North America. Once it did, it didn't take long for chefs to learn how versatile the vegetable is. Potatoes can be boiled, baked, or fried; they can be mashed, sliced, or powdered; they can be used to make sauces thicker and stop ice crystals from forming; and they can be used to make pasta and baked goods. After hundreds of years of distrust and suspicion, by the beginning of the 20th century, the potato had become one of America's staple crops.

## THIS SPUD'S FOR YOU

In the 1920s, Idaho was emerging as "The Potato State." Why Idaho? Because of its altitude, the days are warm and the nights are cool, creating the perfect growing climate. There is also plenty of irrigation water to soak tubers submerged in the porous volcanic soil. And because few people lived in Idaho at the time, millions

---

The French name for potato: *pomme de terre,* or "earth apple."

of acres of land were available for potato farms.

The most successful of the farmers was J. R. Simplot. He started working on a potato farm in Declo, Idaho, when he was just 14. With a keen mind for business and understanding of distribution, Simplot became the potato baron of Idaho and the main supplier of potatoes to the western United States, as well as to the U.S. Armed Forces in the 1930s and '40s. (Simplot now has annual revenues of $3 billion—he is McDonald's #1 potato supplier.)

Through the Great Depression and into World War II, potatoes thrived as an inexpensive, easy-to-grow crop that could easily feed the masses—and the troops. This was crucial during wartime. Most crops only grow in specific climates or terrains, which means that they have to be cultivated in one place and delivered to another. Ships carrying fresh produce overseas were always in danger of being sunk by the enemy. Potatoes, on the other hand, could be grown almost anywhere. In Europe and the Americas, thousands of farmers grew nothing else during those years. By the end of World War II, the all-American meal was simply "meat and potatoes."

The vegetable that was first revered by the Incas, then used as pig feed in the Western world, is now a $100 billion-a-year business.

## POTATO FACTS

• Potatoes produce 75% more food energy per acre than wheat and 58% more than rice.

• Potatoes can also be used to make ethyl alcohol (ethanol). "There's enough alcohol in one year's yield of an acre of potatoes," said Henry Ford, "to drive the machinery necessary to cultivate the fields for one hundred years." Potatoes are used in manufacturing medicines, paper, cloth, glue, and candy.

• It's the only vegetable that can be grown in desert regions and in mountains above 14,000 feet.

• The average American eats about 80 pounds of potatoes a year, but that has health advocates worried. Why? Because they're usually deep fried or buried under butter and cheese. The skin of the potato—which contains half its fiber—is usually discarded.

• In 1995 potatoes became the first vegetables grown in space. In the future, NASA plans on using spuds as the main crop to feed space travelers on long voyages.

# SHAKE THE TREES AND RAKE THE LEAVES

*Some of the most colorful CB expressions of the 1970s came from the cat-and-mouse game played by truckers who hated the 55 mph speed limit, and the cops, who tried to catch them speeding.*

**Convoy:** a group of trucks traveling together for safety (from state troopers), often exceeding the speed limit.

**Front door:** the lead truck in a convoy. Its job is to "shake the trees"—spot any state troopers up ahead and warn the other trucks in the convoy to slow down.

**Back door:** The last truck in a convoy "rakes the leaves"—keeps an eye out for troopers sneaking up from behind.

**Rocking chair/easy chair:** a truck in the middle of the convoy. (They can relax, since they're not shaking the trees or raking the leaves.)

**Hitting the jackpot:** getting pulled over for speeding. (The flashing lights on a patrol car look like a slot machine.)

**Feeding the bears:** After hitting the jackpot, a trucker has to pull over to the side of the highway to feed the bears, i.e., receive a speeding ticket.

**Brush your teeth and comb your hair:** Slow down to 55 mph—a state trooper with a radar gun is "taking pictures" up ahead.

**Plain brown wrapper:** an unmarked patrol car.

**Tijuana taxi:** a marked police car.

**Bear in the air:** state trooper in a helicopter or airplane.

**Someone spilled honey on the road:** The bears are everywhere!

**All clean:** No bears in sight.

**Bear in the bushes:** a state trooper hidden from view.

**Christmas card:** speeding ticket.

**One foot on the floor, one hanging out the door, and she won't do no more:** driving as fast as you can.

**In the pokey with Smokey:** in jail.

---

Dumb prediction: In 1983 *Billboard* magazine declared Madonna a "flash in the pan."

# BILLY MITCHELL'S BATTLE, PART III

*Here's the final installment of our story about the man who may have done more than any other individual to prepare the United States for World War II. (Parts I and II are on pages 185 and 399.)*

## PAYING ATTENTION

Brigadier General Billy Mitchell had proven his point four different times with four different ships: Battleships that were once the unrivaled, unsinkable masters of the sea could now be defeated by aerial bombing. The lesson was not lost on the foreign observers aboard the USS *Henderson* who came to watch the experiment. One of them, a Japanese naval attaché named Captain Osami Nagano, took careful notes during the tests while two companions snapped away with cameras. "There is much to learn here," one of his companions explained to a reporter for the *Hartford Courant*.

Nagano eventually rose to the rank of admiral…and helped plan the Japanese attack on Pearl Harbor in 1941.

## LET'S PRETEND IT NEVER HAPPENED

The foreign observers understood what they had witnessed, and so did many of the American officers who were present. So, too, would the public, when newsreel footage of the sinking ships began appearing in movie theaters across the country.

Everyone got the message except for the people who mattered most—the military brass. A joint Army-Navy board studied the tests and decided that the results were "inconclusive." So a second test, this time using two decommissioned Navy warships as targets, took place in September 1923. Mitchell's pilots sank them both; unbelievably, the military again dismissed the results.

The media certainly didn't ignore them: Mitchell, or the "flying general," as he'd become known, was a popular public figure even before the tests. Coverage of his efforts to repair a serious and obvious defect in America's national defense turned him into a hero. As his public profile grew, however, so did the number of his enemies inside the military. And Mitchell was anything but a diplomat—he pushed his ideas so forcefully and was so contemptuous of people who disagreed with him that he alienated a lot of colleagues who might otherwise have been his allies.

## TAKE A HIKE

In late 1923, the Army sent Mitchell on an eight-month inspection tour of U.S. military installations in the Pacific to get him out of the headlines. Mitchell paid particular attention to the facilities in Hawaii, and when he returned home he wrote a 324-page report that included a prediction that the Japanese would one day attack Pearl Harbor. In his report Mitchell correctly predicted the day of the attack (Sunday), and estimated it would begin at 7:30 in the morning (the first bombs actually fell at 7:53 a.m.). He also correctly predicted where the Japanese aircraft carriers would be positioned, and warned that U.S. forces in Hawaii were unprepared to defend against such an assault.

Not many people bothered to read Mitchell's report; those few who did ignored it. "Many of the opinions expressed are based on the author's exaggerated ideas of the powers and importance of air power, and are therefore unsound," an officer assigned to the Army General Staff wrote in response.

## INTO THE WILDERNESS

Mitchell had been the deputy director of the Army's Air Service since 1919, and as such he had been able to retain his "temporary" wartime rank of brigadier general. But he'd made so many enemies pushing for air power that when his term as deputy director expired in 1925, it was not renewed. He reverted back to his lower, permanent rank of colonel and in June 1925 was transferred to Fort Sam Houston in Texas to keep him out of the newspapers. He was still there three months later when two naval air disasters put him right back in the headlines.

In early September 1925, a Navy seaplane, called a flying boat, crashed into the Pacific after attempting to fly nonstop from San Francisco to Hawaii. A few days later, the dirigible USS *Shenandoah*, pride of the U.S. Navy, crashed after it flew into a thunderstorm, killing 14 crewmembers. Both trips had been ill-advised: the flying boat did not have the necessary range to fly to Hawaii without refueling and had crashed 200 miles short of its destination. The

*Shenandoah* was in the middle of a 27-city publicity tour when its captain, under pressure to stick to a tight schedule and against his better judgment, flew into bad weather. (Ironically, both trips were attempts by the Navy to prevent its air program from being over-shadowed by the Army Air Service.) Secretary of the Navy Curtis Wilbur summed up the tragedies by saying that they demonstrated the limits of air power: If an enemy tried to mount an air attack from across the Atlantic or the Pacific, they were sure to crash before they got to North America.

## WAR OF WORDS

Mitchell had put up with a lot over the years, but the two accidents and the Navy's response to them were too much. "My opinion is as follows," he said in a public statement, "These terrible accidents are the direct result of incompetency, criminal negligence, and almost treasonable administration of the national defense by the War and Navy Departments. As a patriotic American citizen, I can stand by no longer and see these disgusting performances by the Navy and War Departments."

Mitchell's enemies had been waiting for a chance to strike back at him, and this statement handed it to them. The military, probably at the instigation of President Calvin Coolidge, decided to court-martial Mitchell on grounds of insubordination and making public statements that were prejudicial to good order and discipline.

## GOING OUT WITH A BANG

How do you defend yourself against charges of insubordination when you've just called your superiors incompetent, criminally negligent, and practically guilty of treason? Mitchell and his defense team decided that a guilty verdict was almost inevitable, so they turned the trial into a public forum for his belief that the United States was woefully unprepared to fight the next war.

The trial lasted seven weeks. Mitchell defended himself by arguing that the statements he'd made were true. In December 1925, just as he'd expected, he was found guilty on all charges and suspended from active duty without pay for five years. He resigned from the Army a week later.

For a time, Mitchell hoped to capitalize on the publicity generated by his court-martial, and continued to speak out and publish articles in favor of air power. But now the "flying general" was just another civilian, and his arguments had become repetitive and shrill. Then, in 1927, Americans turned their attention to a new and more exciting aviation hero when 25-year-old Charles Lindbergh became the first person to make a nonstop solo flight across the Atlantic.

## THE END

Mitchell once said that if the U.S. were ever drawn into another full-scale war, he wanted to "see the color of the faces of those who opposed our military aircraft program." But he didn't live long enough to see his dire predictions about the nation's vulnerability come true. In 1936, at the age of 56, he died of heart disease —five years before the attack on Pearl Harbor.

Still, though he died overshadowed and largely forgotten, he hadn't lived his life in vain. The sinking of the *Ostfriesland* had made an impact—not with senior officers, but with younger ones working their way up through the ranks. One by one, Mitchell's skeptics retired and were replaced by officers who understood the importance of air power.

## JUST IN THE NICK OF TIME

Whatever doubts remained about the role of military air power ended in 1939, when Germany used fighters and bombers to devastating effect during the invasion of Poland. As with the First World War 25 years earlier, the United States lagged behind its opponents in air power.

But, thanks in large part to Billy Mitchell's battle, the U.S. military now understood the importance of air power, knew how to use it effectively, and was in a position to build a much larger, stronger air force. Luckily, the nation had two years between the invasion of Poland and America's entry into World War II, and the military made good use of the time, arming rapidly and building what would ultimately become an 80,000-plane Army Air Force and a 35-carrier Navy, both of which would be decisive in winning the war.

Where would America be now if Billy Mitchell hadn't been willing to sacrifice his career to drag the U.S. military kicking and screaming into the aviation age?

Maybe it's better not to think about it.

# THE PILGRIMS, PT. IV: THE NEW WORLD

*The Pilgrims' landing in Massachusetts is without question one of the most important moments in North American history. Here's Part IV of the story. (Part III starts on page 396.)*

## LANDING ON PLYMOUTH ROCK

The Pilgrims didn't land on "Plymouth Rock." They didn't land on any rock at all. They didn't even land at Plymouth. Their original destination was "Northern Virginia"—but not the same region that currently resides next to Washington, D.C. In the 1600s, many maps referred to the entire eastern seaboard as Virginia, because the Virginia Company laid claim to it. The Pilgrims' actual destination was the Hudson River area in what is now New York, where they had been granted a land claim from the Virginia Company. But they didn't land there, either.

As the *Mayflower* headed for the Hudson, yet another squall tossed and turned the ship, forcing it off course. When one of Master Jones's men sighted a peninsula that they could safely reach, William Bradford begged Jones to land there. Jones agreed, so the battered ship immediately turned its rudders and headed for safety. On November 11, 1620, after more than two months at sea, the *Mayflower* dropped anchor off the sandy tip of Cape Cod, near what is now Provincetown, Massachusetts. William Bradford describes the landing in his journal:

> Being thus arrived in a good harbor and brought safe to land, they fell upon their knees and blessed the God of heaven, who had brought them over the vast and furious ocean, and delivered them from all the perils and miseries thereof, again to set their feet on the firm and stable earth, their proper element.

## THE MAYFLOWER COMPACT

It was there that 41 Pilgrims signed the Mayflower Compact—the first set of written laws in America. The Pilgrims realized during the voyage that if they were to survive in this new land, their congregation would need to form a government and draft laws. They didn't want a repeat of the lawlessness they had heard existed in Jamestown. And, in spite of their faith, they knew they were only human—a few squabbles had already broken out between the London and Leiden Separatists. These power struggles, they felt, would only escalate without a governor and arbiters.

In the hopes of creating a "city upon a hill" that would serve as a beacon to the rest of the world, the Pilgrims elected the most learned and respected member of their group, William Bradford, to be governor. "This day," he later wrote,

> before we came to harbour, observing some not well affected to unity and concord, but gave some appearance of faction, it was thought good there should be an association and agreement, that we should combine together in one body, and to submit to such government and governors as we should by common consent agree to make and choose, and set our hands to this that follows, word for word.

Bradford then drafted what he called "An Association and Agreement" (it would be renamed the Mayflower Compact in 1793). The document set forth that

> in the name of God, Amen, We, whose names are underwritten... during a voyage to plant the first colony in the northern parts of Virginia; do by these presents, solemnly and mutually in the Presence of God and one of another, covenant and combine ourselves together into a civil Body Politick, for our better Ordering and Preservation, and Furtherance of the Ends aforesaid.

## BY THE PEOPLE, FOR THE PEOPLE

The Mayflower Compact was a covenant so well conceived that its basic principle would later be written into the United States Constitution: For a government to be legitimate, the people who are being governed must first agree to the structure of that body and pledge to follow its laws. Without that agreement firmly in place, the government will founder.

As important a document as it was, though, the Mayflower Compact lasted only a year. It was a temporary fix designed to get the community through those first few difficult months while maintaining civility. And although the Pilgrims all agreed to the terms of the Compact, it lacked one important detail: the approval of the British government. So a year later they drafted the 1621 Pierce Patent, a more detailed contract that was approved by the Crown, and enabled the Pilgrims to live peacefully in the place newly christened "New England."

## FINDING HOME

But back to that first winter of 1620. The joy of having reached the New World safely was short lived. Because of the delays the Pilgrims encountered leaving England, the bite of winter was already in the air when they arrived in America. They had to find a home—a place with reliable food and shelter—fast.

The Pilgrims spent the first few weeks exploring the sandy beaches and inlets around Cape Cod, and then the *Mayflower* took up anchor and sailed farther north up the coast until they found an inviting harbor. According to a surveying map, the harbor had been visited by Captain John Smith seven years earlier. He named it Plymouth, the same name as the town in England from which the Pilgrims had set sail more than three months earlier. Plymouth Harbor, it was agreed, would be their new home. They landed there on December 21, 1620...the first day of winter.

While the snow fell, the colonists quickly sawed lumber and built clapboard houses. The *Mayflower*'s crew dropped anchor off shore, judging that a return trip to England in winter would be too dangerous, and they spent that winter with the Pilgrims. Neither group fared well. Food supplies ran perilously low and more than half of those who arrived—including Oceanus Hopkins, the baby boy who was born on the *Mayflower*—did not survive to spring. (The other *Mayflower* baby, Peregrine White, lived into his 80s.)

## MEET THE LOCALS

The English settlers referred to their new home as Plymouth, but the area was known as "Patuxet" to the native people. Only one member of the Patuxet nation remained, however; the rest had been wiped out by smallpox two years earlier. The lone survivor, a man named Tisquantum—the Pilgrims called him "Squanto"— had spent several years in Europe after being kidnapped by British sailors (which is how he avoided the smallpox outbreak). Squanto befriended the Pilgrims and became their interpreter, helping them negotiate with the two other area tribes—the Nauset and the Wampanoag.

Also aiding the Pilgrims was a professional soldier named Myles Standish. The Pilgrims weren't fighters, but, because they were going into unknown lands, Pastor John Robinson thought it prudent to hire a military captain. The decision turned out to be crucial to the Pilgrims' survival. Although Standish lost his wife that first winter, he remained loyal to protecting those who made him their captain. Standish also impressed the neighboring Indians with his wisdom and prowess as a warrior, and even fought alongside them when another tribe attacked…a tribe who had vowed to wipe out the English next.

## THE FIRST THANKSGIVING

Without the aid of Squanto and Captain Standish, the Pilgrims would not have been safe in their new home. But, thanks to their protection, the Pilgrims lived in peace with the Indians for nearly 75 years, until the Wampanoag challenged the Pilgrims' claim to the land. In the meantime, they coexisted, traded goods and services, and in 1621 they celebrated their first (and only) Thanksgiving together. It wasn't a solemn religious affair, as many history books have portrayed it—it was a lively three-day harvest feast. The Pilgrims, having survived the journey over the ocean and the harsh winter that followed, were very thankful for their new home—and new friends—in Plymouth.

An account of that Thanksgiving survives, and it sheds even more light on what life was like for these early Americans. The celebration was described by a Pilgrim named Edward Winslow in a letter dated December 12, 1621.

> Our harvest being gotten in, our governor sent four men on fowling, that so we might after a special manner rejoice together after we had gathered the fruit of our labors. They four in one day killed as much fowl as, with a little help beside, served the company almost a week. At which time, amongst other recreations, we exercised our arms, many of the Indians coming amongst us, and among the rest their greatest king Massasoit, with some ninety men, whom for three days we entertained and feasted, and they went out and killed five deer, which they brought to the plantation and bestowed on our Governor, and upon the captain and others. And although it be not always so plentiful as it was at this time

with us, yet by the goodness of God, we are so far from want that we often wish you partakers of our plenty.

## THE FATE OF THE *MAYFLOWER*

Master Jones and his beleaguered crew set sail for England on April 5, 1621. The *Mayflower* never carried Pilgrims again. She returned to her life as a merchant ship, but for only a short time—after a few more trading runs, Christopher Jones died in 1622. The battered ship was docked for more than two years in an English harbor, then appraised for probate while Jones's estate was settled. The ship's official condition: "In ruins."

So in 1624 the *Mayflower* was sold as scrap. A farm in the Quaker village of Jordans, in Buckinghamshire, England, claims that the *Mayflower's* hull and keel still exist in the barn's frame and outer walls, but no evidence exists to support this claim. The barn is definitely made from an old wooden ship, but no markings verify it was the *Mayflower*. Still, the "Mayflower Barn" remains a popular tourist destination.

## DESCENDANTS AND LEGACIES

The Pilgrims' journey to the New World was a major turning point in history for both England and North America. It marked the beginning of structured society in America, as well as the beginning of a mass exodus of English people to the new land of opportunity. And to say the Pilgrims were fruitful and multiplied would be an understatement: Experts say that as many as 35 million people around the world are descended from those few dozen who settled in Plymouth in 1620.

Today, a state park in Plymouth with a monument to those who landed there memorialize the Pilgrims' accomplishments. And although Pilgrim Memorial State Park is the smallest state park in Massachusetts, it is by far the most visited, receiving more than a million tourists every year—people who want to stand in the same spot as those weary travelers whose only wish was to create a society where the citizens were free to live and worship as they chose.

\*　　\*　　\*

"One accurate measurement is worth a thousand expert opinions."

—Grace Hopper

The Four Horsemen of the Apocalypse: Conquest, Slaughter, Famine, and Death.

# VAUDEVILLE

*If you've ever faked a soft-shoe or yelled out, "One more time!"
at the end of a song, you're doing vaudeville—America's
favorite form of entertainment for half a century.*

**B**OWERY BOY

Although theater-going has been part of American cultural
life since the 18th century, it was a pleasure reserved mostly
for the upper classes, and found only in major cities like New York
and Philadelphia. Most Americans lived in rural areas, with neither
the time nor the money to attend shows on a regular basis. The
Industrial Revolution changed all that: By the mid-1800s, more
Americans were living in cities than on farms and, more importantly, they had extra money and one day off every week to spend it.

Tony Pastor was a New York entertainer and entrepreneur who
produced raunchy variety shows in the city's working-class Bowery
district. Pastor knew that the big money to be made in show business lay in getting the growing middle class into the theater. But
few respectable New Yorkers, especially women and children,
would be caught dead at Pastor's bawdy shows. So he created a
new kind of variety show in a "clean"—meaning no sacrilegious
language or overtly sexual content—family-friendly format. And
he moved it uptown.

In 1881 Pastor opened the 14th Street Theatre in New York
City's Union Square and launched a style of entertainment that
dominated American theater for the next 50 years—vaudeville.

## FAMILY FUN

Strictly speaking, vaudeville was a variety show: seven or eight
acts, featuring singers, sketches or routines by comedians and
actors, and novelty acts like escape artists, high divers, quick-
change artists, strong men, jugglers, and animal acts.

The origin of the name itself is obscure. It may be a corruption
of the phrase *voix de ville*, French slang for "songs of the town," or
it may have come from *vau-de-Vire*, a valley in Normandy that
became known for satiric songs full of double-entendres written by
street singers in the 15th century.

---

Hey, sports fans—how big is an NFL football field? (It's 360 feet long by 160 feet wide.)

But Tony Pastor never called his shows "vaudeville." The term was given to the new form of entertainment by impresarios Benjamin Franklin Keith and Edward F. Albee. Keith and Albee were two of the most cutthroat producers in a business full of rascals and sharks. In 1883, using money they'd made with unauthorized productions of Gilbert and Sullivan operettas, they built a chain, or "circuit," of lavish theaters across the northeast. Then they stole Pastor's format, instituted the practice of playing two shows a day, and called it vaudeville. Other producers jumped on the bandwagon, and soon there were other successful vaudeville circuits—the Pantages and Loew's, to name two—but Keith and Albee dominated the industry, gobbling up the other circuits one by one.

## HULLY GEE!

Not only did Keith and Albee control the theaters, they also controlled the performers. Acts were required to uphold strict codes of behavior. Fred Allen, the radio superstar who started out as a juggler in vaudeville, recalled a warning sign posted backstage:

> Don't say slob or sonofagun or hully gee [19th-century slang for "Holy Jesus!"] on the stage unless you want to be canceled peremptorily. If you are guilty of uttering anything sacrilegious or even suggestive you will be immediately closed and will never again be allowed in a theater where Mr. Keith is in authority.

They meant business. Acts that violated the rules were blackballed from the circuit. Keith and Albee eventually controlled the bookings in most of the 17,000 vaudeville theaters from coast to coast. Acts who didn't play by their rules didn't work.

## BIRTH OF "BLUE"

Over time, as social conventions relaxed, the rules were bent, especially for big stars like Sophie Tucker and the Marx Brothers, who made pushing the envelope part of their act. But that process took years. In the meantime Keith and Albee dutifully watched the Monday matinee of every new act. After the show, they wrote out terse instructions on what improper line or scene each performer was to cut before the evening performance. Those instructions were put in little blue envelopes, which would appear in the performers' mailboxes backstage. To this day, raunchy jokes and sketches are known as "blue" material.

There was no arguing with the orders. Performers had two choices: obey or quit. And if they quit, they never worked for Keith and Albee again. "During my early years on the Keith Circuit," wrote veteran vaudeville star Sophie Tucker in her memoirs, "I took my orders from my blue envelope and—no matter what I said backstage (and it was plenty)—when I went on for the Monday night show, I was careful to keep in bounds."

The work was grueling. Acts played a minimum of two shows a day (2:00 p.m. and 8:00 p.m.), but sometimes as many as four. The only days off were when there were no bookings. Producers never hesitated to call rehearsals on short notice any day of the week. There was no holiday pay, no overtime pay, no rehearsal pay. Performers were also expected to supply their own costumes and maintain them for the season, which ran 42 weeks a year.

Why did performers put up with such harsh conditions? Money. The pay was good in vaudeville. In 1910 the average American factory worker was lucky to make $1,300 a year; a small-time vaudevillian could make more than twice that. For women, uneducated immigrants, and the poor, vaudeville was one of the few ways they could earn a good living.

## THE DEATH TRAIL

Performers worked their way up (or down) three tiers of vaudeville:

• **Small-time:** Theaters at this level were sometimes no more than a storefront with benches, often out in the middle of nowhere. The pay was as low as $15 a week, especially on the "Death Trail," which was what players called a tour of one-nighters in towns like Butte, Montana, or Winnemucca, Nevada. Small-time was a training ground for new acts, or the last stop for old-timers on the skids.

• **Medium-time:** Good theaters in a wide range of cities, and good money—$200–$300 a week. This is where most acts earned their bread and butter.

• **Big-time:** The best theaters, the best cities, the best money. Headliners could easily earn $1,000 a week—a fortune at the time.

## THE BILL

The formula for a vaudeville performance was honed and perfected by producers like Keith and Albee to make sure the audience (called "the big black giant," by impresario Oscar Hammerstein) always got its money's worth.

• **Opening act:** Usually a "silent" act—a juggling troupe or trained dogs, for example—that wouldn't be ruined by the noise of the audience settling in. (Some silent acts, like juggler W.C. Fields and rope trick artist Will Rogers, went on to become headliners when they added comedy to their bits.)

• **Second act:** A juvenile brother or sister act, like the Gumm Sisters (Frances Gumm became famous later as Judy Garland) or the dancing Nicholas Brothers.

• **Third act:** A one-act play or comedy sketch featuring "legit" actors, like Sarah Bernhardt, Helen Hayes, or the Barrymores. Famous writers, such as J. M. Barrie (*Peter Pan*) and Jack London (*The Call of the Wild*), often provided material.

• **Fourth act:** A novelty act, like a magician or mind reader. Escape artist Harry Houdini started in this slot but quickly rose to headliner status.

• **Fifth act:** Celebrity guest stars held down this spot, which came right before intermission. Sports figures such as boxer John L. Sullivan or baseball's Babe Ruth would come out to answer questions from the crowd. Helen Keller appeared with a translator, who signed questions into the palm of Keller's hand. Carrie Nation, the famous temperance crusader, came onstage wielding the axe she'd used to break up saloons. Convicted murderesses were always a big hit.

• **Sixth act:** The act right after intermission was always something big and flashy—a lavish production number with lots of dancers and elaborate costumes, or a novelty orchestra. Tiger and lion acts were popular too.

• **Seventh act:** Called "next to closing," this spot was reserved for the headliners. It was the star spot, and only the top acts earned it. They also made the most money—at a time when a laborer might earn $40 a week, Eddie Cantor was getting $7,700.

• **Closing act:** Being the closer was the worst. It meant you were on the way down and out. No one paid attention to you as the crowd put on their coats and headed for the aisles.

Producers often purposely put bad acts in the closing slot to help clear the theater faster, before the next performance. Occasionally the policy backfired with happy results. The Cherry Sisters were possibly the worst act ever to star in vaudeville. They sang so horribly off-key that they were booed and pelted with rotten fruit. Then a smart producer realized that the audience actually loved to hate the Cherry Sisters. So he set up a fruit stand in the lobby and sold "ammo" to the audience as they came in. When the sisters went on, they found themselves performing from behind a protective wire screen. As they sang, the crowd howled with laughter and fired away. The Cherry Sisters soon became one of the hottest acts in vaudeville, commanding top dollar, and remained a big draw for decades.

## THE PALACE

For a vaudeville performer, playing the Palace Theatre in New York City was like being in the World Series for a baseball player. Built in 1913 by impresario Martin Beck, who dubbed it the "Valhalla of Broadway," the Palace was the pinnacle of vaudeville success. Monday matinees were packed with theater managers, booking agents, talent scouts, and other performers. A good response not only meant instant fame but also, more importantly, bookings all across the country. Performers would often take a lower fee just to get on the bill.

Unemployed players would hang out on the triangular patch of sidewalk outside the Palace, trading gossip and tips about possible work. So many of them "vacationed" there that the spot came to be known as "the beach." Today it's the site of the TKTS discount ticket booth in Times Square.

## "WEEDING OUT THE CRAP"

It took discipline and stamina to make it on the vaudeville circuit. Sketches like Abbott and Costello's classic "Who's on First?" were polished by the continuous grind of playing "two-a-days." Singers and comedians had to create material that would play coast to coast, for everyone from sophisticated urban audiences to rural hayseeds. "It took two years to get seven solid minutes to put in an act," recalled Milton Berle. "You weeded out the crap, and then deleted and edited stuff that wouldn't play."

And acts had to be quick-witted to survive. Fred Allen was playing a show in Bayonne, New Jersey, when a cat walked onstage

during his act, howled…and gave birth to a litter of kittens. "I thought this was a monologue," quipped Allen, "not a catalogue."

## FORGOTTEN LEGENDS

Many legendary names in show business—Bob Hope, Jack Benny, Al Jolson, Mae West, Burns and Allen, the Marx Brothers, W.C. Fields, Buster Keaton, Bill "Bojangles" Robinson, Bessie Smith, Judy Garland, Jimmy Durante, and Bert Lahr, to name a few—cut their teeth in vaudeville. We remember them today because they made a successful transition to movies and radio in the 1930s and '40s, and to television in the 1950s. But many of the biggest vaudeville stars didn't cross over.

• **Eva Tanguay** (1879–1947): Known as "the girl who made vaudeville famous." She had a so-so voice but knew how put across a song. Audiences loved this Canadian's brassy personality and racy numbers. Billed as the "I Don't Care" girl, after her biggest hit, "I Don't Care What Happens to Me," she followed it up with, "It's All Been Done Before but Not the Way I Do It."

• **Bert Williams** (1874–1922): The first black performer to become a national star. He made a dance called the "cakewalk" famous; his hit songs, "Nobody" and "All Going Out and Nothing Coming In," were admired for their wry wit. And although his act was popular with blacks and whites, he still had to navigate a segregated society. He pulled it off with style: After a show in Chicago he stepped into a nearby bar and ordered a drink. When the bartender smugly told him drinks for "coloreds" were $50 each, Williams pulled out a wad of $50 bills and told the guy to buy a round for everyone at the bar.

• **Smith and Dale**, a.k.a. Charles Marks (1882–1971) and Joseph Sultzer (1884–1981): The top comedy team for 20 years. Legendary for their perfect timing and "rat-a-tat" delivery, they were Neil Simon's inspiration for his hit play *The Sunshine Boys*. Here's a sample from their signature sketch, "Doctor Kronkheit and His Only Living Patient":

> **Smith:** "Are you the doctor?"
> **Dale:** "I'm the doctor."
> **Smith:** "I'm dubious."
> **Dale:** "Hello, Mr. Dubious. So what's your problem?"
> **Smith:** "It's terrible. I walk around all night."

---

Name 3 people on U.S. money who weren't presidents. (Hamilton, Franklin, and Sacagawea.)

**Dale:** "Ah! You're a somnambulist!"
**Smith:** "No, I'm a night watchman."

Ba-dum-pum.

## CURTAIN DOWN

On Friday the 13th in May, 1932, the Palace Theatre did the unthinkable. It replaced its two-a-day vaudeville bill with a movie double feature. Most historians mark that date as the death of vaudeville. Several factors were to blame—the growing sophistication of audiences, who now saw vaudeville as old-fashioned, and the reliance of theaters on ever more lavish and expensive shows. Mostly, though, it was the movies. Films were easier and cheaper for producers to present, and ticket prices were much lower for audiences. Vaudeville limped on until the 1950s, but by 1926, nearly all of the great vaudeville theaters had been converted to moviehouses.

But vaudeville didn't really die—its influence continued on in the new medium of television. Variety shows were a staple on early TV, and programs like Sid Caesar's *Your Show of Shows* and *The Ed Sullivan Show* were pure vaudeville. Where does the ghost of vaudeville linger today? On *Saturday Night Live* and late-night talk shows like Leno and Letterman, which continue to be a collage of comics, singers, dancers, and even jugglers. As writer Larry Gelbart (M*A*S*H) said, "If vaudeville is dead, TV is the box they put it in."

## VAUDEVILLE TERMS WE USE TODAY

• *Hoofers.* A nickname for dancers, who would beat their feet on the stage before their entrance to give the conductor the right tempo. It sounded like a horse stamping its hooves.

• *Corny.* Unsophisticated comedy routines were considered "stuck in the corn," meaning they appealed only to rural audiences. The term became shortened to "corny."

• *Tough act to follow.* When an act got a huge response, the next act had to work twice as hard to win over the audience. So it was a great compliment to a performer to be called "a tough act to follow." For W. C. Fields and Jack Benny, both masters of their craft and never shy about taking on the competition, there was only one act they dreaded following: the Marx Brothers. Benny said after a while he gave up worrying about whether he could top the zany comics: "I just stood in the wings and laughed like hell."

---

The average temperature on Mars is –81°F.

# HOW TO FIND YOUR WAY HOME

*In 1978 Uncle John journeyed to the Himalayas, searching for the world's highest outhouse. Did he bring a map? No. Extra supplies? No. Did he find the outhouse? No. Did he have to be rescued? Yes. Don't be like Uncle John. Read this article so you'll know how to survive in the wilderness.*

**A**RE YOU PREPARED?

What would you do if you suddenly found yourself stranded—lost in the woods or alone in the desert? The more civilized we become, the less armed we are with the skills needed to survive off the land. And too often, people on outdoor adventures put themselves in harm's way because of poor planning and a lack of basic knowledge about their surroundings. We pored over our library of survival books to bring you these general rules to follow any time you go on a trip—by car or on foot.

### TIP #1: PLAN BEFORE YOU LEAVE HOME

• Whether you're going on a long vacation or just a day trip, tell more than one person where you plan to go, what route you plan to take, and when they should expect you to return.

• Always have an up-to-date map in your possession. If you're taking a long road trip, bring an atlas. If you're hiking in the wilderness, bring a detailed topographic map of the area.

• A basic knowledge of where you're going may save your life, especially if you're heading into nature. What's the terrain? What predators, poisonous plants, or insects live there? What kind of weather should you expect? Example: If you're heading to the mountains—even in August—an unexpected storm could roll in and drench you with rain or even snow.

• Pack adequate food (some of it nonperishable), water, and warm clothes, including socks, gloves, and a hat. Basic survival kits with matches, a knife, and a compass can be found in any outdoor equipment or recreation store.

• Keep extra supplies in your car: two gallons of water (one for you, one for your car), nonperishable food, detailed maps, water-proof matches, a flashlight, spare batteries, flares, a dashboard cover that has "Emergency—Need Help" printed on one side, a whistle, first aid kit, rope, pocket knife, tools, blanket, extra cloth-ing, jumper cables, and tire chains.

## TIP #2: STAY CALM AND ASSESS THE SITUATION

So the unthinkable has happened: You find yourself stranded or lost, and your cell phone doesn't work. Should you stay where you are, or try to find civilization? In most cases, experts say you should stay put, especially if you told someone where you were going. That will make it easier for rescuers to find you. If you're lost because you survived a car crash in a remote area, stay near the wreckage—it's easier to spot from the air than a person. Only go looking for help if you absolutely have to—either because you're in unsafe conditions or because you're sure there's a settlement or road nearby.

• Which do you look for first—food, water, or shelter? It depends on the conditions. If it's extremely cold, hot, or stormy, make a shelter so you don't succumb to exposure, then rest until you have the strength to find water. If you're not injured and conditions are safe, look for water first, then deal with shelter, then food. (More on that later.) If you do stay put, make yourself visible to rescuers.

• The universal distress signal is three fires in a triangle. Any passing plane that sees this will alert the authorities.

• Another good signal is a shiny object reflecting the sun. Rescuers are trained to look for light flashes like these.

## TIP #3: DON'T GET MORE LOST

• If you've decided to go find help, leave some kind of note at your starting point with your condition and intentions, or at least con-struct an arrow pointing in the direction you're heading.

• Stay on marked trails, if there are any. It's almost never a good idea to stray into the bush.

• The general rule about finding civilization: Head downhill until you find a creek or river, then head downriver until you find peo-ple. But first, depending on your surroundings, you may want to go to a higher elevation to scan the landscape for any sign of settlements. If it's not too dangerous or cold, do it at night when it's easier to see the lights of a distant town or city.

• Take your time (unless you or someone in your group is in immediate danger). "Rest," says the *U.S. Army Survival Guide*, "can be more valuable than speed. Whether you are struggling through jungle undergrowth, facing a dwindling water supply in the desert, or making your way across arctic ice, plan and make your way carefully; do not dash blindly on."

## TIP #4: FIND DRINKING WATER

• Assume all creek or pond water is polluted. If you don't have a filtration system or a way to boil water, try to find the clearest, fastest-moving water you can.

• Collecting rainwater is your safest bet. Search around for makeshift containers and save as much water as possible.

• Morning dew can provide you with enough water to keep you alive, but you have to know how to collect it. One way is to carefully place leaves around a container in such a way that any water that gathers on them will flow into the container. Big leaves or flowers also collect water; get to them just after dawn before the water evaporates.

• If you suddenly find water after going a long time without, sip it rather than drinking it fast. Gulping it could cause you to vomit, which will dehydrate you even more.

• In the desert, look for water at the base of cliffs or deep in the sand near a dry stream bed. Or follow animal tracks—animals know where water is.

• You can make a dew trap in the desert. Dig a hole in the ground and place a makeshift container inside it, then cover the hole with clothing or leaves. Condensation will pull water from the air. A piece of fabric left in the hole may even collect enough water for you to wring out in the morning.

• The stems of desert plants and cacti store water, but be careful—some of these plants are poisonous. The saguaro cactus, common in the southwestern United States, is a good source of water. Cut through the stem with a knife or hard-edged rock. Then carefully suck the water out of the soft, middle part (the pith). Do not eat the pith, and watch out for the spines—they can cause severe rashes if they prick you.

• And, in case you're wondering, urine is *not* a good source of drinking water—much too salty. It is, however, effective for cleaning wounds (only your own) and keeping cool in extreme heat.

## TIP #5: FIND FOOD

Some plants are edible, others aren't. If you don't know the difference, here's a simple test you can do, outlined by John "Lofty" Wiseman in his *SAS Survival Handbook*:

**1. Inspect.** What's the plant's condition? If it's past ripe, slimy, or worm-ridden, don't eat it.

**2. Smell.** If it looks healthy, crush a part of it to release the pores and then sniff. If there's even a hint of bitterness, don't eat it.

**3. Touch.** Crush a small portion of the plant and rub it between your armpit and elbow. Wait a few minutes. If your skin starts itching or swelling up, don't eat it. (And remember that if it has three shiny leaves, it's most likely poison oak or poison ivy.)

**4. Taste.** Place a small portion on your lips, work it into your mouth, and then let it touch your tongue. If there is no immediate reaction, then chew a small portion. If you notice any discomfort whatsoever, don't eat it.

**5. Swallow.** If your plant has passed all of the tests so far, then eat a *very* small portion…and wait at least five hours. Don't eat or drink anything else in that time period. Symptoms to look for: soreness in the mouth, burping, nausea, stomach and/or abdomen pains, hallucinations, or anything else that doesn't feel right.

**6. Eat.** If after five hours you haven't felt any ill effects, the plant is most likely safe to eat. But don't eat a lot at one time—ration it and keep a very close eye on yourself for the next few days.

We don't have enough room to go into trapping animals, but here's a quick tip: Pound for pound, insects have more protein than cows. The larger bugs, such as beetles and grasshoppers, are usually (but not always) safer then the smaller bugs, such as ants, which may be poisonous. Earthworms are excellent sources of protein.

*One more important tip:* If you have food but no water, don't eat it, because that will start up your digestive system, which requires

Prickly subject: The world's largest cactus plantation is in Edwards, Mississippi.

a lot of water. Unless you drink at least one pint of water per day, eating dry food by itself will dehydrate you much faster than not eating at all. Also, drinking beverages such as beer or soda can dehydrate more than hydrate you.

## TIP #6: FIND OR BUILD SHELTER

In *Outdoor Survival Skills*, Larry Dean Olsen, who also wrote the requirements for the Boy Scouts' outdoor survival merit badge, writes, "Building for survival requires more than a minimum of effort and careful planning. Most essential to this planning is the selection of a campsite."

• Find as flat an area as you can, preferably with trees to one side. But if you're camped next to the only trees in sight, be careful: you may get unwanted four-legged visitors.

• Don't build or seek shelter in dry gullies, at the base of unstable cliffs, or in any spot that may be prone to flash floods or landslides. Remember that flash floods can occur many miles away from a thunderstorm.

• Inspect your area thoroughly before you set up. Move on if you find anthills, poisonous plants, or signs of predators.

• While there are many types of shelters, the easiest to build is a lean-to. Find three large sticks or branches and lean them against each other in the shape of a teepee. Anchor each into the ground by digging a hole at least eight inches deep, and surrounding each base with packed dirt and rocks. Then lean more sticks on the foundation, leaving one side open, facing away from the wind.

• Be careful where you seek shelter in the woods. A tree snag (a felled tree leaning on a cliff or another tree) may look like a ready-made shelter, but can give way and collapse at any time.

• Caves are good, but make sure nothing else is living in them. If you see droppings or bones, move on.

• If there's snow, use it to your advantage. Dig a trench, insulate it with branches and leaves, and huddle inside to keep warm.

## TIP #7: DETERMINE WHICH DIRECTION IS NORTH

Sometimes, finding your way back to civilization can be as simple as knowing which way is north. Then, if you're sure there's a town somewhere to the southeast, for example, you can head in that direction. If you don't have a compass, here are some ways to determine north:

• In the daytime, look at plants. They tend to lean toward north, so the highest abundance of leaves will face south. (It's the opposite in the southern hemisphere.)

• On a clear night, look for the Big Dipper and find the two "pointer stars" that make the forward edge of the cup. Draw a line from the star at the bottom of the cup through the top star and keep going to the first bright star—that's Polaris, the North Star.

• The sun rises in the east and sets in the west. It's not always *due* west or *due* east, but the sun's position can give you a general sense of direction.

### TIP #8: IN EXTREME HEAT, STAY COOL

• The hotter you get, the more difficult it is to think clearly. Heat stroke will kill you quicker than thirst, so find shade and avoid exposure by covering your entire body with clothing, especially your face.

• Although sweat is undrinkable, it *can* keep you cool. Wear a headband to collect sweat, then wring it out down your back.

### TIP #9: IN EXTREME COLD, STAY WARM

• Your best defense against frostbite is to stop it before it starts. The key is movement. Jump up and down, wave your arms, extend your fingers, wiggle your toes, pull on your ears, make funny faces. Do whatever you can to keep your blood flowing.

• Moisture combined with cold can be deadly. Stay as dry as possible. If your clothes are wet, wring them out. If all that moving around made you sweat, wipe it off.

• Excessive cold causes mucus to leak from your nose. Don't give it a chance to freeze—wipe it away.

• Find anything dry to create layers around your body, such as leaves or newspapers. Loose clothes are better than tight ones.

• If your feet get frostbitten, you can usually keep walking on them for a while. But if you find shelter and warm them up, it's better to stay put—walking again could cause severe damage.

A male sea catfish keeps the eggs of his young in his mouth until they are ready to hatch.

• Once you've made it to safety, go straight to a hospital. If that's not an option, soak any frostbitten areas in warm (not hot) water, then wrap yourself in warm blankets. Avoid direct heat from a fireplace, stove, or heating pad.

• Never rub or scratch frostbite; dress it loosely with a sterile cloth. If fingers or toes are affected, wrap each one individually.

## THE WILL TO SURVIVE

Of course, this chapter only scratches the surface of what you can do to survive in the wilderness until you're rescued or you find your way to safety. For more information, read some survival books and how-to guides on your favorite outdoor activity (hiking, camping, skiing, etc.), which often have good tips on what to do if you get lost. And if you're a novice, it's a good idea to head out with an experienced guide or friend before you try it on your own.

Ultimately, though, knowledge alone may not be enough. Many people who survived wilderness ordeals report that they simply *wanted* to survive…and, just as importantly, kept a clear head. We'll end with the opening words of the *U.S. Army Survival Manual*:

> Many survival case histories show that stubborn, strong willpower can conquer many obstacles. One case history tells of a man stranded in the desert for eight days without food and water: he had no survival training, but he wanted to survive, and through sheer willpower, he did. With training, equipment, and the **will to survive**, you will find you can overcome any obstacle you may face.

Now get out there and have fun…but stay safe.

\*        \*        \*

### POSITIVELY NEGATIVE

During a lecture, a linguistics professor said to his students, "In English, a double negative forms a positive. For example, 'He doesn't have no apples' actually means he *does have* apples. In some languages, such as Russian, a double negative is actually still a negative. However, there is *no* language in which a double positive can form a negative."

Just then, one of the students huffed and said, "Yeah, right."

# MAKING
# *THE GODFATHER, PT. III*

*Here's the third installment of our story on how the most popular novel of the 1970s ended up as one of the greatest films of the 20th century. (Parts I and II are on pages 91 and 354.) Salud!*

## THOSE EYES

T HOSE EYES
Coppola had his heart set on Al Pacino for the role of Michael Corleone, and, as he had with Marlon Brando, he just kept pushing until he finally got his way. Paramount forced him to test other actors for the part, and every time he did he had Pacino come in and do another screen test, too. Robert Evans got so sick of seeing Pacino's face that he screamed, "Why the hell are you testing him again? The man's a midget!"

But Coppola would not back down, not even when Pacino grew discouraged filming test after test after test for a part that he knew the studio would never give him. Ironically, it may have been that very frustration that got Pacino the part—in some of the screen tests he appears calm but also seems to be hiding anger just below the surface. This moody intensity was an accurate reflection of his state of mind, and it was just the quality he needed to convey to be successful in the role.

Did the screen tests convince Paramount that Pacino was right for the part, or did Coppola finally just wear them down? Whatever it was, Pacino got the job. "Francis was the most effective fighter against the studio hierarchy I've ever seen," casting director Fred Roos told one interviewer. "He did not do it by yelling or screaming, but by sheer force of will."

## YOU LOSE SOME, YOU WIN SOME

By the time Paramount finally got around to approving Pacino for the role, he'd signed up to do another film called *The Gang That Couldn't Shoot Straight*. To get him out of that commitment, Coppola made a trade: He released another young actor from appearing in *The Godfather* so that he could take Pacino's place in *The Gang That Couldn't Shoot Straight*. The actor: Robert De Niro—

The famous "horse's head" seen in *The Godfather...*

he'd been cast as Paulie Gatto, the driver and bodyguard who betrays Don Corleone. Losing the part may have been disappointing to De Niro at the time, but it also cleared the way for him to play the young Vito Corleone in *The Godfather: Part II*, the role that won him his first Oscar, for Best Supporting Actor, and made him an international star.

## FAMILY PROBLEMS

As if fighting Paramount wasn't bad enough, Coppola also had to contend with the real-life Mafia, which wasn't too pleased with the idea of a big-budget Italian gangster movie coming to the screen. Joe Colombo, head of one of the *real* "five families" that made up the New York mob, was also the founder of a group called the Italian-American Civil Rights League, an organization that lobbied against negative Italian stereotypes in the media.

The League had won some impressive victories in recent years, successfully lobbying newspapers, broadcast networks, and even the Nixon Justice Department to replace terms like "the Mafia" and "La Cosa Nostra" with more ethnically neutral terms like "the Mob," "the syndicate," and "the underworld." The League was at the height of its powers in the early 1970s, and now it set its sights on *The Godfather*.

## I'M-A GONNA DIE!

How would you deal with the Maf...er, um...the "syndicate" if they were trying to stop the project you were working on? Albert Ruddy, the producer, decided to face the problem head on: He met with Colombo in the League's offices to discuss mutual concerns, and he even let Colombo have a peek at the script. Colombo's demands actually turned out to be fairly reasonable: He didn't want the film to contain any patronizing Italian stereotypes or accents—"I'm-a gonna shoot-a you now"—and he didn't want the Mafia identified by that name in the film. Ruddy assured Colombo that Coppola had no plans to use that kind of speech, and he even promised to remove all references to "the Mafia" from the script.

Colombo didn't know it at the time, but removing the word "Mafia" from the script was an easy promise to keep because it wasn't in there to begin with—guys who are in the Mafia don't sit around discussing it by name.

In effect, Colombo had agreed to end the Mob's opposition to the film and even to make some of his "boys" available for crowd control and other odd jobs, and had gotten next to nothing in return. (In 1971, during filming of *The Godfather*, Colombo was gunned down in a Mob hit and lingered in a coma until 1978, when he finally died from his wounds.)

## LASHED TO THE MAST

One of the nice things about winning so many battles with studio executives is getting to make the film you want to make; the bad thing is that once it becomes your baby, if things start to go wrong it's easy for the studio to figure out who they need to fire—*you*.

Filming of *The Godfather* got off to a rough start—Brando's performances in his first scenes were so dull and uninspired that Coppola had to set aside time to film them again. Al Pacino's earliest scenes didn't look all that promising, either. His first scenes were the ones at the beginning of the film, when he's a boyish war hero determined to stay out of the family "business." Pacino played the scenes true to character—so true, in fact, that when the Paramount executives saw the early footage, they doubted he'd be able to pass as a Mafia don.

For a time the set was awash with rumors that Coppola and Pacino were both about to be fired. How true were the rumors? Both men were convinced their days were numbered—that was one of the reasons Coppola cast his sister, Talia Shire, as Don Corleone's daughter, Connie: He figured that if he was going to lose his job, at least *she'd* get something out of the film.

## FAIR-WEATHER FRIENDS

More than 30 years later, it's difficult to say how true the rumors were, especially now that the film is considered a classic—the executives who would have wanted to fire the pair back then are now more likely to take credit for discovering them. But the threat was real, and Marlon Brando saved Coppola by counter-threatening to walk off the job if Coppola was removed from the film.

Al Pacino saved his own skin when he filmed the scene where he murders Virgil Sollozzo and Captain McCluskey (Al Lettieri and Sterling Hayden) in an Italian restaurant. That was the first scene in which he got the chance to appear as a cold-blooded killer, and he pulled it off with ease. Finally, Paramount could see that he could indeed play a Mafia don.

## PUTTING IT ALL TOGETHER

Once these early problems were resolved, the production made steady progress and remained more or less on schedule and on budget. Marlon Brando behaved himself on the set and delivered one of the greatest performances of his career; the other actors gave excellent performances as well. As Paramount executives reviewed the footage after each day of shooting, it soon became clear to everyone involved that *The Godfather* was going to be a remarkable film.

In 62 days of shooting, Coppola filmed more than 90 hours of footage, which he and six editors whittled down to a film that was just under three hours long. (Paramount made Coppola edit it down to two and a half hours, but that version left out so many good scenes that the studio decided to use Coppola's original cut.) By the time they finished—and before the film even made it into the theaters—*The Godfather* had already turned a profit: So many theaters rushed to book it in advance that it had already taken in twice as much money as it had cost to make.

## LARGER THAN LIFE

The advance bookings were the first sign that *The Godfather* was going to do really big business; another sign came on March 15, 1972, the day the film premiered in the United States. That morning when Albert Ruddy drove into work, he saw people waiting in front of a theater that was showing *The Godfather*. It was only 8:15 a.m., and the first showing was hours away, but the fans were already lining up around the block—not just at that theater, but everywhere else in America, too.

The long lines continued for weeks. As *The Godfather* showed to one sold-out audience after another, it smashed just about every box-office record there was: In April it became the first movie to earn more than $1 million in a day; in September it became the most profitable Hollywood film ever made, earning more money in six months than the previous record holder, *Gone With the Wind*, had earned in 33 years. In all, it made more than $85 million during its initial release. (How long did it hold the record as

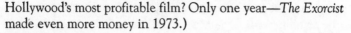

Hollywood's most profitable film? Only one year—*The Exorcist* made even more money in 1973.)

Nominated for 10 Academy Awards, *The Godfather* won for Best Actor (Brando), Best Adapted Screenplay (Coppola and Puzo), and Best Picture.

*The Godfather* revived Marlon Brando's career and launched those of Francis Ford Coppola, Al Pacino, Robert Duvall, Diane Keaton, James Caan, Talia Shire, and even Abe Vigoda (who later starred in TV's *Barney Miller* and *Fish*), whom Coppola discovered during an open casting call. "The thing that I like most about the film's success is that everyone that busted their hump on this movie came out with something very special—and good careers," Albert Ruddy said years later. "All of these people came together in one magic moment, and it was the turn in everybody's careers. It was just a fantastic thing."

## SERENDIPITY

*Two memorable scenes in* The Godfather *came about only by chance:*

### • Luca Brasi Memorizes his Speech

It wasn't unusual for real-life wiseguys to hang out around the set during location shoots; one day during filming in the Little Italy neighborhood of New York, a mobster visited the set with an enormous bodyguard in tow. The bodyguard, a onetime professional wrestler named Lenny Montana, was 6'6" and must have weighed over 300 pounds. Albert Ruddy spotted him and pointed him out to Coppola, who cast him on the spot as Luca Brasi, the hit man who is garroted early in the film and ends up "sleeping with the fishes."

Montana had no acting experience, and in his scene with Marlon Brando he was so nervous that he kept stumbling over his lines. Rather than replace him with someone who could act, Coppola made Montana's fumbling a part of the story by creating the scene where Luca Brasi rehearses and repeatedly flubs the few words he wants to say in his meeting with Don Corleone at Connie and Carlo's wedding. For the meeting with the Don, Coppola used one of Montana's actual blown takes.

### • The Don's Death Scene

On the day that Coppola was supposed to film the scene in which

Don Corleone dies while playing with his grandson, they were having trouble getting the young boy playing the grandson to perform his part. Brando mentioned a trick that he liked to use with his own small children: He would cut up the peel of a slice of orange into teeth, stuff it into his mouth, and play "monster" with his kids. Coppola liked the sound of it, so he tossed the script aside and filmed Brando playing monster with the boy. That was the scene that ended up in the movie.

## THREE BITS OF *GODFATHER* TRIVIA

• **Foreboding fruit:** One of the best-known uses of foreshadowing in all three *Godfather* films is the use of oranges to hint at upcoming scenes of violence and death. The Godfather buys a bag of oranges just before he is gunned down; later in the film, he dies while playing "monster" with his grandson with an orange peel stuffed in his mouth. The character Sal Tessio (Abe Vigoda), who betrays Michael and is murdered at the end of the film, is introduced at the beginning of the movie playing with an orange. According to production designer Dean Tavoularis, oranges didn't start out as symbolic of anything. Cinematographer Gordon Willis, who worked on all three *Godfather* films, is known as "the Prince of Darkness" because he likes to film in low light, so Tavoularis put oranges in some sets for contrast—just to brighten scenes that would otherwise have been extremely dark and devoid of color.

• **Hits:** The scene where Sonny Corleone beats up his brother-in-law, Carlo Rizzi, contains a famous blooper that has become known as "The Miss": Sonny takes a swing at Carlo and obviously misses, but there's a sound effect, and Rizzi still reacts as if he's been punched. (Ever notice that Rizzi is wearing an *orange* leisure suit?) The entire fight sequence, including The Miss, was reenacted in a 2003 episode of *The Simpsons* titled "Strong Arms of the Ma."

• **Name game:** Francis Ford Coppola was named after his grandfather, Francesco Pennino. Where'd the "Ford" come from? The Ford Motor Company. They sponsored a radio show that employed his father, Carmine Coppola, as a conductor and musical arranger.

---

First movie to earn $100 million: *Jaws* (1975). First movie to earn $200 million: *Jaws* (1975).

# ANSWER PAGES

## G.E. COLLEGE BOWL
### (Answers for page 61)

**LITERATURE**

**Tossup:** *Animal Farm*, the title of the 1945 novel by George Orwell

**Bonus Questions:**

**1.** Lord Alfred Tennyson

**2.** Percy Bysshe Shelley and Mary Wollstonecraft Shelley were husband and wife.

**3.** Santiago

**4.** Jack Kerouac, in his 1957 novel *On the Road*

**5.** O. Henry

**SCIENCE & MATH**

**Tossup:** Time (your watch is a chronometer)

**Bonus Questions:**

**1.** They're traveling at almost exactly the same speed—1 knot is equal to 1.151 miles, which means the ship is traveling at

46.04 mph.

**2.** The funny bone

**3.** You made $20—$10 on the first sale; $10 on the second.

**4.** The moon and its physical features

**5.** 10° Celsius or Centigrade (to convert Fahrenheit to Celsius, subtract 32 and then multiply by ⅝).

**GENERAL KNOWLEDGE**

**Tossup:** Wild Bill Hickok

**Bonus Questions:**

**1.** In your pancreas (they produce insulin)

**2.** A countess

**3.** Pain

**4.** Ships or boats

**5.** Kill it—the *musca domestica* is the scientific name for the common housefly.

## G.E. COLLEGE BOWL
### (Answers for page 303)

**SCIENCE & MATH**

**Tossup:** 18 feet (300 yards/10 seconds = 30 yards per second. 30/5 = 6 yards per fifth of a second = 18 feet per second)

**Bonus Questions:**

**1.** James drank sulphuric acid.

**2.** Liquid

**3.** James Van Allen—he discovered the Van Allen belts in 1958.

**4.** Only one—the number 2. Every other even number is divisible by 1, itself, *and* 2, which means it is not prime.

**5.** Call 911—you're having a heart attack!

## U.S. HISTORY

**Tossup:** Treason (Article 3, Section 3)

**Bonus Questions:**

**1.** Andrew Johnson; Dwight D. Eisenhower

**2.** Aaron Burr (he shot Alexander Hamilton in a duel in 1804)

**3.** Abraham Lincoln

**4.** Bulgaria, Hungary, and Romania

**5.** To put down the Whiskey Rebellion and resume collection of the federal tax on whiskey in Pennsylvania

## GEOGRAPHY

**Tossup:** Afghanistan

**Bonus Questions:**

**1.** The (U.S.) Virgin Islands

**2.** Vaduz

**3.** Australia

**4.** The Caspian Sea—the world's largest landlocked body of water

**5.** The Aleutian Islands, in Alaska

## GENERAL KNOWLEDGE

**Tossup:** Massachusetts, Kentucky, Pennsylvania, and Virginia

**Bonus Questions:**

**1.** A tomato

**2.** General John Joseph "Black Jack" Pershing

**3.** A map of the moon

**4.** By planting thousands of apple trees and giving seedlings and seeds to everyone he met. (He's better known as Johnny Appleseed.)

**5.** Maid Marian

# U.S. CITIZENSHIP TEST (EASY)

## (Answers for page 177)

**1.** The White House

**2.** 13

**3.** The original 13 colonies

**4.** 50

**5.** The 50 states. A new star is added to the flag every time a state enters the union. Originally the plan was to add a star *and* a stripe every time a state entered the Union, but that would have made the flag taller than it is wide; either that or the stripes would have become so thin that the appearance of the flag would have changed drastically. In 1818 the number of stripes was dropped from 15 to 13, and after that, only stars were added to the flag.

**6.** The Congress

**7.** The president

**8.** Germany, Italy, and Japan

**No two lions have the same pattern of whiskers.**

**9.** Alaska (49) and Hawaii (50)

**10.** To escape religious persecution (see page 44).

**11.** The *Mayflower*

**12.** 18

**13.** George Washington

**14.** The Congress

**15.** The House of Representatives and the Senate

**16.** The Democratic Party and the Republican Party

**17.** "The Star-Spangled Banner"

**18.** Francis Scott Key

**19.** November

**20.** January

**21.** Thanksgiving

**22.** Thomas Edison

**23.** England

# U.S. CITIZENSHIP TEST (MEDIUM)
### (Answers for page 334)

**1.** A veto

**2.** The adoption of the Declaration of Independence

**3.** Freedom of religion, of speech, of the press, of assembly, and to petition the government

**4.** Nine. The number varied from six to ten in the 19th century; then in 1869 the number was set at nine. An odd number was chosen to prevent tie votes.

**5.** The president of the United States

**6.** The Congress. However, as commander in chief, the president can order soldiers into combat without a declaration of war from Congress. The Korean War (1950–53), the Vietnam War (1957–75), and the Persian Gulf War (1991) were all undeclared wars.

**7.** The citizens of the United States

**8.** The electoral college. Each state has as many votes, or *electors*, in the Electoral College as it has U.S. senators and representatives in Congress (and the District of Columbia has three votes). In some states, the ballot may only show the names of the presidential candidates. In those states, you are actually casting votes for the elector, who will vote for the presidential candidate you prefer. In most states, all of the electoral college votes go to the presidential candidate who wins the highest number of the state's popular votes.

**9.** The legislative, executive, and judicial branches

**10.** The president

**11.** Slavery and states' rights

---

In Florida, it's against the law to hunt or kill deer while they're swimming.

**12.** To interpret laws

**13.** 435. In addition, four "delegates" represent the District of Columbia, Puerto Rico, American Samoa, the U.S. Virgin Islands, and Guam, and a "resident commissioner" represents Puerto Rico. These officials can cast votes in committee and on some votes that come before the full House, but they are not full voting members.

**14.** 100

**15.** Each of the 50 states has two senators.

**16.** The Bill of Rights

**17.** 6 years

**18.** 2 years

**19.** 2 full terms. When the Constitution was written, there was no limit to how many terms a president could serve. Before Franklin Delano Roosevelt (1933–1945), no president had ever run for more than two consecutive terms, out of respect for the precedent set by George Washington, who declined to run for a third term. FDR broke the tradition—he ran (and won) four times.

The 22nd Amendment, ratified in 1951, limited presidents to two terms, or only one term in the case of a vice president who has served more than two years of another president's term, such as when a president dies in office or is impeached and removed from office.

**20.** There is no limit.

**21.** Patrick Henry. According to tradition, Henry said it in 1775 during the Virginia Provincial Convention. The following year he became independent Virginia's first governor, and he was largely responsible for the passage of the Bill of Rights, the first 10 amendments to the U.S. Constitution.

# U.S. CITIZENSHIP TEST (HARD)
## (Answers for page 473)

**1.** The right to vote. (All other rights depend on it.)

**2.** Thomas Jefferson. Jefferson wanted his friend John Adams to write it, but Adams believed Jefferson was the better man for the task, and gave three reasons: "Reason first: You are a Virginian, and Virginia ought to appear at the head of this business. Reason second: I am obnoxious, suspected and unpopular; you are very much otherwise. Reason third: You can write 10 times better than I can."

**3.** 27 (so far)

**4.** The speaker of the U.S.

House of Representatives. Next in the line of succession is the president pro tempore of the Senate (traditionally the majority-party senator with the longest history of continuous service), followed by the members of the cabinet in the order in which their departments were established: the secretary of state, followed by the secretary of treasury, secretary of defense, the attorney general, and the secretaries of the interior, agriculture, commerce, labor, health and human services, housing and urban development, transportation, energy, education, veterans affairs, and homeland security. The secretary of bathroom reading is not an official member of the cabinet; Uncle John sits upon his throne but will probably never be president.

**5.** Virginia, New Hampshire, Massachusetts, Rhode Island, Connecticut, North Carolina, South Carolina, Pennsylvania, New Jersey, New York, Maryland, Delaware, and Georgia

**6.** The president must: 1) be a native-born citizen; 2) be at least 35 years old; and 3) have lived in the U.S. for at least 14 years.

**7.** 1787

**8.** You'll have to answer this yourself—Uncle John has no idea where you live!

**9.** The 15th, 19th, 24th, and 26th amendments

**10.** The president, the cabinet, and the departments under the cabinet members. Here's an easy rule of thumb: If it's part of the federal government but isn't part of the federal courts or the Congress, it's part of the executive branch.

**11.** The Preamble. It lays out the purpose of the Constitution in clear language, and establishes that the new government being established gets its powers from the people, and not vice versa. The Preamble reads:

"We the people of the United States, in order to form a more perfect Union, establish justice, insure domestic tranquility, provide for the common defense, promote the general welfare, and secure the blessings of liberty to ourselves and our posterity, do ordain and establish this Constitution for the United States of America."

**12.** Everyone who lives in the United States, whether they are citizens or not

**13.** Abraham Lincoln

**14.** The Mississippi River

**15.** A *republican* form of government—that means that the citizens elect representatives who form the government. This is also known as a *representative democracy*. In a *direct* or *pure* democracy, the voters would make the laws themselves instead of electing representatives to do it for them. The ancient Greek city-state of Athens was governed by a direct democracy.

**16.** That all men are created equal.

**17.** 1600 Pennsylvania Avenue NW, Washington, D.C.

## RIDDLE ME THIS

### (Answers for page 232)

**1.** Stars
**2.** A wheelbarrow
**3.** A splinter
**4.** A lawsuit

**5.** A pillow
**6.** A hearse
**7.** Heroine
**8.** Your lap

**9.** A nail
**10.** Your temper
**11.** Your leg
**12.** Asteroids

## OL' JAY'S BRAINTEASERS

### (Answers for page 167)

### 1. BRIGHT THINKING

Standing in the hallway, Amy turned on the first light switch. She waited two minutes and then turned on the second light switch. Then after another minute she turned them both off. When she walked into the library, one was very hot, the other was slightly warm, and the other was cold—making it easy for her to tell Uncle John which switch turned on which lamp.

### 2. MYSTERY JOB

Brian works at a library.

### 3. SIDE TO SIDE

The river was frozen.

### 4. SPECIAL NUMBER

*8,549,176,320*

It contains each number—zero through nine—in alphabetical order.

### 5. TIME PIECES

An hourglass. It is filled with thousands of grains of sand.

### 6. WORD PLAY

If you remove the first letter of each word and place it on the end of the word, it will spell the same word backwards.

\*     \*     \*

"Everything flows and nothing stays." —**Heraclitus**

Only father & son to hit back-to-back home runs in major-league baseball: Ken Griffey Sr. & Jr.

# UNCLE JOHN'S BATHROOM READER CLASSIC SERIES

Find these and other great titles from the *Uncle John's Bathroom Reader* Classic Series online at **www.bathroomreader.com**. Or contact us at:

Bathroom Readers' Institute
P.O. Box 1117
Ashland, OR 97520
(888) 488-4642

# NOW AVAILABLE!

# NOW AVAILABLE:

*Uncle John's Bathroom Reader*
*Extraordinary Book of Facts*

*Uncle John's Journal*

*Uncle John's Monumental*
*Bathroom Reader*

*Uncle John's Puzzle Book #4*

*Uncle John's Bathroom Reader*
*Cat Lover's Companion*

*Uncle John's Bathroom Reader*
*Sudoku Challenge*

*Uncle John's Bathroom Reader*
*Plunges Into National Parks*

*Uncle John's Wonderful World of Odd*

*Uncle John's Bathroom Reader*
*Book of L-O-V-E*

*Uncle John's Quintessential*
*Collection of Notable Quotables*
*for Every Conceivable Occasion*

To order, contact:
Bathroom Readers' Press
P.O. Box 1117, Ashland, OR 97520
Phone: 888-488-4642   Fax: 541-482-6159

*www.bathroomreader.com*

Hiya, Sam! Hiya, Gideon!

# BONUS PAGE: DOG-ENGLISH DICTIONARY

*Somehow we wound up with an extra page. So we thought we'd use it to help you improve your interspecies communication skills.*

"I'm hungry." *Woof!*

"I'm not hungry." *Woof!*

"Feed me." *Woof!*

"Don't feed me *that*." *Woof!*

"What do you mean, the litter box isn't a snack bar?" *Woof!*

"Let me out." *Woof!*

"Let me in." *Woof!*

"Let me out." *Woof!*

"Let me in." *Woof!*

"Mind if I just stand here and look out the open door for a few minutes?" *Woof!*

"I'll tell *you* when you're done petting me." *Woof!*

"Exactly who is this 'Poopsie' you keep referring to?" *Woof!*

"Here's an idea. Let's run around in a circle." *Woof!*

"Please accept this dead Frisbee as a token of my esteem." *Woof!*

"Hey, I threw up! Wait... it's OK, I took care of it." *Woof!*

"The cat did it." *Woof!*

"Personally, I'm more of an existentialist than a—OOH, A BALL!" *Woof!*

"Just because I'm your best friend doesn't mean I'll guard your sandwich." *Woof!*

"Look! My tail! Get it!" *Woof!*

"These new shoes will be a lot more comfortable now that I've chewed them up for you." *Woof!*

"Bath? Isn't that against the law?" *Woof!*

"No, I don't know who made that stain on the carpet." *Woof!*

"Hey, you lost this stick again." *Woof!*

"Nice leg!" *Woof!*

# THE LAST PAGE

F ELLOW BATHROOM READERS:
The fight for good bathroom reading should never be taken loosely—we must do our duty and sit firmly for what we believe in, even while the rest of the world is taking potshots at us.

We'll be brief. Now that we've proven we're not simply a flush-in-the-pan, we invite you to take the plunge: Sit Down and Be Counted! Become a member of the Bathroom Readers' Institute. Log on to *www.bathroomreader.com*, or send a self-addressed, stamped, business-sized envelope to: BRI, PO Box 1117, Ashland, Oregon 97520. You'll receive your free membership card, get discounts when ordering directly through the BRI, and earn a permanent spot on the BRI honor roll!

---

If you like reading our books...
## VISIT THE BRI'S WEB SITE!
### *www.bathroomreader.com*

- Visit "The Throne Room"—a great place to read!
  - Receive our irregular newsletters via e-mail
    - Order additional *Bathroom Readers*
      - Become a BRI member

*Go with the Flow...*

---

Well, we're out of space, and when you've gotta go, you've gotta go. Tanks for all your support. Hope to hear from you soon. Meanwhile, remember..

*Keep on flushin'!*